Toward a New Political Humanism

Toward a New Political Humanism

Edited by

Barry F. Seidman

and

Neil J. Murphy

Prometheus Books

59 John Glenn Drive
Amherst, New York 14228-2197

Published 2004 by Prometheus Books

Toward a New Political Humanism. Copyright © 2004 by Barry F. Seidman and Neil J. Murphy. All rights reserved. No part of this publication may be reproduced, stored in a retrieval system, or transmitted in any form or by any means, digital, electronic, mechanical, photocopying, recording, or otherwise, or conveyed via the Internet or a Web site without prior written permission of the publisher, except in the case of brief quotations embodied in critical articles and reviews.

Inquiries should be addressed to
Prometheus Books
59 John Glenn Drive
Amherst, New York 14228–2197
VOICE: 716–691–0133, ext. 207
FAX: 716–564–2711
WWW.PROMETHEUSBOOKS.COM

08 07 06 05 04   5 4 3 2 1

Library of Congress Cataloging-in-Publication Data

Seidman, Barry F.
    Toward a new political humanism / Barry F. Seidman & Neil J. Murphy.
        p. cm.
    Includes bibliographical references.
    ISBN 1–59102–271–1 (hardcover : alk. paper)
    1. Political psychology. 2. Humanism. I. Murphy, Neil J., 1978– II. Title.

JA74.5.S445 2004
320'.01—dc22

                                                                2004007252

Printed in the United States of America on acid-free paper

This book is dedicated to the late Edward Said (1935–2003),
who epitomized humanism by giving voice
to the oppressed and disenfranchised everywhere.

Contents

PART I: TOWARD A HUMANIST POLITIC

PART II: POLITICAL HUMANISM IN AMERICA

PART III: GLOBAL HUMANISM

PART IV: REVISIONING HUMANISM

For the world of the twenty-first century, humanistic values must project the vision of a peaceful world in which no man, woman or child, or class of men, women, or children shall live as servants or slaves existing simply to fulfill the whims and wishes and desires of others, a world in which no man or woman or child shall be used as a tool to satisfy the lusts or greed or ambitions of others, a world in which every human life, the life of every man, woman, and child shall be a wanted, welcomed, and esteemed member of the one human family.

—Gerald A. Larue

Acknowledgments

Barry would like to acknowledge all those who have supported him on this project, including, first and foremost, his wife, Susan Seidman, and Dr. Paul Kurtz. He would also like to thank all those who contributed essays to this book, for they are among humanism's best hope.

Neil would like to acknowledge all those political historians and philosophers who shaped the humanist and progressive landscape and led him to enter their world of ideas.

INTRODUCTION

The Natural Symbiosis of Progressive Politics and Humanism

Barry F. Seidman and Neil J. Murphy

ARE HUMANISTS PROGRESSIVE?

Just as organized religion in almost any form—particularly in its marriage with government—can be seen as the most dangerous threat to humanism from without, the battle over where humanism stands with regard to real-world politics may be the most dangerous—at least the most divisive—argument from within . . . especially in the post–9/11 world.

The question at hand is, Can humanism, as put forth via the Affirmations of Humanism and the *Humanist Manifestos I, II, III,* and *2000*,[1] continue to stay neutral on political issues not so obviously tied in with religion or superstition—issues that nevertheless shape our daily lives and our collective future?

Many within the humanist movement, unlike most other competing philosophies, have claimed that political ideologies such as left/right, liberal/conservative, or progressive/regressive should not, dare we say *cannot*, be addressed via humanist philosophy. The argument has been that humanists of conscience can differ widely on any number of sociopolitical issues.

Although we recognize that different people do indeed come to humanism from different launching points and expect different things from the movement (e.g., tough stands taken against religion, a nonreligious community, a place where science is respected), we feel that humanism cannot reach its potential unless it becomes a universal philosophy. And that cannot happen unless humanists are willing to enter the real world of politics.

First, let us make a disclaimer right here. As with so many other *isms*, if we put twenty self-identifying humanists into a room and asked almost any question of them, we'd get fifty different answers. Indeed, even the very definition of humanism seems to alter with every generation—indeed, with each "humanist." Our position in this book argues for the humanism we can find in the *Humanist Manifestos;*[2] that is, humanism to us is a secular, planetary, and active philosophy whose aim is to build a cooperative human society in which science, reason, compassion, and the use of evidence in every decision are paramount. For easy reference, the condensed version of the *Humanist Manifesto 2000* is included in this book; but we strongly advise the reader to read all four full manifestos before reading this book, as they act as the foundation for most of the viewpoints expressed within these pages.

Humanists love to debate, and not just our opponents. We love even more to debate each other. Debate and discussion are key to the humanist lifestyle—sometimes, to the discomfort of some of us, the dominant part of the humanist lifestyle. Perhaps the main reason debate is so prevalent is that humanists often start out as atheists or skeptics looking for a philosophy to attach their ideas to. These people despise dogma . . . and this is a good thing, we admit.

However, this disregard for accepted "truth" very often leads to so much philosophizing and granting open arms to so many different political and economic ideas that the humanist community never *does* anything—not anything powerful, at least, to create social change and make humanism the world's philosophy. However, if humanism is indeed a coherent philosophy as laid out in the various manifestos, then what follows must become a pragmatic and powerful humanist activism based on the ideas written in these defining works.

To us, this attitude is a bit obsessive-compulsive, even absurd, and just plain bad business. If humanism throughout the centuries has meant anything at all, if the manifestos of modern humanism are worth the weight of their ideas, then we do indeed already have a humanist position on many sociopolitical-economic human endeavors. And, to those of you who wish to call even the manifestos and affirmations we humanists base our philosophies on dogma, then we might as well call everyone—or no one—a humanist.

However, we believe that humanists can indeed fall upon their philosophical and ethical principles as stated in those works to inform themselves as to what actions in the political realm they need to take: actions to promote and defend the humanist worldview and actions to give humanism a chance to become the world's worldview, a goal all humanists maintain if indeed we feel that humanism is the healthiest philosophy for the human species.

THE GOALS OF HUMANISM

The late Edward Said once said that "humanism is the only, and I would go so far as saying, the final resistance we have against the inhuman practices and injustices that disfigure human history."[3] We in the freethinking community understand all too well the moral and political responsibility which that sentiment implies. Humanism represents the binding social, political, and cultural thread that can unite people of different cultures, beliefs, and values into a common framework of respectful coinhabitance, while at the same time articulating a vision of a shared humanity in which all the peoples of the world can prosper and function in an environment where their humanity is valued more than profit or another's usefulness as a pawn.

For instance, humanists should understand the need for media reform in America and that corporate control of information is a threat to democracy. And, yes, at this time, it seems that democracy is the form of government that can best allow humanism to flourish (although democratic socialism might indeed work better). Also, humanists should deplore the documented and very real effects of neoliberal privatization as manifested though undemocratic organizations such as the World Trade Organization (WTO), the International Monetary Fund (IMF), and the World Bank. These entities, as the evidence has shown, are creating a tremendous amount of suffering, poverty, and unfettered exploitation of peoples that are vehemently opposed in the several Humanist Manifestos. Indeed, the unethical practices of visceral self-interest of the few at the expense of the many is most antihumanistic.

On other issues such as the environment, civil liberties, and civil rights for gays/lesbians, blacks, and other minorities, humanists have always fought on the front line for the hearts and minds of committed people who struggle for a cleaner, safer, and freer society. Though we cannot go through each of these examples in this opening essay, most of them are indeed covered in this book.

Of all the words describing humanism, perhaps the one we see as most important is *evidence*. Our adherence to the scientific method, accuracy, and consequentialism—whether it concerns human behavior and nature, religious or paranormal claims, or political and economic agendas—is key to the foundation of the humanistic philosophy. So why, then, are we so afraid to apply evidence to the ways politics and the economy function as well as to science, religion, ethics, or human nature? We have beaten the rap that it is not polite to talk about religion, so why not politics?

The invasion of Iraq in 2003, for example, was argued for by the Bush administration with a series of "facts" that justified to US citizens, and indeed the entire world, the "duty" to go to war. The Bush administration argued that Saddam Hussein possessed weapons of mass destruction (WMDs), that Hussein was trying to get material to build such weapons from Africa, and that Hussein was partly behind the tragic events of 9/11.

Before any humanist can discuss the moral and ethical implications of acting on such claims, he or she must first test these claims for accuracy. Neither the American press nor most Americans took this crucial step. If they had, they would have found out that the international inspection teams (UNSCOM and UNMOVIC), had determined that 95 percent of Iraq's weapons were successfully disarmed as a result of these inspections long before 2003. As former inspection team leader, Scott Ritter (forced to resign by the Bush administration due to his openness about the findings of the inspection teams), pointed out, "Iraq had in fact, been disarmed to a level unprecedented in modern history."[4] Similarly, the claim that Iraq was trying to purchase uranium from Nigeria was demonstrated by agent Joseph Wilson to be false. Wilson's reward for speaking contrary to the wishes of the Bush administration was the blowing of the CIA cover of Wilson's wife (an action which, by the way, is a prosecutable felony).

And what of the acclaimed connection between Saddam Hussein and the Al Qaeda network. . . a claim that much of the media and many Americans still believe? Daniel Benjamin, who served on the National Security Council from 1994 to 1999, wrote on September 30, 2002, in the *New York Times*, "Iraq and Al Qaeda are not obvious allies. In fact they are natural enemies."[5] Indeed, both regimes stand drastically apart in their goals and ideologies. Saddam's Baathist party was ruthlessly secular, in contrast to Al Qaeda, which is a fundamentalist Islamic terrorist group. Richard Butler, former head of the UNSCOM weapons inspectorate, testified in July 2002, "I have seen no evidence of Iraq providing weapons of mass destruction to non-Iraqi terrorist groups. I suspect that, especially given his psychology and aspirations, Saddam would be reluctant to share with others what he believes to be an indelible source of his own power."[6]

Another specific example might concern humanism and economics. The last twenty years have seen a complete elimination of the social welfare policies enacted by Franklin Delano Roosevelt during the New Deal. The belief in giving the working-class citizens of America guaranteed social protections such as Social Security, the right to form unions and collectively bargain, full-time labor with benefits, unemployment compensation, and disability payments and pensions has given way to a return to what the sociologist Charles Derber calls "the second gilded age," in which all forms of social protections are either eliminated outright or sold to the highest bidder.[7] This eradication of the notion of the common good has caused a drastic increase in the gap between rich and poor, an increase in homelessness, poverty, joblessness, hunger, and many other social problems.

Internationally, the triad of global economic institutions known as the World Bank, the WTO, and the IMF purport to help third-world countries that are having severe economic problems and are collapsing under debt by proposing solutions designed to solve their economic ills. The IMF proposes the following methods by which third-world country solutions are to get themselves out of debt:

1. Massive deregulation.
2. Privatization of state institutions.
3. Removal of trade barriers.[8]

What are the consequences of these policies?

1. The benefits and resources of these institutions are transferred from the public governments to private enterprise.
2. The gap between rich and poor widens as economic power concentrates.
3. Poverty and hunger escalate.
4. Farmers are driven out of business.[9]

The humanist who believes, as mentioned in the Amsterdam Declaration, that "Humanism supports democracy and Human rights,"[10] cannot simply support political democracy and human rights as articulated in the United States Constitution while ignoring issues of economic democracy and the right of each human being to a decent wage, which reflect basic biogenic and sociogenic needs. Current progressive values of economic democracy and social welfare protections to "the least of these" should be an integral part of a humanist's thinking since that is where the evidence leads us and that is what most closely represents humanist thinking.

Likewise, waging a unilateral, preventive war against the innocent civilian population of Iraq—and don't think that only "combatants" were targeted as we don't know what the Daisy Cutter Bomb is, if not a civilian killer—is unjustified according to the humanistic moral perspective. If indeed the intention of the United States had been merely to remove Saddam Hussein from power—reversing a wrong the United States committed in the 1980s—for humanitarian reasons, then a nonwar removal of Saddam with voluntary aid from the United Nations and the International community would have been attempted . . . and Iraq would not be in the mess that US destruction and occupation have caused.

So, what can humanists do to put all this into practice? What we think needs to occur is a change in the type of social structures that we view as most beneficial to the human race. It is ironic that humanists—who believe that religion is a fascist, antihuman, immoral, anti-intellectual, unscientific ideology that is responsible for unimaginable suffering—would support economic and political institutions that engage in the same practices. Humanists need to embrace more cooperative structures that expand the humanist ethic from a libertarian, individualistic framework to a more universalistic framework that, while retaining the belief in personal freedom, seeks to bring about a global ethic that values interconnectedness as much as individualism. These goals and others are represented in the essays found in this book.

Humanism is also in need of a coherent definition. In an age in which religious (and other) fundamentalisms have taken over the minds of so many people, it is time for humanists to articulate their political vision of a better world and have their voices represented in the political arena. Speaking up does not mean, as some writers have suggested, that humanists should vote for any candidate regardless of party affiliation who publicly comes out as a secular humanist or an atheist. The issue should be not whether to vote *any* humanist into political office but what *type* of humanist to vote into office. Indeed, humanists should support candidates whose platform articulates a vision of the United States, and the world, in which people build cooperative structures instead of competitive ones; a world in which humanistic economics, universal human rights, and respect for human needs take precedence over corporate capitalism, religious intolerance, and ultraconservative ideologies.

In sum, it is our opinion that in order for humanism to have a real-world impact on society—especially American society—humanists must move beyond (but not forgo) our basic foundation of skepticism, atheism, and agnosticism into the world of human endeavors. To do so, humanists must do more than write impressive manifestos and affirmations; they must live by them.

NOTES

1. There are many sections in all three manifestos that attest to a progressive humanism. In *Humanist Manifesto I,* affirmation 14 states ". . . humanists are firmly convinced that existing acquisitive and profit-motivated society has shown itself to be inadequate and that a radical change in methods, controls, and motives must be instituted. A socialized and cooperative economic order must be established to the end that the equitable distribution of the means of life be possible. The goal of humanism is a free and universal society in which people voluntarily and intelligently cooperate for the common good. Humanists demand a shared life in a shared world."

Although in *Humanist Manifesto II,* a strictly Socialist economic agenda was backed away from to a degree—no doubt due to the anti-Communist agenda of the US government and the anti-Communist feelings of the American people—socialism's polar opposite, free-market capitalism, was to be regulated in a humanist society. Indeed, on page 20 of *Humanist Manifesto 2000,* it is acknowledged that "the belief in some quarters that the free market will cure all social problems remains a *faith.* How to balance the demands of the free market with the need for equitable social programs to assist the disadvantaged and impoverished remains an unsolved issue in many countries of the world."

The editors of this book feel that in light of the obvious problems with the World Bank and the International Monetary Fund, much more work must be done to eradicate the inequalities that are born of free-market capitalism. Perhaps *Humanist Manifesto I* got it right in the first place?

Also, there are other affirmations stated in *Humanist Manifesto II,* later repeated in *Humanist Manifesto 2000,* that lean toward progressive politics. Here are just a few such affirmations:

Affirmation 8 states: "We are committed to an open and democratic society. We must extend participatory democracy in its true sense to the economy, the school, the family, the workplace, and voluntary associations. Decision-making must be decentralized to include widespread involvement of people at all levels—social, political, and economic. All persons should have a voice in developing the values and goals that determine their lives. Institutions should be responsive to expressed desires and needs. The conditions of work, education, devotion, and play should be humanized. Alienating forces should be modified or eradicated and bureaucratic structures should be held to a minimum. People are more important than decalogues, rules, proscriptions, or regulations."

Affirmation 12 states: "We deplore the division of humankind on nationalistic grounds. We have reached a turning point in human history where the best option is to transcend the limits of national sovereignty and to move toward the building of a world community in which all sectors of the human family can participate. Thus we look to the development of a system of world law and a world order based upon transnational federal government. This would appreciate cultural pluralism and diversity. It would not exclude pride in national origins and accomplishments nor the handling of regional problems on a regional basis.

Human progress, however, can no longer be achieved by focusing on one section of the world, Western or Eastern, developed or underdeveloped. For the first time in human history, no part of humankind can be isolated from any other. Each person's future is in some way linked to all. We thus reaffirm a commitment to the building of world community, at the same time recognizing that this commits us to some hard choices."

And finally, affirmation 13 states: "This world community must renounce the resort to violence and force as a method of solving international disputes. We believe in the peaceful adjudication of differences by international courts and by the development of the arts of negotiation and compromise. War is obsolete. So is the use of nuclear, biological, and chemical weapons. It is a planetary imperative to reduce the level of military expenditures and turn these savings to peaceful and people-oriented uses."

2. *Humanist Manifestos I* and *II* can be found in book format, published by Prometheus Books, as can *Manifesto 2000*, written by Paul Kurtz.

3. Edward Said, "*Orientalism* Twenty-five Years Later: Worldly Humanism versus the Empire-Builders," Arabic Media Internet Network, August 6, 2003, http://www.amin.org/eng/edward_said/2003/aug06.html (accessed June 2004).

4. Scott Ritter, "The Case for Iraq's Qualitative Disarmament," *Arms Control Today* 30, no. 5 (June 2000).

5. Daniel Benjamin, "Saddam Hussein and Al Qaeda Are Not Allies," *New York Times*, September 30, 2002.

6. "Testimony by Richard Butler on Iraq and Weapons of Mass Destruction," statement at the Senate Foreign Relations Committee, Washington, DC, July 31, 2002, Council on Foreign Relations, http://www.cfr.org/pub4687/testimony/testimony_by_richard_butler_on_iraq_and_weapons_of_mass_destruction.php (accessed June 2004). Butler is the diplomat in residence at the Council on Foreign Relations and the former executive chairman of the United Nations Special Commission (UNSCOM), charged with inspecting weapons and disarming Iraq after the Gulf War.

7. Charles Derber, *Corporation Nation* (New York: St. Martin's, 1998).

8. Clark F. Ford, "Myth #7: The Free Market Can End Hunger," World Food Issues: Past and Present course outline, http://www.public.iastate.edu/~cfford/342myth7.htm (accessed June 2004).

9. Ibid.

10. "Amsterdam Declaration 2002," International Humanist and Ethical Union, http://www.iheu.org/adamdecl.htm (accessed June 2004).

Humanist Manifesto 2000
A Call for a New Planetary Humanism

Drafted by Professor Paul Kurtz,
International Academy of Humanism, USA

> *If we are to influence the future of humankind, we will need to work increasingly with and through the new centers of power and influence to improve equity and stability, alleviate poverty, reduce conflict, and safeguard the environment.*
>
> —Paul Kurtz

I. PREAMBLE

Humanism is an ethical, scientific, and philosophical outlook that has changed the world. Its heritage traces back to the philosophers and poets of ancient Greece and Rome, Confucian China, and the Charvaka movement in classical India. Humanist artists, writers, scientists, and thinkers have been shaping the modern era for over half a millennium. Indeed, humanism and modernism have often seemed synonymous for humanist ideas and values express a renewed confidence in the power of human beings to solve their own problems and conquer uncharted frontiers.

Condensed from *Humanist Manifesto 2000: A Call for a New Planetary Humanism*, drafted by Paul Kurtz. Amherst, NY: Prometheus Books, 2000.

II. PROSPECTS FOR A BETTER FUTURE

For the first time in human history we possess the means provided by science and technology to ameliorate the human condition, advance happiness and freedom, and enhance human life for all people on this planet.

III. SCIENTIFIC NATURALISM

The unique message of humanism on the current world scene is its commitment to scientific naturalism. Most worldviews accepted today are spiritual, mystical, or theological in character. They have their origins in ancient preurban, nomadic, and agricultural societies of the past, not in the modern industrial or postindustrial global information culture that is emerging. Scientific naturalism enables human beings to construct a coherent worldview disentangled from metaphysics or theology and based on the sciences.

IV. THE BENEFITS OF TECHNOLOGY

Humanists have consistently defended the beneficent values of scientific technology for human welfare. Philosophers from Francis Bacon to John Dewey have emphasized the increased power over nature that scientific knowledge affords and how it can contribute immeasurably to human advancement and happiness.

V. ETHICS AND REASON

The realization of the highest ethical values is essential to the humanist outlook. We believe that growth of scientific knowledge will enable humans to make wiser choices. In this way there is no impenetrable wall between fact and value, is and ought. Using reason and cognition will better enable us to appraise our values in the light of evidence and by their consequences.

VI. A UNIVERSAL COMMITMENT
TO HUMANITY AS A WHOLE

The overriding need of the world community today is to develop a new Planetary Humanism—one that seeks to preserve human rights and enhance human freedom and dignity, but also emphasizes our commitment to humanity as a whole. The underlying ethical principle of Planetary Humanism is the need to respect the dignity and worth of all persons in the world community.

VII. A PLANETARY BILL OF RIGHTS
AND RESPONSIBILITIES

To fulfill our commitment to Planetary Humanism, we offer a *Planetary Bill of Rights and Responsibilities*, which embodies our planetary commitment to the well-being of humanity as a whole. It incorporates the *Universal Declaration of Human Rights*, but goes beyond it by offering some new provisions. Many independent countries have sought to implement these provisions within their own national borders. But there is a growing need for an explicit *Planetary Bill of Rights and Responsibilities* that applies to all members of the human species.

VIII. A NEW GLOBAL AGENDA

Many of the high ideals that emerged following the Second World War, and that found expression in such instruments as the *Universal Declaration of Human Rights*, have waned through the world. If we are to influence the future of humankind, we will need to work increasingly with and through the new centers of power and influence to improve equity and stability, alleviate poverty, reduce conflict, and safeguard the environment.

IX. THE NEED FOR NEW
PLANETARY INSTITUTIONS

The urgent question in the twenty-first century is whether humankind can develop global institutions to address these problems. Many of the best remedies are those adopted on the local, national, and regional level by voluntary, private, and public efforts. One strategy is to seek solutions through free-market initiatives; another is to use international voluntary foundations and organizations for educational and social development. We believe, however, that there remains a need to develop new global institutions that will deal with the problems directly and will focus on the needs of humanity as a whole. These include the call for a bicameral legislature in the United Nations, with a World Parliament elected by the people, an income tax to help the underdeveloped countries, the end of the veto in the Security Council, an environmental agency, and a world court with powers of enforcement.

X. OPTIMISM ABOUT THE HUMAN PROSPECT

Finally, and perhaps most importantly, as members of the human community on this planet we need to nurture a sense of optimism about the human prospect. Although many problems may seem intractable, we have good reasons to believe that we can marshal our talent to solve them, and that by goodwill and dedication a better life will be attainable by more and more members of the human community. Planetary humanism holds forth great promises for humankind. We wish to cultivate a sense of wonder and excitement about the potential opportunities for realizing enriched lives for ourselves and for generations yet to be born.

Part I
Toward a Humanist Politic

1.

Toward a Humanist Politic

Joe Chuman

I often think about what a future humanist world might look like. How would people treat each other? How would the government and the economy function? And what about individual freedom and creativity, work, health care, education, morality, and the environment? [But] before we can take our final baby-steps toward a humanist society, however, we need to change the way we think. We must learn to make decisions and sacrifices today knowing that we will not be around to reap the benefit. This will be a difficult transition for those of us living in the industrialized countries who are used to instant gratification, so we must therefore keep our eyes on the prize and never forget that we are working for the betterment of society.

—Jaime York

THE CHALLENGES WE CONFRONT

Our times cry out for a vigorous humanist politics. More than forty years ago, *Humanist Manifesto II* declared, "The next century can be and should be the humanistic century."[1] It was a statement of contingency and hope. It revealed neither certainty nor assertive confidence. Events of the intervening four decades have done little to bolster the faith of humanists that historical currents favor the emergence of a society guided by humanistic ideals.

Those events have been staggering, and, peering forward from the dawn of the new century, severely challenge the triumph of a humanist future.

While for humanists the future is always open, and therefore eludes predictive certainty, political assessment unavoidably is based on impressions drawn from current trends that are projected into the future. A sketch of major events over the past forty years makes concerted action by humanists especially urgent. What are the greatest challenges that humanists confront?

Challenges on the International Scene

The fall of the Soviet bloc in 1989 opened the societies of Eastern Europe to the promises of democracy and liberal freedom. But the collapse of the centrist state has left an ideological vacuum in the former Communist world that is being filled by virulent nationalism, xenophobic ethnic violence, and religious revival, often of a very conservative kind. The universalism implicit in socialist and communist ideologies is being succeeded by varieties of political parochialism that negate humanist values no less than the totalitarianism that it is replacing.

Political ideologies of Western origin are undergoing a parallel backlash as secular nationalism is challenged by competing forms of religious nationalism. Most dramatic is the emergence of radical Islam in both its nationalist and terrorist manifestations. The Islamic Revolution in Iran led by the Ayatollah Khomeini in 1979 was the watershed event that recharged Islamic movements in Algeria, the Sudan, Egypt, Pakistan, and elsewhere in the Muslim world. Secular government, which is among the crowning humanistic glories of the Enlightenment, is seen as the matrix of depravity and ungodliness among Islamic resurgents. It is also interpreted as a legacy of Western imperialism that has been tried and failed in the Muslim world, leaving oppressive and corrupt military dictatorships in its wake.

The emergence of religious nationalism and despair with the secular state extends beyond Muslim movements. Hindu nationalism threatens the secular character of Indian society and its constitution. In neighboring Sri Lanka, some elements in the dominant Sinhalese population have called for the creation of a Buddhist state in the face of an especially bloody civil war waged with Hindu Tamil secessionists, which seems as I write to be feeling its way toward a tentative peace. On the West Bank, Jewish nationalists, who comprise the trenchant hard core of the settlement movement, seek to establish a "halachic" state on territory deeded to their ancestors by divine will. These global movements directed by visions of religious glory severely and all too violently compete with the humanist legacy of secular political arrangements, including democracy based on the equality of all individuals, respect for minorities, and human rights.

The most calamitous expression of this parochialism on the world scene is the unspeakable horror of genocide targeting ethnic and religious minorities. While the decades between World War II and the Second Humanist Manifesto of 1973 witnessed politically generated mass slaughter in China, Indonesia, Guatemala, Chile, and elsewhere as virulent expressions of the Cold War, growing awareness of the Holocaust suggested that the genocide of ethnic and religious minorities might be relegated to the past. But this hope was tragically short-lived. The killing fields of Cambodia in the "auto-genocide" of the late 1970s, the extermination of two hundred thousand Iraqi Kurds in the 1980s, the murder of as many Bosnian Muslims in the 1990s, and the unfathomable slaughter of almost nine hundred thousand Rwandans in less than a year in 1994 provided ghastly evidence that the arrival of the "humanist century" would suffer a torturous postponement.

Domestic Challenges: From the Right

Though spared the violence, American society is also succumbing to the despair over the alleged barrenness and moral depravity wrought by the removal of religion from the public square.[2] The result is an American *kulturkampf*, with battle lines drawn more starkly than they have been in more than a century. The political, legislative, and judicial divisions are the most obvious, and therefore, most accessible to public debate and struggle. But they represent the tip of the iceberg, beneath which seethes a cultural schism, pitting religiously infused and hitherto silent occupants of America's southern and midwestern outbacks against liberal elitists residing on the coasts.

In the late 1970s, with the emergence of the Moral Majority under the leadership of Rev. Jerry Falwell, the sleeping giant of evangelical and fundamentalist Christianity entered the activist fray and has subsequently transformed the American political landscape. No shift in American politics has been as consequential both at the grassroots level and in the citadels of power within the Washington beltway. The United States, especially since the presidency of Ronald Reagan, has shifted far to the right, a move which is growing in intensity and is fueled primarily by the conservative and ultraconservative churches.

While identifying "secular humanism" as its adversary, the enemies of the Religious Right range far more broadly to encompass groups, movements, and cultural values that violate the Religious Right's patriarchal, authoritarian, and antimodernist sensibilities. An analysis of its positions uncovers a profound anxiety with issues driven by sexual freedom, especially the egalitarian initiatives of women epitomized by the accessibility, since the early 1970s, of legal abortion. Additional issues filling the agenda of the Religious Right include cutting government-supported social programs, augmenting the military budget, demanding a balanced federal budget, restoring organized prayers to the public schools, promoting the teaching of "scientific creationism," vetting federal judges for their conservative opinions, opposing gun control, and lending strong support to Israel as a vehicle toward fulfillment of biblical end-time scenarios.

In accordance with its analysis of the moral erosion of American society resulting from the triumph of secular culture, the Religious Right, together with its secular allies, has sought to undermine the separation of church and state, which has served as normative jurisprudential doctrine for more than half a century. Seeking to replace the Jeffersonian wall of separation with a doctrine of religious accommodationism, the Right can count in its corner at least three Supreme Court judges, as well as several major national political figures, who within the current climate ride the winds of the religious resurgence.[3]

While the failure of Protestant evangelicals and their allies in the Catholic and orthodox Jewish communities to undo *Roe v. Wade*, as well as other legislative gains they deem crucial to their success, has caused some fracturing of the Religious Right on the national scene, progressives and humanists can nevertheless find little room for comfort or optimism. The indisputable indicator of the Religious Right's success is the fact that the leader of its minions is the current occupant of the White House. Neither Jerry Falwell nor Pat Robertson nor Ralph Reed is the de facto head of the Christian Right. As a born-again Christian who laces his rhetoric with biblical allusions recognizable to conservative Christians, George W. Bush has sealed the trust of this huge constituency. From attacking family planning in the international arena to war making to opposing gay marriage, the president is devoted to pushing ahead their agenda.

Perhaps no program better represents Bush's allegiance to the Religious Right's interests than his aggressive pursuit of faith-based initiatives. This ill-conceived drive to open federal coffers for direct aid to churches in pursuit of their social missions is the most frontal assault on church-state separation, and hence religious freedom, imaginable. Despite the efforts of conservative Christians to revise the religious views of America's founders, Bush's "Charitable Choice" initiative categorically violates the establishment clause of the First Amendment as the framers understood it. The perils of melding religion with the economic and political power of the state, as we have noted, grow severely ominous in the light of the dangers wrought by such unholy marriages elsewhere in the world. After three hundred years of prodding the tiger into the cage, it has been let loose once more.

It is a tragic irony of the American evangelical subculture (excluding its African American sector) that its prevailing identification with conservative politics and the growing strength of the Republican Party has placed it in the position of supporting an economic agenda that counters its own class interests. Yet this contradiction is a testament to the symbolic power that sketches the fault lines of the contemporary culture war. Conservatives have promoted themselves as the political movement that preserves American military hegemony, wrests individualism from the hands of intrusive government, and reinforces the pillars of religion, family, and values. It is the success of this political juggernaut, engined by conservative and triumphalist religion, that has placed humanists on the defensive and makes humanist political action imperative.

Domestic Challenges: From the Left

Postmodernism was born out of the failures of the New Left. While much has been made of the countercultural values of the 1960s, the political dynamics of the era, which included the civil rights struggle and ending the war in Vietnam, also sustained a strong commitment to economic justice. Its sustaining critique, whether Marxist, democratic socialist, or reformist, was to that extent economist and implied a baseline of universal values. In its assault on capitalism and its excesses, the Left assuredly has lost. The attack on the New Left, which has become a commonplace of conservative polemics (although often severely caricatured and distorted by the Right), was completed by the Reagan presidency. Right-wing ideology has triumphed in the public mind over the liberal politics of the Great Society programs of the 1960s.

The effect of this defeat was to virtually cede the bread-and-butter issues that had characterized the Old Left, and parts of the New, in favor of "identity politics," including a preoccupation with multiculturalism and "tolerance." Rather than subordinating ethnic differences to the universal imperatives of economic justice, the new politics has seen the expression of political interests through one's ethnic, religious, and gender identity, be it black, Latino, Jewish, female, or gay. The political Left had morphed into the "cultural Left" with its emphasis on "political correctness."

It certainly is true that the politics of the 1960s spoke the language of equality while greatly overlooking the historic oppression of women, minorities, and gays. To its credit, the cultural Left has chastened and humanized the rough edges of a politics that too often omitted subjective sensitivities from the political equation. As philosopher Richard Rorty has argued, the cultural Left "has reduced the amount of sadism in our society."[4]

While humanists can appreciate these developments as welcome and progressive ones, it is hard to escape the conclusion that they have done little to alleviate the grievous economic conditions that confront American society and are becoming intolerable under the second Bush administration. Never has the gap between the poor and the wealthy corporate elite been greater. The middle class, which has sustained liberal and humanistic values in America, is experiencing greater pessimism and stress than at any time since the Second World War. While the politics of multiculturalism has done much in enabling America to grapple with its historical legacies of racism, sexism, and homophobia, the dour feeling remains that each parochial group, with its attendant claims of "victimization," is left to scramble for its piece of the diminishing pie, while corporate hegemons and their political allies continue to appropriate wider swaths of the American economy as their private domain.

The emergence of identity politics on the ground has been theoretically legitimated by postmodernism nurtured in the academy. Contemporary humanism is a child of the European Enlightenment. As such, it intellectually rests on the sturdy pillars of reason, scientific method, and the search for truth, which presuppose objectivity. Humanism is most comfortable in an environment of theoretical consistency and fact.

Postmodernism is built on the presumption that such values are historicist in character and declares that the sun has set on the modern era. While humanists and postmoderns may agree that there are no transcendental "Truths" beyond the realm of sensory experience, the postmodern claim that negates objectivity and relegates knowledge of it to subjective assertions of power is a reductionism unacceptable to the axioms on which the humanist worldview is grounded. In its starkest sense, postmodernism dissolves objectivity into subjectivity, fact into opinion, and ethics into matters of taste.

It is in the field of epistemology that postmodernism most tightly allies itself with identity politics. While eschewing fixed points, postmodernism claims that people are socialized within their specific ethnic, religious, and cultural communities. This socialization shades inevitably into a relativism of knowledge and the reinforcement of parochial boundaries separating disparate communities. In its most extreme manifestations, postmodernism suggests an incommensurability of discourse that denies any meaningful communication across group lines.

From the political standpoint, in its denial of any objective anchors outside the interests of communities by which to adjudicate competing claims, the postmodern worldview condemns the relations of these groups to eternal power struggles. To the humanist, the world defined by postmodernism is a grim world, lacking in inspiration and grandeur—and, ultimately, hope.

SKETCHING A HUMANIST POLITICS

Humanism has a long pedigree. Its origins can be found in the East in aspects of early Buddhism, Taoism, and Confucianism. In the West, humanism can be traced to elements in the Bible, fifth-century Athens, Stoic and Epicurean philosophies of the Hellenistic period, the Renaissance, and the European Enlightenment. In the Enlightenment period, inclusive of the Age of Science in the seventeenth century and the political theorizing of the eighteenth, the pillars of modern humanism were set in place. Yet throughout Western history and up until the nineteenth century, humanism remained a tendency within Jewish and Christian thought and society, rather than a self-conscious and clearly defined movement. It is only since the emergence of Auguste Comte's short-lived "Religion of Humanity" in the 1840s and 1850s and the creation of agnostic movements, primarily in Britain in the second half of the nineteenth century, that humanism has coalesced into a philosophy assuming organizational form.

In the United States, humanism emerged after the Civil War among thinkers influenced by, among others, the radical theology of the left-wing Unitarian and transcendentalist Theodore Parker. Humanism moved away from its transcendentalist roots toward a philosophy based on philosophical naturalism in the twentieth century, via the influence of such pragmatists as Charles S. Peirce, William James, and especially John Dewey. Contemporary American humanism finds organizational expression in the Ethical Culture movement, the American Humanist Association, the Council for Democratic Humanism, the Society for Humanistic Judaism, and sectors of the Unitarian Universalist movement. It is to these associations and individuals who share kindred worldviews that this chapter refers in its call for political activism among humanists.

Humanism is ineluctably political. On occasion one still hears the plea that humanists confine their interests and activities to discussion centered primarily on reinforcing humanist identity, yet efforts to exclude political activity are a logical contradiction that debases the humanist project. All associations, organizations, and movements are unavoidably political, either by intent or default, and there can be no stance of innocence. Opponents of political action within humanist groups contend that by taking sides humanists risk fracturing their small and fragile organizations.

These putative risks frame the challenges; they of themselves do not exempt humanist groups from the mandate to actively join the political struggle. The reluctance to assert its small but distinctive voice in the political arena equates to a position of quietism, which in any time, but especially in our time of conservative and ultraconservative triumphalism, lends whatever political capital humanists possess to the maintenance of a perilous status quo. Moreover, quietistic humanism resembles the characteristic nonengagement, especially the preoccupation with individual salvation, that humanists frequently seeks to condemn, rightly or wrongly, in the traditional faiths.[5] Humanism is an activistic worldview and needs to express itself as such lest it stagnate as a middle-class indulgence preoccupied with refining metaphysical correctness.

Naturalistic humanism philosophically covers a broad range of values that characteristically resist doctrinal formulations. As a product of the Enlightenment, humanism emphasizes the primacy of reason[6] in the process of problem-solving, underscores the autonomy of the individual, cherishes democracy, recognizes the social character of human beings, appreciates (though some would argue not sufficiently) our dependence on and interaction with the natural world, and eschews determinisms of any sort as it projects a future that is open to human development and cultural evolution. Humanism also posits a strong emphasis on ethical values—the foundational commitment from which a humanist politics emerges.

As we confront the difficult challenges to humanism in the twenty-first century, we inevitably search for theoretical handles by which to leverage our activism. The catastrophic consequences of applied determinisms and ideologies in the century just past should incline us toward the reformist rather than revolutionary approach that has historically characterized political initiatives within humanist movements. In this sense, there is wisdom in mining the gold of theorists from within the humanist movement itself.

Mining Our Sources:
Inspiration From Felix Adler and John Dewey

Two thinkers of extraordinary scope, originality and theoretical brilliance were Felix Adler and John Dewey. Though different in temperament and philosophical approach, Adler and Dewey shared much in common and complemented each other in areas where they differ.

Born in Germany of Jewish heritage in 1851, Adler was the founder of the Ethical Culture movement. Dewey, eight years Adler's junior, was a Vermont Yankee who became the prevailing luminary of Columbia University's philosophy department in its golden age. Although Deweyan thought is experiencing a renaissance in the academy, Adler has never achieved the place in American philosophy that his brilliance and creativity merit.

Both Adler and Dewey developed theoretical bases for progressive social change. Both were reformist educators and apostles of democracy. Of great relevance to their social theory is that each held to an organic notion of human society and the social basis of individual development. Consequently, both viewed social action as not merely a matter of transforming society but an ethical obligation. The work toward social betterment transformed the actor in the process of applying himself or herself to the task of improving the world beyond one's immediate interests. Adler and Dewey identified democracy not with the formal rituals of civic duty, but as a character style that led to the growth of individuals who participated in the life of the community.

Ethical Culture was founded in 1876 in New York City. Adler, who came out of Reform Judaism and was greatly influenced by Emerson, situated Ethical Culture on the extreme left-wing of theological speculation. In Ethical Culture he sought to create a religious movement, founded exclusively on ethics, that would be "ultra-scientific without being anti-scientific." Indeed, Ethical Culture is completely modernist in its assumptions, viewing social reform as intrinsic to its mission. The animating spirit of Ethical Culture in its founding decades was a felt need to redress the evils wrought by the industrial revolution. Though Adler was a neo-Kantian idealist who spurned naturalistic humanism as an insufficient philosophical ground for ethics, he created Ethical Culture as a "broad tent" that attracted freethinkers who, in accordance with Adler's maxim, shared a common commitment to place "deed above creed." Though Ethical Culture from its founding until the 1930s did not identify itself as a humanist movement, Adler's idealism could be construed epistemically as humanistic, and the movement attracted humanists in all but name.

John Dewey was the premier American humanist thinker of the twentieth century. Dewey, as noted, has experienced a revival in academic circles in the past dozen years,[7] in part in response to the aridity of logical positivism. Dewey's pragmatism, antifoundationalism, and affirmative activism also render him attractive to those postmoderns who recoil from the nihilist conclusions of an extreme postmodern outlook.[8] Renewed interest in Dewey also results from reasons that coincide with this chapter: the desire to find theoretic moorings for a humane progressive politics in an era that has seen the demise of Marxism and recoils against the reactionary movements we encounter at home and abroad.

Though Dewey never joined the Ethical Culture movement, his influence on it was transformative. Under the pressures of Deweyan instrumentalism in the early decades of the twentieth century, and in response to the influx into Ethical Culture of newly arrived immigrants from Eastern Europe, who brought with them commitments to socialism and Marxism, Ethical Culture increasingly moved into the humanist camp. By the time of Adler's death in 1933, it could be noted "Ethical Culture [was] the movement that Adler built and Dewey, through his followers, so quickly inherited."[9]

Adler's orientation to social justice was reformist rather than revolutionary. To underscore the need to transform social institutions in a progressive direction, he referred to his approach as "social reconstruction." His prevailing theoretical contribution to social change was twofold: As an ethicist, Adler made central a commitment to the unconditional worth of the person while he posited the organic unity of all individuals within a web of interconnecting and reciprocal relations. In the latter commitment, Adler's theory had a pronounced similarity to the directions in which Dewey was moving, though Adler was more preoccupied than Dewey in validating human worth. Indeed, his idealism lent itself to that process more readily than did Dewey's naturalism. Adler was explicit that the positing of human worth resonated with the traditional Hebraic and Christian concern for the "holiness" or "sacredness" of the person, for which he attempted to find a modern justification through his reworking of Kantian metaphysics. I contend that the centrality of human worth needs to serve contemporary humanists as the foundational principle around which to organize political theory and action, even if Adler's idealism no longer serves as its validating metaphysics.

The centrality of worth furnishes the seminal ideal from which other basic values emerge. It validates a bedrock commitment to rights and a need for their safeguarding. It also implies a commitment to human autonomy. However, as I will discuss below, if we invoke Adler's theory of organic unity, individual autonomy does not connote absolute independence. Rather, individual freedom is played out within the context of communal relations and responsibilities.

In a broader sense, a guiding commitment to human worth propels action in a progressive direction. If we posit respect for human inviolability, and subsequently survey the empirical conditions in which humans live, the gap between the " is" and the "ought" becomes immediately manifest. The ensuing tension can, and for many humanists does, serve as the inspiration to narrow the gap through a commitment to progressive action.

In the spirit of both Adler and Dewey, political analysis is radical from an ethical perspective, but its praxis is reformist. The emphasis that humanism places on rational method, its reliance on empiricism, and its affinity for science require that a humanist politics eschew determinisms and view the human situation as flexible but not infinitely malleable, experimental, and open to the future. The unprecedented bloodletting of the twentieth century should make the humanist wary of revolutionary responses to systemic injustice although oppression *in extremis* may leave no other recourse. Though slogans such as "the perfectibility of man" have often been invoked in humanist literature[10]—indeed Adler's idealism led him to frequently speak of "building the perfect society" as a prevailing human end—we would be wise to interpret this aspiration as serving a heuristic purpose only, not to be taken literally. Though utopianism may arouse the imagination and lift the spirit, it has also been the source of the most gratuitous destruction of human life in the modern era.

The experience of the century we have recently left strongly commends that a humanist politics be principled but liberal and reformist. It needs to be democratic and seek to reconstruct social institutions that create and reinforce structural oppression. In its view of social change, a humanist politics is committed to both justice and direct service, though it is biased in favor of the former.

Above all, contemporary humanism needs to be an ethical humanism. Only a humanism that places ethics at its center can create the philosophical foundations and engage the energies of humanists to respond to the challenges we confront. And an ethical humanism can do no better than to borrow from Adler's guiding concern of defending human worth as its prevailing principle.

A worth-based politics speaks against all political, economic, social, and intellectual forces that threaten dehumanization. It agitates for an open and democratic society as the only society compatible with human dignity. The inviolability of the person militates against political oppression and propels us in the direction of a society in which economic and political equality is the goal. The demand to respect human dignity is also a demand to respect human rights.

A humanist politics is inspired by ideals but remains meliorist and pragmatic in its application of those ideals. While demanding individual freedom, it does not demand radical freedom, nor does it assert radical individualism. Inspired by the organic philosophies of both Adler and Dewey, it recognizes that freedom of the individual emerges out of social context and that it requires commensurate engagement with and responsibilities toward the community. While Adler was a philosophical idealist and held to an essentialist view of the human person and of human rights, a contemporary humanism rooted in naturalism need not do so.

Here we can look to Dewey to complement Adler. Unlike Adler, Dewey does not recognize human dignity or view rights as devolving from an ideal or transcendental understanding of personhood. Rather, Dewey recognizes the "sanctity" of the person, and human rights that are correlative to it, as *claims* made on society that are rooted in human beings as natural and social beings. As Dewey notes, "[W]e reach the conclusion that Right, law, duty, arise from the relations which human beings intimately sustain to one another, and that their authoritative force springs from the very nature of the relation that binds people together."[11] We can also recognize these claims as bases for establishing the social, economic and political conditions necessary for human flourishing.[12] Though Adler and Dewey said little about the natural world, one can take their theories of organicism and develop and apply them to responsibilities that we have to the environment on which human survival and flourishing intimately depend.

Organicism and the Challenges it Confronts

Adler's organicism, to which we find parallels in Dewey's naturalism, sketches a basis for an activist response the challenges humanists face. In their philosophies, the human being is neither radically individual nor collectivist. Rather, for Adler and Dewey, the self is social, but individuality is not submerged within the collectivist whole. The person remains an individual whose development results from active and reciprocal engagement with others to the fulfillment of common ends. The self is individual and social at the same time.

In the political sense, this conception of the self translates into a defense of individual rights as a prevailing humanist concern. But it no less speaks to the recognition of and devotion to social duties in the service of the common good. It seeks to bring into being a society that increasingly allows for the flourishing of individual human potential while safeguarding and respecting the inherent dignity of all. This organic and reciprocal ideal, which is intrinsically and methodologically dynamic and democratic, sketches the humanist vision and inspires action toward its fulfillment. In its commitment to freedom, rights, and democracy, it stands against authoritarianism, patriarchy, and all other forces—political, social, and religious—that oppress and demean the individual. In its appreciation for the social dimension of experience, it recognizes the importance of solid human relations—inclusive of families, friendships, social institutions, and communities—that are essential for nourishing, sustaining, and transmitting what is best in the human experience.

While not necessarily pacifist, an organic humanism is deeply skeptical of war, which it views as a very last resort. It focuses on seeking to redress the root causes of human conflict, recognizing the imperatives of social and economic justice and the creation of those institutions that open vistas to a hopeful future. It tempers nationalism and parochial ideologies with a vision of a harmonious world order.

Finally, an organic humanism lays the foundation for an expanding ecological consciousness through an abiding appreciation of our place in the interactive biosphere. Although humanism, in great measure because of anthropocentric preoccupations inherited from earlier centuries, has much work to do to incorporate a substantive environmental ethic, nothing within humanism, organically understood, obviates such theory and practice. Indeed, it is imperative.

CONCLUSION: COMMITMENT OVER THE LONG RANGE

In a certain sense, the prevailing problem we confront at the beginning of the twenty-first century is the major ethical problem people have always confronted in society, namely, how do we not hold the human being cheaply? How do we create a social order that will respect the dignity of human beings? Both questions and both answers are humanistic. They are questions that implicitly guided John Dewey's far-ranging work and explicitly inspired the thoughts and deeds of Felix Adler. Humanists can do no better than consult these sources and build upon them in order to construct a contemporary humanist politics.

But a question remains: How can a humanist politics, so sketched, differentiate itself from liberal, progressive politics in general? Here I think Adler, the idealist, improves upon Dewey, the instrumentalist.

There can be little doubt that Dewey was a visionary who had faith in the possibility of progress and an improved human future. But Dewey is primarily a thinker, as his biographer, Alan Ryan, has noted, "of the here in now."[13] His philosophy is dedicated to problem solving at the expense of explicating grander visions. Dewey's prose, as has been often noted, is dry, difficult, and devoid of metaphor. To be inspired by Dewey is to synthesize a coherent vision after long reflection on the specifics and details of thought. There is so much that is right and useful in Dewey, but there is not much to appeal to the heart.

Adler, speaking in a different idiom, was only incrementally a more accessible thinker, but as an idealist, his thought reached out to the infinite. For him, the improvement of the here and now was guided by a long-range vision—to create a society "in which no men or class of men shall be mere hewers of wood and drawers of water for others; in which no man or woman, or class of men or class of women shall be used as tools for the lusts of others, or for the ambitions of others, or for the greed of others."[14]

Adler believed that a person who devotes himself or herself to the cause of justice and labors under a vision of a perfect society—never to be attained but only approached—is armed against the frustration that inevitably results from the grit of political struggle. To be committed to short-range, material goals is to quit in the face of immediate failure. But to see oneself as an actor in the drama of creating a just world, to assess oneself as a component of a grand narrative, is to be fortified for the long haul. It is to build oneself into justice and transform oneself by the light of the ideal.

The method and aims of a humanist politics are therefore twofold, and this twofold character differentiates it from progressive political action in general: It is to appreciate that in working for a better society in the moment, one is inspired by the far-off ideal of an ethically improved human condition. But this work, so undertaken and inspired, does not call upon us to deplete our energies in unending acts of self-sacrifice, for it recognizes that in dedicating oneself to those ideals, one is rewarded with a sense of purpose and sublime satisfaction that ennobles the inner life.

NOTES

1. *Humanist Manifesto II* (Amherst, NY: Prometheus Books, 1973), p. 14.

2. See especially Richard John Neuhaus, *The Naked Public Square: Religion and Democracy in America* (Grand Rapids, MI: W. B. Eerdmans, 1984) and Stephen L. Carter, *The Culture of Disbelief: How American Law and Politics Trivialize Religious Devotion* (New York: Basic Books, 1993). Both authors claim that religion has been marginalized in American life, leaving a vacuum of values. Neuhaus's treatise has become a major source of conservative ideology and polemics on the issue.

3. Chief Justice William Rehnquist and Associate Justices Antonin Scalia and Clarence Thomas support the accommodationist doctrine. In the 2000 presidential campaign, all four major-party candidates—George W. Bush, Dick Cheney, Al Gore, and Joe Lieberman—declared their support for governmental alliances with religion.

4. Richard Rorty, *Achieving Our Country: Leftist Thought in Twentieth-Century America* (Cambridge: Harvard University Press, 1998), pp. 80–81.

5. Marx's assertion that "religion is the opiate of the people," which induces passivity as it substitutes a wishful world for the concrete benefits of this one, lingers as an unexamined cliché for many humanists. Classic scholars, such as Max Weber, and contemporary thinkers, such as Garry Wills, have documented the positive correlation between progressive activism and religious faith. The activism of such exemplars as Mohandas Gandhi and Martin Luther King Jr. cannot be understood without explicating their immersion in Hinduism and the theology of the black Baptist Church, respectively.

6. Critics of humanism, both within and outside of humanist movements, contend that contemporary humanism overdetermines the function of reason and underappreciates the epistemic value of human emotion, imagination, intuition, and faith, all of which humanists apologetically support as "add-ons." I generally concur with this assessment, but this issue is not central to my endorsement of humanist activism.

7. See especially Robert B. Westbrook, *John Dewey and American Democracy* (Ithaca, NY: Cornell University Press, 1991); Steven C. Rockefeller, *John Dewey: Religious Faith and Democratic Humanism* (New York: Columbia University Press, 1991); and Alan Ryan, *John Dewey and the High Tide of American Liberalism* (New York: W.W. Norton, 1995).

8. The American philosophers Richard Rorty and Cornel West are among the most prominent among them.

9. Edward Ericson, quoted in Horace L. Friess, *Felix Adler and Ethical Culture: Memories and Studies*, ed. Fannia Weingartner (New York: Columbia University Press, 1981), p. 259. By the 1950s, through collaboration with the American Humanist Association, a manifestly secular humanist organization grounded on philosophical naturalism, Ethical Culture moved closer to adopting a humanist

rubric. In 1966, the professional leaders drafted a statement explicitly identifying Ethical Culture with humanism.

10. For example, one finds this phrase strewn throughout the writings of humanist psychologist Erich Fromm.

11. John Dewey, *Theory of the Moral Life* (New York: Irvington, 1980), pp. 69–70.

12. See the work of the contemporary economist Amarya Sen and the philosopher Martha Nussbaum for their work on "capabilities theory" as a basis for grounding human rights.

13. Ryan, *John Dewey and the High Tide of Liberalism*, p. 369.

14. Felix Adler, *Life and Destiny* (1903; repr., New York: American Ethical Union, 1944), p. 71.

JOE CHUMAN has served as the professional leader of the Ethical Culture Society of Bergen County, New Jersey, since 1974. He has a doctorate in religion from Columbia University, where he teaches graduate seminars on religion and human rights. He also teaches human rights courses at the United Nations University for Peace in Costa Rica, Hunter College, and Fairleigh Dickinson University. Chuman served as the chairperson of Amnesty International USA's Death Penalty Committee and is currently on the advisory board of New Jerseyans for a Death Penalty Moratorium.

2.

A Humanist Theory of Ethics
Inference to the Best Action

Theodore Schick

One of the great tragedies of mankind is that morality has been hijacked by religion.

—Arthur C. Clarke

ew people would claim that there can be no science without God. Most realize that making correct judgments about the way the world is doesn't require any beliefs about the supernatural. Yet many Americans claim that there can be no morality without God. In a recent poll conducted by the Pew Research Center, 47 percent of the respondents said that a belief in God is necessary to be moral.[1] According to this group, making correct judgments about the way the world should be does require having a belief in the supernatural. The notion that morality depends on God, however, is demonstrably inadequate. Not only is there no causal relation between belief in God and moral behavior, there is no logical relation, either. Any attempt to define morality in terms of God turns out to be circular or false. Consequently, we cannot solve our moral problems by appeal to God.

How, then, can we solve them? I suggest that we can employ a variant of the inference procedure used to identify good explanations. When faced with a choice among competing hypotheses, scientists and laymen alike use a procedure known as "inference to the best explanation" to decide which hypothesis to accept. Similarly, I believe that we can use a similar procedure—inference to the best action—to decide what to do when faced with a choice among competing courses of action. Both procedures involve applying and weighing various criteria. But because these criteria can be specified without reference to anyone's beliefs (including God's), the conclusions arrived at through inference to the best action can be considered just as objective as those arrived at through inference to the best explanation. Thus, there is no more reason to be skeptical about the existence of an objective humanist ethics than there is about an objective humanist science.

THE DIVINE COMMAND THEORY

The theory behind the view that morality requires God is known as "the divine command theory." According to this theory, what makes an action right is that God wills it to be done. The problem with this theory is that if the god referred to is the traditional God of theism, the theory is vacuous. If not, it's false. Either way, it cannot be considered an adequate theory of morality.

Traditional theism maintains that God is all-powerful, all-knowing, and all-good. If being all-good is a defining attribute of God, however, God cannot be used to define goodness because the definition would be circular; the concept being defined would be contained in the concepts doing the defining. In this respect, all the divine command theory tells us is that something is good if it is willed by a supremely good being. While this idea is undoubtedly true, it is uninformative, because it doesn't tell us what it is about God that makes him so good. If we try to eliminate the circularity by taking goodness out of the definition of God, we have no guarantee that what such a being commands will be good. Infinite power and knowledge do not necessarily incline one to the good, as the story of Satan illustrates. So the divine command theory does not provide a plausible account of the nature of morality.

Those who accept the divine command theory are committed to the view that nothing is right (or wrong) prior to or independent of God's willing it to be done (or refrained from). But if no moral principles exist apart from God's will, God's moral choices cannot be principled, and a being that makes unprincipled choices, as Leibniz, the philosopher and inventor of calculus, realized, is not a being worthy of worship:

> In saying, therefore, that things are not good according to any standard of goodness, but simply by the will of God, it seems to me that one destroys, without realizing it, all the love of God and all his glory, for why praise him for what he has done, if he would be equally praiseworthy in doing the contrary? Where will be his justice and his wisdom if he has only a certain despotic power, if arbitrary will takes the place of his reasonable-

ness, and if in accord with the definition of tyrants, justice consists in that which is pleasing to the most powerful? Besides it seems that every act of willing supposes some reason for the willing and this reason, of course must precede the act.[2]

Leibniz's point is that if actions are neither right nor wrong independent of God's will, then God cannot choose one over another because it is morally better. Thus, any moral choices God makes must be arbitrary. But a being who acts arbitrarily does not deserve our praise. So not only is the divine command theory implausible, it is impious as well.

Perhaps the most serious failing of the divine command theory, however, is that it sanctions obviously immoral actions. The Ten Commandments appear in chapter 20 of the Book of Exodus. These are not the only commandments recorded in the Bible, however. In Exodus 21:15, for example, we read, "He that smiteth his father or his mother shall surely be put to death," and in Exodus 21:17, "He that curseth his father or his mother shall surely be put to death." Elsewhere in the Bible, God mandates the death penalty for adulterers (Lev. 20:10), homosexuals (Lev. 20:13), those who worship other gods (Deut. 13:6–11), those who work on the Sabbath (Exod. 35:2), and those women who are not virgins on their wedding night (Deut. 22:13–21). Obviously, the prohibition against killing found in the Ten Commandments is not absolute since, according to the Bible, all of these people should be killed. We know, however, that anyone obeying these commandments would be acting immorally. The defense "God told me to" would carry no weight in either a court of law or the court of public opinion. The fact that we know such actions to be wrong even though they are supposedly commanded by God shows that there must be standards of morality that are independent of God. One of the jobs of ethics is to identify those standards.

Before we undertake that task, however, let's take a look at the standards that we use to judge the truth or falsity of beliefs so that we have a better idea of how such standards function.

INFERENCE TO THE BEST EXPLANATION

Inference to the best explanation is probably the most widely used form of nondeductive inference. Doctors, detectives, and auto mechanics—as well as scientists, lawyers, and laymen—use it every day. Anyone who tries to figure out why something happened uses inference to the best explanation. It has the following form:

1. Phenomenon P.
2. Hypothesis H explains P.
3. No other hypothesis explains P as well as H. (H is the best explanation of P.)
4. Therefore, probably, H is true.

What determines whether one explanation is better than another, however, is not simply the amount of evidence it its favor because all hypotheses are undetermined by their data. Given any set of data, an infinite number of hypotheses can be constructed to account for those data. So the choice between competing hypotheses can never be made on the basis of the evidence alone. The criteria that we use to distinguish among competing hypotheses are known as "cognitive criteria of adequacy."

We seek explanations because we want to understand the world. The amount of understanding produced by an explanation is determined by how well it systematizes and unifies our knowledge. We begin to understand something when we see it as part of a pattern; the more that pattern encompasses, the more understanding it produces. The extent to which an explanation systematizes and unifies our knowledge is determined by such criteria as

- *simplicity*: the number of independent assumptions made by a hypothesis,
- *scope*: the number of diverse phenomena explained by a hypothesis,
- *conservatism*: the fit of a hypothesis with existing theory,
- *fruitfulness*: the ability of a hypothesis to successfully predict new phenomena.

Neurophysiologist Barry Beyerstein provides a useful example of these criteria at work.

Psychologists have accumulated a diverse set of data relating mental states to physical states. Beyerstein classifies these data as follows:

Phylogenetic: There is an evolutionary relationship between brain complexity and species' cognitive attributes.

Developmental: Abilities emerge with brain maturation; failure of the brain to mature arrests mental development.

Clinical: Brain damage from accidental, toxic, or infections sources, or from deprivation of nutrition or stimulation during brain development, results in predictable and largely irreversible losses of mental function.

Experimental: Mental operations correlate with electrical, biochemical, biomagnetic, and anatomical changes in the brain. When the human brain is stimulated electrically or chemically during neurosurgery, movements, percepts, memories, and appetites are produced that are like those arising from ordinary activation of the same cells.

Experiential: Numerous natural and synthetic substances interact chemically with brain cells. Were these neural modifiers unable to affect consciousness pleasurably and predictably, the recreational value of nicotine, alcohol, caffeine, LSD, cocaine and marijuana would roughly be equal to that of blowing soap bubbles.[3]

These data can be explained in many different ways. They are even consistent with the Cartesian view that the mind is a nonphysical substance that interacts with the body. Very few neurophysiologists accept this view, however, because it does not provide the best explanation of the data. Beyerstein explains:

Despite their abundance, diversity, and mutual reinforcement, the foregoing data cannot, by themselves, entail the truth of the psycho-neural identity thesis. Nevertheless, the theory's parsimony [simplicity] and research productivity [fruitfulness], the range of phenomena it accounts for [scope], and the lack of credible counter evidence [conservatism] are persuasive to virtually all neuroscientists.[4]

In other words, although the hypothesis that the mind is the brain is not the only explanation of these data, it is the best one because it does better with regard to the criteria of adequacy than any competing explanation.

These criteria are values or virtues, if you will. The more virtues a hypothesis exhibits, the better it is. Harvard professor Hilary Putnam explains:

Like the paradigm value terms (such as "courageous," "kind," "honest," or "good"), "coherent" and "simple" are used as terms of praise. Indeed, they are action guiding terms: to describe a theory as "coherent, simple, explanatory" is, in the right setting, to say that acceptance of the theory is justified; and to say that acceptance of a statement is (completely) justified is to say that one ought to accept the statement or theory.[5]

To claim that a hypothesis provides the best explanation of something is to make a value judgment. Thus, contrary to popular belief, science is not value-free.

But that doesn't mean that scientific judgments are not objective because the criteria used to decide among competing hypotheses can be specified without reference to anyone's beliefs. What determines the simplicity of a hypothesis, for example, is not what anyone thinks about it but how many independent assumptions it makes. People may disagree about how simple a hypothesis is, but their disagreement is over an objective feature of the hypothesis, not about someone's subjective state of mind. The same goes for the other cognitive criteria of adequacy. People may disagree about how to rate a hypothesis in terms of these criteria, and they may disagree about how to rank the criteria in order of importance. Nevertheless, a judgment based on these criteria can be considered objective because the criteria themselves are not determined by anyone's subjective mental state.

INFERENCE TO THE BEST ACTION

When we're faced with a moral problem, there are usually a number of different courses of action open to us. To decide which action is the best, we can make an inference similar in form to that found in inference to the best explanation. Inference to the best action has the following form:

1. Moral problem P.
2. Action A would solve P.
3. No other action would solve P as well as A.
4. Therefore, probably, A is the best action.

To decide among competing courses of action, we appeal to various ethical criteria of adequacy. These include:

- *justice*: the extent to which an action treats equals equally,

- *mercy*: the extent to which an action alleviates unnecessary suffering,

- *beneficence*: the extent to which an action promotes happiness and well-being,

- *autonomy*: the extent to which an action respects individual rights.

Just as cognitive criteria of adequacy are values that help us determine which hypothesis we should believe, ethical criteria of adequacy are values that help us to determine which action we should perform. Cognitive criteria help us to evaluate the truth or falsity of a hypothesis while ethical criteria help us to evaluate the rightness or wrongness of an action.

These criteria should be viewed as *ceteris paribus* clauses. Other things being equal, we should choose the action that is the most just, the most merciful, the most beneficent, or the most respectful of individual rights (the least coercive). Unfortunately, things are not always equal. The most just action may be the most cruel, or the most beneficent may be the most coercive. In these cases, we must use our judgment to determine which criterion should take precedence.

"Where do these criteria come from?" a divine command theorist might ask. The proper response, I believe, is to claim that they are contained in our concept of morality. Not everyone knows the difference between right and wrong. Our society has a label for that kind of person; we call them "criminally insane." Anyone who has the concept of morality, however, knows that other things being equal, the best action is the one that is the most just, the most merciful, the most beneficent, and the most enabling. That's just part of what we mean when we say that something is moral.

Another way to look at it is this. Some truths are self-evident. A self-evident truth is one that, if understood, is obviously true. Consider, for example, the statement "Whatever has a shape has a size." If you understand that statement—if you have the concepts of shape and size—you know that it's true. You don't need any additional evidence to support your belief. Self-evident truths provide their own evidence; they do not stand in need of any further justification.

This country was founded on the belief that there are self-evident moral truths, and I think that the Founding Fathers were on to something. The statement "Other things being equal, the most just action is the one that should be performed" is self-evident to anyone who has the concept of morality. You can't refute this statement by simply asserting you don't believe it, any more than you can refute the claim that whatever has a shape has a size by simply asserting that you don't believe it. If you believe that the statement is false, then the burden of proof is on you to provide a counterexample. If you are unable to do so—if you cannot cite a situation in which, other things being equal, the most just action is *not* the one that should be performed—then your assertion is irrational, because you have no reason to make it.

One of the primary reasons people are attracted to the divine command theory is that they believe that if God is not the author of the moral law, then morality is relative and anything goes. As the existentialist saying has it, "If God is dead, everything is permitted." The foregoing considerations indicate that this conditional statement is mistaken. There can be an objective morality, one that applies to all people at all times, even if it doesn't have a divine origin. What's more, we have seen that unless there is such a morality, there is no reason to worship God.

THE "I CARE" METHOD

The foregoing ethical criteria of adequacy can be used to formulate the following procedure for arriving at an ethical judgment. The acronym for this procedure is the "I CARE" method:

- Identify the relevant facts.

- Consider the Alternative courses of action

- Rate the various alternatives in terms of the moral criteria of adequacy.

- Effect a decision based on the rating.

Let's consider each of these steps in turn.

1. *Identify the relevant facts.* Moral judgments follow from moral principles together with factual claims. Many moral disagreements involve the facts of the case rather than the principles. To minimize disagreement, then, the first step involved in making a moral judgment involves identifying the relevant facts.

2. *Consider the alternative courses of action.* When faced with a moral dilemma, you can usually perform a number of different actions. The problem is deciding which one of those actions is best from a moral point of view. To make sure that you haven't overlooked a possible course of action, you should take the time to consider all of the different options available to you. This process involves not only identifying the different courses of action, but also considering their consequences. Who will be affected by the decision? How will they be affected? Those affected by a decision are

known as "stakeholders." So good ethical decision making involves identifying the possible courses of action, identifying the stakeholders, and considering the effects that the different actions will have on the stakeholders.

3. *Rate the various alternatives in terms of the ethical criteria of adequacy.* Once the relevant facts are known and the possible courses of action have been specified, the next step is to rate the different actions in terms of the ethical criteria of adequacy. How well does each action do in terms of treating people fairly, avoiding unnecessary harm, promoting the steakholders' well-being, and respecting their rights? You can assess this by asking a series of questions: Does the action treat people fairly and lead to a just distribution of goods and services? Does it alleviate unnecessary suffering? Does it maximize happiness and minimize harm? Does it respect the right to self-determination? If the answer to all of these questions is yes, and if no alternative action does better with regard to these criteria, then the action is morally permissible.

4. *Effect a decision based on the rating.* Once you've identified the best action, the final step is to perform it. After you've performed it, however, you should continue to monitor the situation to see whether things turned out the way you expected. If not, you need to analyze the situation to determine what went wrong. You can then use the results of that analysis in future decisions so that you don't make the same mistake again.

Using this procedure, it's easy to see why the biblical commandments cited earlier are immoral. Although striking or swearing at one's parents is rarely commendable, these actions are not capital offenses. Anyone who killed someone for commiting either of these transgressions would be acting immorally, because such an action is not sanctioned by the ethical criteria of adequacy. It would not be just because it would run afoul of the fundamental principle of retributive justice, which says that the punishment should fit the crime. As the Bible informs us, we should take an eye for an eye, a tooth for a tooth, a life for a life. Since the children in question did not take a life, they should not have to pay with their own. Killing the offenders would not be merciful because doing so would not prevent unnecessary suffering. It would not be beneficent because the harm would outweigh the good. And it would not respect individual autonomy because it would permanently take away the power to choose from those who were executed.

This procedure also makes it clear why any form of discrimination, including discrimination against homosexuals, is immoral. To discriminate against someone is to make an adverse decision about them because of their membership in a group. Discrimination violates the principle of justice because membership in a group is morally irrelevant to the treatment of an individual. What's relevant from a moral point of view is how well someone performs his or her assigned tasks. Making an adverse decision about a competent person simply because that person belongs to a particular group fails to treat equals equally. Discrimination violates the principle of beneficence because it serves to promote the less competent over the more competent, thus lowering productivity and reducing social welfare. It violates the principle of autonomy because it limits the choices of those discriminated against and diminishes their ability to advance according to their own merit. It violates the principle of mercy because it makes the victims of discrimination suffer unnecessarily. All those who practice discrimination, including racists, sexists, homophobes, and anti-Semites, should be ashamed of themselves because they are engaging in immoral behavior, regardless of what the Bible or any other sacred text says about it.

When a practice is in the best interests of everyone involved, treats people fairly, and doesn't violate anyone's rights, it should be considered morally permissible. This is the basis of the case for euthanasia. As long as euthanasia is confined to those who not only are suffering unmitigable pain but also choose it freely and willingly, it is consistent with the ethical criteria of adequacy. Those who oppose euthanasia fear that legalizing it will lead to involuntary killing: Families may subtly coerce those facing death to end their lives sooner rather than later in hopes of preserving their inheritance, and doctors may covertly take the lives of those they consider to be medically hopeless. These are legitimate concerns because they suggest that legalizing euthanasia may violate the principles of autonomy and justice. But those who make this argument owe us some empirical evidence establishing the existence of the cause-effect relationship they posit. In the absence of such evidence, their objection is ungrounded.

Obviously, much more could be said about these matters. But I hope I have shown not only how an objective humanist theory of ethics is possible but also how it can be used to solve moral problems.

NOTES

1. The Pew Research Center for the People and the Press, "Americans Struggle with Religion's Role at Home and Abroad," Pew Forum on Religion and Public Life, March 20, 2002, http://pewforum.org/publications/surveys/religion.pdf.

2. Gottfried Wilhelm von Leibniz, "Discourse on Metaphysics," in *Leibniz: Selections*, rev. ed., ed. Philip Wiener (New York: Scribner, 1982), p. 292.

3. Barry Beyerstein, "The Brain and Consciousness: Implications for Psi Phenomena," *The Hundredth Monkey and Other Paradigms of the Paranormal*, ed. Kendrick Frazier (Amherst, NY: Prometheus Books, 1991), p. 45.

4. Ibid.

5. Hilary Putnam, *Realism with a Human Face*, ed. James Conant (Cambridge: Harvard University Press, 1990), p. 138.

THEODORE SCHICK is a professor of philosophy and the head of the Department of Philosophy at Muhlenberg College. He is also the director of the Muhlenberg Scholars Program and coauthor (with Lewis Vaughn) of *How to Think about Weird Things: Critical Thinking for a New Age*, currently in its fourth edition.

3.

Common Ground

Finding Our Way Back to the Enlightenment

Thomas De Zengotita

Postmodernism is a stance of pure criticism. . . . [I]t avoids making any claims, asserting any values or acknowledging its own implicit system of values, in particular its orientation toward sophistication and aesthetics. Left politics requires a conception of a better society and an assertion of a better set of values than those that now prevail. This does not mean that any particular vision of society or any particular definition of those values is the last word; a left perspective requires ongoing discussion and debate. But it is not possible for a purely critical stance to serve as the basis for left politics.

—Barbara Epstein

First an anecdote. A friend of mine, very committed and active, a teacher of postcolonial history—he responded immediately and passionately to 9/11. He spoke out loud and clear, holding the United States' support for corrupt and terrorizing regimes historically responsible for the conditions that produced the terrorists and shaped the views of the millions who applauded their action. He insisted on the difference between explanation and justification, but the intensity of his convictions made him controversial—anonymous denunciations to the administration, that sort of thing—and I often found myself defending him.

Now, it happens that my friend had lost a brother to terrorism on Flight 103 over Lockerbie in 1988, something I was quick to point out, since it tes-

© December 2002 by *Harper's Magazine*. All rights reserved. Reproduced from the January 2003 issue by special permission.

tified to the authenticity of his convictions. And that's essential, because people inclined to go with the flow want to believe that outspoken critics are striking self-important poses. One woman I talked to, who understood traumatic loss from personal experience, zeroed in on this piece of information: "That's what I don't get," she said. "How could Mr. D. think the way he does after what happened to him? It doesn't seem natural."

"Natural." That's the word to watch.

Like most decent people living normal lives, this woman has no interest in social and economic history. No serious study informs her political opinions. For Ms. S. life is about job and family and friends, and if events in the world occasionally intrude, she takes account of them as best she can, gleaning impressions from media coverage, from chance encounters with persuasive people, from her personal feelings for public figures, and from the mood in her immediate milieu. That's why she could put her finger so precisely on the reason most people don't pay attention to radical critics. It just doesn't seem natural to be so intensely involved with events in distant times and places at the expense of living the way most people do—invested in one's daily surroundings. It seems almost perverse.

Inspired by some passing muse, my reply to her went something like this: "Mr. D.'s core belief is that every human life is as valuable as every other human life, that every mother's loss, every brother's loss, is as terrible as any other. He also believes that, beginning with the conquest of the world by invading Europeans, we have inflicted untold millions of such losses and have continued to do so up through the Vietnam War and, more indirectly, to this day. . . ."

Ms. S. nodded as I went along, but I could see she thought I was evading the issue until I added, "and I am sure that within a few days, maybe a few hours, of hearing the news about his brother, Mr. D. thought about all those millions of anonymous losses, thought about how each one was like this one, the one that happened to be his."

At first she wanted to reject this whole notion, find some way to disbelieve it, call it crazy. But then she said, "I didn't know politics could go that deep."

The more I think about it, the more striking it is that politics does go that deep for some people. As a matter of life habit, they identify intensely with (and against) multitudes of represented strangers—reading about them constantly, hating these, supporting those while other people, most people, just don't. Except during a crisis, when fear is upon them, when they rally around the obvious rallying point, swept along in whatever direction the powers that be want to go.

Political activists need to think about this. It isn't right to assume that anyone who isn't engaged is somehow impaired, corrupted by propaganda, distracted by sports and sitcoms. That bread-and-circuses stuff just doesn't cut it anymore. Noam Chomsky's 9/11 book got better shelf position at Barnes & Noble than Dr. Phil, and basic information about the rape of the planet has been endlessly disseminated. No, let's face it. People aren't interested. They don't care. That's the truth.

It's also important to notice that political engagement is not a function of education—if only people knew this or that, then surely they would rise up and demand. . . etc., etc. Droves of highly educated citizens are indifferent to events unrelated to their immediate concerns, and many a news junkie ranting away on call-in radio never went past high school.

This is all quite mysterious, having to do with hidden confluences of circumstance and character. But this much is clear: deep political engagement is, if not unnatural, at least unusual. It takes something extra to influence people in this way, to cause them to extend their sense of self to encompass multitudes of strangers.

The most extensive such identification possible, the one I attributed to Mr. D., is an identification with all humanity and each human being. In its secular form, that identification is rooted in the ideals of Enlightenment humanism, ideals articulated by Locke and Rousseau and Kant, and brought to bear on historical events in the Bill of Rights and the Declaration of the Rights of Man—all familiar, if disputed, territory. However miserably partisans of these principles failed to fulfill them in practice, the principles themselves are unambiguous, and they all depend on that fundamental identification of each of us with all of us, with the sheer human being abstracted in the ideal from concrete contexts of history and tradition.

That's what ideals are. Abstract.

I am using "identity" precisely because it isn't part of the Enlightenment vocabulary. I've imported it from now-dominant postmodern rhetorics (multiculturalism, gender, sexual orientation) that derive from a critique of modernity in general and Enlightenment humanism in particular. We owe that critique to Adorno and Heidegger, Bataille, Benjamin, Foucault, Lyotard, Derrida, Fish, Butler, Haraway, and Said, and to a generation of educators, inspired by them to shape the academy we know today. College graduates since the seventies have learned to associate progressive politics with a deconstruction of concepts such as "natural rights," "natural reason," "human progress," and even "human being." No longer self-evident and universal, they were exposed as self-serving constructions of a dominant interest group (white bourgeois males), and politics was refigured as a struggle for access to power by other groups, by those whom moderates had exploited and marginalized. And all those Others were to propose constructions of their own—"discourses," they were called, in deference to the French—and deploy them against the hegemony of Western, especially modern, ideas and institutional arrangements. Hence, the culture wars of the last thirty years. Familiar ground, again.

On this familiar ground, I want to argue that no matter how justifiable the emphasis on identity, no matter how empowering the turn to specifics of experience that go with being black or gay—that is, in spite of all the undeniable gains we owe to identity politics[1]—I want to argue that progressive politics is still, as a matter of fact rather than of rhetoric, based on Enlightenment principles and has been all along. And I want to argue that progressives should acknowledge this basis explicitly and stand together on this foundation once more—or that'll be all she wrote. Time is not on our side.

It has been possible, even convenient, to deny a foundation in Enlightenment humanism while fighting to establish African American studies programs and rid the workplace of sexism. It has been easy to imagine that sheer Foucauldian power struggles were being won or lost by this or that constituency. But in the crisis we now face, with the lives of millions at stake, with the United States embracing an open policy of empire—in these desperate circumstances, such renderings seem suddenly parochial. It did and does matter that Jenny feels inhibited in math class because the boys are so aggressive, and it did and does matter that the CEO of AOL Time Warner is a black man. But so many people don't have any schooling at all, and AOL Time Warner is part of the problem, not the solution. The level of engagement demanded of us now is much deeper than the issue of access within the overdeveloped world, and Enlightenment principles are the only conceivable anchor for the cause of human progress in general—the cause we must take up once again.

The foundational priority, the logical and emotional necessity, of these principles should be evident to any progressive willing to admit to some confusion since 9/11, to anyone feeling that it is not enough to nod when Scott Ritter talks, to mock John Ashcroft, and so on down the list of typical gestures—that is, to any progressive feeling the need for a coherent position in this new context and finding it difficult to fashion one. For we experience the foundational priority of Enlightenment principles, if we are sincerely trying to work out such a position, because these principles are what orient our judgments before we make them.

Before you are informed, before you know what weapons Iraq actually has, before you read up on Pashtun history—what is your attitude? As you begin to educate yourself, before you have made up your mind, as you look into the histories and commitments of the parties, what guides your inquiry, especially when your customary prejudices don't apply neatly—when, for example, your multicultural impulses and your feminist commitments diverge? What are you looking for when you really have to think and decide, rather than just hit the replay button on your polemic deck?

Doesn't it work this way? One may not know what distinguishes Sunni from Shi'ite at first, but the inclination to progressive politics comes down to one's willingness to find out. But more than that. In the end, when deciding what position to take, you are also prepared to judge those differences according to—let's call it the degree of their humane commitments. That's the criterion. When the big chips are down, identity considerations yield to humanist principles, because, as an articulated value, the acceptance of difference depends upon them, logically, emotionally, and historically. You don't need a philosophical argument to "prove" that humanist principles are real if they are actually at work in you.[2]

And this all holds for diversity practices closer to home as well. When we acknowledge the Other as truly other, it can seem as if we leave the abstract Enlightenment equation of the sheer human being behind. But if we also insist upon access to power for others, it turns out that we have only postponed our dependence on that equation. With the emphasis on groups we added an intervening layer, a very potent layer of concrete signs—race, sex, idiom—and that layer can obscure the underlying, axiomatic conviction, but it still holds: all else being equal, every human life is, by nature—that is, simply by virtue of being human—equal in value to every other and therefore entitled to whatever benefits or protections are at issue in the struggle for access.[3]

Everything hangs on the "therefore," on whether or not it actually operates this way in our political thinking. If it does, then we have found what we need—the basis for a coherent ideology that promises unity for progressives at this critical hour.

But isn't that just what postmodern theory, in all its variety, taught us—that all else is never equal? That nobody actually exists outside a context, outside history? That the Enlightenment axiom, the sheer human being, is a figment, a reduction of the socially constructed settings in which real people always already live? That this abstraction is, at best, a projection of modern Western ideas onto other ways of life? Or, at worst, an expression of an imperial mind-set, a God's-eye view of nature and humanity that may carry connotations of justice but actually serves to rationalize Western domination of the world? So, surely, we can and must do without it?

Yes. Yes. Yes. Yes. Yes. No.

How could the postmodern critique get it right on all but the last question? By misunderstanding the nature of modern abstractions—especially those associated with nature (natural law, state of nature, etc.), to whose authority the Enlightenment appealed for leverage out of Europe's Middle Ages. The reasons for this misunderstanding are complex, but it comes down to this: you don't have to believe in an abstract ideal the way you believe in the chair under your butt in order to believe in that ideal. Ideals are real in a different way from the way chairs are real, and furthermore, in the case of Enlightenment ideals, they are universally real. That is, every human being, consulting what early moderns liked to call "natural reason," would come up with something like those ideals, given the opportunity. "Natural reason" just means what an unbiased person would hold to be the case, where "unbiased" means free of historical conditions and local attachments.

Now, the postmodern critique of such ideals rests on the undeniable fact that there is no such person. Pretty devastating at first glance. But even Enlightenment thinkers (contrary to stereotype) understood this. Natural reason was a possibility—hence, the "would." Possibility is the mode of existence appropriate to an ideal. Did they also tend to reify? That is, to believe that God built natural reason into us and ordained natural laws for this reason to access? Did they sometimes imagine that humanity had fallen away from an historical state in which those laws actually held sway? They did a lot of that, yes—but you don't have to.[4] You can just say, Okay, people are and always have been thrown into concrete circumstances that determine their evaluations and attachments; people are and always have been shaped by linguistic and cultural structures, etc. And then you can say that it would be a good thing if everyone would try to get over that. It would be a good thing if people got past the relatively superficial differences between them, put them in perspective, and came together on common ground—of which there is a lot, by the way—this common ground being what matters most in the end. Even if it is an abstraction.

It's as simple as that, actually.

Put it this way: If your concrete gayness is sufficient to propel your identificational attachment to millions of gay people you don't know, isn't that an abstraction, too? And likewise for women, ethnicities, etc. Compared with the Enlightenment abstraction of universal humanism, the abstractions of identity politics are middle-range, it's true, and it's very important. It means they are packed with vivid specifics that bind people together, especially in the context of oppression or marginalization. In such contexts, race and sexuality and the life experiences they implicate can turn an out-group into an in-group overnight and motivate collective action with a force that also has to be called natural—in some sense, in some pre- or post-Enlightenment sense.

There was a moment for me, it became iconic, it was at some political conference, years ago. A black woman, a commanding presence, rose to declare by way of closing down the discussion, in the tone of one whose patience is exhausted, that she had tried to read Marx once and couldn't understand what all that verbiage meant—but she knew damn well what being black meant.

A burst of heartfelt applause. It went on and on.

I've been haunted by that moment ever since.

The quasi-erotic power of tangible signs of identity and the mores that accompany them (the ways of gayness) explains the gradual displacement of socialist agendas by diversity agendas over the last thirty years. But the Enlightenment abstraction is based on some pretty tangible markers, too, if you stop and think about it—as people must if they are to be persuaded to identify with Afghan refugees, for example, or victims of the bombing of Baghdad. Here's a partial list: Food, dreaming, safeness, humor, the sky, music, greetings, snakes, death, fire, stories, dignity, pain. . . .

Very concrete, and quasi-erotic too, in its own way. And identification with all of humanity by abstraction through markers like these has this add-on: a commitment to universal rationality, to making judgments based on our common humanity in spite of the differences—a commitment that is natural in the Enlightenment sense.

So what's the problem? If the Enlightenment abstraction is in fact operating at the core of diversity politics anyway, why have so many very smart people invested so much in deconstructing, denying, and otherwise undermining these universal foundations?

Here is what it comes down to: Progressives don't want to break with the postmodern critique of the Enlightenment because, if they do, if they explicitly reassert modern principles of a secular and universal humanism, they might have to face the possibility that the modern Western tradition has a real claim—a superior claim—upon the allegiance of humanity after all. Western progressives defined themselves in just this way, of course, for most of the modern era, but not anymore. Few of us want to go there now.

That's what it comes down to.

The price we pay for our unwillingness to face this possibility (and it is only a possibility; there may be other sources for these principles) is high, and getting higher. A case in point: How many people who think of themselves as on the left have lapsed into virtual paralysis in relation to the war on terror because they are privately wondering things about Islam that would be difficult to bring up publicly, for the reason just mentioned? Besides, such a stance has the feel of a tactical disaster. It feels like it would lead immediately to a break in the coalition of identity groups that has represented progressivism since the rise of access politics.

Anyone promoting Enlightenment ideals risks being associated with heirs of Allan Bloom, with Lynne Cheney's cohort. You're haunted by the possibility that you might wake up the next day and find yourself agreeing with Samuel Huntington, find yourself signing up for a war to save Western civilization from polygamous barbarians with dubious dress codes.

But none of this follows logically or ethically or even emotionally—or it wouldn't, if our political conversation could rise to this occasion. Polygamy matters, the headwear doesn't, the veils maybe. Enslaving children counts, food prohibitions don't, and women eating separately—well, again, maybe and maybe not, you have to assess that on a case-by-case basis. And so on. But the universal wrongness of inhumane coercion is the principle you apply to all of them. Will that sometimes be hard to do? Will it be really hard to know how to proceed toward reform of inhumane customs without seeming to revive the imperial project of "civilizing" others? Sure, but so what? Debate the means; the ends are clear. The principle is still valid.

Face it. You respect difference, but only up to a point.

Distinctions can be drawn and maintained, in other words, but only on the basis of the universal principles. We can't afford to hide from this simple truth just because we might "sound like" some smug elitist at the *New Criterion* if we admit to such an allegiance openly.

We actually rely on these principles anyway, don't forget—that's the essential claim here. We leave that foundation obscure, but we operate out of it. This has become especially evident with respect to women's issues that have an international or cross-cultural dimension—clitoridectomy being an outstanding example. Every time feminists assert that women's rights are human rights, they are, in effect, overriding cultural contexts on the basis of a universal humanism derived, as a matter of historical fact, from Enlightenment concepts. Why not just say so?

This is so simple—maybe that's the problem. Maybe intellectuals who spent decades in obscure hermeneutical debate over the illusion of Presence just can't see their way to resolutions this simple. You can align yourself with humanist ideals of modern progress without committing yourself to defending what modernity actually did. What's wrong with that? You can say that science provides a truer account of the material world than myth does, but you can also say that the dualistic worldview that made science possible is implicated in a devastating exploitation of nature, in a degradation of the earth, that may already be irreversible. In effect, you don't have to believe that astrology is as good as astronomy to defend the rights of people who believe in astrology. You can say that the Bill of Rights provides a better foundation for a just society than any theology provides but that the selectivity of its application has been a monstrous injustice. What's wrong with saying these things?

In fact, isn't a lot of the anti-American feeling you have stored up actually based on the disparity between those principles and reality? Between the noble words and daily routines of slave-holding Founding Fathers? Between saccharine-sweet ads for pharmaceutical companies and their vile patent-profiteering in Africa? Between pious blather about leaving no child behind and the reality of resource distribution in our schools? In your heart of hearts, do you in fact hold the West to a higher standard, not just because you live here but because the standard set forth is higher? Isn't the betrayal of humanist principles what gets to you, at bottom? Wasn't that what outraged you initially, in your youth, when you first realized what was going on behind the facade, when you first set out on the path of progressive political engagement?

You certainly don't approve of the way China harvests organs from executed prisoners, for example. Ten thousand sentenced to death last year, and some were still alive when the organs were extracted (the fresher the kidney, the more customer satisfaction—and not mainly for Western markets, sorry). Imagine if our privatized prison systems were doing that. Imagine the uproar, imagine how you would feel. You just don't feel that outrage when it's China. Why not? Is it really just because it's another place, far away, a place in which you have no direct stake or responsibility? Or is it also because that outrage just doesn't kick in, the way it did, for example, if you read descriptions of Governor Bush mocking a condemned woman to whom he had refused clemency? Or, if you do feel a comparable outrage, isn't it because China once seemed to represent the socialist experiment, itself derived from the secular humanist principles in question? In that case, the betrayal of those principles is once again a factor. There is a lot of slavery in Africa and Asia right now. Figures show more slaves there right now than were taken from Africa during the transatlantic slave trade. But somehow that doesn't get you that worked up. Maybe in some way you don't—as a matter of emotional fact—blame the slaveholders so much in this case as you blame postcolonial contexts? So, somehow, African slaveholders in Sudan aren't full moral agents? How could that be?

So what's the answer? Do you or don't you hold the modern West to a higher standard, and is that standard more or less the classic Enlightenment standard of human equity or not? I'm not saying you shouldn't do this, by the way—just in case your mind is so pulverized by pragmatist attacks on the idea of ideals that you think that's where I'm going. My point is that you should start doing it explicitly and affirmatively, because your political convictions are actually grounded in this ideal, no matter how ensnared your rhetoric may be in the intricacies of postmodernism.

Try it this way: If you are a member of an historically marginalized group, doesn't the outrage that motivates your politics derive from a gut sense of the violation of basic justice inherent in historical arrangements as well as from the harm that you and yours have suffered? It's hard to distinguish the sources, but try. And if you are not a member of such a group, ask yourself this: Why do you even care? If you are a straight white man with middle-class advantages, why aren't you a Republican? That would obviously be in your interest, in any Nietzschean sense of the word that might be accepted by postmodern political thought. So what's the story here? Isn't it true that your politics are, at bottom, motivated by Enlightenment ideals?

It will only hurt for a minute if you confess. And the benefits will be many.

For example. Notice that when you confront the right with Europe's genocidal imperialism and the hypocrisy of the Founding Fathers, and argue for restitutional policies based on that history, then they start up about different historical periods, standards of the time, and so on. But there is no systematic way for progressives to unmask this outrageous maneuver from these supposed critics of relativism, because we have relinquished the principles that would expose this hypocrisy. We have, in effect, allowed the right to abscond with the very categories of political philosophy that have nourished progressive movements since the seventeenth century.

Think of the leverage we lost when we gave up on that simple story of progress, especially in relation to the young, for whom "fairness," embryo of the ideal of justice, is so fundamental. What a relief it would be if we could once again summarize modern political history by describing it as a struggle to apply the principles of Enlightenment humanism in accordance with their inherent logic. Because isn't that what we were doing in the movements for civil rights, women's rights, gay rights, and in the labor movements of long ago as well?[5] Isn't that what has been going on all along?

And yet we refuse to describe it that way anymore. No wonder so many of us are reduced, once again, but even more so, to ad hoc mockery and purely negative critique. No wonder those pictures of women shedding their burkas could do so much to dilute a progressive response to Bush's conduct of that war—even though, as of this writing, and in spite of all the bogus promises, essential supplies are still not reaching untold numbers of desperate Afghans, however dressed. And is that not obviously what should be concerning us, according to that deepest principle, the equal worth of every human life?

This appeal will not reach everyone. Some people process every event automatically. Whatever scheme they already have always applies. This argument will mean nothing to them, unless it accidentally supplies some grist for their omnivorous mill. Other people really are locally motivated. Their politics are based entirely on the experience of being gay or the loss of a loved one to handgun violence or empathy for animals in pain, and they really aren't moved by general principles. So be it.

Pragmatists like [Richard] Rorty and [Stanley] Fish may also decline this proffer. They will say, Sure, let's invoke that Enlightenment principle when it works for us, but not when it doesn't. So be it, again. Welcome to the coalition, whenever it suits you. There is no ontological litmus test.

But this argument is really meant for people who find themselves genuinely troubled by questions—and they are questions—like these:

- Is there no progressive figure or movement with mass indigenous support in the Islamic world to serve as a rallying point for Western progressives, analogous to Mandela's ANC, say? If not, why not?
- Why do so many critics of US policy and corporate depredation habitually exaggerate when drawing up their bill of particulars? The truth is bad enough; why the litany of ultimately counterproductive exaggerations?
- At the end of the day, what should overdeveloped countries actually be doing in the area of immigration? Can progressives afford to confine themselves to supporting due process against the INS on the one hand and disdaining Pat Buchanan on the other? What should our immigration policies actually be?
- What about the utter failure of the Democratic Party to represent the interests of a dwindling middle class, not to mention the poor, in the face of corporate hegemony? Why is there not even one likely candi-

date for the Democratic nomination in 2004 who can risk the charge of "class warfare" and lead a movement against those malefactors of great wealth? Not one. That gaping void should give pause to progressives who followed Bill and Hillary and Jesse Jackson as they followed the money down their pragmatical path.

Should progressives consider resurrecting their traditional hostility toward religious literalism? Think about it—in Israel and Palestine, India and Pakistan, Islamic fundamentalism all over the world, Christian fundamentalism at home—this is a horrific force, and the tide is rising. We are talking mass delusion here, aren't we? Maybe it's time to say so again.

Similarly for belief systems in general. Have we collaborated too much with irrationality? Has anthropological relativism and philosophical constructivism, once so liberating, returned to haunt us in the form of an indiscriminate possibilism? Are we responsible for the fact that our top graduate schools are now full of people who think, Hey, alien abductions, psychic readings—it's possible, who knows, who really knows anything? And what about the youthful apathy and irony we so regularly lament? Progressives were running a lot of educational institutions while those attitudes were taking root. Why did our deconstruction of dominant discourses not inspire our students the way it inspired us? Was it because we were taken in by a canon that celebrated Western achievements and marginalized the others of the world while they've been exposed to the Other ever since we had them include the Native American point of view in their kindergarten Thanksgiving project and taught them why they shouldn't say that Columbus discovered America? Was it because, for them, what we have been deconstructing was never really a construct? Because, for them, all constructs have become options on a leveled playing field of optionality, so that after a while—well, who's to judge? Is that why a group of bright high school seniors of my acquaintance, after twelve years of exposure to emancipatory multicultural curricula, could watch the film *Gandhi* and then discuss whether or not it was "biased" because it didn't give the "British point of view"?

Enlightenment principles could inform progressive responses to these questions, and to many more, but they will not provide the deductive certainty to which Bentham once aspired. In fact, the first consequence of a discussion of specifics among people committed to the equity axiom will be to expose what remains of our affirmative agenda for what it is: a shallow and selective laundry list that caters to the short-term interests of various constituencies claiming space under the umbrella, no matter how incoherent the net effect. As when, for example, the largest gay-rights organization in New York cuts a deal to support George Pataki against the first African American in that state ever to have a real shot at becoming governor.

Hopeful imagery involving mosaics and rainbows can no longer mask the truth. Except for undeniable gains made by certain members of certain groups in privileged Western countries, things are getting steadily worse for the wretched of the earth and for the earth itself. In the face of this trend, the response has been—incredibly—to repudiate the very notion of ideological unity, though the cause of progress will surely suffer if only fanatics and imperialists can achieve it. The obvious move is to work out such an ideology, one that embraces diversity and transcends it.

Outlining in any detail what such ideological unity would look like goes far beyond the scope of this essay. Unresolved philosophical issues— essentially pitting sheer material need in some places against customary expectations in other places—would divide progressives at the outset. At the level of policy, judgments about probable outcomes for citizens of the world would have to be made, and very technical disputes would immediately arise. But the commitment in all these debates would be to all those citizens equally. That would be the common ground. That would be the criterion to which all were bound. And that would be a major step forward.

On a tactical level, the advantage of returning to this foundation is immediately apparent. It would allow us to force the bully boys of American Empire to deny the equal value of every human life. They would have to stand up in public forums, in schools and colleges, and explain why the lives of our babies are more valuable than the lives of other peoples' babies. To take it to the root, they would be forced to admit that, when they call people on the American left "decadent" because they didn't react "naturally" to an attack on their own country, the "natural" they are invoking is not the natural of the Second Treatise of Government. Quite the contrary. The "natural" they are invoking is the natural of Darwinian selection and tribalism, the natural of passion and vengeance, the natural of what the Enlightenment called "faction."[6] This "natural" Locke associated with the Fall, and a cosmopolitan Enlightenment explicitly set out to overcome it with modern ideas of rights and reason. Let us force self-appointed defenders of the Western tradition to this admission: It is they who are betraying its highest claim to universality. We remain true to it.

But let us confront ourselves at the same time, along these lines: Have you actually become (or were you always) just a liberal after all? Were your pretensions to radicalism mostly a matter of style, of self-image? Have you been working for the realization of something beyond bourgeois democracy—or have you just been aiming for reform? If what your politics really envisions is Global New Deal meets Respect for Diversity, that's one thing. That means you are a liberal. That means you basically accept a world system of private enterprise and technological innovation and consumer culture, and you want to see it managed so that no one is excluded, the environment is protected, free expression flourishes, and so on. And you can be very active in all sorts of obvious ways, if this is what you are.

If, on the other hand, you are a radical, the ironic implication is this: There isn't much to do right now to distinguish yourself from liberals. Toss a few rocks at a Starbucks during the next WTO meeting if you want, but don't mistake such gestures for genuinely radical responses. What radicals should be doing right now is studying and thinking. You need to put in your ten years at the library, the way Marx did. You need to be figuring out what makes human beings tick and what, if any, direction is to be found in history. And I don't mean some half-assed sci-fi anarcho-Gaia nonsense you cobbled together before you dropped out of Bard; I mean serious study, working toward an alternative to a global bourgeois democracy. What radicals need most right now isn't action but theory.

But to any progressive, liberal or radical, inclined to do more than claim that you were right all along, to anyone inclined to rethink politics in a serious way, to anyone for whom the humanist revelation at the heart of the idea of progress still lives—to you I say, if you can't make a move without support from a French intellectual, put down your Foucault. Take up your Voltaire.

NOTES

1. To take just the most salient case in point: Were it not for identity politics, the degree of xenophobic racism in the American response to 9/11 would have been much worse—more indiscriminate bombing in Afghanistan, more attacks on innocent Muslims in this country, more stereotyping in the press, the whole she-bang. We owe what tolerance we did display to institutionalized values of diversity and to the people who have worked for that institutionalization, especially in education. The insistence of the authorities, however condescending, on distinguishing between terrorists and Muslims was driven by strategic and tactical calculations, but good old political correctness paved the way.

2. Which is not to say that establishing the ontology of such principles is easy

or unimportant. Heavy philosophical lifting will be required. The Enlightenment analysis depended on a no-longer-credible belief in natural design. Providing an alternative account—perhaps a phenomenological account—should be a primary task for progressive intellectuals. But the question here is not, What are these things we call "principles"? It is only, Are these principles actually at work in us?

3. Commitment to this principle does not entail indiscriminate approval of anything anybody says or makes. Arguments about relativism and objectivism, intellectual and aesthetic standards, and so forth, can go on quite consistently between people otherwise committed to political equity.

4. Did they also deploy the most outrageous justifications and rationalizations for excluding women and "savages" from the purview of their principles? They did that, too, yes, but once again, you don't have to. It's the principles themselves to which I am appealing.

5. There is a direct line from Locke's natural right to property based on the value of an individual's labor as against the institutionalized claims of monarchs and Marx's evaluation of social labor as against the institutionalized claims of capitalists. The Hegelianized subject of socialism is as modern as the bourgeois individual, and the narrative of progress, rooted in Enlightenment humanism, comprehends both—in spite of the political and philosophical differences between them.

6. And, it must be admitted, the "natural" to which postmodern identity discourses unwittingly acceded as they jettisoned the very concept.

THOMAS DE ZENGOTITA is a contributing editor of *Harper's* magazine. He also teaches at The Dalton School and in the Draper Graduate Program at New York University. He holds a PhD in anthropology from Columbia University.

4.

The Importance of
Church-State Separation

Edd Doerr

> *During almost fifteen centuries has the legal establishment of Christianity been on trial. What have been its fruits? More or less, in all places, pride and indolence in the clergy; igno- rance and servility in laity; in both, superstition, bigotry, and persecution.*
>
> —James Madison, *Memorial and Remonstance*

Separation of church and state, of religion and government, is prob- ably the United States' most important single contribution to polit- ical theory and practice. That separation, though generally supported by most Americans over the past two centuries, is nonetheless in serious jeopardy today. In order to understand the current threats to separation and to promote strategies for defending that vitally important principle, it is necessary to take a deep and broad historical perspective, however con- densed it must be for the purposes of a chapter of reasonable length. This chapter, then, will sketch the origins of the principle, trace its development from theory to practice, summarize the very real current threats (in no spe- cial order), and offer suggestions for action.

BACKGROUND

Throughout history and throughout the world, religion and government have been closely intertwined. In some cultures there was/is no distinction between these two powerful forces. Some Islamic and even some Christian fundamentalists insist today that there should be no separation. While in

Western history, of which the United States is a product, religion and government came to be distinguished or distinguishable in theory, in actual fact they were/are linked in a variety of ways and to varying degrees.

For example, some Western countries provide tax support to religious schools; some still have established churches (in the United Kingdom the monarch is titular head of the Church of England, a fact that resulted in the curious anomaly of the governor of Maryland enjoying the same titular status, even when the governor was Jewish); some still have compulsory or semicompulsory church taxes.

Established churches were the rule when the first Europeans—British, French, Dutch, German, Swedish, and even Jewish—settled the east coast of North America. Although many of these Europeans came to America for freedom of religion, they brought the European established church tradition with them. By the end of the seventeenth century, the Anglican (Episcopal) Church was established in all colonies from Maryland to Georgia, while Puritan Congregationalism was established in all the New England colonies except Rhode Island.

By the start of the American Revolution, the colonies had become fairly pluralistic and included Anglicans, Congregationalists, Roman Catholics, Baptists, Methodists, Presbyterians, Lutherans, Quakers, Unitarians, and Jews. This pluralism set the stage for the development of church-state separation. The idea was first articulated by Roger Williams, the Rhode Island maverick, who seems to have influenced John Locke, and finally flowered under Thomas Jefferson and James Madison in Virginia during and immediately after the Revolution. By 1786, thanks in part to Madison's brilliant 1785 pamphlet, *Memorial and Remonstrance against Religious Assessments*,[1] the church-state separation principle became law in Virginia, setting the pattern that the other states would sooner or later follow.

In 1787, the United States Constitution created the country's present form of government. Significantly, it implies the principle of church-state separation by granting to the national government no authority whatever to meddle with religion. Indeed, the only mentions of religion are in Article VI, prohibiting religious tests for public office and mandatory oaths of office.

The new Constitution would be ratified, but only after Madison and politicians in Virginia and elsewhere promised to add a Bill of Rights to it. Indeed, Madison's good friend Jefferson, then ambassador to France, stressed the importance of such an action. The first Congress, meeting in 1789, drafted twelve amendments, ten of which were approved and ratified. After much discussion, the two houses of Congress settled on the following wording for what became the First Amendment: "Congress shall make no law respecting an establishment of religion, or prohibiting the free exercise thereof; . . ."

In recent years, there has been much debate over whether the First Amendment supports the "separationist" side, as most Supreme Court justices have held since the first major case on the issue in 1947, or the "accommodationist" or "nonpreferentialist" side, represented today by Chief Justice William Rehnquist and Justices Antonin Scalia and Clarence Thomas and on Patrick Henry's losing side in Virginia in the 1780s. An examination of the debates over the text of the amendment shows that the separationists, following Jefferson and Madison, won.[2]

The "separation of church and state" metaphor was popularized by President Jefferson's January 1, 1802, letter to the Baptist Association of Danbury, Connecticut, a letter that Jefferson cleared with Attorney General Levi Lincoln. Jefferson wrote, "I contemplate with sovereign reverence that act of the whole American people which declared that their legislature should 'make no law respecting an establishment of religion, or prohibiting the free exercise thereof,' thus building a wall of separation between church and state."[3]

In 1878, the US Supreme Court noted that "Jefferson's use of the term 'wall of separation between church and state' may be accepted almost as an authoritative declaration of the scope and effect of the amendment thus secured."[4]

Not until 1947, however, did the Supreme Court actually apply the separation principle. The decision in *Everson v. Board of Education* put it this way:

> The "establishment of religion" clause of the First Amendment means at least this: Neither a state nor the Federal Government can set up a church. Neither can pass laws, which aid one religion, aid all religions, or prefer one religion to another. Neither can force nor influence a person to go to or remain away from church against his will or force him to profess a belief or disbelief in any religion. No person can be punished for entertaining or professing religious beliefs or disbeliefs, for church attendance or non-attendance. No tax in any amount, large or small, can be levied to support any religious activities or institutions, whatever they may be called, or whatever form they may adopt to teach or practice religion. Neither a state nor the Federal Government can, openly or secretly, participate in the affairs of any religious organizations or groups and vice versa. In the words of Jefferson, the clause against establishment of religion by law was intended to "erect a wall of separation between church and state."[5]

Backtracking a bit, Jefferson acknowledged in his 1802 letter to the Danbury Baptists that the First Amendment applied only to the federal government, not to state and local governments. It was only in the aftermath of the Civil War that Congress approved and the states ratified the Fourteenth Amendment, which was intended to make the Bill of Rights applicable to state and local governments.[6]

Meanwhile, following the example of Virginia, the rest of the states adopted the separation principle.[7] It is significant that the last two states admitted to the Union in 1959, Alaska and Hawaii, included the separation principle in their constitutions.[8] Perhaps even more significant is the fact that in 1952 Congress considered and approved the Constitution of the Commonwealth of Puerto Rico, which not only reiterates the language of the First Amendment but also adds these words, "There shall be complete separation of church and state."[9]

Church-state separation, then, is, as they say, as American as apple pie. Nonetheless, hurricane winds are blowing that would topple Jefferson's wall.

THE THREATS TODAY

Storm warnings need to be posted for all to see. The threats to the wall are very real and very serious. Led by sectarian special interests and by televangelists such as Pat Robertson, Jerry Falwell, and numerous others, the Religious Right has virtually taken over one of our major political parties on the national and state level, a great many politicians feel that they are beholden to the Religious Right, the media have been shifting steadily to the right, and the Supreme Court itself has drifted away from the strong separationist position it held for so long after 1947.

A complete catalogue of all the threats to the "wall of separation," great and small, would stretch this chapter to intolerable length, so it will concentrate on the most serious threats: tax aid to faith-based schools and charities, dealing with religion in public schools, and reproductive freedom of conscience.

SCHOOL VOUCHERS AND THEIR ANALOGUES

Since around 1960, there has been a rising chorus of demands for tuition vouchers, tuition tax credits (sometimes referred to as "tax code vouchers"), and other forms of federal and/or state tax aid for nonpublic schools. About 90 percent of US kindergarten through twelfth-grade students attend public schools in some fifteen thousand local school districts. Of the remaining 10 percent, about 90 percent attend Catholic, fundamentalist, Quaker, Jewish, Adventist, Muslim, and other "faith-based" schools. The religious demands originally came mainly from the Catholic-school sector, which claimed about 90 percent of the enrollment in faith-based schools in 1965, about 5.5 million students. By 2004, for reasons to be discussed later, Catholic school enrollment had plunged to about 2.5 million. Since 1965, then, total nonpublic school enrollment has declined both proportionally and in absolute numbers. The rise in evangelical or fundamentalist schools, which began with the desegregation of public schools, has not equaled the decline in Catholic schools.[10]

Nonreligious support for vouchers and their analogues started with economist Milton Friedman, soon joined by others of like mind. The usual rationale given for vouchers, and similar programs, is that parents should be able to choose where to educate their children and that competition among schools will somehow improve all schools. The literature on this subject is too vast even for a short bibliography, so this discussion will be as comprehensive as possible in as little space as possible.[11]

Parental choice in schooling is largely a chimera. A 1998 US Department of Education study found that there are not all that many seats available in nonpublic schools, that almost invariably nonpublic schools practice forms of discrimination in admissions that would be intolerable in public schools and which would not be abandoned, and that very few faith-based schools would be willing to exempt tax-supported voucher students from denominational religious instruction.[12] The report, for reasons unknown, neglected to mention that faith-based schools frequently use faith criteria in hiring and firing teachers. Further, faith-based schools tend to be pervasively sectarian and often ideology-oriented.[13] Thus the pervasively sectarian nature of the vast majority of nonpublic schools and their admissions and hiring policies would tend to homogenize student bodies by religion and perhaps less often by social class, ethnicity, ability level, and other ways. A large-scale voucher plan, then, would tend to fragment school populations and communities along religious and other lines to a far greater degree than at present. As for competition improving all schools, it should be obvious that Catholic, Jewish, Muslim, Lutheran, and Protestant fundamentalist schools do not really compete with one another.

Nor does the evidence support the claims that voucher plans, whether public or private, improve all schools, whether in the United States or in other countries with some form of "school choice." In the two cities that already have voucher plans as of 2004, Milwaukee and Cleveland, state laws do not permit meaningful evaluation of the supposed benefits of tax support for nonpublic schools.

So much for the case for school vouchers or their analogues. The case *against* vouchers is so much stronger that in the twenty-five statewide referendum elections on vouchers or their analogues from coast to coast between 1967 and 2000, vouchers were rejected by an average margin of two to one, most recently in California and Michigan in 2000.[14]

Tax aid to nonpublic schools through vouchers, at anything close to current per capita spending on public schools, would necessarily either increase taxes or decrease support for public education. In an era of severe strain on federal and state budgets, we are not likely to see the necessary tax hikes. Moreover, it is already well known that US public schools are seriously underfunded and that within virtually every state, funding for public education has long been inequitably distributed. And just to repair or replace broken-down public school buildings throughout the country, according to one federal study, would cost far more than the $87 billion that President George W. Bush requested in mid-2003 for the reconstruction of Iraq.

And the preceding does not factor in the $2 billion or so in federal and state funds going to faith-based schools annually, the huge cost of simply transporting students to a growing proliferation of nonpublic schools, or the fact that voucher costs would impact adversely on rural and smaller communities. In Pennsylvania, for example, the state's 501 public school districts are required by state law to transport students up to ten miles beyond school district boundaries, which has already imposed a heavy burden on many districts.

We might remember, too, that the Fleischman Report to New York governor Nelson Rockefeller more than thirty years ago concluded that it would be cheaper for the state to take all nonpublic school students into public schools than for the state to support the nonpublic schools.[15]

Economics aside, vouchers would force all taxpayers to support the forms of discrimination and religious indoctrination common in nonpublic schools, the sort of thing that Jefferson labeled "sinful and tyrannical."

We come at last to the question of constitutionality. Unfortunately, during the last decade or so, the Supreme Court has moved away from the fairly strict separationism of 1947. In June 2002, the Court even held that the Cleveland school voucher plan does not violate the First Amendment, a ruling that defied logic, common sense, and the facts.[16] So, as civil libertarians have learned in recent years, the Supreme Court is no longer a reliable defender of the fundamental liberties of citizens.

Fortunately, public opinion and most state constitutions continue to maintain a wall of separation although the Wisconsin and Ohio courts have not seen fit to do so. However, a new effort by voucher advocates is under way to remove state constitutional barriers to vouchers, tied to a grossly exaggerated claim that state constitutional barriers to vouchers are the product of nineteenth-century anti-Catholic bigotry.[17] It is to be hoped that this effort will not succeed, as in 1972 the Supreme Court turned back an effort to do the same thing in Missouri.[18] The charge of anti-Catholic bigotry is refuted by the fact that in 1986 voters in 50 percent Catholic Massachusetts voted 70 percent to 30 percent to defeat an attempt to change the state constitution to allow vouchers.[19] According to exit polls in California and Michigan in 2000, Catholic voters rejected vouchers by about the same two-to-one margin as non-Catholics.

It is worth mentioning that the decline in Catholic school enrollment from half of American Catholic children in 1965 to less than 20 percent in 2004 is due to several factors: the election of a Catholic, pro-separation president in 1960; the Supreme Court's 1962–63 rulings against the essentially Protestant practice of school-sponsored prayer and Bible reading in public schools; the liberalization of the Catholic Church under Pope John XXIII and Vatican Council II, 1962–65; negative reaction to the 1998 papal encyclical condemning contraception; and Catholic achievement of proportionate representation in politics.

Another ace in the hole in the struggle over vouchers may well be a seldom-mentioned 1973 Supreme Court ruling that held that even textbook loans "are a form of tangible financial assistance benefiting the schools themselves" and that "a state's constitutional obligation requires it to steer clear not only of operating the old dual system of racially segregated schools but also of giving significant aid to institutions that practice racial or *other invidious discrimination*" (emphasis mine).[20]

The last chapters in the battle over school vouchers have yet to be written.

CHARITABLE CHOICE

There is no doubt that religion-related charities have done enormous good in this country and elsewhere. Sometimes this is done entirely with voluntarily donated funds but more recently with at least partial public funding. Until 2003, however, religion-related charities receiving tax aid were required by civil rights laws to avoid discrimination in hiring and providing services and to avoid proselytizing.

However, beginning with President George W. Bush, efforts are being made to eliminate the nondiscrimination requirements, either by law or executive order, and to allow these charities to promote religion itself if that is their wish, as in drug or alcohol counseling or prisoner rehabilitation. As I have pointed out elsewhere, this new movement, if not checked, will create a growing proliferation of "unregulated, unaccountable charities of uncertain efficiency competing for scraps of a shrinking public pie" as well as "violating Madison's 1785 warning that using 'religion as an engine of civil policy' would be 'an unhallowed perversion of the means of salvation.'"[21]

A colleague and I have summarized the objections to the new movement, evidently introduced to President Bush by Texas fundamentalist writer Marvin Olasky, as follows:

> President Bush's "charitable choice" expansion would clearly violate the church-state separation principle; it would have government pay religious groups for what they have always done on their own; religious minorities could suffer discrimination under the plan; it could radicalize the delivery of services and threaten the religious freedom of recipients: participating churches could lose their "prophetic edge" and become domesticated branches of the civil bureaucracy; government will be forced to choose among competing religious programs, with the most politically connected getting more than their "fair share"; nonsectarian and secular programs could become second-class and underfunded; religious programs are not necessarily superior to secular services; the promoters of "charitable choice" often use the idea for partisan political advantage; President Bush has used dishonest tactics and appeals to religious prejudice to win support for his program.[22]

These objections could be expanded upon, but that would require a great deal of space. Suffice it to note that a study of the deleterious effects of charitable choice in Texas under then-governor George W. Bush was released by the Texas Freedom Network late in 2002.[23]

RELIGION IN PUBLIC SCHOOLS

Given the astonishing and growing pluralism of religion and other lifestances in the United States and the constitutional requirement of separation of church and state, it should be obvious that the public schools serving American children must be religiously neutral. The courts have dealt with some of the issues involving public schools,[24] but not all, and with fifteen thousand locally responsible school districts in the country, there is no accurate way of surveying all the possible problems and their permutations. So we will have to make do with a hopefully not too superficial overview.

Contrary to popular opinion, government-sponsored prayer and Bible reading, essentially nineteenth-century Protestant affairs, were never universal. They were confined mainly to the East Coast and the South. The practice was halted by the Supreme Court in 1962 and 1963 rulings.[25] Despite tremendous exertions by the Religious Right, all subsequent attempts to amend the Constitution to authorize school-sponsored devotions failed to obtain the necessary two-thirds vote of either house of Congress, thanks in large measure to opposition to such amendments by leaders of mainstream religious denominations. Controversies continue, but even a weakened Supreme Court has not shown signs of caving in on this issue.

Controversies still erupt, however, over the teaching of evolution in public school science classes. Despite the fact that in 1987 the Supreme Court ruled that Fundamentalist biblical "creationism" is religion, not science, and therefore has no place in public school science classes,[26] creationists have not given up. They exert every effort, especially in the South, to water down the teaching of evolution or to get public schools to promote the notion of "intelligent design," a modified form of creationism that has no significant scientific support.

On the whole, as most of the witnesses (including this writer) who testified before a mid-1998 hearing before the US Commission on Civil Rights agreed, "the relevant Supreme Court rulings and other developments have pretty much brought public education into line with the religious neutrality required by the First Amendment. . . ."[27] In August 1995, the US Department of Education issued advisory guidelines to all school districts on religious expression in public schools. At the 1998 Civil Rights Commission hearing, Julie Underwood, general counsel for the National School Boards Association, told the hearing that inquiries to the NSBA about what is or is not permitted in public schools declined almost to the vanishing point once the guidelines were published.[28]

The guidelines grew out of a document titled "Religion in the Public Schools: A Joint Statement of Current Law," issued in April 1995 by a broad coalition of thirty-six religious and civil liberties groups. Declaring that the Constitution "permits much private religious activity in and around the public schools and does not turn the schools into religion-free zones," the statement went on to detail what is and is not permissible in the schools.[29]

On July 12, 1995, President Clinton discussed these issues in a major address at—appropriately—James Madison High School in northern Virginia and announced that he was directing the secretary of education, in consultation with the attorney general, to issue advisory guidelines to every public school district in the country. The guidelines were issued in August. In his weekly radio address of May 30, 1998, anticipating the June 4 House debate and vote on the Istook (R-OK) school prayer amendment, President Clinton again addressed the issue and announced that the guidelines, updated slightly, were being reissued and sent to every school district. This effort undoubtedly helped to sway the House to vote down the Istook amendment.

The guidelines, based on fifty years of court rulings (from the 1948 *McCollum* decision to the present), on common sense, and on a healthy respect for American religious diversity, have proved useful to school boards, administrators, teachers, students, parents, and religious leaders. Following is a brief summary:

> *Permitted:* "Purely private religious speech by students"; nondisruptive individual or group prayer, grace before meals, religious literature reading; student speech about religion or anything else, including that intended to persuade, as long as it stops short of harassment; private baccalaureate services; teaching *about* religion; inclusion by students of religious matter in written or oral assignments where not inappropriate; student distribution of religious literature on the same terms as other material not related to school curricula or activities; some degree of right to excusal from lessons objectionable on religious or conscientious grounds, subject to applicable state laws; off-campus released time or dismissed time for religious instruction; teaching civic values; student-initiated "Equal Access" religious groups of secondary students during noninstructional time.

Prohibited: School endorsement of any religious activity or doctrine; coerced participation in religious activity; engaging in or leading student religious activity by teachers, coaches, or officials acting as advisors to student groups; allowing harassment of or religious imposition on "captive audiences"; observing holidays as religious events or promoting such observance; imposing restrictions on religious expression more stringent than those on nonreligious expression; allowing religious instruction by outsiders on school premises during the school day.

Required: "Official neutrality regarding religious activity."[30]

In reissuing the guidelines, Secretary of Education Richard Riley urged school districts to use them or to develop their own, preferably in cooperation with parents, teachers, and the "broader community." He recommended that principals, administrators, teachers, schools of education, prospective teachers, parents, and students all become familiar with them.[31] As President Clinton declared in his May 30, 1998, address, "Since we've issued these guidelines, appropriate religious activity has flourished in our schools, and there has apparently been a substantial decline in the contentious argument and litigation that has accompanied this issue for too long." The incoming Bush administration in 2001 reissued the guidelines in a somewhat weakened and confusing form.[32]

As good and useful as the guidelines are, especially the original versions, there remain three areas in which problems continue: proselytizing by adults in public schools, music programs that fall short of the desired neutrality, and teaching appropriately *about* religion.

In addition, conservative evangelists such as Jerry Johnston and Jerry Falwell have described public schools as "mission fields." In communities from coast to coast, proselytizers from well-financed national organizations, such as Campus Crusade and Young Life, and volunteer "youth pastors" from local congregations have operated in public schools for years. They use a variety of techniques: presenting assembly programs featuring "role model" athletes, getting permission from school officials to contact students one-on-one in cafeterias and hallways, volunteering as unpaid teaching aides, and using substance abuse lectures or assemblies to gain access to students. It is not uncommon for these activities to have the approval of local school authorities. Needless to say, these operations tend to take place more often in smaller, more religiously homogeneous communities than in larger, more pluralistic ones.

Religious music in the public school curriculum, in student concerts and theatrical productions, and at graduation ceremonies has long been a thorny issue. As Secretary Riley's 1995 and 1998 guidelines and court rulings have made clear, schools may offer instruction about religion, but they must remain religiously neutral and may not formally celebrate religious special days. What, then, about religious music, which looms large in the history of music?

There should be no objection to the inclusion of religious music in the academic study of music and in vocal and instrumental performances, as long as the pieces are selected primarily for their musical or historical value, as long as the program is not predominantly religious, and as long as the principal purpose and effect of the inclusion is secular. Thus there should be no objection to inclusion in a school production of religious music by Bach or Aaron Copland's arrangements of such nineteenth-century songs as "Simple Gifts" or "Let Us Gather by the River." What constitutes "musical or historical value" is, of course, a matter of judgment and controversy among musicians and scholars, so there can be no simple formula for resolving all conflicts.

Certain activities should clearly be prohibited. Public school choral or instrumental ensembles should not be used to provide music for church services or celebrations, though a school ensemble might perform a secular music program in a church or synagogue as part of that congregation's series of secular concerts open to the public and not held in conjunction with a worship service. Hymns should not be included in graduation ceremonies. Students enrolled in music programs for credit should not be compelled to participate in performances that are not primarily religiously neutral.

As for teaching *about* religion, while one can agree with the Supreme Court that public schools may, and perhaps should, alleviate ignorance in this area in a fair, balanced, objective, neutral, academic way, getting from theory to practice is far from easy. The difficulties should be obvious. Teachers are very seldom adequately trained to teach about religion. There are no really suitable textbooks on the market. Educators and experts on religion are nowhere near agreement on precisely what ought to be taught, how much should be taught and at what grade levels, and whether such material should be integrated into social studies classes, when appropriate, or offered in separate courses, possibly electives. And those who complain most about the relative absence of religion from the curriculum seem to be less interested in neutral academic study than in narrower sectarian teaching. Textbooks and schools tend to slight religion not out of hostility but because of low demand, lack of time (if you add something to the curriculum, what do you take out to make room for it?), lack of suitable materials, and fear of giving offense or generating controversy.

The following questions hint at the complexity of the subject:

- Should teaching about religion deal only with the bright side of it and not with the dark side (religious wars, controversies, bigotry, persecutions, and so on)?
- Should instruction deal only with religions within the United States, or should it include religions throughout the world?
- Should it be critical or uncritical?
- Should all religious traditions be covered or only some?
- Should the teaching deal only with sacred books—and, if so, which ones and which translations?
- How should change and development in all religions be dealt with? To be more specific, should we teach only about the Pilgrims and the first Thanksgiving, or also about the Salem witch trials and the execution of Quakers?
- Should schools mention only the Protestant settlers in British North America or also deal with French Catholic missionaries in Canada, Michigan, and Indiana and with the Spanish Catholics and secret Jews in our Southwest?
- Should we mention that Martin Luther King was a Baptist minister but ignore the large number of clergy who defended slavery and then segregation on biblical grounds?
- Should teaching about religion cover such topics as the evolution of Christianity and its divisions, the Crusades, the Inquisition, the religious wars after the Reformation, the long history of anti-Semitism and other forms of murderous bigotry, the role of religion in social and international tensions, the development in the United States of religious liberty and church-state separation, denominations and religions founded in the United States, controversies over women's rights and reproductive rights, or newer religious movements?

The probability that attempts to teach about religion will go horribly wrong should caution public schools to "make haste very slowly" in this area. Perhaps other curricular inadequacies—less controversial ones, such as those in the fields of science, social studies, foreign languages, and world literature—should be remedied before we tackle the thorniest subject of all.

The American landscape has no shortage of houses of worship, which generally include religious education as one of their main functions. Nothing prevents these institutions from providing all the teaching about religion that they might desire.

The late Supreme Court Justice William Brennan summed up the constitutional ideal rather neatly in his concurring opinion in *Abington Township S.D. v. Schempp,* the 1963 school prayer case:

> It is implicit in the history and character of American public education that the public schools serve a uniquely public function: the training of American citizens in an atmosphere free of parochial, divisive, or separatist influence of any sort—an atmosphere in which children may assimilate a heritage common to all American groups and religions. This is a heritage neither theistic nor atheistic, but simply civic and patriotic.[33]

REPRODUCTIVE RIGHTS

Freedom of conscience and freedom of choice in reproductive matters are often regarded as just "women's issues." They are that, but they are also religious liberty and church-state issues and, beyond that, have a direct bearing on the global problems of overpopulation and sustainable growth. That they are religious liberty and church-state issues is attested to by the existence of the Religious Coalition for Reproductive Choice, founded in 1973, a coming together of forty Catholic, Protestant, Jewish, Unitarian Universalist, and humanist denominations and groups that embrace a wide spectrum of views on reproductive matters but which agree on the importance of reproductive choice as a religious liberty issue. Arrayed on the other side of the question are powerful religious leaders representing the more conservative end of the Catholic, Protestant, and Jewish spectrum.[34] It should also be noted that conservative religious opposition to choice has less to do with theology (the Bible is silent on abortion) than with a patriarchal bent toward male dominance.

The Supreme Court's 1973 rulings in *Roe v. Wade* and *Doe v. Bolton* recognized a constitutional right to privacy that covered not only the right to use contraception but also the right of a woman to choose to terminate a problem pregnancy. *Roe* has so far stood the test of time and public opinion, but the Supreme Court has allowed state legislatures to impose some restrictions on the right to choose, such as waiting periods, mandatory presentation of misinformation to women seeking abortions and burdensome or excessive regulation of reproductive health clinics.

Although the Supreme Court has dealt with reproductive choice as a "constitutional right to privacy" matter, the issue also clearly has to do with "establishment" and "free exercise." Government restriction of choice is tantamount to establishing or preferring one religious perspective over all others, that is, the theological notion that "personhood" begins at conception as opposed to the view that "personhood" begins much later, such as after the cerebral cortex is sufficiently developed to permit the possibility of consciousness or at birth. Governmental restriction on choice also runs counter to "free exercise," which is largely synonymous with freedom of conscience.

As for the relation between reproductive choice and global population/sustainability, the Reagan, Bush I, and Bush II bans on US aid to overseas reproductive health agencies that might provide abortions or abortion counseling with other than US tax monies represent political cave-ins to sectarian special interests, which exacerbate population/sustainability problems and actually endanger the health and lives of countless women and children in developing countries.

One tragic consequence of conservative religious influence on public policy was what happened to a report titled "Implications of Worldwide Population Growth for US Security and Overseas Interests" ordered by President Nixon and approved in 1974 by President Ford.[35] Had this report not been classified and suppressed for fifteen years, it might have helped prevent the Rwanda massacre in the early 1990s, which it essentially predicted, and allowed the United States and other countries to get a more timely start on dealing with the population/sustainability problem. The report actually anticipated the proposals that the Clinton administration brought to the 1994 UN population conference in Cairo. Another consequence was President George W. Bush's withholding of $34 million that Congress had appropriated for the United Nations Population Fund.

WHAT TO DO?

Though the preceding discussion is admittedly sketchy and incomplete, it does present a bird's-eye view of a major set of problems. Added to the plate of other concerns of thoughtful citizens in the arena of politics, civil liberties, civil rights, environment, economics, and so forth, we clearly face a concern overload. No one person or group can deal with all of these issues, but each of us, I think, has a moral and social obligation to become involved to the extent of our ability and resources.

We can all participate in the political process, not merely by voting but also by working in and supporting the political organizations and candidates we prefer. We also need to bear in mind that no religious tradition is monolithic. Liberals and progressives in all traditions can, do, and must cooperate in the defense of fundamental liberties, while fundamentalist factions in many traditions work for opposite ends.

We can work in and through—and provide financial support to—the local, state, and national organizations that we consider important. A few of the groups actively dealing with the problems treated in this article are the American Civil Liberties Union, People for the American Way, Americans for Religious Liberty, the Interfaith Alliance, teacher and school administrator organizations, NARAL Pro-Choice America, Planned Parenthood, the Religious Coalition for Reproductive Choice, and the Texas Freedom Network, to name but a few. As the old proverb has it, it is better to light a candle than to curse the darkness.

NOTES

1. James Madison, "Memorial and Remonstrance against Religious Assessments," in *The Papers of James Madison*, ed. William T. Hutchinson and William M. E. Rachal (Chicago: University of Chicago Press, [1962]–1991), 8:298–304;"Amendment I (Religion)," The Founders' Constitution, http://press-pubs.uchicago.edu/founders/documents/amendI_religions43.html. Also published in its entirety in *Great Quotations on Religious Freedom*, comp. and ed. Albert J. Menendez and Edd Doerr (Amherst, NY: Prometheus Books, 2002), p. 209.

2. Although a whole library has been devoted to this issue, the most concise treatment of it is probably Robert S. Alley's *Public Education and the Public Good* (Silver Spring, MD: Americans for Religious Liberty, 1996), reprinted from Alley's long article in *William and Mary Bill of Rights Journal* 4, no. 1 (Summer 1995).

3. Jefferson to the Baptist Association of Danbury, Connecticut, January 1, 1802, in *Writings* (New York Literary Classics of the US, 1984), p. 510.

4. *Reynolds v. United States*, 98 U.S. 145 at 164.

5. *Everson v. Board of Education*, 330 U.S. 15, 16.

6. Irving Brant, *The Bill of Rights: Its Origin and Meaning* (Indianapolis: Bobbs-Merrill, 1965), pp. 318–43.

7. Edd Doerr and Albert J. Menendez, *Religious Liberty and State Constitutions* (Amherst, NY: Prometheus Books, 1993).

8. Ibid., pp. 20, 35.

9. Ibid., p. 16.

10. See, for example, Edd Doerr and Albert J. Menendez, *Church Schools and Public Money: The Politics of Parochiaid* (Amherst, NY: Prometheus Books, 1991); and Edd Doerr, Albert J. Menendez, and John M. Swomley, *The Case against School Vouchers* (Amherst, NY: Prometheus Books, 1996).

11. Ibid.

12. U.S. Department of Education, *Barriers, Benefits, and Costs of Using Private Schools to Alleviate Crowding in Public Schools* (Washington, DC: November 3, 1999), cited in Edd Doerr, "Give Us Your Money . . . ," *Phi Delta Kappan* (June 1999).

13. See Albert J. Menendez, *Visions of Reality: What Fundamentalist Schools Teach* (Amherst, NY: Prometheus Books, 1993); Edd Doerr, *Catholic Schools: The Facts* (Amherst, NY: Humanist Press, 2000); Frances R. A. Patterson *Democracy and Intolerance: Christian School Curricula, School Choice, and Public Policy* (Bloomington, IN: Phi Delta Kappa Educational Foundation, 2003).

14. Albert J. Menendez, "Voters Versus Vouchers: The Forgotten Factor in the Debate," *Americans for Religious Liberty Newsletter* 86, no. 1 (2004).

15. *The New York State Commission on the Quality, Cost, and Financing of Elementary and Secondary Education* (Albany, NY: February 9, 1972), cited in *Church and State* (April 1972).

16. *Zelman v. Simmons-Harris*, 122 S. Ct., at 2460 (2002). The dissenting opinion showed how the majority played word games to dilute the Cleveland program, 96 percent of whose funds went to sectarian schools.

17. See Albert J. Menendez, "Blaming Blaine: A Distortion of History," *Voice of Reason*, no. 2 (2003).

18. *Brusca v. State of Missouri*, 332 F.Supp. 405 US 1050.

19. Albert J. Menendez, "Voters versus Vouchers."

20. *Norwood v. Harrison*, 93 S. Ct. 2804.

21. Edd Doerr, letter to the editor, *New York Times*, May 2, 2001.

22. Albert J. Menendez and Edd Doerr, *The Case against Charitable Choice: Why President Bush's Faith-Based Initiative Is Bad Public Policy* (Silver Spring, MD: Americans for Religious Liberty, 2001).

23. Texas Freedom Network Education Fund, "The Texas Faith-Based Initiative at Five Years: Warning Signs as President Bush Expands Texas-Style Program to National Level," Texas Freedom Network, October 10, 2002, http://www.tfn.org/issues/charitablechoice/report02.html.

24. Perhaps the most useful summary of leading Supreme Court rulings in this area is Robert S. Alley, ed., *The Constitution and Religion: Leading Supreme Court Cases on Church and State* (Amherst, NY: Prometheus Books, 1999).

25. Ibid., pp. 171–93, 195–218, 249–69.

26. Ibid., pp. 219–31.

27. Edd Doerr, "Religion and Public Education," *Phi Delta Kappan* (November 1998): 223–25.

28. Ibid., p. 224.

29. American Civil Liberties Union et al., "Religion in the Public Schools: A Joint Statement of Current Law," April 1995, Religious Liberty, American Civil Liberties Union Freedom Network archives, http://archive.aclu.org/issues/religion/relig7.html.

30. Doerr, "Religion and Public Education," p. 224.

31. Ibid.

32. American Civil Liberties Union et al., "Religion in the Public Schools."

33. *Abington Township S.D. v. Schempp,* 374 U.S. 203, at 224–25.

34. While there is an abundance of literature on this subject, two useful books are Edd Doerr and James W. Prescott, eds., *Abortion Rights and Fetal "Personhood"* (Centerline Press, 1990), and John M. Swomley, *Compulsory Pregnancy: The War against American Women* (Amherst, NY: Humanist Press, 1999).

35. Stephen D. Mumford, *The Life and Death of NSSM 200: How the Destruction of Political Will Doomed a U.S. Population Policy* (Raleigh, NC: Center for Research on Population and Security, 1996).

EDD DOERR served as president of the American Humanist Association from 1995 to 2002 and previously served as vice president under Isaac Asimov for six years. An AHA member since 1950, he is a signer of *Humanist Manifesto II* in 1973 and *Humanist Manifesto III* in 2003. Doerr received the AHA's Humanist Pioneer Award in 1984 and its Distinguished Service Award in 1992. He has represented the AHA on the board of the International Humanist and Ethical Union, the National Committee for Public Education and Religious Liberty, and the Religious Coalition for Reproductive Choice. He is a former board member of the American Civil Liberties Union of Maryland and the National Abortion and Reproductive Rights Action League (NARAL).

Doerr is a prolific writer, the author, coauthor, editor, or translator of twenty books that include *Great Quotations in Religious Freedom*. His editorials and letters to the editor regularly appear in such major newspapers as the *New York Times,* and he has addressed audiences in more than thirty states and five countries and led workshops at humanist conferences and Unitarian Universalist general assemblies, to which he has often been a delegate.

5.

Putting the
Humanist Manifesto 2000
into Practice

Gerry Dantone

For the first time in human history we possess the means pro-
vided by science and technology to ameliorate the human
condition, advance happiness and freedom, and enhance
human life for all people on this planet.

—Humanist Manifesto 2000

How would a planetary society implement a humanistic political
program? I'm not simply talking about an single avowed humanist
elected official making judicial, legislative, or executive decisions
humanistically, although that, in and of itself, would be a rarity and therefore big news in the United States. No, I'm talking about taking the
processes and goals of a government or the governments of the world into
a humanistic direction. What would it mean to do this?

GOALS

Rather than personally define what a political humanism might look like,
it may be more valuable to adopt as a reference a well-known and well-
accepted statement on this subject: the *Humanist Manifesto 2000; A Call for
a New Planetary Humanism*, drafted by Paul Kurtz [see this volume].
Although no one claims that it is an inerrant and irrefutable statement of
humanistic purpose, it is a compelling and detailed vision well suited to
serve as a basis for the question at hand.

The *Humanist Manifesto 2000* defines a "planetary humanism" as one that seeks to preserve human rights and enhance human freedom and dignity, as you might expect; but it also emphasizes a commitment to human well-being as a whole—on the *planetary* scale. According to the manifesto, human suffering should be mitigated, the sum of human happiness should be increased, divisive multicultural parochialism should be avoided, equality of rights should be accorded to all, and these considerations should be applied to future generations as well as our own. These are fairly obvious goals for the global family.

What goals embody enhancing human well-being for the purposes of a political movement? Among the items that *Humanist Manifesto 2000* cites are ending poverty and hunger; providing adequate shelter and health care for all; economic security and adequate income opportunities for everyone; protection and security from various dangers; reproductive freedom; freedom to form families of one's choosing; adequate educational opportunities; equality of opportunity and equality under the law regardless of race, ethnicity, nationality, culture, caste, creed, gender, or sexual orientation; and a wide range of personal freedoms and choices.

These goals are difficult to argue with in principle. Although some may claim that adequate health care, as an example, is not a "right," natural or otherwise, it can be argued that it is humanistic to seek to ensure that health care is available for all, particularly for children, and that societies and their governments should agree by democratic consensus to make some standard of health care a legislated right to which all are entitled. This consensus and a successful implementation of universal health care would most likely increase the sum of human happiness, making this right authentically humanistic.

To be fair, however, if such universal health care plans, to continue the example, were to end up increasing misery in the real world, they would prove to be antihumanistic in practice and would require reversing. Such is the lot of an empirically based ethics. This possibility should not discourage us from pursuing paths on which failure is a possibility—failure is possible no matter what is chosen. The key is to make as objective and well-considered a decision as possible and be prepared to change course if necessary. The absence of a 100 percent guarantee, along with the willingness to accept new evidence, is actually an advantage of a humanistic approach to political issues that typical political ideologies lack. In fact, a consistent ideological approach to political issues *no matter the results* leads to tyranny and only reinforces the need for the consequentialist humanistic approach.

This planetary brand of consequentialism opens the door to consideration of many social programs. Debt relief, environmental laws that span continents, controlling multinational corporations, and resolving disputes in an international court with real enforcement power have obvious benefits—if applied fairly and legitimately. The precise agenda for such a humanism will not be enumerated in further detail here; my concern is putting into place the structure for beneficial policies to be implemented.

It therefore seems difficult to argue against a planetary humanism that seeks to improve the human condition, even if we can argue about the best way to achieve specifics or even which specifics to pursue. All proposals are tentative and to be tested by their actual results. In this spirit, it may be possible to support a policy that one has doubts about, since, in a humanistically run world, we all agree to accept the evidence as it unfolds. An experimental policy that may improve the human condition without taking an undue risk may be worthwhile to attempt. Letting go of discredited political policies is mandatory. In other words, if we're pursuing a planetary humanism, let the reasoned and compassionate debates begin, not end.

CALLS TO ACTION

The *Humanist Manifesto 2000* suggests a number of actions that could be implemented to realize the goals of a planetary humanism. As one would expect, these suggestions are more controversial than the humanistic goals they hope to realize. They are not guaranteed to work as expected since, at this point, they are propositions that will have to be tested in the real world.

They are not revelations handed down from on high by an omnibenevolent and omniscient being, nor are they dogmatic solutions demanded by a particular secular political dogma; they should not become dogma, either. Other suggestions, while having merit, may end up being improperly executed or corrupted by greed or irrationality and fail as well. Finally, other calls to action will require certain preexisting conditions for their implementation that may not be attainable now or in the near future. These caveats are not reserved exclusively for the execution of a planetary humanism; all political theories can experience these pitfalls.

A nondogmatic politics, which the *Humanist Manifesto 2000* seeks to promote, should be aware in advance of these dangers and be ready to react to unforeseen problems without concern for violating a "sacred" principle unrelated to human well-being. We should care about the results of our implementing our principles not about upholding our principles regardless of consequences.

As a methodology, the *Humanist Manifesto 2000* seeks to empower the United Nations or some other instrument of the international community to establish and enforce international law in order to pursue a planetary humanism. It suggests a number of steps to promote security, human development, social justice, globalization, and international law—categories that correspond closely to those items that the *Humanist Manifesto 2000* defines as encompassing human well-being.

To promote national and intranational security, the *Humanist Manifesto 2000* points out that there is no basis under international law for an outside organization or country to interfere in the internal affairs of a member state of the UN without a request by the government of that conflicted country. Going further, it notes that the current structure of the UN's Security Council almost guarantees a veto from one of the permanent members of the council on almost any issue, stifling any action even if there is consensus otherwise. As a result of these problems and the lack of strong enforcement authority by the UN, many countries and alliances have attempted to impose solutions in various situations around the globe by force—often unsuccessfully—and in the process, undermined not only the UN itself but also respect for international law.

The *Humanist Manifesto 2000* calls for a change in the basic structure of international authority by eliminating the veto power of the Security Council's permanent members. In the long run, the injustice of allowing a handful of nations to arbitrarily possess more power in an international forum than others should be obvious. The veto situation in the UN is not and has not been based on population, level of freedom, or any other semi-rational basis but rather on the political power those countries possessed at the time the Security Council was formed. The veto not only impedes the effectiveness of the Security Council, it also makes a mockery of a concept that must be central to any such international forum, equality under the law.

Admittedly, there are strong counterarguments against such a seemingly sensible action as eliminating the veto power. For example, it could be argued that it is hardly fair for India to have only one vote in light of its population—the same representation as Panama. One nation–one vote leads to unequal representation for actual human beings as it does in our own US Senate, where the people from Wyoming or Vermont have inordinate power compared with the citizens of New York or California. It has never been made clear why geographic or political constructs (states) need representation over and above that of the people who live in them. In the United States, this illogical situation has led to a presidential election in which the candidate with the most electoral votes was declared a winner over the candidate with the most popular votes. This is not a trivial matter.

More important, however, it seems ridiculous to give a nation such as a Liberia under a Charles Taylor or a North Korea under a Kim Jong Il any vote at all in light of their dictatorships and lack of personal freedoms. Whom or what can the UN representative of such a country be said to represent? A government in place by force and/or intimidation? Why should free, liberal, secular democratic republics be bound by decisions made even *in part* by enslaved, fascist, and/or theocratic dictatorships?

The *Humanist Manifesto 2000* also calls for international judicial reform—a world court with power to rule on and enforce penalties for violations of human rights, genocide, and transnational crimes. Again the problem of legitimacy arises: Can a free, liberal, secular democratic republic be expected to submit to rulings influenced or perhaps determined by dictatorial governments? There is no doubt that an international or world court is needed. The question is, first, whether the status quo allows for such a court to be created and, second, whether it would be better to set in motion the machinery to change enough governments to achieve legitimacy, or simply to create a world court and hope for the best.

In addition to adjudicating international disputes in a world court, a world union or world government would need enforcement power to oversee environmental and multinational corporate concerns that cross national borders. Rather than the anarchy, often marred by violence or corruption, that is at play in the current world situation, stronger planetary agencies will be needed, perhaps as primary agencies of a future world union. Many of the same problems that would exist for a world court would exist for an international corporate or environmental watchdog agency. Only free and informed electorates can choose a governing body worthy of pursuing and implementing a planetary humanism.

The power to tax is also an indispensable feature of any future world government or union. The *Humanist Manifesto 2000* suggests that a national tax levied on the gross national product of all nations be used for economic assistance and development. Certain UN agencies are already expert in providing the services that can bring developing nations better living conditions in a sustainable manner. A world agency with the power to tax could also levy taxes on international fund transfers or other schemes that multinational corporations use to escape many taxes altogether. In addition, debt cancellation programs could be proposed and administered on an international scale if such a world taxing agency existed, giving hope to those emerging nations making progress in human rights and responsible government but saddled with debt perhaps incurred under illegitimate governments.

With all these responsibilities and powers to be entrusted in it, such a world union must be the result of free, informed societies voting without coercion. This is simply not possible within the current parameters of the UN on any level.

However, the *Humanist Manifesto 2000* hints at the most likely solution to these serious problems of legitimacy of a world government or world union. It suggests a world parliament with an election based on population, thereby representing people, not governments. The UN is an assembly of nations, and as such is held hostage by those member governments hostile to freedom and human well-being at the expense of those nations where freedoms are protected and, ultimately, at the expense of all the citizens of the world who value liberty. The *Humanist Manifesto 2000* mentions the European parliament as a possible model for this world parliament, and perhaps that is precisely the right track.

The European Union (EU) has standards for membership that have led to reforms in nations seeking to become members. Turkey, for example, has improved the situation of women and has improved other freedoms within its borders, though imperfectly at this time. In January 2002, for example, a law took effect giving Turkish women equal rights when marrying. Eventually, if improvement continues to an acceptable level and the existing members agree, Turkey will be able to join the EU and reap the assumed economic benefits, to the further good of its already freer citizens. The admission of Turkey would strengthen the EU further, making it a more formidable force for freedom and democracy around the world. In addition, by becoming more diverse ethnically and religiously, the EU will be forced to become even more secular in approach, another benefit from a humanist standpoint.

The "Unionizing" of the free world frightens fundamentalists more than any other idea and consequently should attract those interested in a planetary humanism. It is no coincidence that Pat Robertson considers the European Union a possible home to a future anti-Christ in his fictional books on the end-times.

It is ultimately futile to believe that true reform can be effected in an organization such as the currently structured UN, which includes non-elected governments that oppress their citizenry. Even if their citizens were given the opportunity to vote in an international election, the accuracy of the vote counts would be suspect, and worse, the ability of a population with no free press, or worse, no women voters, to vote reasonably would be next to nonexistent. It is hard enough to hold fair elections and to inform the electorate in countries with voting rights and a free press; but such a standard must at least be attempted if we are to have a meaningful, democratic world government.

To that effect, it might be easier and far more productive to create an American Union consisting of free countries of the Western Hemisphere, which would include the United States, Canada, and Costa Rica; an African Union, which might have Botswana and South Africa as starting points; and an Asian Union, which might begin with Japan and Australia. These countries could be welfare, socialist, or capitalist economies but would *have* to be secular, free, and democratic governments that meet high standards accepted by member nations. To reform the UN would require the dramatic and unexpected reform of member nations that at present have been given no incentive to change.

Ultimately the various continental unions that would form a popu-larly elected world union or parliament could resolve disputes peacefully, control global megacorporations, protect the environment on a global level, and advance goals consistent with planetary humanism. In the absence of standards requiring equal rights and freedom of dissent, speech, religion, and assembly, any such international entity would be incapable of implementing the visions of the *Humanist Manifesto 2000*. Indeed, the legislating of specific laws and programs would not be the best move toward a planetary humanism: Instead, the construction of a formal foundation of a free, secular, and democratic world government would provide the setting for a peaceful improvement in humanity's condition. And providing an incentive to every nation of the world to move toward the goals of freedom, liberty, secularism, and democracy would be the engine of this reform.

The relative success of the EU should indicate that it is possible to move toward international humanism, and we should go to school on its successes and failures. Unanimity is not required when deciding on spe-cific policies: Reason and the goal of enhancing the human condition *are* necessary. The "federalist" model has worked before in the world's first great experiment in advancing human freedom; perhaps this time around, we can do it even better.

WHAT WE CAN DO

What steps can we, as individuals, take to inch us along the road to a planetary humanism? Our primary assignment is to advance the structural foundations of a free society in our own countries to the best of our abilities. When enough countries have enough elements in place, a union of these countries becomes politically possible within the populace in those countries, as has been shown in Europe. When the union becomes large enough, political power is realized. Hopefully, this power will then be used in a manner consistent with a planetary humanism, but one cannot make this guarantee. The best that can be done is to ensure that the union, its member countries, and their citizens enjoy the blessings of freedom, democracy, and secularism. To *guarantee* a specific agenda would require a kind of tyranny. The antidote to tyranny is freedom.

In the United States, a necessary and completely realizable first step on the road to a better form of government is separation of money and elections: One suggestion has been the public financing of elections. There is real impetus behind this movement, and it has been implemented in some states, such as Maine and Arizona, as of 2003. If a few large states follow, such as New York and California, elections may become more open and less dependent on large donations. The importance of this step cannot be overstated. If elections are largely determined by spending power, democracy is compromised, legitimacy lost, and the voting public disillusioned. Voter turnout in the United States is often below 50 percent. Once again, we are talking about laying a foundation so that planetary humanism can take hold and flourish. Although it is important, in the meantime, to support policies and proposed laws designed to enhance the human condition, in the long run, it will be necessary to ensure fair and free elections free of the influence of big money so that every voter will be motivated and believe that his or her vote matters.

It is also important that the media become more diverse and independent. The trend toward a few large media companies controlling numerous media outlets cannot be good for the general public, and the current regulatory climate under the Bush administration has been very favorable to large corporate interests. Recent events have shown that even the American public, with its access to a free press, is very prone to huge misconceptions on important issues. A press more interested in increasing its market share than in reporting the facts may not be motivated to rock the political and social boat.

Support on the part of our elected officials for international treaties regarding rights for women and children should be encouraged. For example, the United States is among only a handful of countries that have not endorsed the Treaty for the Rights of Women. In Europe and North America, only Monaco and the United States have not ratified the treaty. Many of the other nonratifying countries are Islamic theocracies such as Iran, the United Arab Republic, and Somalia.

In 1989, the UN ratified the Convention on the Rights of the Child. All but two countries in the world have signed the Convention; they are the United States and Somalia. It seems inconceivable that the United States has not also endorsed this convention. Once again, as activist, caring citizens, we must make our elected officials aware of our concerns.

Countries also cannot go it alone when it comes to protecting the environment. Since the excesses of one country affect others around the world, only internationally enforced environmental standards can protect our planet for future generations. Doing so means working with the international community, as opposed to unilaterally opting out of treaties.

All of these issues are directly related to the influence of money in our electoral system. The money often flows from those who have financial interests in certain policies to those willing to carry out those favorable policies. The amount given to a candidate willing to oppose environmental regulations pales when compared with the dollars saved by a large corporation if those laws do not pass. The incentive therefore exists for large corporations and their executives and owners to influence environmental laws via campaign contributions. Multiply this scenario many times around the world (e.g., agricultural subsidies and other industrial tariffs and subsidies) and one can see how nonpublicly financed elections are a major roadblock achieving a planetary humanism.

SUMMARY

Using the *Humanist Manifesto 2000* as a model, I have defined planetary humanism as a philosophy that emphasizes a commitment to human well-being on the planetary scale and argued that these considerations should be applied to future generations as well as our own. Further, the approach is consequentialist; all policies must be tested by the results: No economic or political principle is to be valued more than improving human well-being as evidenced by the results.

Various actions are suggested by the *Humanist Manifesto 2000*, including the formation of world courts, a world taxing authority, and a world government, all with real enforcement powers. I have suggested that such world authorities or unions need real legitimacy, which would require a free and informed electorate. To that effect, the citizens of free, secular democracies would agree to join in continental unions, perhaps on the model of the European Union. Ultimately when enough "continental unions" are created and share high standards for freedom and democracy around the world, a planetary union can be created, at every step giving incentive for more nonmember nations to improve the structure of their governments so that they meet membership requirements. The UN can continue to serve as a forum for all countries of the world, free or not. Modifications to that organization, particularly in the veto power of the Security Council, could be addressed.

It is important, in the meantime, to support those policies that would serve to enhance freedom and democracy in each country on the individual level. It is not reasonable to expect that a world union or world government can be legitimate if it consists of nonfree and undemocratic nations. To prevent this problem, the movement toward public financing of elections should be considered.

It may disappoint some activists that there is no guaranteed program that will lead to a world where a planetary humanism is the accepted policy. Ending poverty, war, and suffering while promoting the worth and dignity of all persons are goals that we should be anxious to obtain. However, it is unreasonable to expect that closed, theocratic dictatorships can be counted on to assist in achieving these goals: They are too busy staying in power.

In the long run, a world union, built piece by piece by assembling those nations whose citizens have a voice in a workable representative democracy, will realize more goals than can be accomplished otherwise. It took millennia for the concept of democracy and protected freedoms to be implemented in the first place, and even then, the resulting governments were largely imperfect. A world union of free, secular democracies does not guarantee a particular political or social agenda, but it may be the best hope for a noncoercive course to a planetary humanism.

GERRY DANTONE, a humanist activist, has a BS in chemical engineering from Polytechnic Institute of Brooklyn (now Polytechnic Institute of New York) and an MBA in finance from St. John's University, and graduated with honors in economics. He is currently a commercial real estate broker on Long Island, and a musician and songwriter. He has written a humanist rock opera, *My Name Is Thomas*; cofounded the Long Island Secular Humanists—serving as its only president; and is coordinator of the Center for Inquiry–Long Island.

6.

Secular Humanism and Politics
An Unapologetically Liberal Perspective

Massimo Pigliucci

Humanism is a progressive philosophy of life that, without supernaturalism, affirms our ability and responsibility to lead ethical lives of personal fulfillment that aspire to the greater good of humanity.

—Humanism and Its Aspirations; Humanist Manifesto III

OVERTURE: SECULAR HUMANISM VERSUS POLITICS?

Secular humanists are often uncomfortable tackling political issues that do not directly concern the rights of nonbelievers. We can easily rally against patent irrationality and religious fundamentalism, we gladly fight in defense of the teaching of evolution, and we strongly affirm that morality is possible without belief in a god. Yet, when it comes to more practical political debates, such as those about war, social policies, or the environment, we become squeamish indeed. Why?

There are some good reasons for this attitude. Perhaps the most important, and enlightened, of them is that secular humanists don't think they have a monopoly on truth. From this perspective, then, it is understandable how members of humanist groups end up criticizing their leadership if it endorses specific political positions. As oriental mystics would say, there is more than one way to climb a mountain, and the important thing is to reach the summit.

But what's on the top of this common mountain that we all wish to climb while respecting other people's alternative paths? If you're a secular humanist, presumably you are concerned with the welfare of humanity at large, so that the peak of the mountain is reached by whatever means improve—as virtue ethics philosophers have put it since Aristotle—human "flourishing." Since there are many ways for humans to flourish, the argument may go, who is to say that one set of social policies is better than another when it comes to complex social problems?

I believe that this agreement is largely a way to avoid the issue, mostly out of fear of losing a chunk of secular humanists who consider themselves libertarian. The fear is well founded, since libertarians do make up a (small but vocal) component of the political spectrum in general and tend to be relatively more common among humanists because they are usually repelled by the religious rhetoric of mainstream and right-wing currents in modern politics. Nonetheless, secular humanists *ought* to engage in political issues simply because wanting a better world for all human beings is an essential component of the humanist philosophy itself. If this wish means an open dialogue, even an occasional clash, within the humanist movement, so be it. There may very well be more than one way to climb the mountain of human flourishing, but a humanist still needs to find the least painful route(s) and to argue in defense of beneficial social policies.

My personal attitude about libertarianism is rather ambivalent. I do agree that government intervention should be limited, an idea that is largely consistent with leaving the maximum latitude of action (and hence room for flourishing) to the individual. However, it is also undeniable that human beings need some restraint imposed from outside, or they inevitably end up limiting someone else's flourishing in the name of individual freedom.[1] The question, then, becomes not *whether* the government should have the power to impose restrictions on its citizenry, but *how much power* it should have and *what checks and balances* should be put into place to minimize abuse on either side.

In this essay, I briefly examine five compelling social and political issues that I think should be at the top of the agenda for secular humanists. I realize that my particular view of these issues, not to mention the solutions proposed, is and ought to be a matter of debate. But if we don't allow such discussions in the open for fear of endangering the very idea of secular humanism, we will engage in a sterile excercise, proposing a philosophy that has little to say to the world other than that people who don't believe in God should have the same rights as everybody else. While the latter claim is obviously important (and, astonishingly, still needs to be defended even in a democracy like the United States), it had better not be all there is to humanism. Surely, a tradition that can trace its philosophical roots to Socrates, Locke, Hume, John Stuart Mill, and Bertrand Russell, to name but a few, can and ought to do better than that.

CONSTITUTIONAL ISSUES: THE MANIFESTED UNFAIRNESS OF AMERICAN ELECTIONS

The United States of America is the self-professed greatest democracy in the world. Besides the obvious offensiveness of such a claim to countries that are equally democratic and that have had a longer history of civil liberties than the United States, the structure of the American electoral system partly belies the claim as has been painfully demonstrated by the now infamous squabble between George W. Bush and Al Gore as to who really won the 2000 presidential elections.

Let's start with Democracy 101. Ever since ancient Athens, democracy has meant the rule of the people (although for a long time the "people" did not include women, economically "lower" classes, and slaves). By that simple criterion, the American system is undemocratic because it allows someone who lost the popular vote to win the presidential election—as did in fact happen to Bush and a few others before him. This bizarre situation can occur because US citizens don't really vote; electors chosen by each state do. And since each state is guaranteed a certain number of electoral votes that is not commensurate with its population, rural states are overrepresented and Bush won by acreage rather than votes. As a citizen of New Hampshire famously put it during one of many interviews the media broadcast after the 2000 elections, "If we went to a proportional system, New Hampshire would count for nothing." As it should, if the United States were really a democracy (as in "the rule of the people").

According to historians, there was originally a good reason for such a peculiar system. The United States were not really united but rather resembled a Swiss-style confederation of largely independent entities. Under those conditions, it was only natural to give precedence to the abstract entity of a "state," rather than to individual citizens. One could argue that the United States has never really become a nation—witness the harsh debates and court rulings on the limits of state versus federal power—but the fact remains that such a system is anything but democratic.[2]

A second major fault with the electoral system of the greatest democracy in the world is that typically only a minority of its population bothers to go to the voting booth. Furthermore, Republicans in Congress have strenuously fought to keep it that way, for example, opposing bills such as the motor voter registration act, which makes it easier for people to register to vote. In other democracies, the percentage of people casting their ballots is much higher than the American average, and people are automatically registered based on their biographical data (they receive the registration at home when they turn eighteen—but, of course, such a procedure would mean that the government needs to know who you are and where you live).

The American electoral situation is so bad that several years ago the Christian Coalition devised a tactic to get their favorite people elected, called "the 12 percent strategy." Since about 50 percent of eligible Americans are actually registered to vote, and of these little more than half bother to show up to cast their ballots, one needs to get the vote of half of these (roughly 12 percent of the whole population) to be ensured victory. On top of this, add the even stranger primary system, in which only a tiny fraction of really dedicated people vote, thereby dramatically influencing the general election by eliminating candidates who might do well with the population at large but don't fit the opinions of a skewed minority of activists. Here is some food for thought: Twenty million more Americans watched the 2001 Super Bowl than cast their vote in the 2000 elections.[3]

One could go even further and suggest that no current voting system is actually democratic, no matter the country in which it is implemented. An article by Dana Mackenzie in *Discover* magazine (November 2000) clearly demonstrates why. It turns out that people have been studying voting systems for quite a while, and better options than the proportional system adopted by most countries have been clearly devised—indeed, they have been historically used by different cultures in different times.[4]

Perhaps the simplest alternative is approval voting, which dates back to the thirteenth century, when it was used in Venice to elect magistrates. In this system, a person casts one vote for every candidate that he or she considers qualified. It works much like an opinion poll, with the difference that the results are added up to determine the winner. One of the advantages of approval voting is that one can vote for a candidate likely to lose—say, Ralph Nader of the American Green Party—and not feel like one is wasting one's vote: Nader (say) will get a good percentage of points while the voter can also cast a preference for somebody who is more likely to actually win. If approval voting had been used in the 2000 U.S. elections, John McCain would have won, based on polls conducted in February of that year. Furthermore, approval voting would have spared Minnesota from electing professional wrestler and buffoon-at-large Jesse Ventura and New Hampshire from handing the state's primary to radical right-winger Pat Buchanan in 1996.[5]

Another alternative to standard voting systems is the Borda count, named after Jean-Charles de Borda, a French physicist and hero of the American Revolution. This system, which was actually in use in the Roman senate at least since 105 CE, is similar to the method used to rank football and basketball college teams: Each voter ranks all the candidates from top to bottom. If we take a poll by the *Sacramento Bee* during California's open primaries in 2000, McCain would have beaten Gore 48 to 43, Gore would have bettered Bush 51 to 43, and McCain would have surpassed Bush 50 to 45. Overall, the final rank would have been McCain 98, Gore 94, and Bush 88.[6] Quite a different outcome from what actually happened!

With both the approval and the Borda methods, voters are asked to provide information that is missing from the current system: who they will pick if their favorite is eliminated. The result is more power to the voters, a better democracy. Of course, neither of these alternatives is perfect, but the point is that most people in the United States don't even realize that their way is one of the worst among those currently practiced by the world's democracies, and serious discussion hasn't begun in any country (except Australia, which does use a more sophisticated ranking method) on how to improve the actual democratic value of voting. Given that we have to live with the results for several years to come, wouldn't it be worth taking a serious look at the alternatives?

INDIVIDUAL RIGHTS: GAYS IN THE MILITARY AND OUTSIDE OF IT

I have never understood what the "gay problem" is all about. As far as I am concerned, the moral aspect is simple: As long as the people involved are consenting adults, what they do in their bedrooms is exclusively their own business. Unfortunately, many people who are otherwise adamantly against any government interference in the private lives of citizens (e.g., business practices or gun control) cry out loudly for a government-imposed "morality" that extends from the treatment of gays to abortion practices and school prayer.

It was therefore no surprise when in November 2002 the US Army dismissed nine of its linguists—all experts in crucial languages for the "war" against terrorism, such as Arabic, Korean, and Mandarin Chinese—invoking that most unfortunate Clinton doctrine, the "don't ask, don't tell" policy that has regulated dismissal of gays from the military over the past few years.

As readers may remember, President Clinton started out his first term with two bold moves, one of which was an executive order that would have made it as normal for gays as it is (now) for blacks to be in the army (the other was the call for a universal health care system, which ended in catastrophe despite Democratic control of both the House and Senate). Soon came harsh criticism from the Far Right, coupled with the obvious fact that the gay community can't muster more than a limited number of votes, which usually go to the Democrats, anyway. The predictable result was that Clinton "moderated" his stance and ended up proposing his infamous "don't ask, don't tell" compromise.

From a moral perspective, the new policy makes no sense: One either thinks that a gay lifestyle is incompatible with the "values" of the military, in which case allowing gays to stay just because they don't declare themselves is simple opportunism; or one thinks that the sexual habits of soldiers have no relationship to the functionality of an army, in which case the policy is an example of moral cowardice. Either way, Clinton, gays, and rationality lose, while bigotry scores points.

From a pragmatic viewpoint, of course, not only is there no evidence that the presence of gays in the military has any negative effect on the troops' morale (remember, the same was said of blacks and women before those issues were settled), but at least one army—that of the Netherlands—openly embraces gay culture and doesn't seem to be any worse for it.

More interesting, this and similar discussions (e.g., those about abortion and school prayers) show that the standard distinction between "liberals" and "conservatives" in terms of being respectively in favor of and opposed to a large role of government in our lives just doesn't cut it. In reality, we need to consider at least two major axes along which political positions and public opinions can be distinguished: the "economic" axis and the "social" axis.

One can—apparently without contradiction—call for little governmental interference in economic matters and at the same time cry out for a large role for Big Brother in people's bedrooms and public schools. Such a person would be a religious conservative. But it is also possible to be a libertarian and favor little or no government influence in any sphere of life (except perhaps national defense). A third position is occupied by people who want a large role of government in the control of the economy (to balance the natural tendency of big business to act amorally or even immorally and with reckless disregard for the public good) but little in the sphere of personal life. Such a person would be a progressive liberal, like me. Then there is the strawman "pink" liberal that most people in America seem to love to hate, the person who wishes for governmental control of everything, communist style. This fourth position is essentially empty in this country (though certainly not throughout the world).

Reality, of course, is more complicated than this simple classification may hint at, but thinking along the two axes of economy and social issues at least brings us beyond the simplistic dichotomy of liberal versus conservative. It also strongly suggests that we should have at least three, and possibly four, parties to represent the four positions just sketched. Instead, we are forced to choose between two alternatives that don't quite fit what a growing number of Americans actually think. I therefore propose to split the Republican Party into one branch of economic conservatives but social moderates and another branch of economic and social conservatives (the latter populated mostly by the Christian Right). Democrats could split into social and economic liberals on the one hand and social liberals but economic conservatives on the other. But who is going to force such healthy multiplication of political choices: the people, or the government? Alas, probably neither.

SOCIAL ISSUES: IT'S THE FUNDAMENTALISM, STUPID!

At the risk of oversimplifying a very complex situation, I propose that the major threat to modern democracies is not terrorism per se but ideological fundamentalism, particularly (but not exclusively) of a religious nature. Political fundamentalism has essentially disappeared, at least for now, with Fidel Castro as one of the few pathetic remnants, destined to natural oblivion, like all mortals.

The real problem now is religious fundamentalism, and in particular fundamentalism rooted in the twin monotheistic branches of Christianity and Islam (with Judaism ranking as a distant third only because it is numerically much less represented worldwide). This is not, of course, because all (or even the majority of) fundamentalist Christians, Muslims, and Jews are willing to blow themselves into pieces to achieve a political goal or because they are all bent toward the destruction of everything and everyone that disagrees with them. Far from it. But the fact remains that fundamentalism of any sort, by definition a form of extremism and therefore ill-suited to exist within a democratic and pluralistic society, easily breeds intolerance, self-righteousness, and even terrorism, of which the world has experienced the consequences all too clearly during the past few years.

Let us not make the mistake of dismissing the problem as simply a modern incarnation of the old (and certainly true) observation that political power exploits religious feelings and therefore the problem is with the desire for power and with people like Saddam Hussein (or George W. Bush), who want power and find it easy to manipulate the masses using religious appeals. Admittedly, that is happening, but Bush, I think, really believes that God is on his side, and so do Tony Blair, Hussein, bin Laden, and a host of other characters who are making a mess of the just-born twenty-first century.

The extremes to which Islamic fundamentalists (including Palestinians and their leader, Yasser Arafat, currently as pathetic as, but much more dangerous than, Castro) can go in the name of their version of the universal truth are well known and need not be belabored here. But the *New York Times* reported in the spring of 2003 about some comments by "mainstream" politicians in the United States and Israel that should be chilling to the bone of every rational and truly compassionate human being. For example, Benyamin Elon, a minister with the Israeli government, has been quoted as referring to cardinal principles of a possible Palestinian-Israeli accord, such as the idea of land for peace, as "clichés" to be overcome and has essentially called for ethnic cleansing of Palestinians. As an exponent of the latter has pointed out, can we imagine what would happen if somebody made the same casual suggestion about moving Jews out of their unhappy "holy" land?[7]

On this side of the Atlantic, things aren't much better. The extremes of the Christian Right are now documented in book upon book, but a recent addition is a declaration by Gary Bauer of American Values, who said that conservative Christians must accept the Abrahamic covenant as described in Genesis, by which God personally promised the land of Israel to the Jews, and that's that.[8] Tom DeLay, the House majority leader, has been quoted in the same newspaper as referring to the West Bank using the biblical names of Judea and Samaria.[9]

It is simply astounding that a species that has conquered space, split the atom, figured out the essentials of its own origins, and invented democracy is currently in the hands of people who still believe in the literal reading of a book written several thousand years ago. How can we vote into office, support, and take seriously a political class that on the one hand uses computers and jet airplanes but on the other hand firmly believes in the actual existence of heaven and hell—concepts invented by barely civilized human beings who slaughtered each other with swords and arrows? How much longer will we leave the future of the world in the hands of people so sure of their own viewpoint that they constantly affirm that God is on their side (on all of their sides, of course)?

I keep hearing of the existence of a "silent majority" of moderately religious people in Western democracies, and even among Muslims and Jews, who apparently have a distaste for the outrages of the extremists who govern them. Where is this silent majority? Isn't it time they woke up and kicked these men out of office (or, if not elected, out of mosques, churches, and synagogues)? The worldwide antiwar demonstrations in 2003 may have been a signal that people are in fact waking up. But let's keep the alarm clock ringing loudly, or Bush, bin Laden, and company will plunge us all back into the Dark Ages, and soon. And we call them "dark" for reasons other than the fact that electricity hadn't been discovered yet.

DOMESTIC POLICY: ECONOMIC VERSUS SOCIAL HEALTH

Money can't buy happiness. Apparently, everybody knows this except Americans, who keep thinking that economic prosperity automatically brings all sorts of goodies, from democracy in the former Eastern Bloc to satisfaction with one's own life here at home. Well, the data are in, and the conclusion is that money really cannot buy happiness.

Perhaps the most astounding indication of this truism is a simple but powerful graph published by the Fordham Institute for Innovation in Social Policy in 2002: it shows a steady increase of the US Gross Domestic Product from 1959 to the late 1990s. No question about it, America has obviously gotten richer. However, equally impressive—and much more disturbing—is the trend of the institute's Index of Social Health, based on eleven indicators including child abuse, child poverty, high school dropout rates, average weekly earnings, unemployment, health insurance coverage, senior citizen poverty, health insurance for the elderly, food stamp coverage, access to affordable housing, and the gap between rich and poor.

The social index went up in parallel with the economic index until the late 1970s, when it began on a downward spiral that continues almost uninterrupted to this day.[10] Apparently, there is no automatic link between economic prosperity and social health or, as a Brazilian general famously commented on that country's economic boom during the 1970s: "The economy's doing fine; it's just the people that aren't."

This discrepancy can be glimpsed by the comparison of a few simple facts. The "good" news is that, in the period covered by the Fordham analysis, the average size of a new home has expanded from 1,500 to 2,190 square feet; the number of cars has risen from one for every two Americans sixteen or older to one for every person of driving age (which basically means that the market is saturated); the number of Americans taking cruises each year has risen from 500,000 to 6.5 million; the production of recreational vehicles has soared from 3,000 to 239,000 per year; and the number of amusement parks has leaped from 363 to 1,164.[11]

Now for the bad news: Suicide among America's young people has increased 36 percent since 1970 and is triple the rate of 1950; the gap between rich and poor in the United States is approaching its worst point in fifty years and is the largest such gap among eighteen industrialized nations; average weekly wages, in real dollars, have declined 19 percent since 1973; the United States still leads the industrial world in youth homicide; America has more children living in poverty (14.3 million) than any other industrial nation; 43 million Americans are without health insurance (the worst performance since records have been kept), and the number has increased by more than one third since 1970; and finally, violent crime remains almost double what it was in 1970, even with substantial improvements during the 1990s.[12]

This picture makes little sense if one insists on accepting the equation "more money = better life." Of course, money does make a difference for both individuals and societies. After all, the economic and social health indices did grow in parallel for almost two decades. To paraphrase Karl Marx, before you can work on the meaning of your life, you have to have enough food in your stomach. But once peoples and societies reach a certain degree of economic prosperity, things become a bit more complex.

One of the complicating factors in the United States is that the huge gap between the rich and poor is not counterbalanced by a social net to help the poor improve their health, obtain an education, and, therefore, find a job. This deficiency relates to what is perhaps one of the most dangerous myths of American society: that this is the land of opportunity. Sure, it is if you are in the highest socioeconomic classes and you wish to keep accumulating wealth across generations, as several dynasties of magnates have done since the beginning of the industrial history of this country and continue to do now (Vanderbilt and Trump come to mind as just two examples among many). This is also the land of opportunity in a rather more limited fashion, for example, if you are a poor immigrant aiming at saving your family from starvation, perhaps even getting to possess your very own VCR. But upward mobility in the United States (or the myth of "from the log cabin to the White House," as it is sometimes referred to) is actually no different, or even worse, than that in most other industrialized countries, when one bothers to use real data instead of political rhetoric. The American poor are actually locked into their status: 54 percent of those in the bottom 20 percent in the 1960s were still there in the 1990s, and only 1 per cent had migrated to the top 20 percent. The United States has the lowest share of workers moving from the bottom fifth into the second fifth, the lowest share moving into the top 60 percent, and the highest share of workers unable to sustain full-time employment.[13]

Next time you are told that you live in a society where everybody can become president or, better, the CEO of a large company, ask about the actual numbers instead of unrepresentative anecdotes. You'll be surprised to find out that the American dream is closer to a nightmare for too many people. Isn't it time to wake up?

FOREIGN POLICY: IS THE UNITED STATES A ROGUE STATE?

The United States is without a doubt one of the best places in the world to live, and I am grateful that I am here. It is a fairly liberal democratic republic, which—even though by no means perfect—seems to be the best that humankind has been able to engineer so far. This said, let me make a case for the idea that the United States is, in fact, a "rogue" state and that it, therefore, cannot rationally use the label on other nations as an excuse to attack them, as it did with Iraq in 2003. Let's start from the basics: The *Oxford English Dictionary* defines *rogue* (first meaning) as "Dishonest or unprincipled person; mischievous child." I assume that we can transfer this definition to the level of state although that raises interesting philosophical questions about the "character" of a nation, which we will need to set aside for now.

Here, then, is my evidence that the United States is the mother of all modern rogue states. First, arguing for a preemptive strike against another sovereign nation is in direct violation of the United Nations charter and therefore puts the United States outside of the international community. For a nation to vow to abide by a certain code of conduct and then refuse to do so when it is inconvenient for its self-interest surely qualifies as "mischievous" behavior.

Second, the United States has consistently avoided joining the international community in a number of treaties that have—ironically—seen it side with "rogue" states such as Libya, Iran, and Iraq (in other words, seen from outside, America looks like part of the "axis of evil"). Examples include backpedaling on the Kyoto accord on the environment; refusing to join the anti–land mine treaty; refusing to join and actively sabotaging the international tribunal. It is "dishonest" and "unprincipled" to ask other nations to respect international law and then arrogate for one's own nation the right to violate it.

Third, before the onset of the second Iraq war, the United States allocated funds to train anti-Iraqi militias recruited among the many dissenting minorities harassed by Saddam Hussein. How, exactly, is this not equivalent to setting up a terrorist training camp? Is it just because these people will be doing the dirty work for and not against the United States? Because we are right and they are wrong? I am reminded of a *Star Trek: The Next Generation* episode in which an otherwise seldom judgmental Captain Picard is reproaching a defecting Romulan general for his past military actions against the Federation. The general reminds Picard that one people's butcher is another people's hero. What should distinguish the United States as a liberal democracy is not only its principles but the way they are defended. If the end justifies the means—Machiavelli-style—then the United States is moving perilously close to the sort of behavior that it condemns in others.

Which brings me to the fourth point: Surely the 2003 aggression against Iraq cannot seriously be framed as a defense of democracy. Doing so would be another example of dishonesty and lack of principles. If the United States is really interested in democracy, why did it decide to attack puny Iraq and at the same time give permanent normal trade relations status to, say, China? Have we forgotten Tiananmen Square? Do we really think that the Chinese leaders threaten their people less than Hussein did his? And don't we know that the Chinese (or the North Koreans, or the Pakistanis) have plenty of weapons of mass destruction, while the ones that were allegedly all over Iraq have never been found? I am not, of course, suggesting that the United States declare war on China, North Korea, or Pakistan—just that it be a bit more consistent (and principled) in its foreign policy.

Being a rogue state in the sense in which the United States surely is can, and has been, defended on rational principles. Robert Kaplan, for example, has written a book entitled *Warrior Politics: Why Leadership Demands a Pagan Ethos*, in which he argues that the United States, as the only superpower in the world, *should* behave outside of international law. Indeed, Kaplan criticizes most American politicians for being held back (ironically, I would add) by their Christian ethos. In fact, he claims that they should explictly embrace Machiavelli's "pagan" attitude and do what needs to be done.[14]

Kaplan's dichotomy is, I think, the real conundrum that the United States has to resolve during the twenty-first century. Does the United States of America want to be seen by the rest of the world as a principled nation, fighting fairly for what it sees as right, or does it want to be viewed as a Machiavellian entity willing to lie and cheat to get whatever it feels is due it? The American people should think hard about the question, because the answer will determine how history will see the United States and, more important, how this country is already affecting the lives of millions of people on this planet.

CODA: WHAT IS A SECULAR HUMANIST TO DO?

As I stated at the beginning of this essay, I don't pretend that this analysis is either comprehensive or beyond reasonable discussion. On the contrary, it is meant to stimulate further thought by my fellow secular humanists (and any other rational persons of goodwill).

The main points that I wish to drive home are these:

1. Secular humanists have a *duty*—if they take their philosophical position seriously—to engage in political discourse, no matter what the consequences, both within and outside of the movement. Not to do so relegates humanism to an irrelevant corner of the human polity.
2. Secular humanism is far more compatible with a liberal view of political issues than with a libertarian one (I assume that the reader will readily agree that religious zealotry and right-wing

Machiavellianism have, by definition, no place within humanism). Liberals and humanists alike view human beings as social animals, which means that our well-being as individuals depends crucially on the well-being of society at large.

To elaborate on the second point, though still simplifying quite a bit, one can think of humanity according to one of three main frameworks—each corresponding to a specific social and political system.[15]

1. If we emphasize the social aspect of the human animal, we may become sympathetic to a Communist view of society. I do not mean here the realized Communist regimes of the former Soviet Union or China—those are much better seen as examples of a dictatorship or an oligarchy (respectively) built on the *excuse* of communism. A true Communist society would work on the assumption that people are genuinely happy to share resources with other people for the common good—no compulsion would be needed. Experiments with "communes" in several Western countries approach this ideal but, of course, are much too small to constitute a realistic political test of the concept.

2. At the opposite extreme, one can think of human beings as essentially individualistic and put forth the libertarian ideal that the more people are left alone to do what they wish, the better society at large will be (a social version of Adam Smith's "invisible hand" in economics). There are no historical examples of such societies, but the current situation in the United States comes as close to it as we have ever been.[16]

3. Somewhere in the middle (and, with various possible combinations), we could conceptualize human nature as a mixture of social and individualist instincts—much as is the case with many other social primates. Under such circumstances, it makes sense to build a society that attempts to leave as much space as possible to the individual for flourishing while at the same time striving to guarantee basic necessities and rights to everybody. Most Western nations implement this model although their position on the continuum between total individualism and total socialism varies.[17]

It seems clear to me that option 3 is by far the most desirable, but it presents two major obstacles that secular humanists can help to overcome. First, as I mentioned earlier, a type-3 society can be realized in a variety of ways, with different degrees of balance between individual rights and social good. This balance can be identified by a combination of rational discourse and social experimentation (social problems are usually much too complicated for armchair solutions only). This process has been unfolding during the recent history of Western and non-Western democracies, and it will continue to do so for a long time to come.

Second, and more urgently, we face the risk of moving perilously close to a type-2 society. Now that the realization of type-1 experiments has been (at least temporarily) ruled out by the worldwide failure of "communism," it is the opposite end of the spectrum that naturally attracts the most sympathy. And yet, that sort of society harbors horrors as great and as irreconcilable with human well-being as true communism would.

Secular humanists realize that humans are a kind of animal, partly conditioned by our biological evolution. We also recognize the power of cultural change and of rational thinking. We should therefore use these crucial starting points to engage in public discourse for the betterment of humankind, whenever possible, and regardless of who is sitting on the other side of the aisle. It is the humanistic thing to do.

NOTES

1. I once had a heated conversation with a fellow humanist of libertarian tendencies who wanted to convince me that property rights are natural and absolute. His example was that if he—by whatever "legal" means—happened to own all the water in a certain area, it was his *right* to deny me any, even if I was dying of thirst. Regardless of various obvious objections one could raise here (e.g., who says that water can be "owned"?), I simply don't wish for the world to turn into that sort of selfish nightmare just because of property "rights."

2. Incidentally, history may be about to repeat itself. As of this writing (end of 2003), the European Union is discussing a constitution for political unity. One of the hottest debates surrounding the process is precisely whether Europe should adopt a proportional system of representation for continent-wide elections or give each nation a single vote, regardless of its population. As with the US Constitutional Convention, small nations are arguing for the latter solution, while populous ones are happier with the former. As in the case of the United States in the eighteenth century, I'm afraid that the small nations of Europe will successfully blackmail the rest and inaugurate yet another large, only partially democratic conglomerate of spurious entities.

3. According to the federal government, less than 106 million people voted in the 2000 elections (Federal Election Commission, "Voter Registration and Turnout 2000," http://www.fec.gov/pages/2000turnout/reg&to00.htm); 131 million people watched the 2001 edition of the Super Bowl, according to Nielsen Media Research (quoted in Christopher Stern, "Super Bowl Ads Stir Violence

Debate," *Washington Post*, January 30, 2001, http://www.superbowl-ads.com/articles_2001/html _files/SB_Ads_Stir_Violence.html).

4. Dana Mackenzie, "May the Best Man Lose," *Discover*, November 2000.

5. Ibid.

6. James Bennett, "The Exit that Isn't on Bush's 'Road Map,'" *New York Times*, May 18, 2003.

7. http://www.fordham.edu/index.html.

8. Gary Bauer, quoted in E. S. Herman and N. Chomsky, *Manufacturing Consent: The Political Economy of the Mass Media* (New York: Pantheon Books, 2002).

9. Tom DeLay, quoted in Herman and Chomsky, *Manufacturing Consent*.

10. Herman and Chomsky, *Manufacturing Consent*.

11. Ibid.

12. Ibid.

13. Ibid.

14. Robert D. Kaplan, *Warrior Politics: Why Leadership Demands a Pagan Ethos* (New York: Random House, 2002).

15. I am assuming here that the reader is not seriously considering a dictatorship or absolute monarchy as forms of government that in any way further human flourishing, and I will therefore not consider them at all.

16. I can already hear the protests of libertarians, but I am not claiming that the United States actually *is* a libertarian state (fortunately!), only that it has managed to approach that condition more closely than any other democracy. (It goes without saying that a libertarian state could exist only in a democracy, not in a dictatorship—be the latter secular or religious.)

17. Canada and several northern European nations seem to have reached a happy compromise in this sense. I would have moved there long ago if it weren't for the climate.

MASSIMO PIGLIUCCI teaches ecology and evolutionary biology at Stony Brook University, Long Island. He has his doctorate in genetics, a PhD in botany, and a PhD in philosophy. He has published seventy-two papers and two books on evolutionary biology, as well as numerous essays for magazines, including *Philosophy Now, Skeptic* and *Skeptical Inquirer*. He is also a regular columnist for *Free Inquiry* magazine and has written two books, one on evolution and Creationism and one on nature and science.

Part II
Political Humanism in America

7.

Political Humanism in America
Speaking Out

Paul Kurtz

> *I submit that at the present moment in American society, our
> cherished values and beliefs are indeed at stake. They are
> under threat. This being the case, then declining to speak
> out would be an affront to our deepest convictions.*
>
> —Paul Kurtz

Should secular humanism as a movement ever take political positions?
Surely individual humanists, as citizens in a democracy, may participate in the political process. They can vote for candidates and support
the political party/ies of their choice. Many humanists, to be sure, are
intensely committed to a political point of view. We have a responsibility
to speak out on issues that we consider vital to our scientific humanist outlook. Primarily, we have an obligation to make ourselves heard when vital
moral issues are at stake. There is no sharp divorce between ethics and politics. If, as Carl Von Clausewitz argued, the purpose of war is to fulfill political purposes, then the purpose of politics is to fulfill the ends and values
that we consider desirable—especially when politics impinges on our fundamental ethical values.

That there is an intrinsic continuity between ethics and politics is a
classical idea. It was first expressed in Athens, most notably by Plato and
Aristotle. The theme reappears throughout the history of political thought.
Machiavelli took another approach, maintaining that the goal of politics
was to secure and maintain power. For Machiavelli, there were certain policies that a ruler should adopt, many of them brutal, in order to achieve

From *Free Inquiry* 23, no. 3 (Summer 2003): 5–6, 63. Reprinted with permission.

political aims. I readily grant that governing a nation is complicated, and that technical rather than moral issues are often relevant. Nonetheless, the overall aim of politics is to realize certain long-range moral goals deemed desirable.

Accordingly, secular humanists should speak out and act when they believe that their cherished values and beliefs are at stake; they should seek to persuade their fellow citizens about the principles that they consider important to endorse and defend.

I submit that at the present moment in American society, our cherished values and beliefs are indeed at stake. They are under threat. This being the case, then declining to speak out would be an affront to our deepest convictions. German theologian Dietrich Bonhoeffer (1906–1945) eloquently stated that he should have protested earlier in the 1930s when the Nazis first began to implement their repressive policies.

Many Americans are today deeply disturbed about political developments. They are frightened by what they view on the domestic front as a drastic threat to our cherished democratic civil liberties, and internationally to the entire framework of international law and order so painstakingly developed over past decades. They are concerned about the unilateral preemptive war undertaken by the United States in Iraq, its abrogation of the test ban and Kyoto treaties, its bypassing of the United Nations, and its refusal to endorse the International Court of Justice.

In the face of such dangers, how can we hold silent?

Getting our theories straight is important, but it is praxis, the practical consequences of our actions, that is the best test of our efficacy and influence. Purely theoretical humanism is a mere abstract concept, without content, of no moment for the real life of humans as lived; thus, the relationship of humanism to praxis is central. (I have called this in my writings "eupraxsophy.")

If "God is dead," as Nietzsche proclaimed at the beginning of the twentieth century, then at the dawn of the twenty-first century we must affirm that "humans are alive." The power of the humanist message is that life itself is intrinsically worthwhile, that we aspire to achieve the best of which we are capable, including the expression of our highest talents and creative excellences, that we cultivate the common moral decencies, that our goal is exuberant happiness. To achieve all this we need to develop a just social order for our own society, regionally and on the planetary scale. We humans are responsible for our own destiny: "No deity will save us; we must save ourselves."[1]

The key message of humanism is not that humanists are nonbelievers in theistic religion—atheists, agnostics, or skeptics—but that we are believers, for we believe deeply in the potentialities of human beings to achieve the good life. Indeed, we wish to apply the virtues and principles of humanist ethics to enhance the human condition. If we indict the theological/messianic claims of the ancient religions for providing false illusions of salvation, then we also need to state that we are concerned with improving the conditions of human life, with improving the cultural, social, economic, and political institutions in which human beings find themselves at various times in history. The underlying premise here is our emphasis on humanist ethics: how we create a better life for ourselves and our fellow human beings in the real world, here and now, and in the foreseeable future.

Let me hasten to say that there is no single humanist response to every complex social or public issue that may arise. But we *are* interested in cognitive and ethical questions, in achieving, especially at the present juncture, a cultural renaissance or cultural reformation. We should concentrate on that. We offer a distinctive set of intellectual and normative values. We emphasize the importance of reason and critical thinking, and we wish to use these methods in order to reformulate and refashion our values, and to raise the quality of taste and the level of appreciation in society. Humanism is life-affirming; it is positive and constructive.

If applied, it would enable us to reform human culture by transcending the ancient religious, racial, ethnic, and ideological dogmas of the past that so adversely affect human civilization in the present. We thus call for a New Enlightenment, a rediscovery and a reaffirmation of the highest values of which humans are capable.

Where does this leave us on the key principle of politics? I think that secular humanists need to speak out critically about present trends in the United States. I would identify at least three areas in which we have taken stands on political issues.

First, we have objected to the recent threats to our liberties on the part of the George W. Bush administration: the Homeland Security and PATRIOT acts, the suppression of civil liberties, the erosion of our liberties by moneyed interests and lobbies, the control of the media by conglomerates with their smothering of dissent, and the emergence of a plutocracy based on wealth and property. All of these trends will, if unchecked, undermine our democratic institutions. We are especially concerned about the growing apathy of the young in politics, perhaps as a result of the pervasiveness of mass media violence, sensationalism, and mind-numbing entertainment.

Second, we have questioned the current direction of American foreign policy, with its broad-ranging antipathy to a peaceful world order, to the United Nations, and to the development of institutions of world government. Apparently, US foreign policy is to be driven by a greedy "National Security Strategy," under which we may carry out preemptive strikes anywhere in the world. Does this mean that a new and imperial Pax Americana shall dominate the world, replacing the policies of deterrence and the balance of power? Our unilateralism has offended our friends all over the world, for we have abandoned many of the ideals that inspired the American dream—ideals of individual freedom, equality of opportunity, human rights, and democracy.

Third, and perhaps least controversially for humanists, we have objected to this administration's egregious violation of the separation of church and state by championing faith-based charities and similar measures. It distresses us that the president uses his office as a bully pulpit to further the ends of Evangelical Christianity. Surely President Bush has the right to his own religious convictions, but it is disturbing when he and his administration invoke them to establish policies that threaten our secular democracy. In our view, the Bush presidency has been captured by the Radical Right and an alliance of Protestant Evangelicals, conservative Roman Catholics, and neoconservative Orthodox Jews. This alliance is bringing into being a new monotheistic quasi-theocracy. Its moral-religious outlook spills out into the political sphere in the nomination of archconservative judges and also in such policies as the administration's opposition to any support for population assistance to the developing world. A political posture that affects every aspect of American life has been inspired by a theological-moral outlook, and we have every right to protest.

The secular humanist movement does not have a narrow political agenda or a party platform and we recognize that many sociopolitical problems are very complex and often difficult to solve. There are no simple solutions. We appeal to committed naturalists and secular humanists who accept our basic scientific, philosophical, and ethical premises yet may sincerely disagree with any of the above political choices: Do not abandon us but rather argue your convictions with equal intensity.

Humanists bring to the bargaining table a unique kind of optimism about the human prospect. We respect diversity of opinion, including differences among ourselves. We believe that rational discourse is preferable to violence and warfare, that compromise is superior to conflict, that debate and deliberation comprise the best method for resolving differences.

We should, as best we can, raise our voices loud and clear in the current maelstrom of conflicting opinions. The secular humanist position is an honorable one. It is based on deeply held convictions, rooted in reason and focused on an ethical concern to enhance, fulfill, and realize human happiness, peace, and tranquility on the globe. This point, though so brilliantly apparent to us, remains a minority position in the world today. Yet we need to affirm it. And in that sense, we need to need to take strong moral-political stances when basic values are endangered.

NOTE

1. *Humanist Manifesto II* (Amherst, NY: Prometheus Books, 1973).

PAUL KURTZ is professor emeritus of philosophy at the State University of New York at Buffalo, founder and chairman of the Committee for the Scientific Investigation of Claims of the Paranormal (CSICOP), the Council for Secular Humanism, and Prometheus Books, and editor-in-chief of *Free Inquiry* magazine. A former copresident of the International Humanist and Ethical Union (IHEU), he has a BA from New York University and an MA and PhD from Columbia University. He is a fellow of the American Association for the Advancement of Science and humanist laureate and president of the International Academy of Humanism. Dr. Kurtz's many books include *Embracing the Power of Humanism*; *The Courage to Become: The Virtues of Humanism*; *The Transcendental Temptation: A Critique of Religion and the Paranormal*; and *Forbidden Fruit: The Ethics of Humanism*.

8.

Identity Politics from a Humanist Perspective

Norm R. Allen Jr.

Blacks are often depicted as relying upon their faith and religious institutions to cope with the considerable impediments which have been placed in their way. Victims need faith. The helpless and hopeless need faith. The less able are almost expected to appeal to a "higher power" to guide them through this bewildering world.

—Patrick Inniss

M any people are primarily attracted to humanism because it offers human-centered solutions to complex problems. Because human beings are political animals, humanistic ideals will continue to shape the political landscape. Humanists, like religionists, can be found among all political parties. Most humanists, however, tend to be essentially progressive. They favor universal human rights, social and economic justice, equal opportunity, church/state separation, and so forth.

African American humanists, like their religious counterparts, tend to vote heavily Democratic. They believe that the Democratic Party offers them the best chance of achieving their progressive conception of society. Like most Americans, they usually believe that it is a colossal waste of time and votes to support third-party candidates—even when it is abundantly clear that their Democratic candidate will lose an election.

African American voters therefore have no real political leverage or power within the Democratic Party. This point was driven home in the controversial film *Bulworth*, starring Warren Beatty and Halle Berry. In one scene, Beatty, who plays the Democratic candidate, arrogantly told his black supporters to stop threatening to withdraw their support because such threats were empty and meaningless. "Where else are you going to go?" he asked. This is a fictional example, but sadly, there is no reason to suppose that it could not happen in reality. No major voting bloc in the United States supports any political party in such vast numbers as blacks support the Democrats.

Jesse Jackson, Maxine Waters, and other influential blacks in the world of politics have repeatedly warned white Democrats not to take black voters for granted. Yet, though their warnings are repeatedly ignored, they continue to give their unwavering support to the Democratic Party.

Black and black-led independent political parties have not had much success in attracting black voters. Most blacks do not trust the Republican Party, and some view black Republicans as race traitors. Why then, would white Democrats *not* take black voters for granted, and what credible threat could black voters use to assure that this does not happen?

Though most black voters are progressive, an authoritarian streak runs throughout African American history. During the heyday of Marcus Garvey and the Universal Negro Improvement Association (UNIA) in the 1930s, millions of blacks supported the African redemption movement. Garvey advocated racial pride, self-help, black independence, and black unity. However, he regarded himself as a sort of black savior and had authoritarian tendencies.

Some of Garvey's followers engaged in acts of violence against his critics. Garvey invited Klansmen to his rallies, and some of his followers formed loose alliances with the KKK in the South. Garvey even accused Hitler of stealing his organizational ideas as Nazism was spreading throughout Germany. Garvey described himself as "brutally a Negro," just as he described one major white segregationist as "brutally a White man."

During the 1950s and 1960s, the Nation of Islam (NOI) became a major force in black communities throughout the United States. Under the autocratic leadership of Elijah Muhammad, the group was much like Garvey's. The Nation taught racial pride, black unity, self-reliance, and black independence. Yet they went much farther than Garvey and his followers.

Though the Nation used a lot of progressive-sounding rhetoric and fought against white supremacy, the organization was reactionary to the core. Preaching female submission and railing against homosexuals, it taught that whites were "a filthy race of devils" grafted by an evil "big-headed scientist" and that blacks were the superior race. Like the UNIA, the Nation loosely flirted with the KKK, as well as with George Lincoln Rockwell's American Nazi Party. All of these groups believed in racial separation and that blacks and whites should live in separate nations.

Muhammad taught his followers to shun politics. He insisted upon blind loyalty and obedience from his followers—and he usually received it. Many former NOI members complained of harassment, beatings, and other forms of mistreatment from the paramilitary group known as the Fruit of Islam (FOI). According to Malcolm X, NOI members firebombed his home. Later, NOI members were sentenced to prison for his assassination.

In the 1980s, minister Louis Farrakhan revived the Nation of Islam, speaking to thousands of black people throughout the world. In public, he dispensed with talk of "white devils," leaving many Americans to believe that he had moderated his views. NOI members no longer complained about beatings, and the NOI provided security in apartment buildings in poor neighborhoods.

However, the organization never ceased to be reactionary and author-itarian—and in some cases, it took turns for the worse. The NOI continued to flirt with white supremacist groups such as the White Aryan Resistance, headed by George Metzger. On September 10, 1996, the Fruit of Islam pro-vided security for the anti-Jewish racist and Holocaust denier David Irving in downtown Oakland, California. The meeting was kept secret until the day it occurred.

In the 1990s the Nation sold copies of Martin Luther's 1543 text, *On the Jews and Their Lies.* Luther calls Jews a "miserable and accursed people" and "truly stupid fools." Claiming that Christ called them "a brood of vipers," he argues that these "thieves and robbers" should be run out of Europe. He says that "their synagogues must be burned down" and argues that their religious texts should be banned and seized.

Along with such paranoid anti-Jewish conspiracy theories, pseudo-science is a constant companion of reactionary thinking. In the 1990s, the Nation promoted a supposed anti-AIDS miracle drug. A special segment on the ABC news show *20/20* exposed the fraud, and the Nation seemed to abandon the idea with no formal explanation as to why.

The Nation promotes theocracy as part of its worldview. In an inter-view with Stephen Barboza, Farrakhan stated that he favors a government run according to the teachings of the Qur'an.[1] In a 1996 interview in the *Arizona Republic,* Farrakhan blamed modernism and humanism for America's ills. While in Iran shortly before the interview—and before the Taliban caught the world's attention—Farrakhan referred to Iran as "the only government in the world run according to God's laws."[2]

Farrakhan has made very strong statements against progressive programs. Speaking to about two thousand people at the Renaissance Center in downtown Detroit in 1997, Farrakhan said that the slashing of welfare, affirmative action, and other social programs was a blessing in disguise to black America. He compared the cuts to God's prophetic command to Pharaoh to free the children of Israel. According to Farrakhan, blacks had been delivered into a position to free themselves and usher in a new world order based on peace.[3]

Perhaps the most disturbing position that the Nation has taken is the defense of Arab slavers in Sudan. In May 2003, researchers covered the northern Bahr-el Ghazal province of Sudan by bicycle and on foot, recording detailed information on thousands of missing persons. It is now known who has been abducted, how many, where, and when. Yet until the ethnic cleansing became front-page news in the mainstream media, NOI spokespersons served as apologists for the slaveholders.[4]

In October 1995, Farrakhan—with the aid of countless thousands of black progressives—had his defining moment. With the support of such notable progressives as Cornel West and Michael Eric Dyson, he called for, organized, and led the Million Man March. Farrakhan and other NOI spokespersons asked black women to "stay home." Farrakhan claimed that his idea for the march came from God, and further stated that the march's success was proof of God's endorsement. No influential progressives publicly challenged this dogmatic claim.

Though seemingly benign, this claim has serious antiprogressive implications. If the claim is true, God must be a reactionary, authoritarian, male chauvinist deity because his call was issued through an internationally renowned leader harboring these traits. Furthermore, it follows logically that such a God favors a reactionary, authoritarian, male chauvinist politics. Those who disagree failed to speak out, possibly favoring a display of black unity over an aggressive defense of progressive politics.

This was not the first time in recent years that black progressives united with reactionary forces. During the hearings involving Clarence Thomas and Anita Hill, Thomas claimed that he was the victim of a "high-tech lynching." By referring to an act that has left a deep scar on the collective psyche of black America, Thomas garnered widespread support among black Americans. In a show of unity, blacks began to support Thomas in large numbers, and he was eventually appointed to the Supreme Court.

However, black unity sometimes comes with a very high price. Just a cursory example of Thomas's career shows that he is a progressive's worst nightmare. In early 2003, Thomas was the only Supreme Court Justice to vote *against* giving a black death row inmate a new chance to defend his claim that prosecutors placed whites and death penalty supporters on his jury. The Court ruled 8–1 in favor of Thomas Miller-El, sparing his life as he tried to prove that he was a victim of discrimination.

In *Reno v. American-Arab Anti-Discrimination Committee*, Thomas and five other justices voted to greatly curtail the First Amendment rights of illegal immigrants. According to the ruling, illegal immigrants may not fight deportation by arguing that the government is trying to remove them just because they advocate provocative political ideas.[5]

Immigrant advocates say that the ruling could potentially threaten immigrants and prevent them from voicing political views due to fear of being identified as illegal aliens. Though the ruling is specifically targeted at illegal immigrants, immigrant advocates say that it could threaten the rights of legal immigrants because it threatens the final determination of their legal status. According to Marc Van Der Hout, an attorney representing the National Lawyers Guild, "It relegates immigrants to second-class citizens and it's reminiscent of the political witch hunts of the McCarthy era."[6]

Dissenting justices noted that a 1945 court ruling determined that "freedom of speech and of press is accorded aliens residing in this country," although the majority opinion by Justice Antonin Scalia did not deal with this case.[7]

Thomas was part of a 5–4 majority decision against affirmative action. He was also part of a 5–4 ruling that makes it more difficult for an employee to legally prove discrimination. And in an Arizona ruling that reduces prisoners' right to use prison law libraries, Thomas was the only judge to argue that inmates should not have the right to use government-funded law libraries.

In *Hudson v. McMillian*, the Supreme Court issued a 7–2 decision in favor of prisoner Keith Hudson. Hudson was placed in handcuffs and leg irons. One officer punched him in the eyes, chest, mouth, and stomach. Another officer kicked and punched him. Hudson suffered injuries, including loosened teeth and a cracked partial dental plate, rendered unusable for many months. Hudson sued, alleging that his Eighth Amendment right was violated—the protection against cruel and unusual punishment. The US Justice Department agreed that Hudson was the victim of cruel and unusual punishment. However, Thomas wrote the dissenting opinion, claiming that the beating was not an example of cruel and unusual punishment but usual prison policy. The seven justices subsequently rebuked him for his position.[8]

Many conservative Christians strongly support Thomas. Pat Robertson secretly donated $1 million to support his Supreme Court nomination. Religious liberals, in contrast, have denounced Thomas. On September 12, 1995, a group of ministers led by the Reverend Al Sharpton and the Reverend Dr. Wyatt Tee Walker, former chief of staff to Martin Luther King Jr., held a national clergy prayer vigil in front of Thomas's residence. Before the march, Sharpton said: "History should not record that while the biggest traitor in American history since Benedict Arnold helped rob [us of] our rights, we responded with inaction and silence. Too many people have died and suffered to allow this to happen."[9]

Thomas demonstrates no genuine connection toward black people anywhere in the world. He voted with the majority to send Haitian refugees back to Haiti, where many Americans believe that the refugees were tortured and put to death. He has hired few black law clerks since joining the court. He refuses to hire clerks who have taken black studies courses. He told one young black man to steer clear of "that African American studies stuff." He added, "You'll find a lot of classes and orientation on race relations. Try to avoid them. Try to say to yourself, 'I'm not a Black person. I'm just a person.' You'll find a lot of so-called multicultural combat, a lot of struggle between ethnic and racial groups wanting you to sign on, to narrow yourself into some group identity or other. You have to resist that."[10]

Sadly and ironically, "black unity" helped to bring this damage about. Farrakhan supported Thomas's nomination, and Thomas has voiced admiration for Farrakhan. They are both reactionary and share similar views. Farrakhan, however, is militant, while Thomas is safe and acceptable to white conservatives. Farrakhan's hatred of white supremacy meshes with the goals of progressives. For this reason, many black progressives have embraced him. Moreover, many black progressives do not believe that Farrakhan will ever gain enough power to implement his authoritarian vision for society, and that he is therefore worth following.

However, Farrakhan has proved to be disastrous for progressive Black politics. For example, he helped to derail Jesse Jackson's Democratic presidential campaign in 1984. He provided security for Jackson with the Fruit of Islam, and even registered to vote. However, after a black reporter from the *Washington Post* reported that Jackson referred to New York City as "Hymie Town," Farrakhan went on the warpath. He considered the reporter a traitor and said that one day the black nation would put such traitors to death. Many people believed that the statement was a veiled death threat. Adding fuel to the fire, Farrakhan charged that Jackson's Jewish critics practiced a "gutter religion." The fallout was strong and swift. Jackson started losing support, and his campaign never recovered.

It could be easily and persuasively argued that Jackson would never have won the election. But we will never know how far he could have gone, or how great his impact could have been if not for this unfortunate turn of events.

Some black progressive politicians supported Farrakhan's call for the Million Man March. However, the march was not tied to any major political or social movement, nor was any overriding progressive political agenda presented by the speakers. The march was a smashing success in terms of numbers, but what lasting impact did it have on black America? A demonstration of such magnitude should have been tied in some serious way to a progressive agenda, but aside from a show of black unity and a lot of feel-good speeches, the march did not accomplish much.

Black unity is certainly important, but what is most important is unity with the right people and for the right reasons. Black unity is not important as an end itself. It is a vehicle to get black people to the true goals of freedom, justice, and equality. This is what it means to "keep your eyes on the prize."

The leaders of the civil rights movement understood this well. Many black militants criticized them for allegedly selling out because they refused to work with reactionary black nationalists. But the civil rights leaders understood that reactionary politics and movements could only enslave black people in countless unforeseen ways. Moreover, they probably understood that it was not wise to align themselves with antidemocratic groups in the hope that these groups would never come to power. One can never be certain how influential and powerful reactionary forces might become.

Indeed, Farrakhan has supported and made loose alliances with many powerful and influential groups and organizations. The late African dictators Sani Abacha of Nigeria and Joseph Desire Mobutu of Zaire warmly welcomed Farrakhan. In the 1990s, Lyndon LaRouche praised Farrakhan and the Nation of Islam supported LaRouche's political party. Farrakhan has also forged ties with the Reverend Sun Myung Moon and the Unification Church. Moon, the billionaire publisher of the *Washington Times*, was part of Farrakhan's Million Family March in Washington, DC, on October 16, 2000. During his world tour, Farrakhan met with Saddam Hussein. These are hardly examples of individuals lacking power and influence in world affairs.

Moreover, reactionary and authoritarian leaders often address issues that most blacks want to see addressed. Yet many progressives have simply denounced black demagogues without attempting to understand their wide appeal to the masses. Because many—if not most—progressives do not believe in self-help, they downplay its importance to most black Americans. They believe that the government is almost completely responsible for the welfare of its citizens.

Reactionary leaders and some conservatives, on the other hand, believe that, regardless of the politics of the leaders in power, it is always within the power of black people to improve their plight. They advocate pride; self-respect; business development; the shunning of drugs; violence, and promiscuity; hard work; responsibility; strong families; and other values that could only improve the condition of American blacks. Why so many progressives believe that the promotion of these values is a threat to their worldview continues to be a mystery. Self-help and progressive politics are not mutually exclusive. Moreover, as long as progressives continue to denigrate self-help programs, authoritarian and conservative groups and leaders will continue to fill this void.

Many Democratic candidates seem to believe that they deserve the undying loyalty of blacks and progressive voters simply because they offer the only realistic alternative to the Republican Party. For example, during and after the 2000 presidential election, Democrats blamed Ralph Nader for their defeat. They never blamed themselves at all. They did not feel obligated to offer a candidate with integrity or even a personality.

Instead, they offered the American people Al Gore. However, Gore had serious limitations as an aspiring presidential candidate. One of the main reasons so many Democrats chose to vote for Nader was because Gore had betrayed President Clinton during the Elian Gonzales controversy in South Florida. Rather than support the president's fair and wise decision to return the boy to his father and his native country, Gore tried to gain votes among Florida's Cuban exile community. In light of this act, how could Democrats be blamed for supporting a candidate from another party? Why do Democrats believe that voters should always have to choose the better of two undesirable candidates? And why should voters always feel obligated to vote only for candidates from one of the two major parties? If they can neither trust nor respect either candidate, why should they be expected to support one or the other?

In reality, many Americans are fed up with politics. They will either vote for third-party candidates or they will not vote at all. Poor people are especially apathetic. They are tired of choosing the less objectionable of two candidates. Though there are differences between the Democratic and Republican parties, many poor people continue to suffer, even under Democratic administrations. They continue to receive inferior social services. They continue to live in crime-infested neighborhoods. They continue to face unemployment and underemployment. They continue to receive inferior health care—or no health care at all—and to die earlier than their wealthier American counterparts. And until politicians demonstrate success in dealing with these kinds of problems, voter apathy will continue to plague the US political system. Other voters will continue to support third-party politicians, if only to let the powers that be know that they are fed up with the program.

One of the saddest chapters in American political history occurred during the 2000 presidential election. Blacks were at the center of the controversy. Throughout some precincts in Florida, there were reports of police harassment and intimidation of black voters. Many black voters were required to provide several forms of identification even if they had perfectly legitimate voter registration cards. At some precincts, blacks attempting to vote showed up only to find that their names were not on the lists. Florida governor Jeb Bush—the future president's brother—and Florida secretary of state Katherine Harris played major roles in the debacle. They took advantage of a nineteenth-century law that white supremacists in Florida had used to deny blacks the right to vote, and they hired a computer firm that purged thousands of legitimate black Democratic voters from the lists.

As if this was not enough, voters had to contend with perplexing ballots, faulty equipment, and other problems. All of this should not be surprising, however. Harris was cochair of the Florida drive to elect George W. Bush to the presidency, a blatant conflict of interest.

Eventually, votes in certain Florida districts had to be recounted and Bush was awarded the election. As Justice Stevens pointed out, many voters lost faith in the US political system. Many blacks in Florida who had never voted lined up to cast their ballots. Who could honestly blame them if they revert to apathy and never vote again? At what point will political leaders seriously attempt to prevent these kinds of abuses of power?

Some progressives believe that a demand for reparations for African Americans should be a major political issue. However, this goal may be unrealistic. It would be especially difficult to pursue the matter through the courts. Slavery was not illegal before 1865, and therefore the enslavement of human beings against their will was not a crime punishable by law. More-over, the statute of limitations for such a law would have run out long ago.

An appeal to the moral conscience of white Americans for reparations seems to be another dead end. Most whites do not even believe America should *apologize* for slavery, let alone pay reparations. Furthermore, Rep. John Conyers of Michigan has repeatedly called for a discussion of repara-tions among members of Congress. Most black congresspersons have sup-ported him, but not a single white congressperson has publicly expressed support for the idea.

Ironically, some staunch conservatives, such as Charles Krauthammer, support the drive for reparations. However, they believe that America should pay reparations and then, essentially, tell blacks that the debt has been paid in full. In the view of these conservatives, paying reparations would elimi-nate the need for affirmative action or any other government-sanctioned program to uplift African Americans. Most advocates of reparations do not deal seriously with this proposal. If this becomes the only way to receive reparations, would most of them agree to such a proposal? If so, what kind of future could African Americans and Americans in general expect?

The call for reparations is not practical. Progressives would be wise to pursue more realistic avenues in the ongoing quest for racial justice. Pro-gressives should focus on dealing with the causes behind America's high incarceration rate. Draconian drug laws such as New York State's Rocke-feller drug laws are largely responsible for the high US incarceration rate. In the 1980s, Congress mandated stronger penalties for drug dealers. In 1986, Congress established much longer prison sentences for people using crack cocaine than for those using the powder form. Most crack users were black and became the main targets in the war on drugs.

The high rate of incarceration has dire consequences for the US polit-ical landscape. Due to felony convictions, about 4 million Americans do not have the right to vote. Many are disenfranchised for the rest of their lives even though they have paid their debt to society.

The Sentencing Project, a nonprofit group that fights for sentencing reform, released a report with Human Rights Watch titled "Losing the Vote: The Impact of Felony Disenfranchisement Laws in the United States." The report, published in 1998, found that 36 percent of the disenfranchised are black men. In seven states, one out of four black men will never have the right to vote in the United States. However, the report also found that many countries allow both ex-felons *and* prisoners to vote. These nations include France, Peru, Israel, Norway, Sweden, and Denmark.[11] Progressives should strive to win voting rights for imprisoned Americans. After all, this would be a great way to help them with their transition back into society after they have served their sentences.

Education is one solution to the crime and incarceration problems. Many people are advocating school vouchers as a way of improving education in the United States. The problem is that most American students attend public schools. Though it is true that simply throwing money at a problem will not solve it, taking money *away* is not necessarily the answer either. While some students get a better education in private schools, the majority of students will remain in public schools. Rather than risking the future of public education, Americans must continue to search for solutions to improve the system in which most American students will continue to attend school.

Blacks, many religious conservatives contend, must find solutions to their own problems. They see little or no need for government action. They expect blacks to lift themselves up by their bootstraps. However, doing so is becoming increasingly difficult as industry continues to move out of the nation in general and the inner cities in particular. At one time, inner-city residents could find jobs in steel plants, auto plants, and so forth. Today, higher education is more important than ever. Even some of the most mundane jobs require college degrees. Yet education is more expensive than ever. Many young women feel compelled to work as exotic dancers to pay their way through college.

If college is necessary, why should it not be free? Some of the oil-rich nations of the Middle East provide free education for college students. The noted scholar Adolph Reed has suggested that the same could be done for students in America if the country only had the will. This should be a major progressive goal.

Affirmative action will continue to be a controversial topic in the twenty-first century. Many whites refer to it as "reverse discrimination," as opposed to the traditional forms of discrimination that have served whites for centuries. They continually talk about the need to level the playing field for all Americans.

However, another unexpected phenomenon is receiving coverage in the mainstream media these days. Pundits have begun to notice a "new gender gap" between males and females in education. Girls have surpassed boys in reading and are catching up with them in math. Since 1999, American women have earned more bachelor's and master's degrees than American men. Moreover, this gap is expected to widen much further by 2009.

Not surprisingly, white males are alarmed by this turn of events. Furthermore, some schools have created affirmative action programs for males. In a cover story in *BusinessWeek*, Michelle Conlin writes, "At one exclusive private day school in the Midwest, administrators have gone so far as to mandate that all awards and student positions be divvied equally between the sexes."[12] She continues, "The female to male ratio is already 60–40 at the University of North Carolina, Boston University, and New York University. To keep their gender ratios 50–50, many Ivy League and other elite schools are secretly employing a kind of stealth affirmative action for boys."[13]

In these instances, white males bemoaning discrimination and a lowering of standards are nowhere to be found. Many white males believe that discrimination is good as long as they are the obvious beneficiaries. The hypocrisy is disturbingly clear. If it is fair to discriminate in favor of white males in the area of education, why is it unfair to establish affirmative action for women and minorities?

Affirmative action has had tremendous benefits to society. It has helped to create more diverse newsrooms and police forces, thereby decreasing racial tension and fostering understanding. It has created opportunities for some of its most vociferous opponents—such as Justice Thomas and writer John H. McWhorter. Unless its opponents are able and willing to come up with a more equitable way to level the playing field, it would be foolish and dangerous to tamper with affirmative action.

Many religious conservatives promote abstinence-only "sex education." Moreover, they have supported government funds for the promotion of marriage as a panacea for all that ails dysfunctional families. Though it is true that children are generally much better off in two-parent households, unemployed and underemployed men are much less likely to wed than their gainfully employed counterparts. If religious conservatives take themselves seriously, they will focus on job creation and easy access to education as their primary objectives.

Progressives must not focus only on conditions in the United States. Humanism offers a cosmic worldview and compassion for human beings throughout the world. The global village has arrived. Parochialism, jingoism, and narrow conceptions of nationalism are serious liabilities and threats to world peace. Progressives must continue to strive for economic justice and equal opportunity, but they must also understand that unchecked capitalism and unrestrained consumerism could destroy humanity in the long run.

Many politicians believe that, ideally, world leaders should strive to help all the peoples of the world to live as extravagantly as Americans live. However, though the United States contains only 5 percent of the world's population, its citizens use over 50 percent of its resources. Some experts claim that the human race would need three more earths if the rest of the world shared the lifestyles of Americans. The people of the earth need sane policies geared toward the protection of the environment. "The Affirmations of Humanism," compiled by philosopher Paul Kurtz, puts forth many principles that could be embraced by progressive politicians. One of the principles reads as follows: "We want to protect and enhance the earth, to preserve it for future generations, and to avoid inflicting needless suffering on other species."[14] The Green Party embraces this principle. For that reason it is an attractive alternative for many Democrats who believe that the Democratic Party is too tightly controlled by big corporations that pose serious threats to the environment.

Some humanists have expressed interest in starting a humanist political party. This proposal does not seem necessary or practical, however. Humanists have much in common with progressive religionists. Both groups are committed to church-state separation, good and responsible science, opposition to the teaching of "creation science" in public schools, and so forth. In fact, Americans United for Separation of Church and State is composed mostly of liberal religionists. They are staunch allies of many humanist groups. Rather than trying to start a separate humanist party and weakening progressive politics, humanists should continue to work toward common goals with their religious counterparts.

In conclusion, most blacks will continue to be progressive. However, their interests must be respected and they must not be taken for granted. They must continue to seek progressive allies, but they must not alienate those allies by supporting antidemocratic leaders and organizations. They must establish and maintain moral authority, as did the leaders of the civil rights movement. And like the leaders of the civil rights movement, they must continue to draw upon humanist ideals in their ongoing struggle for freedom, justice, and equality.

NOTES

1. Louis Farrakhan, quoted in Stephen Barboza, *American Jihad: Islam after Malcolm X* (New York: Doubleday, 1994).

2. "Farrakhan Blames Modernism, Humanism for America's Ills," *AAH Examiner* 6, no. 2 (Summer 1996): 8.

3. "Farrakhan Lauds 'End' of Social Programs," *AAH Examiner* 7, no. 3 (Fall 1997): 7.

4. NOI members continue to defend the Sudanese regime in Khartoum in their paper, the *Final Call*, and on their Web site at http://www.finalcall.com. Also, see "Slavery in Our Time: Black America Slowly Rediscovers Slavery—in Africa," by David Aikman, a former correspondent for *Time*, in the *American Spectator*, February 1997, p. 52.

5. *Reno v. American-Arab Anti-Discrimination Committee*, 525 US 471 (1999).

6. "High Court Limits Constitutional Freedoms of Illegal Immigrants," *Buffalo News*, February 25, 1999.

7. *Reno v. American-Arab Anti-Discrimination Committee*.

8. *Hudson v. McMillian*, 503 US 1 (1992).

9. Al Sharpton, speaking at Mt. Nebo Baptist Church in New York City on July 25, 1995.

10. "Justice Thomas Reflects on Youth as He Turns 50," *Buffalo News*, June 23, 1998.

11. Human Rights Watch, "Losing the Vote: The Impact of Felony Disenfranchisement Laws in the United States," The Sentencing Project, 1998, http://www.hrw.org/reports98/vote.

12. Michelle Conlin, *BusinessWeek*, May 26, 2003, p. 76.

13. Ibid., p. 77.

14. "The Affirmations of Humanism: A Statement of Principles," Council for Secular Humanism, http://www.secularhumanism.org/intro/affirmations.html.

NORM R. ALLEN JR. is the executive director of African Americans for Humanism (AAH), an educational organization primarily concerned with fostering critical thinking, ethical conduct, church-state separation, and skepticism toward untested claims to knowledge. He is the editor of the groundbreaking book, *African-American Humanism: An Anthology* and of the *AAH Examiner* and an associate editor of *Free Inquiry* magazine. His most recent book is *The Black Humanist Experience*.

Allen has traveled and lectured throughout North America, Europe, and Africa. His writings have been published in scores of newspapers throughout the United States, and he has spoken on numerous radio and television programs. Allen's writings have appeared in such books as *Culture Wars* and the National Center for Science Education's *Voices for Evolution*.

9.

Humanism, Progressive Politics, and Gay Rights

Brent Bowen

*Too many religions regard human sexuality as a bad fea-
ture—one barely to be tolerated, then only in a very highly
defined and prescribed manner. But it is an enormously
important characteristic of human beings, which finds many
different kinds of expression. To say that we know only one is
"right" shows a degree of intolerance which I find most
objectionable.*

—Sir Hermann Bondi

*If the Supreme Court says that you have the right to consen-
sual [gay] sex within your home, then you have the right to
bigamy, you have the right to adultery, you have the right to
anything.*
       —U.S. Senator Rick Santorum, April 2003, responding to the
United States Supreme Court decision rendering
sodomy laws unconstitutional

ew issues draw the fury of religious conservatives as much as gay
rights. From vitriolic fund-raising letters to organized campaigns to
rescind gay rights measures, religious fundamentalists see gays rights
as a galvanizing force for their base. One reason is that this issue—alongside abortion and capital punishment—invokes religious beliefs far more
than other policial issues. To right-wing believers, gay rights represents
nothing less than an attack on the values they contend form the basis for
civilization. Any breach on these values paves the way for the slippery
slope of the moral nihilism referred to by Senator Rick Santorum (R-PA).[1]

Humanists and progressives believe differently. Both movements view gay rights as another step in social progress, following the civil rights struggles of women, African Americans, and other historically opressed groups. Humanists and progressives reject the hierarchical dualities promoted by conservative religions: men over women, believers over nonbelievers, straights over gays.

Since the gay riots at the Stonewall Inn in New York City in 1968, the last thirty-five years have brought an incredible change in the landscape of gay issues in the United States and worldwide. Gay people sprang out of their secretive lives and suddenly began demanding their right to participate in society. The notion of gay marriage, which would have been considered laughable in the 1900s, has now moved to the forefront of political issues as we begin the twenty-first century. In fact, as of 2004, gays have gained domestic partner benefits in seventeen countries and marriage privileges in two countries, as well as the Canadian provinces of Ontario, Quebec, and British Columbia. As the tide seems to favor more rights for gays, the religious conservatives are mounting a backlash. US legislators have introduced a constitutional amendment codifying marriage as a union between one man and one woman. This action is the latest in a series of organized opposition to gay rights, most notably seen in the recall of city council measures that added gays to the antidiscrimination laws in particular communities.

The debate around "gay rights" incorporates several issues, most notably the right to privacy (sodomy laws), employment rights, and family rights. Here is a rundown of where these issues stand entering 2004:

Privacy rights: Many countries have used sodomy laws to declare unlawful any private sexual conduct besides heterosexual intercourse. The term *sodomy* harkens back to the biblical story of Sodom and Gomorrah, cities whose inhabitants engaged in "sinful" activity, including homosexuality. Legally, sodomy laws have included not only homosexual acts but also oral and anal sex between heterosexuals, but the enforcement of the laws has been overwhelming targeted at gays. Beginning with Illinois's decision to rescind its sodomy laws in 1961, state after state reversed its sodomy laws until only fourteen remained in 2004.[2]

Then, in a historic ruling, the Supreme Court reversed an earlier decision (*Bowers v. Hardwick*, 1986) and declared in *Lawrence v. Texas* that sodomy laws outlawing private, consensual acts among adults were unconstitutional. With that ruling, the United States joined 121 other nations with no sodomy laws. However, eighty-four countries, most of them in Africa and the Middle East, retain sodomy laws. Seven countries have laws in which homosexual acts are punishable by death.[3]

Employment rights: In the United States, fourteen states and hundreds of municipalities have gay antidiscrimination laws or regulations as of 2003. Still, in most areas it is possible for a homosexual person to be denied employment or fired because the employer dislikes gay people. The Employment Non-Discrimination Act (EDNA), which would bar discrimination against homosexuals in most areas of employment, was voted down by the United States Senate in 1996, but efforts to reintroduce the act continue. Worldwide, twenty-two countries have national gay rights laws that ban some antigay discrimination. The right of gays to openly serve in the military is another hotly debated issue. In 1993, President Bill Clinton reneged on his campaign promise to overturn the military ban on homosexuals, but intense political pressure from conservatives forced him to compromise with a "don't ask, don't tell" policy. In other words, gays seeking to serve in the military would not be asked about their sexual orientation, but they would be expected to keep their sexuality a secret or risk discharge. So the military ban remains in the United States, while twenty-five other countries allow homosexuals in their fighting forces.

Family rights: The ability of gay couples to achieve legal recognition in the United States was first granted by the state of Vermont, which allowed gays to enter "civil unions" with many of the same benefits as heterosexual married couples. No other state has passed a similar measure. In fact, most states have adopted "Defense of Marriage" acts that reflect a federal law passed in 1996, which provides that states do not have to recognize domestic partner benefits or same-sex legal marriages granted in another state. Consequently, most gay couples in the United States have no access to more than eleven hundred special privileges afforded to heterosexual married couples by federal laws and statutes. The same holds true for gays in every other nation except Belgium and the Netherlands, both of which recognize gay marriages. The ability of homosexuals to adopt children and gain child custody from prior marriages is greatly hampered by the lack of marital or partnership rights. This issue is constantly evolving, especially since the Massachussets Supreme Court in 2003 found that the exclusion of gays from legal marriage violated that state's constitution. As a result, homosexual couples began to legally marry in Massachusetts in May 2004. More discussion about gay marriage rights follows later in this chapter.

The philosophies of humanism and progressive politics are in close alignment regarding these issues. Both camps respect the rights of individuals to gain and maintain employment and to participate in society without being subject to discrimination. Another shared principle is the right of individuals to engage freely in private behavior, as long as the behavior doesn't adversely affect others.

The *Humanist Manifesto 2000*, drafted by the founder of the Council for Secular Humanism, Paul Kurtz, laid out clear support for gays against discrimination. Kurtz wrote, "Discrimination in job opportunity, education or cultural activities is insupportable. Society should not deny homosexuals, bisexuals or transgendered and transsexuals equal rights."[4]

Similar support for gays was voiced in the *Humanist Manifesto II*, which was first published in 1973 in the *Humanist* magazine. That document states:

> In the area of sexuality, we believe that intolerant attitudes, often cultivated by orthodox religions and puritanical cultures, unduly repress sexual conduct. . . . The many varieties of sexual exploration should not in themselves be considered evil. Without countenancing mindless permissiveness or unbridled promiscuity, a civilized society should be a tolerant one. Short of harming others or compelling them to do likewise, individuals should be permitted to express their sexual proclivities and pursue their life style as they desire.[5]

Progressive political movements have promoted similar viewpoints. Liberal views are often framed in a respect for minority rights, the right to privacy, and the separation of church and state. For example, the 2000 Democratic Party platform offered support for the inclusion of sexual oreintation in antidiscrimination and hate crime laws, increased AIDS funding, and the inclusion of gays in the military.[6] The Green Party went even further than the Democrats, declaring in its party platform: "We affirm the right to openly embrace sexual orientation in the intimate choice of who we love. We support the rights of gays, lesbian, and bisexual people in housing, jobs, civil marriage and benefits, child custody, and in all areas of life, the right to be treated equally with all other people."[7] Not surprisingly, the strongest support for gay rights laws is found in urban settings with high levels of social diversity and education and few adherents to fundamentalist religions.

Flip over that equation and you find the roots of the opposition to gay rights. Many rural communities with conservative religious beliefs are stridently antigay. Nationally, those views are reflected in the Republican Party, whose 2000 platform included language supporting the bans against gays in the military and in the Boys Scouts of America, the definition of marriage as a union "between one man and one woman," and the statement that "we do not believe sexual preference should be given special protection or standing in law."[8]

That last quotation bears significance by its use of certain words. Note the reference to "sexual preference" instead of "sexual orientation." Whereas humanists and progressives believe that sexuality is largely an innate characterisitic, probably a result of genetics influenced by environment, conservatives view homosexuality as a choice—and a choice that can be reversed. That's why religious conservatives trumpet the works of groups like Exodus International and other organizations that support the conversion of homosexuals to a heterosexual or celibate life. The reasoning goes like this: If being gay is a choice, that person can choose to become heterosexual, and consequently there's really no need for antidiscrimination laws.

The notion of "special protection" is also revealing, as gay rights activist Suzanne Pharr illustrates. First, the right wing defines civil rights as a special category for minorities who have suffered discrimination. Second, these legal protections are defined as "special rights" that can be given or taken away by the majority, who have ordinary rights, not special rights. Granting special rights imposes a cost on society and has resulted in reverse discrimination against more deserving people. Third, gay rights opponents argue that homosexuals have not suffered, especially economically, to the same degree as groups that special rights are designed to protect, such as African Americans. Also, gays can avoid discrimination by hiding their sexual identity, unlike African Americans, whose appearance can invite unfair treatment. And finally, returning to the "choice" issue, being gay is not an intrinsic trait like being African American; instead, gays choose their lifestyle and therefore shouldn't be afforded the same minority status and privileges.[9]

The slogan "Equal Rights, Not Special Rights" was adopted by gay rights opponents because the overt references to religion proved divisive in political referendums in the early years of the gay political movement. Still, the formidable voice of fundamentalist religion and its allied associations can be heard amid the civil discours. Political scientist Debra Burrington summarizes the perspective of the religious conservative:

> Religious fundamentalists have a long history of attention to what they consider "traditional moral values." At the center of these traditional moral vlaues is Bible-based religion. Around this core are related values about God-given "natural differences" between men and women, traditional gender roles, the nuclear family, and procreatively-focused sexuality, or what religious right activists have called the heterosexual ethic. From these values emerge political interests in protecting the traditional family, preventing abortion, and prohibiting homosexuality.[10]

From that web of interlocking concerns springs the emotional battle over gay marriage, providing a battleground between religion and secularism.

Spouting biblical references, conservatives cite religious tradition as the cornerstone of their arguments. Christian activist Jim Woodall writes, "Marriage is a covenant established by God wherein one man and one woman, united for life, are licensed by the State for the purpose of founding and maintaining a family. A family that follows biblical principles and cherishes its members."[11] Accordingly only a few religions—Reform Judaism, Universalist Unitarianism, and some sects of Buddhism—support gay marriage and perform commitment ceremonies. Clergy from other religions holding similar ceremonies have been rebuked or expelled by their institutional hierarchies.

In response, gay marriage advocates have stressed that their goal is civil marriage—marriage endorsed by the state but not necessarily by a religious institution. Civil marriages have long been available to heterosexual couples, so the same legal status could be afforded to homosexuals. Gay marriage opponents respond that churches may be forced to recognize same-sex married couples should gay marriage be legalized, a claim that is debatable considering the constitutional separation of church and state and the right of free association reinforced by the 2003 US Supreme Court decision upholding the Boy Scouts of America's ban on homosexuals.

Besides playing the religion card, conservatives paint gay marriage as a gateway to other social ills. If states allow homosexuals to marry, they argue, the definition of marriage would be so watered down that all types of marriages would have to be recognized, including bigamous marriages, incestuous marriages, and marriages between humans and animals. Christian Right groups such as the Family Research Council and Gary Bauer's Campaign for Working Families have loudly voiced this position.

The gay marriage issue also calls into question the purpose of marriage. Conservatives contend that the purpose of marriage is to procreate, and since homosexuals can't procreate naturally, they can't fulfill this purpose. Progressives respond that heterosexual couples who are either unable or unwilling to procreate are still allowed to marry and that gays can parent children through in vitro fertilization, adoption, and other methods. Conservatives try to play a liberal card in this scenario by arguing that parenting by two men actually discriminates against women by making motherhood seem unnecessary, and vice versa regarding lesbians and fatherhood.

The loudest voices within the humanist movement support gay marriage and argue that civil marriage is about commitment, not procreation. Charlene Gomes states:

> The time has come to expand marriage to include same-sex couples. . . . Most human beings at some point in their lives desire to share their fortunes and misfortunes with a partner with whom they have formed lasting bonds, desire to provide emotional stability and economic security for their loved ones, desire to feel secure in the knowledge that their loved ones' emotional and economic secutrity are protected by law. . . . In this respect, and many others, gays and lesbians are no different from heterosexuals.[12]

The largest humanist organization, the American Humanist Association, has supported gay rights and gay marriage for decades, confirming its support in the 1976 publication of its New Bill of Sexual Rights and Responsibilties. In 1997, the AHA board resolved that the organization "reaffirms the validity and supports the legalization of same-sex marriages in all states of the United States."[13] The Council for Secular Humanism has been less forceful, implying but not directly stating support for gay marriage in its *Humanist Manifesto 2000*: "Adults should have the right to marry who ever they wish. . . . Same-sex couples should have the same rights as heterosexual couples."[14]

Of course, there are exceptions to the standard viewpoints of humanists and religious conservatives. Tom Flynn, editor of the humanist magazine *Free Inquiry*, argues that the gay movement should be promoting civil unions instead of gay marriages because civil unions could extend benefits to include unmarried cohabitating heterosexual couples, who outnumber gay couples.[15] Conservative *New York Times* columnist David Brooks defends gay marriage as a way of actually bolstering traditional marriage by fostering commitment and fidelity instead of what he terms a "culture of contingency" in which "the marriage bond . . . is now more likely to be seen as an easily cancelled contract."[16]

When it comes to the gay marriage issue, humanists go where many progressive politicians fear to tread. Of the nine Democratic presidential candidates for the 2004 primary elections, only three support gay marriages; and those three candidates lagged far behind the other candidates in the polls. The eventual presidential nominee, Senator John Kerry of Massachussets, echoes the opinions of his fellow frontrunners by supporting civil unions for gays but not gay marriage because of "tradition." Surely, Kerry and his fellow candidates have a keen eye on the 2003 Pew Research Center poll results, which show that most Americans oppose gay marriage by a 59 percent to 32 percent margin, including a 52 percent to 39 percent split among both Democrats and Independents. The civil union stance appears safer because Democrats and Independents have majorities that agree with the question, "Should gays and lesbians be allowed to have legal agreements with many of the same rights as marriage?" Nationally, however, Americans tilt against that question 51 percent to 41 percent.[17]

The future of the gay marriage debate and the myriad of other gay rights issues will ultimately hinge on the public's perception of religion's role in society. Secular, pluralistic nations with deep religious traditions, such as the United States, will continue to navigate the divide between literalist religious interpretations and the repect for individual rights and freedoms. Theocratic nations such as Afghanistan will likely continue their oppression of homosexuals as the world of democratic values slowly begins to exert its influence.

Through it all, humanists and progressives will continue to fight to end the suffering and hatred that homosexuals have had to endure for centuries. The key differences in their approaches center on the word "politics" in progressive politics. The philosophy of humanism can boldly point to the injustice of religious doctrines and the effects these doctrines had on homosexuals. Progressive politics, in contrast, must respect the mainstream and liberal religious views of the adherents that make up much of its base. Still, the goal of achieving respect and dignity for all humans remains a unifying force.

NOTES

1. Rick Santorum, AP Press interview, April 21, 2003.

2. Rachel Kranz and Tim Cusick, *Gay Rights* (New York: Facts on File, 2000), pp. 46–52.

3. *Bowers v. Hardwick* 478 US 186 (1986); *Lawrence v. Texas* (02-102) 41 S. W. 3d 349; http://www.actw.n.com/eatonohio/gay/worldnrap.htm (accessed June 2004).

4. Paul Kurtz, *Humanist Manifesto 2000: A Call for a New Planetary Humanism*, page 23 in this volume.

5. Paul Kurtz, ed., *Humanist Manifesto II* (Amherst, NY: Prometheus Books, 1973).

6. 2000 Democratic Party Platform, http:// www.thetaskforce.org/election-center/rep2000platform.htm.

7. 2000 Green Party Platform, http://www.gp.org/platform/2000.

8. 2000 Republican Party Platform, http://www.the taskforce/electioncenter/rep2000platform.htm.

9. Suzanne Pharr, "Multi-Issue Politics," *Transformation* 9 (January/February 1994): 3.

10. Debra Burrington, "Competing Visions of Community: The Religious Right and Gay Rights" (paper presented at the annual meeting of the American Political Science Association, Washington, DC, 1993), p. 7.

11. Jim Woodall, "Lawfully Wedded?" *Family Voice* 18 (April 1996): 5.

12. Charlene Gomes, "The Need for Full Recognition of Same-Sex Marriage," *Humanist* (September/October 2003): 15.

13. American Humanist Association, http://www.americanhumanist.org/press/TPGayMarriage.

14. Council for Secular Humanism, *Humanist Manifesto 2000*, page 23 in this volume.

15. Tom Flynn, "Mixed Blessings," *Free Inquiry* 24, no. 1 (December 2003/January 2004).

16. David Brooks, "The Perfect Marriage," *New York Times*, November 22, 2003.

17. Susan Page, "Gay Marriage Looms Large for '04," *USA Today*, November 19, 2003.

BRENT BOWEN is the founder and current president of the Free Inquirers of Northeastern Ohio (FINO), a humanist group based in the Cleveland area. He is the owner of Bowen Library Services, a publishers' representative group marketing to public libraries in the midwestern United States. A resident of Akron, Ohio, he is a supporter of the Gay and Lesbian Service Centers in both Cleveland and Akron.

10.

Humanistic Patriotism

Michael Parenti

For a whole to be strong, its parts must be strong. For plane-tary society to be dynamic, each socio-economic unit must have a sound economy and cultural vitality. Whereas geo-political patriotism arises out of a people's narrow identifica-tion with their nation, humanistic patriotism gets established through identification with the universal humanity.

—ProutWorld.org

The United States has more than its share of what I call "superpa-triots," the hypernationalist, mindless, flag-waving types who are ready to support any overseas US aggression and who tolerate no criticism of our country. For them it's "America, love it or leave it." But a good number of real patriots who care enough about their country to want to improve it also exist. Their patriotism has a humanistic social content. They know that democracy is not just the ability to hold elections but the obligation to serve and fulfill the basic needs and interests of the *demos*, the people. Humanistic patriots educate themselves about the real history of their country and are not satisfied with the promotional fluff and chau-vinism that passes for history in our schools. They find different accom-plishments in our past to be proud of than do the superpatriots—for instance, the struggle for enfranchisement; the abolitionist movement; the peace movement; the elimination of child labor; the struggle for collective bargaining, for the eight-hour day, for occupational safety, for racial justice and gender equality. In the humanistic patriot's pantheon can be found Tom Paine, Harriet Tubman, Frederick Douglass, Mark Twain, Susan B.

Anthony, Mother Jones, Big Bill Haywood, John Reed, Eugene Victor Debs, Elizabeth Gurly Flynn, Jeanette Rankin, Paul Robeson, A. J. Muste, Harry Bridges, Walter Reuther, Martin Luther King Jr.—and the millions in the ranks who brought forth these kinds of leaders.

"More than ever," writes a humanist patriot living in Berkeley, California, "we need to embrace what is best in our history—the democratic principles of free speech, equality and nonviolent activism—while confronting the worst—oppression, degradation of the environment, an oil-driven foreign policy—with eyes wide open. Only by embodying true liberty, justice and equality for all does our country and our world stand a chance of surviving in the 21st century."[1]

Humanistic patriots struggle for fundamental social change. They want to tax the rich, not low-income working people, and they want to eliminate the extremes between very rich and very poor. They want to restructure the use of energy and transportation in order to save our country and the planet on which it exists. In contrast to the profit-oriented conservative superpatriots who repeatedly profess their love for this land called America but seem unconcerned about its forests, rivers, wildlife, wetlands, water supplies, and overall ecological health, the real patriot puts environmental concerns before everything else. Without a livable ecology, nothing else will survive.

Humanistic patriots also advocate more struggle against racism and sexism in all spheres of life. They advocate freedom of speech and freedom of ideas in the major media, ideas that would include dissident left views as well as the usual hard-line right-wing and conventional centrist opinions. They want relief from the evasive, fatuous, mealy-mouthed, know-it-all, anti-Communist media pundits and conservative columnists. They want discussion of worker-controlled enterprises and public ownership. They want a national debate on the oppressive, unjust purposes of US foreign policy in the third world and elsewhere. They want to reclaim the nation's airwaves, which are part of the public domain and belong not to a handful of wealthy conservative network bosses but to the people of the United States.

Some of them want a government that will go directly into not-for-profit goods production. If private industry cannot provide for the needs of the people, cannot build homes and hospitals enough for all, then the public sector should do so—not by contracting out labor to private profiteers but by direct production as during the New Deal when public workers did all sorts of necessary work. They made tents, cots, and shoes, and produced canned foods for the destitute. Not-for-profit production created jobs, served human needs, and expanded individual spending power and the tax base, all without the parasitic private investors making a penny on their labor. No wonder not-for-profit production is not tolerated by the powers that be.

Real patriots of the humanistic variety want to open up our political system to new political parties, not just to capitalist empire-building parties, not just one party that red-baits and liberal-baits and the other that lives in fear of being red-baited and liberal-baited. We need to do what revolutionary Nicaragua did and institute proportional representation, easy ballot access to dissident parties, convenient voter-registration conditions, public campaign funding, and free TV time for minority parties.[2]

Real patriots want the fundamental democratization of the political process and the economy of this country. They say, along with Albert Camus, that they want to be able to love their country and justice, too. In fact, the only way one can be a real patriot is to love justice. A real patriot is not afraid of dramatic and fundamental changes—if those changes are in a democratic direction. As Mark Twain put it more than a century ago:

> You see my kind of loyalty was loyalty to one's country, not to its institutions or its office-holders. . . . I was from Connecticut, whose Constitution declares "that all political power is inherent in the people, and all free governments are founded on their authority and instituted for their benefit; and that they have *at all times* an undeniable and indefeasible right to *alter their form of government* in such a manner as they may think expedient." (Twain's emphasis)[3]

Finally, humanistic real patriots are also internationalists. They feel a special attachment to their own country but not in some competitive way that pits the United States against other powers. They love the people of all nations, seeing them as different representations of the same human family. In 1936, individuals from many countries and all walks of life joined together to form the International Brigade, which fought in Spain to protect democracy from the fascist forces of Generalissimo Franco. Charles Nusser, a veteran of that great struggle, relates this incident of "international patriotism":

> Sam Gonshak and I, both Spanish Civil War veterans, were in Guernica on June 1, 1985, not long after President Reagan's infamous visit to Bitburg. We were there to lay a wreath at the historic Tree of Guernica. I

spoke briefly, saying there are those who lay their wreaths on the graves of the Nazi criminals [an allusion to President Reagan's visit to Bitberg cemetery in Germany], but that we veterans of the Abraham Lincoln Brigade pay our homage at the Tree of Freedom in loving memory of the *victims* of the fascist murderers.

I will never forget the speech of the organizer of the gathering. He referred to Sam and me as "Patriots of the World." Not patriots of the United States but "Patriots of the World." There have always been too many patriots in various countries straining to get at the throats of patriots in other countries. (Nusser's emphasis)[4]

"Patriots of the World" who happen to live in the United States want to stop destroying others with jet bombers and missiles and US–financed death squads and start healing this nation. This is not just a good and noble ideal; it is a historical necessity. Sooner or later Americans rediscover that they cannot live on flag-waving alone. They begin to drift off into reality, confronted by the economic irrationalities and injustices of a system that provides them with the endless circuses and extravaganzas of superpatriotism, heavy tax burdens, bloodletting in foreign lands, and sad neglect of domestic needs, denying them the bread of prosperity and their birthright as democratic citizens. That is what humanistic patriotism is all about: a return to reality, to unveiling the lies and subterfuges that favor the wealthiest 1 percent of the population and pursuing policies at home and abroad that serve the real needs of humanity

NOTES

1. Nancy Carleton, letter to *San Francisco Chronicle*, July 4, 2002.

2. Michael Parenti, "Is Nicaragua More Democratic Than the United States?" *CovertAction Information Bulletin* (Summer 1986): 48–50, 52.

3. Maxwell Geismar, ed., *Mark Twain and the Three R's* (New York: Bobbs-Merrill, 1973), pp. 179–80; the selection is quoted from Twain's novel, *A Connecticut Yankee in King Arthur's Court* (1889).

4. Charles Nusser, letter to the *Nation*, January 6–13, 1992, p. 2.

Michael Parenti received his PhD in political science from Yale University. He has taught at a number of colleges and universities, both in the United States and abroad. Some 250 of his articles have appeared in scholarly journals, political periodicals, and various magazines and newspapers. Parenti appears on radio and television talk shows to discuss current issues and ideas from his published works. Some of the topics he covers include democracy and economic power, imperialism and US interventionism, terrorism and globalization, political bias in the US news media, and fascism of the past and present. Parenti is the author of seventeen books, including *Democracy for the Few*, *The Terrorism Trap*, and *The Assassination of Julius Caesar: A People's History of Ancient Rome*, which has been nominated for a Pulitzer Prize. For further information, visit his Web site, http://www.michaelparenti.org.

11.

An Orwellian Nightmare

Critical Reflections on the
Bush Administration

Douglas Kellner

*In our time, political speech and writing are largely the
defense of the indefensible.*

—George Orwell

After World War II, the United States worked with other nations to produce a set of international institutions, treaties, and multilateral relationships to cope with political conflict and global problems. Internationalist multilateralism was complicated by the cold war, which split the world into competing camps and blocs. Facing a Soviet nuclear threat and challenges on the military, political, and economic fronts, the United States developed multilateral institutions and alliances with European and other allies to provide national security. Doctrines of containment and deterrence, combined with a global system of alliances, protected the United States from military assault and provided outlines of a global system from within which conflicts could be resolved and global problems dealt with.

With the collapse of the Soviet Union, some hoped that a more peaceful and secure world could be produced through strengthened multilateral global alliances and with major countries working together within international law. The first Bush administration and the Clinton administration developed globalist and multilateral politics, and the 1990s exhibited remarkable economic prosperity, at least for those in the overdeveloped countries, and, with some marked failures, began to deal with human rights and violations of international law collectively and multilaterally within a global framework.

The second Bush administration renounced internationalist and multilateralist policies and alliances. From the beginning, it rejected international accords such as the Kyoto treaty on the environment and a series of arms limitations treaties ranging from attempts to cut back on nuclear weapons to controlling the small arms trade. After the September 11 terrorist attacks on the United States, the Bush administration responded with unilateral militarism, developed new doctrines of preemptive strikes, and waged violent but unresolved wars in Afghanistan and Iraq. The result is a highly insecure world wherein human rights are regularly violated, human life is devalued, and military violence is the preferred means for the Bush administration to address political problems and challenges.

On the global front, the United States has never been more isolated from allies and more hated by opponents. Domestically, following the USA PATRIOT Act there have been serious attacks on civil liberties and the democratic and constitutional order in the United States by the Bush advisors and, specifically, from the attorney general's office. The consequences of the Bush administration's failed terror war policies and domestic policy outrages are frightening.[1] The Bush regime seems to be erecting an Orwellian totalitarian state apparatus and plunging the world into ongoing war that could generate a military and police state both domestically and abroad. In his prophetic novel *1984*, George Orwell envisaged a grim condition of total warfare in which his fictional state Oceania ruled its fearful and intimidated citizens through war, police state terror, surveillance, and the suppression of civil liberties. This constant warfare kept Oceania's citizens in a perpetual situation of mobilization and submission. Further, the Orwellian state controlled language, thought, and behavior through domination of the media and was thereby able to change the very meaning of language ("war is peace") and to constantly rewrite history itself.[2]

Orwell's futuristic novel was, of course, an attack on the Soviet Union and therefore became a favorite of conservatives over the years, but it describes the potential dangers of the regime of George W. Bush. Orwell's totalitarian state had a two-way television screen that monitored its citizens' behavior and a system of spies and informers that reported on politically incorrect thought and activity. Bush's police state has its USA PATRIOT Act, which enables the state to monitor the communications of e-mail, cell phones, telephones, and other media, while allowing the state to arrest citizens without warrants, to hold them indefinitely, to monitor their conversations, to examine their library records and book purchases, and to submit them to military tribunals, all of which would be governed by the dictates of the "Supreme Leader" (in this case, a dangerously demagogic figurehead, ruled by right-wing extremists).

The Bush administration also proposed an Operation TIPS (Terrorist Information and Prevention System) program that would turn citizens into spies who would report suspicious activities to the government and would recruit truck drivers, mail carriers, meter readers, and others who would "report what they see in public areas and along transportation routes," thus turning workers into informants. In addition, Attorney General John Ashcroft has proposed concentration camps in the United States for citizens that he considers "enemy combatants."[3] Sign me up, because I'm an enemy of Orwellian fascism, Bush-style. It's clear that the United States needs a regime change if its democracy is to be preserved and a more peaceful and secure world is to emerge in the new millennium.

With its Orwellian-sounding Office of Homeland Security, proposed Office of Strategic Information, Shadow Government, and USA PATRIOT Act, the Bush administration has in place the institutions and apparatus of a totalitarian government. The Bush administration's surprise call on June 6, 2002, for a new cabinet-level Office of Homeland Security was seen by critics as an attempt to deflect attention from investigations of Bush administration and intelligence failures. Indeed, the USA PATRIOT Act pushed through by the Bush administration following September 11 already was erecting powerful trappings of a police state, and fears that it would increase bureaucracy and even provide the apparatus for a Gestapo-type police state have been widespread. These frightening measures included allowing the government the right to eavesdrop on all electronic and wireless communication, to arrest individuals without specific charges and to hold them indefinitely, to monitor conversations between lawyer and client, and to carry out secret military trials of suspected terrorists.[4]

Although the Bush administration has repeatedly warned of imminent terror attacks, keeping the country jittery and attempting to justify its unjustifiable foreign and domestic policies, these actions have done little to make the country safer and have instead exploited the crisis to push through the administration's hard right agenda. The Bush administration assault on civil liberties has weakened constitutional democracy and the rule of law in the United States. On August 15, 2002, Human Rights Watch released a report that claimed: "The U.S. government's investigation of the September 11 attacks has been marred by arbitrary detentions, due process violations, and secret arrests." Human Rights Watch discovered that over twelve hundred noncitizens were secretly arrested and incarcerated and that

> the U.S. government has held some detainees for prolonged periods without charges; impeded their access to counsel; subjected them to coercive interrogations; and overridden judicial orders to release them on bond during immigration proceedings. In some cases, the government has incarcerated detainees for months under restrictive conditions, including solitary confinement. Some detainees were physically and verbally abused because of their national origin or religion. The vast majority is from Middle Eastern, South Asian, and North African countries. The report describes cases in which random encounters with law enforcement or neighbors' suspicions based on no more than national origin and religion led to interrogation about possible links to terrorism.[5]

Yet not only has the Bush administration dangerously undermined the US constitutional order, but its unilateralist and militarist foreign policy has alienated allies, provoked enemies, and increased instability and insecurity throughout the world. Since Election 2000, the Bush clique has practiced a form of Orwellian "Bushspeak" that endlessly repeats the Big Lie of the moment. Bush and his propaganda ministry engage in daily propagandistic spin to push the administration's policies and to attack its opponents while showing little regard for the canons of truth and justice that conservatives have traditionally defended.[6]

Indeed, conservatives have traditionally defended truth and integrity while attacking dishonesty and lying. During the Clinton administration, conservative defenders of truth, such as William Bennett, constantly attacked Bill Clinton for lying and dishonesty. Yet few, if any, conservatives have spoken up to criticize the Bush administration for its systematic policy of deception and lies.

In my books *Grand Theft 2000* (2001) and *From 9/11 to Terror War: The Dangers of the Bush Legacy* (2003), I criticize "Bushspeak" as a mode of systematically engaging in the discourse of deception and lies. I document a wealth of Bush falsehoods in the 2000 election campaign, the thirty-six-day battle for the White House, fallacious claims about his economic policies, and other deception and lies about the economy, the environment, energy policy, and foreign affairs. It has therefore been interesting to see best-selling books emerge by Al Franken called *Lies and the Lying Liars Who Tell Them* and by Joe Conason called *Big Lies: The Right-Wing Propaganda Machine and*

How It Distorts the Truth, with another book by David Corn on *The Lies of George W. Bush: Mastering the Politics of Deception* demonstrating Bush administration mendacity. In addition, Web sites such as www.spinsanity .com expose lies from all sides of the political spectrum, while MoveON.org's Web site www.misleader.org, George Soros's Web site www .wedeservethetruth.com, and www.Bushwatch.com all post examples of Bush administration lying.

As Princeton economist Paul Krugman has demonstrated in his *New York Times* columns and recent books, Bush administration economic policy has been based on "fuzzy math" and outright lying concerning deficit figures, who would get the giant tax cuts, and the effects of the tax breaks for the rich on job production and social services. President Bush said in 2002 that his tax cut would generate eight hundred thousand jobs and repeatedly claimed that "everyone knows" that tax cuts create jobs. Yet major economists took out newspaper ads saying that this simply was not true, and, since Bush's initial statements were made, another million jobs have been lost, with more than 3 million jobs vanished in toto since Bush became president.

Bush administration spokespeople continue to lie about the extent of the deficit and its potential harmful effects. President Bush and Vice President Cheney have repeatedly claimed that the Bush tax cuts constitute only 25 percent of the mushrooming federal deficit, while the White House's own Office of Management and Budget shows that the tax cuts account for 39 percent. As Krugman and others have repeatedly shown, the projected record deficit will be much larger than current Bush administration figures, which do not include skyrocketing expenses for US programs in Afghanistan and Iraq.[7]

To keep the public in a state of fear, Bush and his administration have repeatedly evoked the specter of renewed terrorist attacks and promised an all-out war against an "axis of evil." This threatening "axis," to be defined periodically by the Bush administration, allegedly possesses "weapons of mass destruction" that could be used against the United States. Almost without exception, the mainstream media have been a propaganda conduit for the Bush administration terror war and have helped generate fear and even mass hysteria. The mainstream corporate media have thus largely failed to advance an understanding of the serious threats to the United States and to the global economy and polity from Bush administration policy and to debate the respective merits and possible consequences of a range of possible responses to the September 11 attacks.

In a speech to West Point cadets on June 1, 2002, George W. Bush proclaimed a new "doctrine" that the United States would strike first against enemies. It was soon apparent that this was a major shift in US military policy, replacing the cold war doctrine of containment and deterrence with a new policy of preemptive strikes that could be tried out in Iraq. US allies were extremely upset with this shift in US policy and the move toward an aggressive US unilateralism. *New York Times* reporter David E. Sanger wrote that:

> the process of including America's allies has only just begun, and administration officials concede that it will be difficult at best. Leaders in Berlin, Paris and Beijing, in particular, have often warned against unilateralism. But Mr. Bush's new policy could amount to ultimate unilateralism, because it reserves the right to determine what constitutes a threat to American security and to act even if that threat is not judged imminent.[8]

After a summer of debate on the necessity of the United States going to war against Iraq to destroy its weapons of mass destruction, on August 26, 2002, Vice President Cheney applied the new preemptive strike and unilateralist doctrine to Iraq, arguing, "What we must not do in the face of a mortal threat is to give in to wishful thinking or willful blindness. . . . Deliverable weapons of mass destruction in the hands of a terror network or murderous dictator or the two working together constitutes as grave a threat as can be imagined. The risks of inaction are far greater than the risks of action." Cheney was responding to many former generals and high-level members of the earlier Bush administration who had reservations against the sort of unilateralist US attack against Iraq that hawks in the Bush administration were urging.

Indeed, Bush and others in his circle regularly described the terror war as World War III, while Donald Rumsfeld said that it could last as long as the cold war and Dick Cheney, speaking like a true militarist, said it could go on for a "long, long time, perhaps indefinitely." Such an Orwellian nightmare could plunge the world into a new millennium of escalating war with unintended consequences and embroil the United States in countless wars, normalizing war as conflict resolution and creating many new enemies for the would-be American hegemon. Indeed, as Chambers Johnson writes in *Blowback*, empire has hidden costs. Hegemony breeds resentment and hostility, and when the empire carries out aggression, it elicits anger and creates enemies, intensifying the dangers of perpetual war.[9]

On September 20, 2002, it was apparent that the hawks' position in the Bush administration had triumphed, at least on the level of official military doctrine, when the Bush administration released a document signaling some of the most important and far-ranging shifts in US foreign and military policy since the end of the cold war. Titled *The National Security Strategy of the United States*, the thirty-three-page report outlined a new doctrine of US military supremacy, providing justifications for the United States to undertake unilateral and preemptive strikes in the name of "counterproliferation." Offered as a replacement for the concept of nonproliferation, this clumsy Orwellian concept in effect would legitimate unilateral destruction of a country's presumed weapons of mass destruction. The document renounced global security, multilateralism, and rule by international law, concepts that had informed US thinking since World War II and that appeared to be a consensus among Western nations during the era of globalization.

The Bush administration's language of "preemptive strikes, "regime change," and "anticipatory self-defense" is purely Orwellian, presenting euphemisms for raw military aggression. Critics assailed the new "strike first, ask questions later" policy, the belligerent unilateralism, and the dangerous legitimation of preemptive strikes.[10] Israel, Pakistan, Russia, China, and lesser powers had already used the so-called Bush doctrine and "war against terrorism" to legitimate attacks on domestic and external foes, and there were dangers that it could legitimate a proliferation of war and make the world more unstable and violent. As William Galston, professor of public affairs at the University of Maryland, states:

> A global strategy based on the new Bush doctrine of preemption means the end of the system of international institutions, laws and norms that we have worked to build for more than half a century. What is at stake is nothing less than a fundamental shift in America's place in the world. Rather than continuing to serve as first among equals in the postwar international system, the United States would act as a law unto itself, creating new rules of international engagement without the consent of other nations. In my judgment, this new stance would ill serve the long-term interests of the United States.[11]

In his book *Rogue Nation: American Unilateralism and the Future of Good Intentions*, Clyde Prestowitz, founder and president of the Economic Strategy Institute, argues that Bush's doctrine of preemptive strikes and military supremacy undermines three key pillars of international order and stability: the 1648 Treaty of Westphalia, which established a principle of respect for national sovereignty and noninterference in the affairs of other countries; the UN Charter, which bans the threat or use of military force except in self-defense or under the authority of a UN Security Council mandate; and the Nuremberg Trials, which deemed preemptive strikes to be a war crime.[12]

Moreover, the Bush administration doctrine of preemptive strikes could unleash a series of wars that would plunge the world into the sort of nightmare militarism and totalitarianism sketched out in Orwell's *1984*. The Bush policy is barbaric, taking the global community to a social Darwinist battleground in which decades of international law and military prudence were put aside in perhaps the most dangerous foreign policy doctrine in US history. It portends a militarist future and an era of perpetual war in which a new militarism could generate a cycle of unending violence and retribution, such as has been evident in the Israel and Palestine conflict.[13]

Around the same time that the Bush administration was pushing its new strategic doctrine and seeking to apply it in a war against Iraq, a 2000 report circulated titled *Rebuilding American Defense: Strategies, Forces and Resources for a New American Century*. Drawn up by the neoconservative think tank Project for a New American Century (PNAC) for a group that now comprises the right wing of the Bush administration, including Dick Cheney, Donald Rumsfeld, and Paul Wolfowitz, the document clearly spelled out a plan for world hegemony grounded in US military dominance and control of the Persian Gulf region and its oil supplies.[14] Its upfront goals were a "Pax Americana" and US domination of the world during the new millennium. The document shows that core members of the Bush administration had long envisaged taking military control of the Gulf region, with the PNAC text stating: "The United States has for decades sought to play a more permanent role in Gulf regional security. While the unresolved conflict with Iraq provides the immediate justification, the need for a substantial American force presence in the Gulf transcends the issue of the regime of Saddam Hussein."[15]

The PNAC document argues for "maintaining global US pre-eminence, precluding the rise of a great power rival, and shaping the international security order in line with American principles and interests." The vision is long-range, urging US domination of the Gulf "as far into the future as possible." It is also highly militarist, calling for the United States to "fight and decisively win multiple, simultaneous major theater wars" as a "core mission." US armed forces would serve as "the cavalry on the new American frontier," with United States military power blocking the emergence of other countries challenging US domination. It would enlist key allies such as Britain as "the most effective and efficient means of exercising American global leadership" and would put the United States, and not the UN, as leader of military interventions or peacekeeping missions. Moreover, it envisages taking on Iran after Iraq, spotlights China for "regime change," and calls for the creation of "U.S. Space Forces" to dominate outer space, and positioning the United States to totally control cyberspace to prevent "enemies" from "using the Internet against the U.S."[16]

As 2002 unfolded, the Bush administration intensified its ideological war against Iraq, advanced its doctrine of preemptive strikes, and provided military buildup for what now looks like a long-planned and orchestrated war. Whereas the explicit war aims were to shut down Iraq's "weapons of mass destruction" and thus enforce UN resolutions mandating that Iraq eliminate its offensive weapons, there were many hidden agendas in the Bush administration offensive against Iraq.[17] To be reelected, Bush needed a major victory and symbolic triumph over terrorism to deflect attention from the failings of his regime in both the domestic and foreign policy realms.

Moreover, ideologues within the Bush administration wanted to legitimate the doctrine of preemptive strikes, and a successful attack on Iraq could inaugurate and normalize this policy. Some of the same militarist unilateralists in the Bush administration envisage US world hegemony and the elder Bush's "New World Order," with the United States as the reigning military power and world's policeman. Increased control of the world's oil supplies provided a tempting prize for the former oil executives who maintain key roles in the Bush administration. And, finally, one might note the Oedipus Tex drama, in which George W. Bush's desires to conclude his father's unfinished business with Saddam Hussein and simultaneously defeat Evil to constitute himself as Good helped drive him to war against Iraq with the fervor of a religious crusade.

With all these agendas in play, a war on Iraq appears to have been inevitable. Bush's March 6, 2003, press conference made it evident that he was ready to go to war against Iraq. His handlers told him to speak slowly and keep his big stick and Texas macho out of view, but he constantly threatened Iraq and evoked the rhetoric of good and evil that he had used to justify his crusade against bin Laden and Al Qaeda. Bush repeated the words "Saddam Hussein" and "terrorism" incessantly, mentioning Iraq as a "threat," which he attempted to link with the September 11 attacks and terrorism, at least sixteen times. His frequent use of the word "I" as in "I believe" and his talk of "my government" as if he owned it depicted a man lost in words and self-importance, positioning himself against the "evil" that he was preparing to wage war against. Unable to make a logical and objective case for a war against Iraq, Bush could only invoke fear and a moralistic rhetoric, attempting to present himself as a strong nationalist leader.

Bush's rhetoric, like that of fascism, deploys a mistrust and hatred of language, reducing it to manipulative speechifying, speaking in codes and incessantly repeating the same phrases. Bush's anti-intellectualism and hatred of democracy and intellectuals are clearly evident in his press conferences through his snitty responses to questions and general contempt for the whole procedure. His rhetoric plays to anti-intellectual proclivities and tendencies in the extreme conservative and fundamentalist Christian constituencies that support him. It appears that Bush's press conference was orchestrated to shore up his base and prepare his supporters for a major political struggle rather than to marshal arguments to convince opponents that war with Iraq was a good idea. He displayed, against his will, the complete poverty of his case for war against Iraq. With no convincing arguments and nothing new to communicate, he just repeated the same tired clichés over and over.

Bush's discourse also displayed Orwellian features of Doublespeak, in which war against Iraq is for peace, the occupation of Iraq is its liberation, destroying its food and water supplies enables "humanitarian" action, and the murder of scores of Iraqis and destruction of the country will produce "freedom" and "democracy." In a prewar summit with Tony Blair in the Azores and again in his first talk after the bombing began on March 19, Bush spoke repeatedly about the "coalition of the willing" and how many countries were supporting and participating in the "allied" effort. In fact, however, it was a Coalition of Two, with the United States and United Kingdom doing most of the fighting and with many of the countries that Bush claimed supported his war quickly expressing reservations about the highly unpopular assault, which was strongly opposed by most people and countries in the world.

Moreover, it is by now well known and documented that Bush's policy of launching a preemptive strike on Iraq was based on deception. Bush and others in his administration constantly made false claims about alleged Iraqi "weapons of mass destruction" and the threat that the Iraqis posed to the United States and the entire world. The failure to find such threatening weapons and media exposure of claims that US and UK intelligence agencies were skeptical of these claims have led to critical scrutiny of the case for war offered by the United States and Great Britain. In the latter country, a major inquiry presided over by Lord Hutton into government deception over Iraq was held, and in early 2004, Bush's arms inspector, David Hay, admitted that no Iraqi weapons had been found.

Robert Greenwald's remarkable 2003 documentary *Uncovered* contrasts statements by members of the Bush administration, including Bush, Cheney, Rumsfeld, and Condoleezza Rice, with critical commentary by former members of the US intelligence and political establishment demonstrating that Bush administration claims were utterly bogus. Former intelligence analysts dissect Colin Powell's address to the United Nations, which claims to document Iraqi possession of weapons of mass destruction, and show in detail that key statistics Powell appealed to were simply false, that his satellite imagery pictures claiming to present Iraqi weapons were appallingly misinterpreted, and that his major claims concerning the immediate threat of Iraqi weapons were utterly fictitious. The documentary also presents critics such as former US ambassador to Iraq Joseph Wilson convincingly arguing that Bush administration claims concerning ties between Al Qaeda and the Iraqi regime are completely unproven, while a variety of critics argue that the Iraq occupation has created new terrorist enemies for the United States and has not made the United States safer, as Bush administration officials continually claim.[18]

After the collapse of the Baath regime in April 2003, the Bush administration began threatening Syria and there have been reports that the neoconservatives in the administration have planned five more wars.[19] The Bush administration policy of terror war raises the possibility that Orwell's *1984* may provide the template for the new millennium as the world is plunged into endless war, as freedom and democracy are snuffed out in the name of freedom, as language loses meaning, and as history is constantly revised.[20] As the danger looms that Orwell's dark grim dystopia may replace the (ideological) utopia of the "information society," the "new economy," and a prosperous and democratic globalization that had been the dominant ideology and vision of the past decade, questions arise: Will the Bush administration terror war lead the world to apocalypse and ruin through constant war and the erection of totalitarian police states over the facade of fragile democracy? Or can more multilateral and global solutions to the dangers of terrorism be found that will strengthen democracy and increase the chances for world peace and security?

There is indeed a danger that terror war will be a force of historical regression and the engine of destruction of the global economy, liberal polity, and democracy itself, all to be replaced by an aggressive militarism and totalitarian police state. Orwell could well be the prophet of a coming new barbarism, with endless war, state repression, and enforced control of thought and discourse, and that George W. Bush and his minions will be the architects of an Orwellian future.

It could also be the case, however, that the Taliban, bin Laden, Al Qaeda, Saddam Hussein, and the Bush administration represent obsolete and reactionary forces that will be swept away by the inexorable forces of globalization and liberal democracy. The opposing sides in the current terror war of the Bush administration reactionaries and Al Qaeda could be perceived as representing complementary poles of an atavistic and pre-modern version of Islam and nihilistic terrorism confronted by reactionary right-wing conservatism and militarism.[21] In this scenario, both poles can be perceived as disruptive and regressive forces in a global world that need to be overcome to create genuine historical progress. If this is the case, terror war would be a momentary interlude in which two obsolete histor-ical forces battle it out, ultimately to be replaced by saner and more dem-ocratic globalizing forces.

This is, of course, an optimistic scenario; probably, for the foreseeable future, progressive forces will be forced to confront intense battles between the opposing forces of Islamic terrorism and right-wing militarism. Yet if democracy and the human species are to survive, global movements against militarism and for social justice, ecology, and peace must emerge to combat and replace the atavistic forces of the present. As a new millen-nium unfolds, the human race has regressed into a new barbarism unfore-seeable before September 11. If civilization is to survive, individuals must perceive their enemies and organize to fight for a better future. And now is the time for liberals, conservatives, and all who believe in truth in politics to demand straight talk from the Bush administration and other politi-cians and for the media and critics of the politics of lying to take the Bush administration to task for its big lies. As the history of recent totalitarian regimes demonstrates, systematic deception rots the very fabric of a polit-ical society, and if US democracy is to find new life and a vigorous future, there must be public commitment to truth and public rejection of the pol-itics of lying.

To conclude: As a response to the September 11 terror attacks, the Bush administration has answered with an intensified militarism that threatens to generate an era of terror war, a new arms race, accelerated military violence, US support of authoritarian regimes, an assault on human rights, constant threats to democracy, and destabilizing of the world economy. The Bush regime also provides political favors to its largest supporters, corporate and otherwise, unleashing unrestrained Wild West capitalism (exemplified in the Enron scandals) and a form of capitalist cronyism whereby Bush administration family and friends are provided with government favors while social welfare programs, environmental legislation, and protection of rights and freedoms are curtailed.

Consequently, I would argue that Bush administration unilateralist militarism is not the way to fight international terrorism but is rather the road to an Orwellian nightmare in which democracy and freedom will be in dire peril and the future of the human species will be in question. These are frightening times, and it is essential that all citizens become informed about the fateful conflicts of the present, gain clear understanding of what is at stake, and realize that they must oppose at once international terrorism, Bushian militarism, and an Orwellian police-state in order to preserve democracy and a life worthy of a human being.

NOTES

1. This analysis is an expansion and updating of material from my book *From 9/11 to Terror War: Dangers of the Bush Legacy* (Lanham, MD: Rowman and Littlefield, 2003), which contains fuller documentation of claims and positions taken here.

2. For a discussion of Orwell's prophetic novel, see Douglas Kellner, "From *1984* to One-Dimensional Man: Critical Reflections on Orwell and Marcuse," *Illuminations*, 1990, http://www.uta.edu/huma/illuminations/kell13.htm. In the light of the Bush administration–projected terror war, however, it could well be Orwell rather than Huxley and Marcuse, as I argue in the article cited here, who provides the most prescient templates of the future present.

3. See Jonathan Turley, "Camps for Citizens: Ashcroft's Hellish Vision," *Los Angeles Times*, August 14, 2002. US Attorney General John Ashcroft was awarded the annual 1984 award for "Worst Government Official" by Privacy International. The watchdog group said that the top US law enforcement officer "is responsible for a massive increase in wiretapping of phones and other electronics and for the imprisonment without charge of as many as 1,200 people in the United States after the September 11 attacks on America." See "Reuters: Ashcroft, Ellison, Win 'Big Brother' Privacy Awards," Vigilant TV: Freedom and Technology, April 20, 2002, http://vigilant.tv/article/1343.

4. On the USA PATRIOT Act, see David Cole, *Enemy Aliens: Double Standards and Constitutional Freedoms in the War on Terrorism* (New York: New Press, 2003) and Ronald Dworkin, "Terror and the Attack on Civil Liberties," *New York Review of Books,* November 6, 2003, pp. 37–41.

5. See "Presumption of Guilt: Human Rights Abuses of Post–September 11 Detainees," Human Rights Watch, http://www.hrw.org/reports/2002/us911.

6. See Douglas Kellner, *Grand Theft 2000: Media Spectacle and a Stolen Election* (Lanham, MD: Rowman and Littlefield, 2001) for documentation and a systematic critique of Bushspeak.

7. Paul Krugman, "Fuzzy Math, NY: 2001," *Washington Post,* 2003. See also Thomas E. Ricks and Vernon Loeb, "Bush Developing Military Policy of Striking First," *Washington Post,* June 10, 2002. For a sharp critique of Bush's new preemptive strike policy, see "Werther Report: Is Preemption a Nuclear Schlieffen Plan?" July 20, 2002, http://www.d-n-i.net/fcs/comments/c453.htm.

8. David E. Sanger, "Bush to Formalize Defense Policy of Hitting First," *New York Times,* June 17, 2002.

9. Chalmers Johnson, *Blowback: The Costs and Consequences of American Empire* (New York: Metropolitan Books, 2000; New York: Henry Holt, 2004).

10. See William Saletan, "Shoot First: Bush's Whitewashed National Security Manifesto," *Slate,* September 20, 2002; Peter Slevin, "Analysts: New Strategy Courts Unseen Dangers: First Strike Could Be Precedent for Other Nations," *Washington Post,* September 22, 2002; and Paul Krugman, "White Man's Burden," *New York Times,* September 24, 2002.

11. William Galston, "Perils of Preemptive War," *American Prospect* 13, no. 17 (September 23, 2002).

12. Clyde Prestowitz, *Rogue Nation: American Unilateralism and the Failure of Good Intentions* (New York: Basic Books, 2003).

13. See Gore Vidal, *Dreaming War: Blood for Oil and the Cheney-Bush Junta* (New York: Thunder's Mouth Press/Nation Books, 2003) and *Perpetual War for Perpetual Peace: How We Got to Be So Hated* (New York: Thunder's Mouth Press/Nation Books, 2002).

14. An article by Neil Mackay, "Bush Planned Iraq 'Regime Change' before Becoming President," *Sunday Herald* (September 15, 2002), widely circulated through the Internet, called attention to the sort of militarist global strategic vision that informed Bush administration policy. The 2000 plan is available at "Rebuilding America's Defenses: Strategy, Forces, and Resources for a New Century," Project for the New American Century, September 2000, http://www.newamerican-century.org/RebuildingAmericasDefenses.pdf.

15. Ibid.

16. Ibid.

17. Ibid.

18. Arguments against official Bush administration reasons for going to war,

shredded in Robert Greenwald's 2003 documentary film *Uncovered: The Whole Truth about the Iraq War,* are systematically articulated by Thomas Powers, "The Vanishing Case for War," *New York Review of Books,* December 4, 2003, pp.12–17.

19. See Wesley Clark, *Winning Modern Wars: Iraq, Terrorism, and the American Empire* (New York: PublicAffairs, 2003).

20. Kellner, *Grand Theft 2000.*

21. Tariq Ali captures this dialectic in *The Clash of Fundamentalisms: Crusades, Jihads, and Modernity* (London: Verso, 2002), whose cover pictures George W. Bush shading into the visage of Osama bin Laden—two fundamentalists whose families had long been linked in shady business practices (see chapter 1) and who personally represented the competing fundamentalisms of the ongoing Terror War.

DOUGLAS KELLNER received his PhD in philosophy from Columbia University and is currently the George F. Kneller Chair in the Philosophy of Education, UCLA. He is a member of the American Philosophical Association, the World Sociology Congress, the American Political Science Association, and the Union for Democratic Communications, the Radical Philosophy Association, the Society for the Study of Phenomenology and Existential Philosophy, and more. He has written more than two hundred articles for various journals and has published many books, including *Media Spectacle; Postmodern Adventure: Science, Technology, and Cultural Studies at the 3rd Millennium;* and *From 9/11 to Terror War: The Dangers of the Bush Legacy.*

12.

Resolved:
George W. Bush Is the Worst
President in American History

Laurence Britt

Sooner or later this combustible mixture of ignorance and power is going to blow up in our faces.

—Carl Sagan

Using the debater's format, I will make the case for the stated resolution. You, dear reader, can make the opposite argument if you so choose, as I admit to a one-sided presentation. The arguments to the affirmative will be made based on the humanist worldview as stated most concisely on the inside cover of every *Free Inquiry* issue. The full text of the "Affirmations of Humanism: A Statement of Principles" is included at the end of this chapter as an appendix.

Where to begin? Who have been the worst American presidents according to the considered opinion of the preponderance of historians? The list would include James Buchanan, who allowed the union to dissolve while he was a lame duck; Warren G. Harding, who briefly presided over rampant corruption before he expired in office; and Richard Nixon, the only president to resign just ahead of impeachment, amid scandals of dirty tricks and abuse of power. How can George W. Bush top, or should we say fall below, this unsavory cast? Even though Bush is less than three years into his presidency at this writing, he is definitely in the running in terms of his unmatched record in turning almost all of the country's metrics from a positive to a negative in the shortest possible time. These metrics include the federal budget going from surplus to massive deficit, unemployment up, the trade deficit up, poverty rates up, number of people lacking health insurance up, and international insecurity way up.

And these metrics will not be short lived. As stated at the outset, I will consider the Bush record through the prism of humanist principles.

What considerations will be at least partially omitted from the arguments stemming only from the humanist perspective? Some of these issues, important as they may be and rightly laid directly at the feet of Bush and his neoconservative minders, include the very real and overwhelming issue of America's deteriorating position in the eyes of the world, brought about in record time by the sum total of US actions in the first three-plus years of Bush's presidency. A few countries' leaders may proclaim support for the Bush agenda. The general population in almost every country, however, opposes the Bush agenda, and in many cases, overwhelmingly so. To have the population of almost the entire world adamantly against us is unprecedented in American history.

Also, Bush has implemented an economic policy of deliberately destroying the tax base so as to drown government spending—except, of course, for military spending. The Bush tax policy is a recipe for unprecedented deficits and financial instability far into the future. Jobs and growth are a smoke screen for the real purpose of the huge tax cuts already enacted. In reality this policy is a massive transfer of wealth away from those with little to those who already have much. And those who have much money also have much influence with the Bush administration, which is truly a government of the rich, by the rich, for the rich, to pervert the ideal expressed by the first Republican president. Disdaining virtually every international agreement and thereby projecting the image of a country that is selfish and arrogant, the administration is totally at odds with the statement in our own Declaration of Independence that we sought "a decent respect for the opinions of mankind." The operating assumption seems to be that one set of rules can apply for the rest of the world but a different set, or no set at all, will apply to America.

The waging of war on Iraq is without justification, in violation of the UN Charter, on pretenses proved totally false on all counts. Its execution is a disaster, with nothing but disaster as a conceivable end result. Not only that, but the fight against terrorism has been immeasurably set back. Instead of going after the known terrorist leader Osama bin Laden in his likely hiding place in Northern Pakistan, a war has been launched against a totally contained Iraq with no proven ties to terrorism. Iraq now becomes a magnet for terrorism, with endless new recruits enraged at American actions.

Beyond the policy actions not directly related to the principles of humanism, what about the personal characteristics of Bush that argue strongly for his relegation to the nadir of presidential failure? There is nothing in the public record up to his election to suggest that Bush had the intelligence, insight, curiosity, base of knowledge—or interest in advancing any of these characteristics—to qualify him to hold the most powerful position on the planet.

Little is known about Bush's life before age forty except that he came from great privilege and wealth, drank too much, probably used drugs, was AWOL from a cushy spot in the Texas Air National Guard, and had many questionable business dealings set up through family influence and other people's money. These influences and financial backers garnered him the governorship of Texas, a state whose governor has little real power or executive authority, but the position was nevertheless a convenient springboard to the presidency. One wonders what this man would have made of himself, with his capabilities and personal characteristics, without family name and money. Yet he was elected president of the United States.

Amazingly, he took office having never traveled to Canada, let alone Europe or Asia, despite family wealth and vast international connections. Why? Did he have no curiosity about other countries until he assumed the presidency? But, then, this was a presidential candidate who thought that people from Greece were called "Grecians" and the pronunciation of *nuclear* was "nuke-u-lar." One wonders how long it will take Bush's handlers to teach him how to pronounce this word. As of this writing, it's more than three years and counting.

Here is a man who admittedly does not read newspapers, let alone books, and prefers to get all he "needs to know" from his advisers. Unfortunately, ignorance and horrendous policies are not necessarily at odds with humanist principles. But most Bush administration initiatives assuredly are.

THE CATEGORIES OF HUMANISM

The twenty-one principles of humanism as shown in the appendix to this chapter have been consolidated into seven general categories:

1. Respect for science and our environment.
2. Belief in separation of religion and government (also part of the US Constitution).

3. Support for civil liberties.
4. Opposition to secrecy and promotion of openness.
5. Belief in a just and inclusive society.
6. Support for the right to individual privacy.
7. Reliance on what is good or beneficial in the human experience and in human aspirations and rejection of ignorance, hate, and fear as the driving force.[1]

For each of these general categories, I will provide a more detailed description of the principles involved, followed by a summary of Bush administration policies that run counter to the category.

Respect for Science and the Environment

Secular humanists are committed to the application of science and reason to the understanding of the natural universe. They reject the supernatural as an explanation for life, deny the concept of salvation, and believe in the advancement of knowledge as the key to human betterment.

What about the Bush administration? To an unprecedented degree, the Bush administration has placed scientific principles and the environment in eclipse through an agenda oriented toward the president's financial and religious backers. In no particular order, these policies include:

- Eliminating US aid to family planning in the third world.
- Walking away from promises to reduce CO_2 emissions.
- Walking away from the Kyoto treaty with no substitute proposed and ignoring universal scientific agreement on global warming.
- Allowing an increase in acceptable levels of arsenic in drinking water.
- Rolling back emission standards for power plants.
- Severely restricting stem cell research despite its great promise in combating many diseases.
- Drastically reducing federal support for basic scientific research.
- Opening up the Alaska wildlife preserve for oil drilling.
- Opening up national parks to road building and logging.
- Proposing an energy program with giveaways to industry and no incentives or mandates for conservation.
- Allowing polluters to escape further contributions to the Superfund and allowing it to fall into bankruptcy.
- Allowing fines collected by the Environmental Protection Agency for

environmental law violations to fall by more than 50 percent in three years (2000–2003).[2]

Showing his disdain for science, Bush commented that the jury was still out on evolution. Reacting to the record of the Bush administration, a group of more than sixty prominent scientists, including a dozen Nobel laureates and medical experts, released a statement on February 18, 2004, stating that the Bush administration was distorting scientific fact for "partisan political ends."[3]

SEPARATION OF RELIGION AND GOVERNMENT

Secular humanists firmly believe in the separation of religion and government and look to history for the overwhelming evidence of human misery caused by the union of these entities. Separation of church and state was one of the founding precepts of the US Constitution, whose framers were well aware that European monarchies traditionally used religion as a weapon to cow their subjects.

And the Bush administration?

- Readily accepted major political support from the most fundamentalist elements of the American religious establishment and became an active agent for their agenda.
- Encouraged White House staff in daily Bible study.
- Started faith-based charity initiative with a new White House office with that charter.
- Proceeded with the faith-based initiative even though it didn't get congressional funding, illegally establishing a presence in numerous federal agencies to forward its agenda.
- Strongly supported a voucher system to provide public monies for attendance in private, mostly religious schools. (The proposal is sold as a help to inner-city youth but is clearly aimed at providing the Religious Right with public funds to send their children to Christian schools, which are often right-wing political indoctrination academies.)
- In combination with the voucher program, passed the "No Child Left Behind" initiative and then defunded it to ensure that many children will be left behind because public schools will fail, leaving

religious schools as the recipient of both the children and the public funds.

- Supported the repeal of *Roe v. Wade* in response to the Religious Right.
- Opposed gay marriage and other gay rights, again consistent with the Religious Right agenda.

SUPPORT FOR CIVIL LIBERTIES

The democratic system of government, though imperfect, is the best one yet devised to insure the protection of human rights from authoritarian elites and repressive majorities. These precious rights require extraordinary effort to maintain, especially in times of stress. The Bush administration has shown little regard for civil liberties and has created an atmosphere in which they are deeply threatened. Examples abound:

- The 9/11 catastrophe opened the gates to massive abuses of civil liberties, perhaps understandably, but well beyond an acceptable response by a democratic government.
- Thousands have been held for months without charges, massive deportations have been conducted, suspects, none of whom had any proven connection to the 9/11 disaster, have been deprived of the right to an attorney.
- Overreacting to a threat that had already passed, the USA PATRIOT Act was enacted in an atmosphere of administration-generated hysteria.

The new Patriot Act would not have prevented the 9/11 disasters, but good intelligence and competent security would have. Nevertheless, the act gave the federal government onerous new powers to challenge constitutional protections, including:

- Search warrants used in secret without the target's knowledge.
- Secret review of targets' reading and buying habits.
- Limitations on lawyer-client contact and confidentiality.
- Many new surveillance powers, easily open to abuse.

The administration has also asserted the right to declare anyone an enemy combatant with no proof required, thus stripping the individual of all constitutional protections. Not satisfied, the administration is proposing a PATRIOT Act II, which will further erode civil liberties.[4] Finally, the assault on individual rights was not limited to the domestic scene. Approximately nine hundred enemy combatants were rounded up from Afghanistan in late 2001 and placed in solitary confinement awaiting trial at Guantanamo. As of this writing, more than two years have passed and no charges have been filed. Although this action violates the Geneva Convention, all international protests have been ignored. The scandal at the Abu Ghraib prison is yet another example of the systemic abuse encouraged by an administration tone deaf to the issue of human rights.

Opposition to secrecy and promotion of openness in human society

Secular humanists believe that for a democracy to function effectively, government must operate in the open, not behind a black curtain where abuse of power can go on undetected. A gullible public fed by a government seeking to expand its power unjustifiably easily swallows the term *national security* as a rubric for all secrecy. The Bush administration is probably the most secretive in American history, not only in relation to the "war on terrorism" but in almost every aspect of its operations, foreign or domestic. For instance:

- The administration's energy task force secretly and illegally determined a new energy policy program, keeping all details secret and beyond public scrutiny. It has so far resisted court challenges for open disclosure.
- The administration resisted all efforts to form an independent inquiry into the 9/11 disasters. When overwhelming pressure finally compelled action, it consistently refused to cooperate and withheld information even though half of the commission was administration-friendly.
- The Freedom of Information Act specifically details public documents that must be made available. The Bush administration routinely defies these provisions by withholding documents such as the Iran-Contra papers from the 1980s, which would undoubtedly embarrass members of the current administration.
- A shadow government structure was established shortly after 9/11 to operate under certain emergency conditions. Congress was not even informed.

- The head of the new Department of Homeland Security apparatus refused to testify before Congress on plans and spending requirements.
- In the run up to the war in Iraq, the administration consistently concealed all information that would argue against a preemptive attack and knowingly promoted information to justify the war that was later proved to be false. Those challenging the war or its bungled aftermath were characterized as unpatriotic or "aiding the terrorists."

Seeking a just and inclusive society

Secular humanists believe in the ideals of justice and inclusiveness while recognizing both the difficulty in achieving this ideal and the differences of opinion as to how it can be accomplished. The Bush administration, while never overtly expressing opposition to these principles, follows a different policy agenda, relying on a right-wing support base that is either hostile to the concepts or interprets them in the context of its economic interests or its religious, racial, or sexual prejudices. Numerous administration initiatives overtly favor the rich and large corporations at the expense of those less well off. The link between campaign contributions and payback is obvious and blatant. For example, tax cuts in May 2001 and January 2003 significantly reduce tax rates for upper-income taxpayers with minimal cuts at middle-income levels. Those in the middle also face the need for higher state and local taxes to offset cuts in federal spending resulting from the tax cuts. Net effect: no net tax cuts for middle- and low-income taxpayers and a reduction in services. In addition, deliberately running huge deficits into the future to help cover the gap in federal income tax revenues will drain Social Security and Medicare funds. Those depending primarily on Social Security for retirement will be put at severe risk.

Another example of favoring the few over the many was the California energy fiasco where prices were manipulated by large power companies at the expense of ratepayers. Although price fixing by major energy suppliers was proven, the Bush administration chose to punish the millions of California ratepayers and taxpayers, perhaps seeing a political advantage by embarrassing the Democratic governor, rather than forcing the price fixers to indemnify California.

The Bush administration has also opposed affirmative action, as shown in numerous initiatives such as the University of Michigan admissions case. In the area of judicial appointments, the administration has consistently appointed judges who support the right-wing version of a just society. The impact of these appointments far into the future cannot be overstated.

Support for the right of privacy for the individual

The right to privacy and individual autonomy is fundamental to secular humanists. The Bush administration's views on these principles seem to depend on the constituency it is appealing to at the moment. It opposes a woman's privacy in her right to chose and control her own body and a person's choice to die with dignity. Opposition to these rights is in response primarily to the administration's religious supporters. The right to private gain in economic affairs, no matter how achieved, is a different matter. In this matter, the administration responds to its business and financial supporters. The pattern is quite consistent. When it comes to impinging on the individual's rights versus those of the powerful, the Bush administrations sides with the powerful. For example, it supported more intrusive spying by industry on employees, changed bankruptcy laws to support banks versus individuals, opposed death with dignity initiatives in several states, passed new Medicare "reform" measures strongly supported by industry groups and opposed by consumer advocate organizations, and passed third-trimester abortion prohibition even though virtually all third-trimester abortions result from women's health problems. The many invasions of individual privacy rights have already been discussed under civil liberties.

Reliance on the positives in the human experience and human aspirations and rejection of ignorance, hate, and fear as the driving force

To secular humanists, history clearly records the disastrous impact of cultivated racial, religious, and ethnic hatreds. The wars generated by these hatreds, stoked by unscrupulous leaders capitalizing on ignorance, have caused human suffering almost beyond comprehension. Yet beneath the trappings of spin and propaganda, this tactic is the stock in trade of the Bush administration, especially as it relates to the "war on terrorism."

In the aftermath of the 9/11 attacks, which in their essence were a quintessential act of religious fanaticism, a wave of religiosity swept the country, strongly encouraged by the Bush administration. Instead of attempting to help us understand the forces that could unleash such a hideous attack, the administration simply told us that the attack occurred because we were the "beacon of freedom and opportunity." Faced with a continuous barrage of propaganda, most people came to believe this absurd statement, and the country was psychologically prepared to strike back at whomever was presented as the enemy. Brushing aside the sympathy of the world right after 9/11, the Bush administration unilaterally and arrogantly asserted American power. Ignorance, hatred, and fear were solidly in the driver's seat, perpetuated by the Bush administration: ignorance, exemplified by an obstinate refusal to understand the root causes of worldwide terrorism and its religious base, hatred for the identified "evildoers," and fear of the consequences of not acting. Examples abound of the reliance on this three-headed monster for policy guidance:

- Identification of the "Axis of Evil" as the target—never mind that the three (Iraq, Iran, and North Korea) had nothing in common and had nothing to do with 9/11.
- The color-coded warning system to alert the country to imminent terrorist threats, which was used continuously to maintain the anxiety level and stoke the three-headed monster. None of the dire warnings materialized. Every time a threat was identified, it was blown out of all proportion to keep the populace agitated and willing to accept "strong" administration actions. When arrests were made, perhaps on trumped up charges, draconian prosecutorial methods were employed to assuage the now-agitated public.
- An Office of Strategic Information was established as yet another means of gathering information on members of the public including, among other onerous elements, encouraging neighbors to spy on each other. A public outcry stopped this initiative, which nevertheless abundantly illustrates the Bush administration mindset.

The penchant for identifying anyone who questions administrative actions as unpatriotic or "aiding the terrorists" has become a standard response, both domestically and internationally. Those in Europe who opposed the Iraq war were "old Europe." Other opinions were not welcome. Fifteen million war protesters in the streets in February 2003 were just aiding the

terrorists. In an act of patriotism (or childish pique), French fries were rela-
beled "freedom fries." A "coalition of the willing" consisting of the United
States, the United Kingdom, and a few other countries was cobbled
together. A better label would have been a coalition of the bribed, cajoled,
and intimidated. In none of the countries of this "coalition" did the general population support the war effort.

SUMMARY

At the outset of this chapter, I posited that the negative impact of George
W. Bush would eclipse the failed administrations of those presidents generally regarded as the worst in American history. I understand that history
takes time to judge and assess a presidency and that this assessment is
being done contemporaneously, before Bush's term of office has ended.
Additionally, the views I have developed are juxtaposed with the principles
of secular humanism, not necessarily against the more lenient standards of
Realpolitik. History has passed unfavorable judgments on Presidents
Buchanan, Harding, and Nixon. The long-term impacts of Buchanan's
failure are hard to discern: Although he was a weak president who did not
act to prevent secession, Lincoln did act and the Union was saved. Harding
was also weak and deceived by friends and appointees. The scandals these
people generated came to light when Harding died after only two and one-
half years in office: long-term impact, nil. Nixon lowered partisanship to a
new level of blood sport and dirty tricks and abused power to "get" his
opponents. Unfortunately, these tendencies have continued to this day.
However, the Nixon presidency was not without successes—the opening of
China, creation of the Environmental Protection Agency, federal-state rev-
enue sharing, and a moderate economic policy. Moreover, Nixon's presidency, unlike Bush's, was contained by a Congress under the control of the
opposition. These failed presidencies had limited long-term impact on the
future of the country.

In contrast, the potential long-term damage caused by the Bush
administration and its policies could stretch far into the future, especially
if he is reelected in 2004. The rejection of science typified by the disas-
trously irresponsible attitude toward global warming, and scientific
research beholden to the Religious Right, as well as allowing environmental deterioration, ignoring world population growth, and abandoning
conservation all will have serious consequences in the future, both for the

United States and the world. The position of civil liberties and the ideal of a just society are deteriorating under the Bush administration, and these conditions will extend into the future unless countermeasures are taken. Packing the federal judiciary exclusively with lifetime-appointed judges who view issues according to Bush orthodoxy will help perpetuate these tendencies. The support for religious schools at the expense of public schools will also have long lasting and unknown consequences.

Deliberately destroying the tax base needed to support government obligations will put Social Security and Medicare in extreme jeopardy in the future, as huge deficits will be partially funded from these trust funds. Draconian cuts in federal spending will be needed, with obligations shifted to the financially strapped states. Economic inequality is being enormously increased and perpetuated by the Bush administration's tax cuts, which have yet to kick in to the fullest extent. One can almost envision a future with the affluent few in their gated communities and everyone else struggling economically, a future society more akin to a plutocracy than a democracy, with government bought and paid for by the rich friends of those in power.

In the view of the international community, America has already ceased to be the respected world leader it once was. Our country is seen as an arrogant bully, dangerous and unpredictable, above the rule of international law. The status of America has never been lower in the eyes of people the world over. The combination of all these factors ranks the leader who put them into motion as the worst president in American history.

*   *   *

APPENDIX
THE AFFIRMATIONS OF HUMANISM:
A STATEMENT OF PRINCIPLES

- We are committed to the application of reason and science to the understanding of the universe and to the solving of human problems.
- We deplore efforts to denigrate human intelligence, to seek to explain the world in supernatural terms, and to look outside nature for salvation.
- We believe that scientific discovery and technology can contribute to the betterment of human life.
- We believe in an open and pluralistic society and that democracy is

the best guarantee of protecting human rights from authoritarian elites and repressive majorities.

- We are committed to the principle of the separation or church and state.
- We cultivate the arts of negotiation and compromise as a means of resolving differences and achieving mutual understanding.
- We are concerned with securing justice and fairness in society and with eliminating discrimination and intolerance.
- We believe in supporting the disadvantaged and the handicapped so that they will be able to help themselves.
- We attempt to transcend divisive parochial loyalties based on race, religion, gender, nationality, creed, class, sexual orientation, or ethnicity, and strive to work together for the common good of humanity.
- We want to protect and enhance the earth, to preserve it for future generations, and to avoid inflicting needless suffering on other species.
- We believe in enjoying life here and now and in developing our creative talents to their fullest.
- We believe in the cultivation of moral excellence.
- We respect the right to privacy. Mature adults should be allowed to fulfill their aspirations, to express their sexual preferences, to exercise reproductive freedom, to have access to comprehensive and informed health care, and to die with dignity.
- We believe in the common moral decencies: altruism, integrity, honesty, truthfulness, responsibility. Humanist ethics is amenable to critical, rational guidance. There are normative standards that we discover together. Moral principles are tested by their consequences.
- We are deeply concerned with the moral education of our children. We want to nourish reason and compassion.
- We are engaged by the arts no less than by the sciences.
- We are citizens of the universe and are excited by the discoveries still to be made in the cosmos.
- We are skeptical of untested claims to knowledge, and we are open to novel ideas and seek new departures in our thinking.
- We affirm humanism as a realistic alternative to theologies of despair and ideologies of violence and as a source of rich personal significance and genuine satisfaction in the service to others.
- We believe in optimism rather than pessimism, hope rather than

despair, learning in the place of dogma, truth instead of ignorance, joy rather than guilt or sin, tolerance in the place of fear, love instead of hatred, compassion over selfishness, beauty instead of ugliness, and reason rather than blind faith or irrationality.

- We believe in the fullest realization of the best and noblest that we are capable of as human beings.[5]

NOTES

1. "The Affirmations of Humanism: A Statement of Principles," Council for Secular Humanism, http://www.secularhumanism.org/intro/affirmations.html.

2. *Nation*, March 8, 2004.

3. Robert F. Kennedy Jr., "The White House Plays Dirty with the Environment," *Los Angeles Times*, November 24, 2003, Op-Ed.

4. USA PATRIOT Act.

5. Copyright © Council for Secular Humanism.

LAURENCE BRITT has been a close observer of the political and economic scene in the United States and the world for the past thirty-five years. A former businessman, Britt was an executive of a Fortune Top 40 Corporation and CEO of a worldwide trading company. Britt has written numerous articles on political and economic affairs, was published in *Foreign Affairs*, and is the author of "Fascism, Anyone?" a noted essay written for *Free Inquiry* magazine in 2003. He is also the author of a prophetic political thriller novel written in 1997, which takes place in 2004; it tells the story of the rise of an ultraright-wing fascist government in America, which gains undue respect as the result of a major American tragedy.

13.

The Despoiling of America

How George W. Bush Became the Head of the New American Dominionist Church/State

Katherine Yurica

The death of democracy is not likely to be an assassination from ambush. It will be a slow extinction from apathy, indifference, and undernourishment.

—Robert Maynard Hutchins

THE FIRST PRINCE OF THE THEOCRATIC STATES OF AMERICA

It happened quietly, with barely a mention in the media. Only the *Washington Post* dutifully reported it.[1] And only Kevin Phillips saw its significance in his new book, *American Dynasty*.[2] On December 24, 2001, Pat Robertson resigned his position as president of the Christian Coalition.

Behind the scenes religious conservatives were abuzz with excitement. They believed that Robertson had stepped down to allow the ascendance of the president of the United States of America to take his rightful place as the head of the true American Holy Christian Church.

Robertson's act was symbolic, but it carried a secret and solemn revelation to the faithful. It was the signal that the Bush administration was a government under God that was led by an anointed president who would be the first regent in a dynasty of regents awaiting the return of Jesus to earth. The President would now be the minister through whom God would execute his will in the nation. George W. Bush accepted his scepter and his sword with humility, grace, and a sense of exultation.

© Katherine Yurica. Reprinted by permission of the author.

As Antonin Scalia, associate justice of the Supreme Court, explained a few months later, the Bible teaches and Christians believe "that government . . . derives its moral authority from God. Government is the 'minister of God' with powers to 'revenge,' to 'execute wrath,' including even wrath by the sword. . . ."[3]

George W. Bush began to wield the sword of God's revenge with relish from the beginning of his administration, but most of us missed the swordplay. I have taken the liberty to paraphrase an illustration from Leo Strauss, the father of the neoconservative movement, which gives us a clue of how the hiding is done: "One ought not to say to those whom one wants to kill, 'Give me your votes, because your votes will enable me to kill you and I want to kill you,' but merely, 'Give me your votes,' for once you have the power of the votes in your hand, you can satisfy your desire."[4]

Notwithstanding the advice, the president's foreign policy revealed a flair for saber rattling. He warned the world that "nations are either with us or they're against us!" His speeches, often containing allusions to biblical passages, were spoken with the certainty of a man who holds the authority of God's wrath on earth, for he not only challenged the evil nations of the world, singling out Iraq, Syria, Iran, and North Korea as the "axis of evil," but he wielded the sword of punishment and the sword of revenge *against his own people*: The American poor and the middle class, who, according to the Religious Right, have earned God's wrath by their licentiousness and undisciplined lives.

To the middle class he said, "I'm going to give you clear skies, clean air, and clean water," then he gutted the environmental controls that were designed to provide clean air and water. The estimated number of premature deaths that will result: one hundred thousand.[5] He said to the poor and to the middle class: "I'm going to give you a prescription drug program, one that you truly deserve." Then he gave the drug industry an estimated $139 billion in increased profits from the Medicare funds and arranged for the poorest of seniors to be eliminated from coverage, while most elderly will pay more for drugs than they paid before his drug benefit bill passed.[6] After that he arranged for the dismantling of the Medicare program entirely, based on the method outlined by his religious mentors.[7] He said to the people of America, "I'm going to build a future for you and your children," then he gutted their future with tax breaks to the rich and a pre-emptive war against Iraq, and the largest spending deficit in history.[8]

This essay is the documented story of how a political religious movement called *Dominionism* gained control of the Republican Party, then took over

Congress, then took over the White House, and now is sealing the conversion of America to a theocracy by taking over the American judiciary. It's the story of why and how "the wrath of God Almighty" will be unleashed against the middle class, against the poor, and against the elderly and sick of this nation by George W. Bush and his army of Republican Dominionist "rulers."

HOW DOMINIONISM WAS SPREAD

The years 1982–1986 marked the period Pat Robertson and radio and televangelists urgently broadcast appeals that rallied Christian followers to accept a new political religion that would turn millions of Christians into an army of political operatives. It was the period when the militant church raised itself from centuries of sleep and once again eyed power.

At the time, most Americans were completely unaware of the militant agenda being preached on a daily basis across the breadth and width of America. Although it was called "Christianity," it can barely be recognized as Christian. It in fact was and is a wolf parading in sheep's clothing. It was and is a political scheme to take over the government of the United States and then turn that government into an aggressor nation that will forcibly establish the United States as the ruling empire of the twenty-first century. It is subversive, seditious, secretive, and dangerous.[9]

Dominionism is a natural if unintended extension of social Darwinism and is frequently called "Christian Reconstructionism." Its doctrines are shocking to ordinary Christian believers and to most Americans. Journalist Frederick Clarkson, who has written extensively on the subject, warned in 1994 that Dominionism "seeks to replace democracy with a theocratic elite that would govern by imposing their interpretation of 'Biblical Law.'" He described the ulterior motive of Dominionism as to eliminate "labor unions, civil rights laws, and public schools." Clarkson then describes the creation of new classes of citizens: "Women would be generally relegated to hearth and home. Insufficiently Christian men would be denied citizenship, perhaps executed. So severe is this theocracy that it would extend capital punishment [to] blasphemy, heresy, adultery, and homosexuality."[10]

Today, Dominionists hide their agenda and have resorted to stealth; one investigator who has engaged in Internet exchanges with people who identify themselves as religious conservatives said, "They cut and run if I mention the word 'Dominionism.'"[11] Joan Bokaer, the director of Theocracy Watch, a project of the Center for Religion, Ethics and Social Policy at Cornell University, wrote:

> In March 1986, I was on a speaking tour in Iowa and received a copy of the following memo [Pat] Robertson had distributed to the Iowa Republican County Caucus titled, 'How to Participate in a Political Party.' It read:
> Rule the world for God.
> Give the impression that you are there to work for the party, not push an ideology.
> Hide your strength.
> Don't flaunt your Christianity.
> Christians need to take leadership positions. Party officers control political parties and so it is very important that mature Christians have a majority of leadership positions whenever possible, God willing.[12]

Dominionists have gained extensive control of the Republican Party and the apparatus of government throughout the United States; they continue to operate secretly. Their agenda to undermine all government social programs that assist the poor, the sick, and the elderly is ingeniously disguised under false labels that confuse voters. Nevertheless, as we shall see, Dominionism maintains the necessity of *laissez-faire* economics, requiring that people "look to God and not to government for help."[13]

It is estimated that 35 million Americans who call themselves Christian adhere to Dominionism in the United States, but most of these people appear to be ignorant of the heretical nature of their beliefs and the seditious nature of their political goals. So successfully have the televangelists and churches inculcated the idea of the existence of an outside "enemy," which is attacking Christianity, that millions of people have perceived themselves rightfully overthrowing an imaginary evil anti-Christian conspiratorial secular society.

When one examines the progress of its agenda, one sees that Dominionism has met its timetable: The complete takeover of the American government was predicted to occur by 2004.[14] Unless the American people reject the GOP's control of the government, Americans may find themselves living in a theocracy that has already spelled out its intentions to change every aspect of American life, including its cultural life, its Constitution, and its laws.

Born in Christian Reconstructionism, which was founded by the late R. J. Rushdoony, the framers of the new cult included Rushdoony; his son-in-law Gary North; Pat Robertson; Herb Titus, the former dean of Robertson's Regent University School of Public Policy (formerly CBN University); Charles Colson, Robertson's political strategist; Tim LaHaye; Gary Bauer; the late Francis Schaeffer; and Paul Crouch, the founder of TBN, the world's largest television network, plus a virtual army of like-minded television and radio evangelists and news talk show hosts.

Dominionism started with the Gospels and turned the concept of the invisible and spiritual "Kingdom of God" into a literal political empire that could be taken by force, starting with the United States of America. Discarding the original message of Jesus and forgetting that Jesus said, "My kingdom is not of this world," the framers of Dominionism boldly presented a gospel whose purpose was to inspire Christians to enter politics and execute world domination so that Jesus could return to an earth prepared for his earthly rule by his faithful "regents."

HOW MACHIAVELLIANISM, COMMUNISM, SECULAR HUMANISM, AND NEOCONSERVATISM INSPIRED A NEW MILITANT AND EVIL ANTI-CHRISTIAN RELIGION

In the fifties and sixties, right-wing Christians worried about Communists and communism taking over the world. Along with communism, another enemy to Christianity was identified by ministers. In 1982, Francis Schaeffer, who was then the leading evangelical theologian, called secular humanism the greatest threat to Christianity the world had ever seen. Soon American fundamentalists and Pentecostals were seeing "humanists" everywhere. Appearing on Pat Robertson's *The 700 Club*, Schaeffer claimed that humanism was being forced on Christians; it taught that man was the "center of all things." Like communism, secular humanism was based on atheism, which was sufficient for Schaeffer to conclude that humanism was an enemy to the Kingdom of God.[15] "The enemy is this other view of reality," Schaeffer spoke emotionally. Citing the Declaration of Independence as his authorizing document, he said:

> Today we live in a humanist society. They control the schools. They control public television. They control the media in general. And what we have to say is we live in a humanist society. . . . [Because] the courts are not subject to the will of the people through elections or reelection . . . all the great changes in the last forty years have come through the courts. And

what we must get in our mind is the government as a whole, but especially the courts, has become the vehicle to force this view on the total population, even if the total population doesn't hold the view.[16]

Schaeffer claimed that the major "titanic changes" to America occurred since 1942: "If you don't revolt against tyranny and this is what I call the bottom line, is that not only do you have the privilege but [you have] the duty to revolt. When people force upon you and society that which is absolutely contrary to the Word of God, and which really is tyranny . . . we have a right to stand against it as a matter of principle. And this was the basis upon which the founding fathers built this country."

The appeal to Evangelicals went further. On April 29, 1985, Billy Graham, the respected and world-famous evangelist, told Pat Robertson's audience on *The 700 Club* that: "the time has come when evangelicals are going to have to think about getting organized corporately. . . . I'm for evangelicals running for public office and winning if possible and getting control of the Congress, getting control of the bureaucracy, getting control of the executive branch of government. I think if we leave it to the other side we're going to be lost. I would like to see every true believer involved in politics in some way shape or form." According to Schaeffer, Robertson, and Graham, then arguably the three most famous and influential leaders in the American Protestant Church world, "God's people" had a moral duty to change the government of the United States.[17]

Significantly, at the time, many other fundamentalist ministers were identifying communism and secular humanism as *religions*. However, the equating of a political ideology, on the one hand, and a philosophy that rejects supernaturalism, on the other hand, with *religions* was not accidental.[18] It allowed the preachers to revile an economic-political system as well as a philosophy as *false* religions, even *demonic* religions, which Christians should reject at any cost.[19]

Underneath the pejoratives, however, there was a grudging admiration on the part of Pat Robertson and the other politically astute Dominionists, for they saw that a political agenda that wrapped itself in religious robes had the innate power to explode exponentially into the most politically dynamic movement in American and world history.

The result of the new religion was that by the year 2000, 35 million Americans would declare war on the remaining 245 million. Karl Rove, President Bush's political advisor, told the Family Research Council in 2002, "We need to find ways to win the war."[20] One is tempted to respond,

"Wait a minute, they're in power so why do they need to continue the war?" That is the salient question. The answer is frightening.

Starting with a simple idea, Robertson perceived the enormous advantage of placing an otherwise unacceptable political theory into a religious context. By doing so, it would stand Christianity upside down and end American democracy.

A MACHIAVELLIAN RELIGION WAS BORN

American Christianity had already seen extremes. For Dominionists, perhaps the single most important event in the last half of the twentieth century occurred when the Reverend Jim Jones proved that the religious would follow their leader to Guyana and even further, to their deaths. That fact could hardly have escaped the notice of even the dullest of politically minded preachers.

Indeed, Jim Jones's surreal power over his congregants leaps out from the grave even today. If a man desired to change the laws in America—to undo Franklin Delano Roosevelt's New Deal, for instance, and allow corporations the unbridled freedom they enjoyed prior to the Great Depression (which included the freedom to defraud, pillage, and destroy the land with impunity on the way to gathering great fortunes), what better way to proceed than to cloak the corruption within a religion? If a few men wanted to establish an American empire and control the entire world, what better vehicle to carry them to their goal than to place their agenda within the context of a religion? Jim Jones proved religious people would support even immoral political deeds if their leaders found a way to frame those deeds as "God's Will." The idea was brilliant. Its framers knew they could glorify greed, hate, nationalism and even a Christian empire with ease.[21]

The religion the canny thinkers founded follows the reverse of communism and secular humanism. It poured political and economic ideology into a religion and that combustible mixture produced "Dominionism," a new political faith that had the additional advantage of insulating the cult from attacks on its political agenda by giving its practitioners the covering to simply cry out, "You're attacking me for my religious beliefs and that's religious persecution!"[22]

But how could a leader get away with a religious fraud that barely hides its destructive and false intent?

Jim Jones's history holds the answer. He not only proved the obvious fact that people are blinded by their religious beliefs and will only impute goodness, mercy, and religious motivations to their leader, but Jim Jones proved the efficacy of the basic teaching of Machiavelli: A leader must only *appear* to have the qualities of goodness—he need not actually possess those attributes.

In fact, Machiavelli taught that it is dangerous for a leader to practice goodness. Instead, he must *pretend* to be good and then do the opposite. Machiavelli taught that a leader will succeed on appearances alone. A good leader puts his finger to the wind and changes course whenever it is expedient to do so. Machiavelli wrote this revealing passage that could be applied not only to false religious leaders but to a false president: "Alexander VI did nothing else but deceive men, he thought of nothing else, and found the occasion for it; no man was ever more able to give assurances, or affirmed things with stronger oaths, and no man observed them less; however, he always succeeded in his deceptions, as he well knew this aspect of things. . . . Everybody sees what you appear to be, few feel what you are, and those few will not dare to oppose themselves to the many, who have the majesty of the state to defend them; and in the actions of men, and especially of princes, from which there is no appeal, the end justifies the means."[23]

Chillingly, Machiavelli advises his readers: "Let a prince therefore aim at conquering and maintaining the state, and the means will always be judged honourable and praised by every one, for the vulgar is always taken by appearances and the issue of the event; and the world consists only of the vulgar, and the few who are not vulgar are isolated when the many have a rallying point in the prince."[24] Machiavelli also wrote how to govern dominions that previous to being occupied lived under their own laws. His words eerily reflect the Bush administration's decisions on how to rule Iraq:

> When those states which have been acquired are accustomed to live at liberty under their own laws, there are three ways of holding them. The first is to despoil them;[25] the second is to go and live there in person; the third is to allow them to live under their own laws, taking tribute of them, and creating within the country a government composed of a few who will keep it friendly to you. Because this government, being created by the prince, knows that it cannot exist without his friendship and protection, and will do all it can to keep them. What is more, a city used to liberty can be more easily held by means of its citizens than in any other way, if you wish to preserve it.[26]

However, Machiavelli has second thoughts and follows with this caveat: "[I]n truth there is no sure method of holding them except by despoiling them. And whoever becomes the ruler of a free city and does not destroy it, can expect to be destroyed by it, for it can always find a motive for rebellion in the name of liberty and of its ancient usages. . . ."[27]

Machiavelli's books *The Prince* and *The Discourses* are not abstract treatises. Christian Gauss, who wrote an important introduction to the Oxford edition, called them by their rightful name: They are in fact a "concise manual—a *handbook for those who would acquire or increase their political power.*" Gauss tells us that a long line of kings and ministers and tyrants studied Machiavelli, including Mussolini, Hitler, Lenin, and Stalin.

HOW CAN EVIL DEEDS BE RECONCILED WITH CHRISTIAN BELIEFS?

It's important to understand that the founders of Dominionism are sitting on the horns of a moral dilemma: How can a leader be both good and evil at the same time? For if biblical moral proscriptions are applicable to him, he will certainly suffer some form of censure. And if proscriptions are applicable, the leader could not lie to the citizenry with impunity or do evil so that "good" could be achieved. The answer to the dilemma of how a Dominionist leader could both do evil and still maintain his place of honor in the Christian community lies in the acceptance and adoption of the Calvinistic doctrine that James Hogg wrote about in *The Private Memoirs and Confessions of a Justified Sinner.* This novel, published in 1824, is concerned with psychological aberration and, as such, anticipates the literature of the twentieth century. The protagonist is a young man named Robert, who, drenched in the religious bigotry of Calvinism, concluded that he was predestined before the beginning of the world to enter heaven; therefore no sin he committed would be held to his account. This freed Robert to become an assassin in the cause of Christ and his church.[28]

Fifty years ago a variation on the concept was expressed disapprovingly as, "Once saved—always saved." In this view, salvation had nothing to do with "good works or a holy life." A drunk who had a born-again experience would be among God's chosen elect whether he stopped drinking or not. But the logical extension of the reasoning is the idea that Christianity could have within itself not ex-sinners but active sinners: as Christian murderers, Christian pedophiles, Christian rapists, Christian thieves, Christian arsonists, and every other kind of sociopathological behavior possible. As we have sadly witnessed of late, the concept is broadly accepted within the American churches.

But the Dominionists needed the aberrant extension of Calvinism; they believe, as did Calvin and John Knox, that before the creation of the universe, all men were indeed predestined to be either among God's elect or unregenerate outcasts. And it is at this point Dominionists introduced a perversion to Calvinism—the same one James Hogg utilizes in his *Private Memoirs and Confessions of a Justified Sinner*—its technical name is "supralapsarianism." It means essentially that the man called from before the foundation of the world to be one of the elect of God's people *can do no wrong*. No wonder, then, observers noted a definite religious swing in George W. Bush from Wesleyan theology to Calvinism early in his administration.[29]

How comforting the Calvinistic idea of a "justified sinner" is when one is utilizing Machiavellian techniques to gain political control of a state. It's more than comforting; it is a required doctrine for "Christians" who believe they must use evil to bring about good. It justifies lying, murder, fraud, and all other criminal acts without the fuss of having to deal with guilt feelings or to feel remorse for the lives lost through executions, military actions, or assassinations.

If this doctrine seems too wayward to believe, as it might have done had I not heard a recent interview with a Pentecostal minister—rest assured that the twisted doctrine is horribly alive and thriving in America today.

The interview, conducted by Brian Copeland, a news talk show host for KGO, San Francisco, on September 5, 2003, was with the Reverend Donald Spitz of Pensacola, Florida, who is involved with a pro-life group in Virginia and with the Army of God. The occasion was the execution of Paul Hill, another Pentecostal minister who murdered a doctor and his bodyguard outside an abortion clinic. Hill was caught and convicted of the crimes. Spitz admitted that he was Paul Hill's spiritual counselor. He said Hill died with the conviction that he had done the Lord's work. Spitz, who approved of the murder, said, "Someone else is going to handle the publishing of Paul Hill's book on how to assassinate."

Spitz believed that Hill was completely justified in murdering the physician because, according to him, "twenty-six babies' lives were saved by the killing." When Copeland pointed out that the scheduled abortions for the morning of the murders would have simply been postponed to another day—and that the lives of the fetuses were only extended for a day or so—Spitz refused to accept the argument. Not surprisingly, Spitz opposed the use of birth control methods. Copeland asked, "If a woman is raped should she be forced to carry the fetus to term?" Spitz said, "Yes."

"What if the pregnancy will kill the mother?" Spitz replied that under no circumstances could "the baby be killed." When Spitz was asked, "Why haven't you gone out and killed an abortionist?" he replied calmly, "God hasn't told me to do the killing."[30]

THE NEOCONSERVATIVE CONNECTION WITH DOMINIONISTS AND MACHIAVELLI

I suspect that most Americans have never heard of Machiavelli. Nevertheless, it should be no surprise to us that Machiavelli has been accepted, praised, and followed by the neoconservatives in the White House and that his precepts are blindly adopted by the so-called Christian Dominionists. Kevin Phillips tells us in his masterful book *American Dynasty* that Karl Rove, political strategist for President George W. Bush, is a devotee of Machiavelli, just as Rove's predecessor, Lee Atwater, had been for the elder Bush.[31] In fact, there has been an incredible effort to dilute the immoral implications of Machiavelli's teachings. Today's best apologist for Machiavelli is one of the most influential voices in Washington, with direct connections into the Oval Office.

Michael A. Ledeen was a senior fellow with the Center for Strategic and International Studies and a counselor to the National Security Council and special counselor to former secretary of state Alexander Haig in 1985. His relationship with Pat Robertson goes back at least to the early 1980s.[32] Like Robertson, Ledeen was an advocate for military intervention in Nicaragua and for assistance to the Contras. (Ledeen was also involved in the Iran-Contra affair.)[33]

Today, in 2004, Michael Ledeen is a fellow at the conservative think tank the American Enterprise Institute and, according to William O. Beeman of the Pacific News Service, "Ledeen has become the driving philosophical force behind the neoconservative movement and the military actions it has spawned."[34]

Ledeen made a number of appearances on the *700 Club* show during the 1980s, always presented as a distinguished guest. Robertson interviewed him on April 30, 1985, and asked him on this occasion: "What would you recommend if you were going to advise the president [Ronald Reagan] as to foreign policy?"

Ledeen responded: "The United States has to make clear to the world and *above all to its own citizens, what our vital interests are.* And then we must make it clear to everyone that we are prepared to fight and fight fiercely to defend those interests, so that people will not cross the lines that are likely to kick off a trip wire" (emphasis added).

If Ledeen's advice sounds ruthless and Machiavellian—it may be because it *is* Machiavellian. (By definition his statement presupposes the existence of something or several things that are *life-threatening* to the nation by the use of the word "vital." Yet, Ledeen asserts, that which is life-threatening must be made manifest or defined. If an interest must be defined, then it is not apparent; yet the nation will nevertheless ask its sons and daughters to fight and die for something that is not apparent. Therefore, whatever "interests" Ledeen wanted to be defined cannot have been *vital* interests, which are apparent—so in reality he advised the president to call *discretionary* interests vital—which is a lie.)

Be aware that Ledeen is in complete accord with Machiavellian thinking. And so is Pat Robertson.[35] Robertson agreed to virtually every nuance Ledeen presented. In fact, it's not clear which of the two first proposed invading Syria, Iran, and Iraq back in the 1980s,[36] a refrain that also echoed in the reports of the Project for the New American Century (PNAC), one of the major homes for neoconservatives in the 2000s. Both Ledeen and Robertson targeted the same nations that the PNAC lists as America's greatest enemies in its paper "Rebuilding America's Defenses" (published in September 2000).[37]

In 1999, Ledeen published his book *Machiavelli on Modern Leadership: Why Machiavelli's Iron Rules Are as Timely and Important Today as Five Centuries Ago.* Here is a sample of how Ledeen smoothes rough edges and presents a modern Machiavelli: "In order to achieve the most noble accomplishments, the leader may have to 'enter into evil.' This is the chilling insight that has made Machiavelli so feared, admired, and challenging. It is why we are drawn to him still. . . ."[38]

Again, Ledeen writes: "Just as the quest for peace at any price invites war and, worse than war, defeat and domination, so good acts sometimes advance the triumph of evil, as there are circumstances when only doing evil ensures the victory of a good cause."[39] Ledeen clearly believes that "the end justifies the means" but not *all* the time. He writes, "Lying is evil," but then contradictorily argues that it produced "a magnificent result," and "is essential to the survival of nations and to the success of great enterprises"[40] Ledeen adds this tidbit: "All's fair in war . . . and in love. Practicing deceit to fulfill your heart's desire might be not only legitimate, but delicious!"[41]

Beeman tells us about Michael Ledeen's influence: "Ledeen's ideas are repeated daily by such figures as Richard Cheney, Donald Rumsfeld and Paul Wolfowitz. . . . He basically believes that violence in the service of the spread of democracy is America's manifest destiny. Consequently, he has become the philosophical legitimator of the American occupation of Iraq."[42]

In fact, Ledeen's influence goes even further. The BBC, the *Washington Post*, and Jim Lobe, writing for the *Asia Times*, report that Michael Ledeen is the only full-time international affairs analyst consulted by Karl Rove.[43] Ledeen has regular conversations with Rove. The *Washington Post* said, "More than once, Ledeen has seen his ideas, faxed to Rove, become official policy or rhetoric."[44]

LEO STRAUSS, THE FATHER OF NEOCONSERVATISM

Leo Strauss was born in 1899 and died in 1973. He was a Jewish scholar who fled Germany when Hitler gained power. He eventually found refuge in the United States, where he taught political science at the University of Chicago. He is most famous for resuscitating Machiavelli and introducing his principles as the guiding philosophy of the neoconservative movement. Strauss has been called the godfather of Newt Gingrich's "Contract with America." More than any other man, Strauss breathed upon conservatism, inspiring it to rise from its atrophied condition and its natural dislike of change and to embrace an unbounded new political ideology that rides on the back of a revolutionary steed, hailing even radical change; hence the name neoconservatives.

The father of neoconservatism had many "spiritual" children at the University of Chicago, among them Paul Wolfowitz and Abram Shulsky, who received their doctorates under Strauss in 1972. Harry V. Jaffa was a student of Strauss and has an important connection to Dominionists like Pat Robertson as we shall see below. However, Strauss's family of influence extended beyond his students to include faculty members in universities and the people his students taught. Those prominent neoconservatives who are most notable are Justice Clarence Thomas, Robert Bork, Irving Kristol and his son William Kristol, Alan Keyes, William J. Bennett, J. Danforth Quayle, Allan Bloom, John Podhoertz, John T. Agresto, John Ashcroft, Newt Gingrich, Gary Bauer, Michael Ledeen, and scores of others, many of whom hold important positions in George W. Bush's White House and Defense Department.

To understand the Straussian infusion of power that transformed an all but dead conservative realm, think of Nietzsche's Overman come to life. Or better yet, think of the philosophy most unlike Christianity: Think of pure, unmitigated evil. Strauss admits that Machiavelli was an evil man. But according to Strauss, his admission is a prerequisite to studying and reading Machiavelli: The acknowledgement is the safety net that keeps the reader from being corrupted. One is tempted to talk back to Strauss and point out an alternative: The admission could be the subterfuge that keeps a person from being ridiculed and rejected for espousing Machiavellian methods.

In one of the most important books for our times, *Leo Strauss and the American Right*, Shadia Drury undertakes to explain the ideas behind Strauss's huge influence and following. Strauss's reputation, according to Drury, rests in large part on his view that "a real philosopher must communicate quietly, subtly, and secretly to the few who are fit to receive his message." Strauss claims secrecy is necessary to avoid "persecution."[45]

In reading Strauss, one sometimes encounters coded contradictory ideas. For example, Strauss *appears* to respect Machiavelli because—as he points out—in contrast to other evil men, Machiavelli openly proclaimed opinions that others only secretly expressed behind closed doors. But we have just noted that Strauss teaches that secrecy is essential to the real philosopher. Strauss concluded, some would say that Machiavelli was, after all, a patriot of sorts, for he loved Italy more than he loved his own soul. Then Strauss warns, but if you call him a patriot, you "merely obscure something truly evil."[46] So Strauss dances his way through the Machiavellian field of evil, his steps choreographed with duplicity and its opposite. The reader cannot let go.

In Strauss's view, Machiavelli sees that Christianity "has led the world into weakness," which can be offset only by returning the world to the ancient practices of the past. (Implied is not a return to the pagan past but rather a return to the more virulent world of the Old Testament.) Strauss laments, "Machiavelli needed . . . a detailed discussion revealing the harmony between his political teaching and the teaching of the Bible."[47] These statements of Strauss, by themselves, were sufficient to send neoconservative Christians to search for correlations between Machiavellianism, radical conservatism, and the scriptures.[48]

Strauss's teaching incorporated much of Machiavelli's. Significantly, his philosophy is unfriendly to democracy—even antagonistic. At the same time, Strauss upheld the necessity for a national religion not because he favored religious practices but because religion in his view is necessary in order to control the population. Since neoconservatives influenced by Strauss are in control of the Bush administration, I have prepared a brief list that shows the radically un-Christian basis of neoconservatism (I am indebted to Drury for the following):

First: Strauss believed that a leader had to perpetually deceive the citizens he ruled.

Second: Those who lead must understand there is no morality, there is only the right of the superior to rule the inferior.

Third: According to Drury, religion "is the glue that holds society together."[49] It is a handle by which the ruler can manipulate the masses. Any religion will do. Strauss is indifferent to them all.

Fourth: "Secular society . . . is the worst possible thing," because it leads to individualism, liberalism, and relativism, all of which encourage dissent and rebellion. As Drury sums it up: "You want a crowd that you can manipulate like putty."[50]

Fifth: "Strauss thinks that a political order can be stable only if it is united by an external threat; and following Machiavelli, he maintains that if no external threat exists, then one has to be manufactured."[51]

Sixth: "In Strauss's view, the trouble with liberal society is that it dispenses with noble lies and pious frauds. It tries to found society on secular rational foundations."[52]

STRAUSS'S STUDENT, HARRY JAFFA, ON *THE 700 CLUB* WITH PAT ROBERTSON

For four days in 1986, from July first through the fourth of July, Pat Robertson interviewed neoconservative Dr. Harry Jaffa, a former student of Leo Strauss, on *The 700 Club*. The topic was the importance of the Declaration of Independence. Joining with Jaffa was Robertson's own man, Herb Titus, the dean of CBN's School of Public Policy. This series of interviews was one of the most important philosophical moments in the development of the political agenda and political philosophy of the Dominionists.

Robertson found in Harry Jaffa the champion he needed, whose reasoning would influence how the Constitution should be interpreted by conservatives and would provide a "Christian" view of the establishment of the United States that excluded the secular social contract view. Jaffa would influence both Clarence Thomas (who would be appointed to the Supreme Court by President George Bush senior in 1991) and Antonin Scalia (who would be appointed to the Supreme Court by President Ronald Reagan on September 26, 1986).

During the four days of interviews, Jaffa and Titus agreed that the Declaration of Independence was the premier document and that it superseded the Constitution. Titus said, "The Declaration . . . is the charter of the nation. It is what you might call the articles of incorporation, whereas the Constitution is the bylaws. The Constitution is the means by which to carry out the great purposes that are articulated in the Declaration."

Robertson asked: "Let's assume that 80 percent of the people are just totally immoral—they want to live lives of gross licentiousness and they want to prey on one another—that's what they want and they want a government to let them do it. How does that square with the Declaration of Independence and its consent of the governed?"

Titus said, "Even the people can't consent to give away that which God says is unalienable."

Robertson then asked, "The principles enunciated in the Declaration of Independence—how far have we gone from it and what can we do to redress some of these problems?"

Jaffa responded cryptically: "I'd say that today, for example in the attorney general's [Edwin Meese's] warfare with the liberals on the Supreme Court, in his appeal to *original intent*, he appeals to the text of the Constitution. Jefferson and Madison said together in 1825, 'If you want to find the principles of the Constitution of the United States, you go first to the Declaration of Independence.'"

First, Jaffa means by the term "original intent" that the Constitution must be interpreted according to what it meant when it was originally adopted. It is a revolutionary and brilliant idea that will allow the Dominionists to effectively repeal most of the judicial decisions made in the last century. [53]

Second, if we take Jaffa and the Dominionists at their word and go to the Declaration of Independence, we can see just how radical the conservative revolution and Dominionism are. The only portion that is ever quoted publicly is these words: "We hold these truths to be self-evident, that all men are created equal, that they are endowed by their Creator with certain unalienable Rights, that among these are Life, Liberty, and the pursuit of Happiness. That to secure these rights, Governments are instituted among Men, deriving their just powers from the consent of the governed,— . . . ."

The quotation stops in the middle of the sentence—the part that is never quoted is this: "That whenever any Form of Government becomes destructive of these ends, it is the Right of the People to alter or to abolish it, and to institute new Government, laying its foundation on such principles and organizing its powers in such form, as to them shall seem most likely to effect their Safety and Happiness."

Dominionism, then, takes its authority to overthrow the government of the United States from our own Declaration of Independence. By the time all Americans wake up to the Dominionists' intent, it may be too late.

Though Harry Jaffa speaks with a high-minded sense of political righteousness, Drury exposes his Machiavellian side. Like Strauss, he "clearly believes that devious and illegal methods are justified when those in power are convinced of the rightness of their ends."[54] Jaffa and Robertson saw eye to eye on more than one topic: for instance, Jaffa, like his host Pat Robertson, found Oliver North to be a hero (and by extension Michael Ledeen) when both North and Ledeen went around the law to provide military aid to the Contras.[55]

HOW DOMINIONISM STEALTHILY SWEPT OVER AMERICA

Within a period of twenty to thirty years, beginning in the 1970s, Dominionism spread like wildfire throughout the evangelical, Pentecostal and fundamentalist religious communities in America. It was aided and abetted by television and radio evangelists. More than any other man, Pat Robertson mobilized the millions of politically indifferent and socially despised Pentecostals and fundamentalists in America and turned them into an angry, potent army of political conquerors.[56]

But it would be a mistake to limit Dominionism to the Pentecostals and fundamentalists alone: Conservative Roman Catholics and Episcopalians have joined and enlarged the swelling numbers.[57] Robertson, like other media preachers, used every form of communication: television, radio, books, and audiotapes available for sale. One book stands out. Originally published in 1982 and written with Bob Slosser, a key Robertson loyalist, Robertson's *The Secret Kingdom* soared on the best-seller charts. It underwent four printings during its first year. By 1984 Bantam had published a mass paperback in cooperation with Thomas Nelson, the original publisher.[58]

However, it was the Pentecostals and fundamentalists who made up the core of Robertson's audience. To a people who were largely uneducated and who often remained ignorant even if they went through college because of their fear of becoming tainted by the "world and worldliness," Dominionism came as a brilliant light that assuaged their deep sense of inferiority. Pentecostals in particular could take comfort from the notion that no longer would the world think of them as "Holy Rollers" who danced in the "Spirit" and practiced glossolalia. This time, they would be on top—they would be the head and not the tail—and the so-called elite, the educated of the world, would be on the bottom.

A new world was coming. To help the transition along, Pat Robertson, along with other pastors, evangelists, and churchmen, founded schools, universities, and colleges throughout the United States to train "Christians" how to run for office, how to win, and how to manage the affairs of government after they gained office. To get an idea of how successful the plan was, Robertson's Regent University now has a $100 million endowment. After watching the Dominionists take over the Republican Party and observing their ruthless methods, it is indeed apparent that Machiavellian principles are the fuel running their "how-to manual."

Starting with a class of only twelve in 1985, Robertson began his journalism department at CBN University, where eight hundred other graduate students were earning master's degrees in a fully accredited institution. Later Robertson changed the name of CBN University to "Regent University"—based on Dominionism's teaching that the national government of America and governments of the world will be ruled by Dominionists, who will act as regents on an interim basis, that is, until the true king—Jesus Christ—will return to earth again and gratefully accept his kingdom from the hands of his faithful regents.

THE DOMINIONIST PLAN: TODAY CONTROL THE UNITED STATES, TOMORROW THE WORLD

Significantly, Dominionism is a form of social Darwinism.[59] It inherently includes the religious belief that wealth-power is a sign of God's election. That is, out of the masses of people and the multitude of nations—wealth, in and of itself, is thought to indicate God's approval on men and nations, whereas poverty and sickness reflect God's disapproval. The roots of the idea come from a natural twist of an Old Testament passage, which I discuss below. Essentially, later in this chapter there were two elements necessary to establish Dominionism among Christians who previously believed that helping the poor was a mandate of Christianity.[60]

First, Old Testament law had to be accepted as an essential part of a Christian's theology. Second, the Christian had to undergo a second conversion-like experience that went *beyond being born again* and demanded not only a commitment to reestablishing the Old Testament legal structure but required the *implementation of that law in the nations of the world* (including the United States) based upon a different understanding of the Great Commission (Matt. 28:18–20).[61] Under this concept, Dominionists are to go into all the world to take dominion and "make disciples," teaching the disciples to "observe all" that Jesus "commanded." All nations under Dominionist's teaching are to convert to biblical laws, which are ranked superior to secular laws that were not God given or God directed and are found wanting. The Christian therefore must be willing to overthrow all laws that are secular.

In other words, a measure of one's spirituality rested upon the individual's willingness to accept the concept of taking dominion over not only the people of America but the people of the entire world. From Dominionists' actual words, the taking of America is perceived as a violent act. Ben Kinchlow, who cohosted CBN's *The 700 Club* with Pat Robertson, told an audience, "We need to *grab* the American dream by the short hairs and *snatch* it back to where it was originally designed to be."

As Robertson wrote approvingly in his book *The Secret Kingdom*, the kingdom of heaven "suffers violence, and violent men take it by force." He explained, "Zealous men force their way in. That's what it means."[62]

WHAT "DOMINION" MEANS

There were an estimated 110,000 Pentecostal and fundamentalist churches in America in the 1980s. Robertson taught them—through his vast television network and through his books—that the role of the Christian is to rule over the wicked. Dominionism's purpose is to create theocrats (a Christian class of rulers). But in order to successfully place only certain Christians in positions of power, Dominionism divides Christian believers into classes based upon *political* ideology and certain hot-point issues such as the privatization of Social Security and Medicare, freedom to decide on medical procedures with one's own physician, freedom of the press and freedom of speech, freedom of the arts, and certain rights like the right to a fair trial and protection from governmental intrusion into the privacy of marriage and adult associations.

The believers who are destined to rule are called the "elect" and are separated from those believers who do not and will not accept the predestined superiority of the chosen ruling class. A Christian who raises his voice against the "elect" could be labeled a "false prophet or a dreamer of dreams," and therefore, according to the Deuteronomic law "shall be put to death."

Placing his own words in the mouth of God, Robertson wrote in *The Secret Kingdom*: "It is clear that God is saying, 'I gave man dominion over the earth, but he lost it. Now I desire mature sons and daughters who will in My name exercise dominion over the earth and will subdue Satan, *the unruly*, and *the rebellious*. Take back My world from those who would loot it and abuse it. Rule as I would rule.'"[63]

On his *The 700 Club* television show (May 1, 1986) Robertson said:

God's plan is for His people, ladies and gentleman to take dominion. . . . What is dominion? Well, dominion is Lordship. He wants His people to reign and rule with Him . . . but He's waiting for us to . . . extend His dominion. . . . And the Lord says, "I'm going to let *you* redeem society. There'll be a reformation. . . ." We are not going to stand for those coercive utopians in the Supreme Court and in Washington ruling over us any more. We're not gonna stand for it. We are going to say, "we want freedom in this country, and we want power. . . ."

Charles Colson, the former special counsel to Richard Nixon, who was called "Nixon's Hatchet Man," pled guilty to charges in the Daniel Ellsberg case during the Watergate scandal. He served a prison sentence and started a prison ministry afterward. Pat Robertson has called him "the most brilliant political strategist in the world." Over the years, Colson made many appearances on *The 700 Club*. On May 21, 1986, he laid out the battle lines: "It always has been a conflict between the kingdoms: the kingdom of God and the kingdom of man. When you really look at what Jesus is saying, He is saying the time is fulfilled, repent and believe, the kingdom is at hand. And He is calling for the kingdom of God to rule over the affairs of man. And so inevitably there's going to be a conflict."

Robertson said on his program the on May 13, 1986: "We've sat idly by long enough and said, 'Well religion and politics don't mix.' Don't you believe it. If we don't have moral people in government then the only other people that can be in government are immoral. That's the only way it goes. Either you have moral people in there or you have immoral people." On another show (May 7, 1986) he revealed a partial list of changes the Dominionists planned for America: "We can change the government, we can change the court systems, we can change the poverty problem, we can change education. . . . We can make a difference."

WHO RULES? AND WHO ARE TO BE THE RULED?

In an earlier section, I discussed the principle held by both Machiavelli and Leo Strauss that religion is necessary as a tool for a leader to control the masses. If conformity—not dissent—is required, then religion is the power tool of choice, for it will ensure a controlled populace. We're about to examine its uses, its ingenious gifts and its powers, in this and the following sections. Be aware that Dominionism is, in fact, a brilliantly executed road that leads to total power.

In his book, which tended to be more formal and less expansive, Robertson began the listing of those Americans not fit for public office: "Obviously the drunk, the drug addict, the lustful, the slothful do not have the discipline to rule the earth and to correct its evils."[64]

"If we remain unrighteous, the Bible says, we will miss the kingdom."[65] Then he quoted Paul's Epistle to the Corinthians: "Or do you not know that the unrighteous shall not inherit the kingdom of God? Do not be deceived; neither fornicators, nor idolaters, nor adulterers, nor effeminate, nor homosexuals, nor thieves, nor the covetous, nor drunkards, nor revilers, nor swindlers, shall inherit the kingdom of God"(1 Cor. 6:9–10).[66]

If "secular humanists are the greatest threat to Christianity the world has ever known," as theologian Francis Schaeffer claimed, then who are the humanists? According to Dominionists, humanists are the folks who allow or encourage *licentious* behavior in America. They are the *undisciplined* revelers.

Put all the enemies of the Dominionists together, boil them down to liquid and bake them into the one single most highly derided and contaminated individual known to man, and you will have before you an image of the quintessential "liberal"—one of those folks who wants to give liberally to the poor and needy—who desires the welfare and happiness of all Americans—who insists on safety regulations for your protection and who desires the preservation of your values—those damnable people are the folks that must be reduced to powerlessness—or worse: extinction.

Dominionists determine who is among God's elect—not solely by a religious experience such as being born again but by a political determination of whether one is a Republican or a Democrat, a liberal or a conservative, or simply a person who questions the deeds of Dominionist political figures. The politics of exclusion, including bigotry, is in fact widespread throughout the United States.

Take, for instance, Sean Hannity's remarks to *Time* magazine: "You can play golf with liberals, be neighbors with them, go out to dinner. I just don't want them in power."[67] Or take Ann Coulter's assertions: "Liberals have a preternatural gift for striking a position on the side of treason." Or, "Whenever the nation is under attack, from within or without, liberals side with the enemy."[68] (It turns out that every single "liberal" in the country is a member of the Democratic Party and therefore is a traitor.)

The Machiavellian nature of the Dominionist cult explains why Bill Clinton, who is a Christian believer, was attacked so viciously for his sexual folly, but Newt Gingrich, Bill Livingston, Henry Hyde, Strom Thurmond, and scores of other Republicans escaped the punishment of public ridicule, verbal abuse, and humiliation for the same sexual peccadilloes. (It appears that only Democratic "liberals" must be held to the fire of biblical standards and biblical *punishments* because, as we all know, they are "unregenerate from the beginning of time.")

Robertson's book acknowledges that his followers, the "Christian" army raised up for political purposes, are the elect chosen to rule. Robertson's transcribed television interviews and dialogues give shocking evidence to the legitimization of greed, hatred, violence, and cruelty by members of the various fundamentalist branches of the American clergy and by elected officials of the Republican Party, which can be cited as evidence that Dominionism is not a Christian religion—that above everything else, Dominionism is synonymous with Machiavellianism: the ends justify the means. Under Dominionism, true Christianity is a target to destroy, not a goal to achieve.

WHO LIVES AND WHO DIES? HOW JUSTICE SCALIA WOULD EXPAND THE DEATH PENALTY

In one of those peculiar moments when a host on television seems to have a disconnect with his guest, I realized that Pat Robertson was using "code" with Herb Titus, his "guest" on the show on May 27, 1985. Titus was the dean of CBN University's School of Public Policy and was a known Christian Reconstructionist (Dominionist) who had written position papers arguing that government has exceeded its authority by requiring individuals such as doctors, lawyers, and teachers to be licensed by the state. Robertson himself revealed what the School of Public Policy was teaching on a later show (July 5, 1985). "What are we going to teach them? We'll teach them the foundation of our government. We're going to teach them how to win elections."

This exchange with Titus occurred on May 27, 1985:

ROBERTSON: We have with us today *constitutional* authority, Herb Titus. Herb, . . . how about the biblical concept of war? You know, there are many people who don't think we should ever fight wars and yet we're talking about brave men who died for freedom. (Emphasis added)

TITUS: Well, I believe the scripture is very clear that if you are attacked by evil whether within the country or outside the country, that it's the duty of the civil authorities to defend the nation and the people of the nation from evil whether it comes from an aggressor outside or an aggressor inside. We can see that in Romans 13, for example.

Curious about the meaning of what was being said, particularly since Robertson had asked a question about war and Titus's answer included war against one's own population, I looked up Romans 13. I had always read this passage to be Saint Paul's concept of a good government providing beneficial services to the governed, and I restricted its meaning to only a lawfully constituted government that rules justly.

But read Romans 13 in the light of Machiavelli's and Leo Strauss's discourses on religion and its uses by a political leader, and one glimpses the danger that Dominionism represents to the American people and to the American way of life. For it can be read to mean that *any* lawful government is ordained by God to execute retribution and punishment upon those who challenge (resist or rebel against) unjust policies of a government. When read this way, it takes on a new and sinister meaning. Or, it can be read to mean that once a *new* government of the United States of America has been established under biblical law—then no citizen will have the right to resist it or rebel against its edicts. In other words, the Declaration of Independence will no longer be applicable to the regency established by the Dominionists. This is how Romans 13 reads in the New English Version:

> Every person must submit to the supreme authorities. There is no authority but by act of God, and the existing authorities are instituted by him; consequently anyone who rebels against authority is resisting a divine institution, and those who so resist have themselves to thank for the punishment they will receive. For government, a terror to crime, has no terrors for good behaviour. You wish to have no fear of the authorities? Then continue to do right and you will have their approval, for they are God's agents working for your good. But if you are doing wrong, then you will have cause to fear them; it is not for nothing that they hold the power of the sword, for they are God's agents of punishment, for retribution on the offender. That is why you are obliged to submit. It is an obligation imposed not merely by fear of retribution but by conscience. That is also why you pay taxes. The authorities are in God's service and to these duties they devote their energies.

This section, if taken literally as fundamentalists are apt to do, appears to prohibit any kind of resistance against the policies of a government, including peaceful protests, petitions, and writings. Supreme Court Justice Antonin Scalia appears to endorse that position, for he quoted this same Romans 13 passage in his article "God's Justice and Ours" to prove that Christian doctrine states "government—however you want to limit that concept—derives its moral authority from God."[69] Government is not only the "minister of God," but it has the authority to "execute God's wrath."

The power of the sword is surely the power to kill or maim and certainly the power to intimidate. Scalia believes that the power of the sword in *this passage* is "unmistakably a reference to the death penalty."[70] At this point, Scalia demonstrates the absolute brilliance of the judicial rule created by neoconservatives, which requires a judge to determine the "original intent" of the writers of the Constitution. As Scalia himself describes it, "The Constitution that I interpret and apply is not living but dead. . . . It means today not what current society . . . thinks it ought to mean, but what it meant when it was adopted."[71] Once the original thinking is determined, the judge can enforce the Constitution only as a document that is bound by the time zone in which a particular passage was written.

When I first read articles by authors who were exposing the Dominionists' intention to extend the death penalty to cover "crimes" like adultery, rebelliousness, homosexuality, witchcraft, or effeminateness, I found the death penalty extension goal to be laughable. It couldn't be done in America.

I was wrong. I now realize that we are very close to seeing the Dominionists achieve their goal. All they need to do is to appoint a majority of judges who will adhere to the "dead Constitution" construction rule of Scalia (or what Harry Jaffa called "the original intent" construction rule). At the point when the Dominionists control the judiciary, that judiciary can roll back America's body of legal jurisprudence to a century or more ago as law professor Patricia J. Williams pointed out.[72]

Scalia spilled the beans when he explained how he would determine whether the death penalty is constitutional or not. His reasoning goes like this: Since the death penalty was "clearly permitted when the Eighth Amendment [which prohibits 'cruel and unusual punishments'] was adopted," and at that time the death penalty was applied for all felonies— including, for example, the felony of horse-thieving, "so it is clearly permitted today."[73] Justice Scalia left no doubt that if the crime of horse stealing carried a death penalty today in the United States, he would find that law constitutional.

All a willing Dominionist Republican–controlled Congress need do to extend the death penalty to those people who practice witchcraft, adultery, homosexuality, heresy, et cetera, is to find those particular death penalty laws existing as of November 3, 1791, and reinstate them. No revolution is required. That's why the battle over Bush's judicial appointments is so crucial to the future of the America we know and love. And that's why the clock is running out on freedom-loving Americans.

Scalia himself appears to be a Dominionist, for he believes that Romans 13 represents the correct view—that government authority is derived from God and not from the people; he asserts that his view was the consensus of Western thought until recent times. Like Pat Robertson, he laments that the biblical perspective was upset by "the emergence of democracy."[74] Taking his cue from Leo Strauss, Scalia argued, "A democratic government, being nothing more than the composite will of its individual citizens, has no more moral power or authority than they do as individuals." Democracy, according to Scalia, creates problems: "It fosters civil disobedience."[75]

As Patricia Williams wrote: "God bless America. The Constitution is dead."[76]

DOMINIONISM'S THEOCRATIC VIEWS

What would a "reconstructed" America look like under the Dominionists? K. L. Gentry, a Dominionist himself, suggests the following "elements of a theonomic approach to civic order," which I strongly suggest should be compared to the Texas GOP platform of 2002, which reveals that we are not just talking about imaginary ideas but some things are already proposed on Republican agendas.[77] Dominionism's concept of government, according to Gentry, is as follows:

1. It obligates government to maintain just monetary policies . . . [thus prohibiting] fiat money, fractional reserve banking, and deficit spending.
2. It provides a moral basis for elective government officials. . . .
3. It forbids undue, abusive *taxation of the rich*. . . . [empashis mine]
4. It calls for the abolishing of the prison system and establishing a system of just restitution. . . .
5. A theonomic approach also forbids the release, pardoning, and paroling of murderers by requiring their execution. . . .
6. It forbids industrial pollution that destroys the value of property. . . .
7. It punishes malicious, frivolous malpractice suits. . . .
8. It forbids abortion rights. . . . Abortion is not only a sin, but a crime, and, indeed, a capital crime.[78]

The fourth item in Gentry's list, "abolishing of the prison system and establishing a system of just restitution" has been worked on extensively by Dominionist Gary North, who holds a doctorate degree in economics. North has written volumes of books, essays, and articles (many of which falsely predicted that the year 2000 computer problem would bring down modern civilization). He is most famous among Dominionists for reconciling economic theory with Old Testament passages.

Gary North describes the "just restitution" system of the Bible, which happens to reinstitute slavery, like this: "At the other end of the curve, the poor man who steals is eventually caught and sold into bondage under a successful person. His victim receives payment; he receives training; his buyer receives a stream of labor services. If the servant is successful and buys his way out of bondage, he re-enters society as a disciplined man, and presumably a self-disciplined man. He begins to accumulate wealth."[79]

THE IMMORALITY OF THE MEDICARE AND MEDICAID PROGRAMS

If the blithe acceptance of slavery isn't shocking enough, here is one of the coldest attitudes I ever heard expressed in an interview on American television. I can't help reading it in light of the coercive bullying tactics resorted to by Dominionist leaders in the House of Representatives to get the necessary votes to pass the controversial new Medicare prescription drug law.[80] The following interview reveals the deep-seated hatred Dominionists have against governmental medical assistance to the elderly. The interview was conducted on August 1, 1985, with Dr. Walter Williams, professor of economics at George Mason University and author of thirty-five books. Danuta Soderman was a cohost on Pat Robertson's *The 700 Club*. She began the interview with a question about Medicare and Medicaid fraud, suggesting they cost possibly "millions and billions" of dollars:

> WILLIAMS: Well, I think that the abuse and fraud in and of itself is a relatively minor problem. That is, the bigger problem is the whole concept of funding somebody's medical care by a third party. And I might also mention here, that is, I saw in the audience many older and senior citizens. Now whose responsibility is it to take care of those people? I think it lies with their children and it also lies with themselves. That is, I think Christians should recognize that charity is good. I mean charity, when you reach into your pocket to help your fellow man for medical care or for food or to give them housing. But what the government is doing in order to help these older citizens is not charity at all. It is theft. That is, the government is using power to confiscate property that belongs to one American and give, or confiscate, their money and provide services for another set of Americans to whom it does not belong. That is the moral question that Christians should face with not only Medicare, Medicaid, but many other programs as well. . . . Well, people should have insurance. But I would say if our fellow man is found in need, does not have enough, well that's a role for the church, that's a role for the family, that's a role for private institutions to take care of these things.

> DANUTA SODERMAN: I thought it was interesting you talked about Medicare and Medicaid as not being a moral issue. A lot of people would think that to want to eliminate the program is rather uncompassionate—that there is something immoral about taking away something that people are relying so heavily upon, but you said that there is no moral issue here.

WILLIAMS: I think the moral issue runs the other way. That is, we have to ask ourselves, "What is the moral basis of confiscating the property of one American and giving it to another American to whom it does not belong for whatever reason?" That is, I think we Americans have to ask ourselves, "Is there something that can justify a legalized theft?" And I think that even if the person is starving in the street that act, in and of itself, doesn't justify my taking money from somebody else.

HOW TO DESTROY THE SOCIAL SECURITY PROGRAM

On August 14, 1985, Pat Robertson unveiled his ingenious program on how to get rid of Social Security. The plan amazingly resembles sections of the Bush administration's Medicare prescription drug bill passed in December 2003. Robertson, however, outlined what to do twenty years ago on his TV program as follows:

1. We should say to all the elderly, "You're going to be taken care of. The government's going to pay you. Don't worry about it. [You'll] get your Social Security like you're expecting, 'cause you're counting on it."
2. There should be a gradual moving [up] of [the retirement] age to reflect the fact that we're healthier and we live longer and people should have dignity and be allowed to work a little bit longer.
3. The last thing we should do is to begin to let the younger workers slowly but surely go into private programs where the money is tax sheltered and over the years build up their own money and that would in turn, through the intermediary organizations, banks, insurance companies, would invest in American industry. They would buy plants and equipment, put people to work and it would help a tremendous boom. Imagine . . . $100 billion dollars a year flowing into American industry. It would be marvelous.

WEALTH IS A SIGN OF GOD'S FAVOR, POVERTY IS A SIGN OF GOD'S DISFAVOR

How did the Dominionists get so far from the Lord's edict to help the poor, the sick, and the elderly? Using the text of Deuteronomy 28, which is a list of God's blessings and curses, Robertson and other Dominionists believe that the chapter reveals God's covenanted economic law. God only bestows "material wealth or blessings" upon those who are among his elect and he does so because these are the individuals and nations who obey his commandments and laws. So what about the poor? Dominionist Gary North explains it this way: "God is sovereign over the poor. He raises them up—not all of them, but some of them. 'The Lord maketh poor, and maketh rich: he bringeth low, and lifteth up.'"[81]

I grant that the verse cited leaves government assistance out of the picture. North claims that the blessings and sanctions of Deuteronomy 28 are historical. He says, "They are predictable. Covenantal rebellion by a society will lead to God's imposition of these sanctions."[82] North then ties the package up neatly: "The blessings and cursings of God under the Mosaic Covenant were sure. They were not disconnected from God's law. There was a bedrock objectivity that united covenant-keepers and covenant-breakers."[83]

To understand what North is talking about, we have to read a portion of the text of Deuteronomy 28: "The Lord shall establish thee an holy people unto himself, as he hath sworn unto thee . . . and the Lord shall make thee the head and not the tail; and thou shalt be above only, and thou shalt not be beneath. . . ." A conclusion drawn by the scripture itself is that a nation that follows the commandments or laws of God will be "high above all nations of the earth . . . and all people of the earth shall see that thou art called by the name of the Lord, and they shall be afraid of thee." On the other hand, the Dominionists believe those who are poor, sick, and weak are so situated because God's wrath has been visited upon them—they are the "wicked" of this earth and they deserve the wrath of God because their behavior is bringing the entire nation under condemnation.

The litany of the curses of God on those who do not keep his laws and commandments is among the most horrendous descriptions of torture in literature. Here is a sample from Deuteronomy 28:

> The Lord shall cause thee to be smitten before thine enemies . . . thy carcass shall be food unto all fowls of the air. . . . The Lord will smite thee with [boils] . . . and with . . . tumors, and with the scab, and with the itch, whereof thou canst not be healed. The Lord shall smite thee with madness and blindness and astonishment of heart [fear]; thou shalt grope at noonday; thou shalt not prosper in thy ways; and thou shalt be only oppressed and spoiled evermore . . . thou shalt betroth a wife and another man shall lie with her; thou shalt build an house, and thou shalt not dwell therein, and thine ox shall be slain before thine eyes, and thou

shalt not eat thereof; thine ass shall be violently taken away from before thy face and shall not be restored to thee; they sheep shall be given unto thine enemies, and thou shalt have none to rescue them. Thy sons and thy daughters shall be given unto another people, and thine eyes shall look, and fail with longing for them all the day long; and there shall be no might in thine hand. The fruit of thy land, and all thy labors, shall a nation whom thou knowest not eat up, and thou shalt be only oppressed and crushed always. . . ."

North explained: "The point of Deuteronomy 28 is this: the way to wealth, both individual and corporate, is through systematic adherence to God's Bible-revealed law."[84] Hence the idea that should a nation minister to the poor or attempt to lift the poor out of poverty or save people from poverty and ill health, that nation is contravening the will of Almighty God and such legislation is contrary to the laws of God. It is only one step further to say that if this is God's attitude toward the poor, it is morally wrong to help them. So it's easy to see how Social Security and Medicare are viewed by Dominionists as "evil" programs that rob money from some citizens to enrich others.

There's one other little trap for the unwary Dominionist; when a government is seen to be the enforcer of the Deuteronomic laws, it's easy to take the next step and say that it is the duty of the "Christian" Dominionist government to subdue the wicked of the world, especially the vast American middle class, because its collective licentious lifestyle is bringing the nation down as a whole; therefore, the government must "minister the wrath of God" against the citizens of America as punishment for "rebelliousness." That the entire scheme is an unending circular argument escapes the notice of the rank and file sitting in the pews.

In their new role as ministers of God's wrath against this nation, Dominionist political strategists are aware that they must not be seen as being cruel and hateful. So at first, until the population is completely subdued and dominated by the elect, Dominionists are forced to devise laws that will create the political, social, and medical environment that will ultimately ensure that the wicked are punished—but it will appear, at first blush, to be a gift. The truth, of course, according to Machiavellian/Straussian dictates, must be hidden from the population; not just once or twice, but over and over again.

In the end, Dominionism should be viewed as a backboard that bounces the New Deal and FDR's social safety net programs, Social Security (as well as Medicare) into their political opposite: laissez-faire economics (the motto of eighteenth-century French economists who protested excessive government regulation of industry). Laissez-faire is a doctrine opposing governmental interference (as by regulation or subsidy) in economic affairs beyond the minimum necessary for the maintenance of peace and property rights. Dominionism opposes the licensing and regulating power of the government.

One last comment on Pat Robertson. On November 3, 1986, *The 700 Club* ran a piece on the use of computers in counting votes. Robertson ended his "Perspective" by saying there should be some kind of control on computer voting to assure an honest count. How prescient this man is! And how worrisome his prescience is.

WHO IS ON THE SIDE OF FREEDOM? LET HIM SPEAK NOW!

There is an infection, a religious and political pathology, that has corrupted our churches. Those we trusted the most have embraced evil. That knowledge is almost more than we can bear. Who among us will stand in the gap and make up the hedge to save our nation?

When we look for help—for the wealthy leaders with the means to help rescue America—we find they have all defected to the Dominionists. They do not realize that if the middle class of America is wiped out, there will be no one to buy their cars, their computers, or their products. Only one or two brave souls like George Soros have made massive contributions to combat the think tanks and the organized political machine of the Dominionists. The corporate press lies sleeping, not realizing they will be allowed to report only what they are instructed to report.

Freedom is under siege. There is only one free major political party still left in America. I know the Democrats look chaotic, unfocused, and generally unsmooth and, thank God, unprogrammed. Make no mistake, these plain ordinary citizens are holding the candles that together form the great torch of liberty. For all their faults, they love America and they love freedom and they love the Bill of Rights. America's independents, its true conservatives, its sensible Republicans, and its Libertarians must join hands together with the homely Democrats and take back America for all Americans.

The livelihood of the working people of America is at stake. The Dominionists have lost more American jobs in the last three years than since the days of Herbert Hoover. And now they want to eliminate the minimum wage laws, too. America's unions have helped to create a better life for millions of workers. The Dominionists want to break all unions apart (especially the teachers' union). As Americans, we love our schools and are proud of our educational system. The Dominionists want to destroy all public education in America and force Americans to be educated in their religious schools. Americans love our culture and the arts. The Dominionists want to destroy that culture.

The election of 2004 is not just another election. It is the battle of the century. It is the gravest political war since the Civil War, which if lost, spells the end of Independence Day and every right in the Bill of Rights that we have fought so hard to preserve. Is there an American, regardless of his or her party, who would not fight for our democracy? It's in jeopardy now. Our friends and cousins in Britain, France, Australia, New Zealand and scores of other nations have seen our jeopardy and have been crying out for months and days and years to wake up America!

Let me see your face and look into your eyes. Let me hear you say, "There is no difference between the two parties." May God help us and grant us discernment when we vote.

NOTES

1. "Religious Right Finds Its Center in Oval Office," *Washington Post,* December 24, 2001.

2. Kevin P. Phillips, *American Dynasty: Aristocracy, Fortune, and the Politics of Deceit in the House of Bush* (New York: Viking, 2004), p. 224.

3. Antonin Scalia, "God's Justice and Ours," *First Things* 123 (May 2002): 17–21, http://www.firstthings.com/ftissues/ft0205/articles/scalia.html.

4. Leo Strauss, *Thoughts on Machiavelli* (Chicago: University of Chicago Press, 1984), p. 9. The actual quotation is: "[O]ne ought not to say to someone whom one wants to kill, 'Give me your gun, I want to kill you with it,' but merely, 'Give me your gun,' for once you have the gun in your hand, you can satisfy your desire."

5. Osha Gray Davidson, "Dirty Secrets," *Mother Jones,* September/October 2003, p. 53. "The Bush administration has been gutting key sections of the Clean Water and Clean Air acts, laws that have traditionally had bipartisan support and have done more to protect the health of Americans than any other environmental legislation." The subtitle reads: "No president has gone after the nation's environmental laws with the same fury as George W. Bush and none has been so adept at staying under the radar."

6. Alan Sager and Deborah Socolar, "61 Percent of Medicare's New Prescrip-

tion Drug Subsidy Is Windfall Profit to Drug Makers," Boston University School of Public Health, October 31, 2003, http://www.healthreformprogram.org. The report is available in a PDF file at http://www.yuricareport.com/Medicare/ Medicare_Rx_bill_windfallprofitBostonU.pdf.

7. See Pat Robertson's prescription on how to eliminate Social Security as described on page 216 of this chapter.

8. Pat Robertson ironically outlined the drastic effects that follow rash government spending in 1985, stating that it will wipe out the middle class and destroy the Social Security and Medicare programs. (Taped and transcribed by the author.) See Katherine Yurica, "Pat Robertson Said 'Congress Is Buying Votes with Your Money and My Money," Yurica Report, http://www.yuricareport.com/Campaign 2004/PatRobertsonCongressBuyingVotes.html.

9. If my words appear extreme, consider that in January 2004, Walter Cronkite broke a lifetime rule, saying, "I must speak out." Cronkite continued, "I am deeply disturbed by the dangerous and growing influence of people like Pat Robertson and Jerry Falwell on our nation's political leaders" (an open letter from Walter Cronkite and the Interfaith Alliance, January 2004). Former governor of Delaware Russ Peterson in his new book, *Patriots, Stand Up! This Land Is Our Land, Let's Fight to Take It Back* (Wilmington, DE: Cedar Tree Books, 2003), wrote:

Our cherished American way of life is under attack by the far right-wing Republicans who are now running the White House, the Senate and the House of Representatives. This is the product of a conspiracy that has been growing over the past few decades through the use of evil tactics and strategies, lies and deceptions to transform America.

Deception is now the hallmark of the Bush administration. Read of the frightening chicanery in furthering an imperial strategy, nurturing the military-industrial complex, waging war on the environment, plunging the nation into debt, demeaning the needy, antagonizing the world and using terrorism to frighten and exploit.

The author calls on patriots to apply the principles of democracy now to retake America from a conservative elite that controls the country.

Peterson's Web site, http://www.governorpeterson.org, provides the following description of his background:

Russ Peterson, scientist, citizen activist, former executive with the DuPont Co., Republican governor of Delaware, assistant to Republican Gov. Nelson Rockefeller of New York, head of the US Council on Environmental Quality under Presidents Nixon and Ford, head of the Office of Technology Assessment, reporting to six Republican and six Democratic members of Congress, president of the National Audubon Society, internationally acclaimed environmental leader, United Nations goodwill ambassador, and faculty member at Dartmouth College, Carleton College and the University of Wisconsin Madison. His numerous national and international awards include 15 honorary doctorates. In 1996 he became a Democrat.

10. Frederick Clarkson, "Christian Reconstructionism: Theocratic Dominionism Gains Influence," *Public Eye*, March/June 1994, part 1 of a four-part series, http://www.publiceye.org/magazine/v08n1/chrisre1.html.

11. Gary North, PhD, president of the Institute for Christian Economics (ICE) and son-in-law of R. J. Rushdoony, the founder of Christian Reconstructionism, advises his followers not to give out his literature to everyone—only to interested people. "Let word of mouth tell the story. You need not become very visible if you choose not to." From "Replacing Evil with Good," chapter 8 of North's *Conspiracy: A Biblical View*, http://reformed-theology.org/ice/books/conspiracy/html/8.htm, p. 9. For a complete understanding of how good and evil are inverted and the "conspirators" become *us*, see the entire book at http://reformed-theology.org/ice/books/conspiracy/index.html. Click on each section of the table of contents, which can be reached only by entering the Web site from the root directory.

12. See Joan Bokaer, "Taking over the Republican Party," The Rise of the Religious Right in the Republican Party, a public information project from TheocracyWatch.org, http://www.4religious-right.info/taking_over.htm.

13. Ben Kinchlow, cohost of *The 700 Club* with Pat Robertson, was made vice president of CBN in charge of CBN's charities program "Operation Blessing." On March 27, 1985, while criticizing farmers for wanting a government bailout, he said: "What's wrong in this country is that so many people have substituted the government for God. Instead of looking to God to supply their needs, they're looking to government." Railing at financially stressed people was very common on the show.

14. Tim LaHaye predicted on Pat Robertson's *The 700 Club* on September 25, 1985, that 110,000 evangelical, fundamentalist, and Pentecostal churches could sponsor one person per church to run for office and win, that *in a decade* they would hold every office in the United States. At the time, he said there were only 97,000 public offices in the United States so "we would have more Christians in office than there are positions." By 1994, for the first time in forty years, Republicans regained control of Congress. Similarly, Ralph Reed predicted that by the year 2000 they would control Congress. Gary North wrote in 1985: "I propose a program. Some variant of this program must be adopted if we are to have any meaningful hope in recapturing the machinery of civil government, the media, and the educational institutions. It will be done. It has already begun. How long it will take is problematical; I think we will begin to see major victories before the year 2005." "Replacing Evil with Good," p. 5.

15. Francis Schaeffer originally appeared on *The 700 Club* with Pat Robertson in 1982. The series of interviews with Schaeffer was repeated on the show in the week of July 7, 1986, as Robertson presented the legal and biblical foundations for Christian political action. Schaeffer, however, died between the first and second airing. The Schaeffer interviews were tape recorded and transcribed; my quotations are from my transcript. The accuracy of my transcript can be compared to the videotapes of the shows. At the time, *People for the American Way* was recording the shows and establishing a Pat Robertson *700 Club* library for future reference.

16. All *700 Club* quotations in this chapter were recorded and transcribed by the author and her assistant unless otherwise indicated.

17. Although neither Robertson nor Schaeffer used the words *Dominionism* or *dominion* in this interview series, both used the word *dominant* when asking which culture was dominant in the United States: the Christian culture or the humanistic culture. They asserted that the humanistic culture was the dominant force in America and "Christians" had to regain dominance.

18. The most successful ministers knew the psychological importance of creating "enemies" that were attacking the church. Jerry Falwell maintains the rule: "To be successful, keep a good fight going all the time."

19. Psychiatrist Scott Peck has written about the phenomena groups resort to almost universally: "There are profound forces at work within a group to keep its individual members together and in line. . . . Probably the most powerful of these group cohesive forces is narcissism . . . group pride. . . . A less benign but practically universal form of group narcissism is what might be called 'enemy creation,' or hatred of the 'out-group.'" *The People of the Lie: The Hope for Healing Human Evil* (New York: Simon and Schuster, 1983).

20. TheocracyWatch.org, "War on Secular Society," The Rise of the Religious Right in the Republican Party, January 2004, http://www.4religious-right.info/introduction2.htm.

21. In short, they needed a religion of their own to justify evil acts and to counter the political acceptance by many Christians who were attracted to the communal and "communistic" principles of the early church (Acts 2:42–47), in which the early Christians sold all their possessions, gave them to the needy, and held "all things [in] common." Such Christian ideas were a direct threat to capitalism's future robber barons. How could great fortunes be amassed if one had to give it all away to the poor and follow Jesus? (Matt. 19:16–30).

22. Pat Robertson is particularly adept at changing the issue from questioning an aggressively religious political agenda into an *attack* on religion. The Constitution prohibits a religious test for office in America (Article VI). However, a battle over the nomination of Herb Ellingwood in 1985 to the position of assistant attorney general for legal policy caused a firestorm. (That office screens candidates for the federal judiciary.) During the same period, Dominionists like Ellingwood and Tim LaHaye were advocating that 25 percent of all government positions

should be handed to Christian fundamentalists (Dominionists) because they made up 25 percent of the nation's population. Pat Schroeder, former Democratic congresswoman from Colorado and chairman of the Civil Service Committee, strongly opposed the view as a religious quota system and a violation of Article VI of the Constitution. She said the questions that were asked of judicial candidates, apparently prepared by Ellingwood, amounted to a religious test for office. She spoke on *Donahue* (the Phil Donahue show) on September 6, 1985:

> If you look at some of the questions that are being asked by some of the senators of judges, they don't have to do with their background, their training, whether or not they understand the law, they have to do with personal beliefs. That's not where we have been in the past, and that's a very dangerous turn. . . .

During the same period (August–September), Pat Robertson easily turned the legitimate questioning of Herb Ellingwood's agenda into an attack on Christianity by framing it this way on his *The 700 Club* on August 9, 1985:

> Can an evangelical Christian hold high office in the United States of America? Now that is the question. Or are evangelical Christians going to be discriminated against? And indeed will there be a religious test for public office which disqualifies anybody who speaks to a religious group? . . . Herb Ellingwood is chairman right now of the Merit Protection Review Board and he has done a superb job. He was the former legal counsel to President Reagan in California and has worked closely with Ed Meese for years. He's been a very distinguished attorney. It just seems like this campaign of assassination that goes on against good men like that should be brought to a stop. . . . And if you feel that Christians ought to be allowed to serve in positions of responsibility in the government . . . and you don't think that Christians should be discriminated against . . . here's the number of the White House: 202-446-7639. . . .

23. Niccolò Machiavelli, *The Prince*, trans. Luigi Ricci, 1903; rev. E. R. P. Vincent (London: Oxford University Press, 1935), p. 93.

24. Ibid., p. 94.

25. One cannot help comparing this passage with the fact that twenty-seven thousand bombs were dropped on Iraq in the 2003 air war and in a demonstration of cold indifference, the Bush administration ignored the advice of prominent archeologists to protect Iraq's museums, which contained the greatest collection of ancient relics, art, and ancient treasures in the world, and in so doing, allowed the looting—the despoiling—of that nation's treasures.

26. Machiavelli, *The Prince*, p. 46.

27. Ibid.

28. James Hogg, *The Private Memoirs and Confessions of a Justified Sinner* (1824; New York: W. W. Norton, 1970).

29. Again, because we will learn in this article that Machiavelli is a handbook in the Bush administration, one must ask if the George W. Bush administration perceives *despoiling* as a plan of action to control the *American* populace. The question must be asked.

30. Donald Spitz, interview by Brian Copeland, KGO, San Francisco, September 5, 2003.

31. See Kevin Phillips, *American Dynasty: Aristocracy, Fortune, and the Politics of Deceit in the House of Bush* (New York: Viking, 2004), pp. 239–40.

32. Ibid., p. 321.

33. Robertson's and Ledeen's relationship continues. For a recent CBN interview of Ledeen conducted by Pat Robertson and transcribed by CBN.com, go to "Protestors Pressing Iran's Shaky Regime," CBN News, 2004, http://cbn.com/CBN News/News/030623e.asp?option=print. Ledeen tried to arrange the sale of arms to Iran in order to divert the profits to the Contra militants who were fighting the Nicaraguan government's Sandinistas. However, Congress had voted to cut off US aid to the Contras and therefore any such transaction was illegal.

34. William O. Beeman, "Who Is Michael Ledeen?" AlterNet.org, May 8, 2003, http://www.alternet.org/story.html?StoryID=15860.

35. Gerard Thomas Straub worked at CBS for eight years before joining *The 700 Club* as executive producer. After leaving CBN's employment, he went to work for ABC's *General Hospital* as associate producer. His 1986 book, *Salvation for Sale* (Amherst, NY: Prometheus Books), offers insights to how Pat Robertson conducted business off camera from the perspective of an insider. The dichotomy between his public friendly "pastoral" role and his actual business conduct is stark evidence that he understood Machiavelli's rule that only appearance counts. Straub wrote: "In reality Pat is a pompous pope of the video Vatican of Christian broadcasting, and he rules his empire with absolute authority. He does not tolerate debate, discussions, or dissent. . . . His television followers never get to see the tough-minded, hard-driving cut-throat leader." In addition, over the years, Pat Robertson revealed his Machiavellian political philosophy repeatedly and openly on his show in discussions of how to handle foreign policy and in his ruthless approach to the poor and needy of America.

36. On June 19, 1985, Danuta Soderman, the second member of Pat Robertson's daily team, asked Pat Robertson how the United States should deal with Middle East terrorist groups: "Speaking about being decisive in dealing with terrorist groups, yesterday you offered some opinion on how Iran should be one of the places we should target our energies on. Any other thoughts on this?" Robertson responded:

Just like the last guest in that clip our news department did, he said it's pretty much undeclared war. Khomeini has declared war against the United States. He has told people that if they die against the infidel, they go to heaven. The Islamic Jihad is controlled out of Iran, and the other factor of course is Syria, which is giving some sanctuary to all of these people. Syria controls the Becca Valley now—practically all of it, since Israel withdrew its forces. So up in the Becca Valley the Shiite Muslims from Iran are forcing the Lebanese women to wear veils and practice the various extreme views of the Islamic faith in the Shiite traditions. We've got to go after the source. *If you want to go after a snake, you don't cut inches off his tail.* (Emphasis mine)

Robertson also focused on the Becca Valley on July 12, 1985, and on several other occasions. The refrain has not changed in nineteen years. A January 2004 article published in the *Jerusalem Post* states that Secretary of Defense Donald Rumsfeld is considering invading the Becca Valley, which as of this writing is still controlled by Syria.

37. See "Statement of Principles," Project for the New American Century, June 3, 1997, http://newamericancentury.org/statementofprinciples.htm and "Rebuilding America's Defenses: Strategy, Forces, and Resources for a New Century," Project for the New American Century, September 2000, http://newamericancentury.org/RebuildingAmericasDefenses.pdf.

38. Michael A. Ledeen, *Machiavelli on Modern Leadership: Why Machiavelli's Iron Rules Are as Timely and Important Today as Five Centuries Ago* (New York: Truman Valley Books, 1999), p. 91.

39. Ibid., p. 93.

40. Ibid., p. 95.

41. Ibid.

42. Beeman, "Who Is Michael Ledeen?"

43. BBC News, "Michael Ledeen," Panorama, 2003, http://news.bbc.co.uk/1/hi/programmes/panorama/3031803.stm. A longer and more important article is Jim Lobe, "Veteran Neo-con Advisor Moves on Iran," *Asia Times*, June 26, 2003, http://www.atimes.com/atimes/Middle_East/EF26Ak03.html. Another very interesting article is John Laughland, "Flirting with Fascism: Neocon Theorist Michael Ledeen Draws More from Italian Fascism Than from the American Right," *American Conservative*, June 30, 2003, http://www.amconmag.com/06_30_03/print/featureprint.html. For a recent interview with Ledeen conducted by Pat Robertson on CBN.com, see note 27.

44. Quoted in Lobe, "Veteran Neo-con Advisor Moves on Iran."

45. Shadia B. Drury, *Leo Strauss and the American Right* (New York: St. Martin's Press, 1997), p. 1.

46. Leo Strauss, *Thoughts on Machiavelli* (Chicago: University of Chicago Press, 1984), pp. 10–11.

47. Ibid., pp. 176–78.

48. The only example of this possibility I have found so far is in the work of Dominionist Gary North, who wrote tirelessly on the correlations between conservative economic principles and the Old Testament laws and rules. See North, "The Covenantal Wealth of Nations," *Biblical Economics Today* 21, no. 2 (February/March 1999), http://reformed-theology.org/ice/newslet/bet/bet99.02.htm. See also J. Ligon Duncan III, "Moses' Law for Modern Government: The Intellectual and Sociological Origins of the Christian Reconstructionist Movement," *Premise*, May 27, 1995, p. 4, http://capo.org/premise/95/may/ssha2.html. Ligon states that "Reconstructionism is attempting to make a systematic and exegetical connection between the Bible and the conservative ideology of limited government and free market economics. For instance, Gary North has written volume after volume deriving principles of economics from his studies of the Pentateuch."

49. Drury, *Leo Strauss and the American Right*, pp. 11–13.

50. Drury, quoted in Jim Lobe, "Strong Must Rule the Weak, said Neo-Cons' Muse," Inter Press Service News Agency, May 7, 2003, http://www.ipsnews.net/interna.asp?idnews=18038.

51. Drury, *Leo Strauss and the American Right*, p. 23.

52. Ibid.

53. I am indebted to Patricia J. Williams, professor of law at Columbia University, for this insight. See her article, "Infallible Justice," *Nation*, October 7, 2002, http://www.thenation.com/docprint.mhtml?i=20021007&s=williams. Not only is the concept of "original intent" brilliant and revolutionary, it in fact goes further than any other political format to legitimize the conversion of present day jurisprudence back to the judicial *weltanschauung* (worldview) of eighteenth-century jurists. It is the key factor in the Dominionists' intent to establish biblical law over all Americans. Two Supreme Court justices subscribe to it already. In other words, as Williams has pointed out, the rule would effectively repeal most of the judicial decisions made in the last century.

54. Drury, *Leo Strauss and the American Right*, p. 106.

55. Ibid.

56. See the online excerpts from my book *The New Messiahs* (1988), http://www.yuricareport.com/Art%20Essays/The%20New%20Messiahs%20Excerpts.htm which trace the political machinations of the Dominionists within the Republican Party and the plot to take over all three branches of the government of the United States.

57. Duncan, "Moses' Law for Modern Government."

58. Although the book has been revised, my quotations are from the original edition.

59. Social Darwinism, the discredited extension of Charles Darwin's evolutionary theory to the human social condition, takes Darwin's concept "the survival of the fittest" and applies it to the idea that the ladder to material wealth and to

the "good life" may be climbed only after one has successfully engaged in group battles and conflicts and prevailed in the pit of life by drop-kicking one's opponents. Those who climb out of the pit and up the ladder become the socially recognized victors in the competition and are considered biologically superior to those who fail. The illogical fallout from this concept is the circular argument that the existence of a socially elite class must be proof that those who possess wealth and power are necessarily superior to those in economic classes below them.

60. Dominionists may argue with some credibility that they do believe in helping the poor; however, they want churches to undertake that task and adamantly fight against government social aid programs funded from tax monies—unless, of course, it is a so-called faith-based initiative. Pat Robertson forgot his objections to the government's handing out money and gratefully accepted the $500,000 President Bush sent him early in his administration for "good faith-based charitable work." Regardless of their protestations, however, the churches of America cannot and do not have the billions of dollars to provide the social safety net for the poor, elderly, and sick among America's population. In 1985, for example, Robertson bragged that CBN gave $50 million worth of food, clothes, and supplies to 8.5 million people, but that was what he called "leveraged" contributions, in which CBN had joined with other charities. Robertson admitted that they gave only $10 million. Deducting the $2 million of CBN's contributions to the Contras in Central America, CBN's total contribution amounted to only about eighty-eight cents to every hungry, needy person he said CBN had helped.

61. Pat Robertson wrote in *The Secret Kingdom* (Dallas: Word Publishing, 1992):

Unhappily, evangelical Christians have for too long reduced the born-again experience to the issue of being "saved." Salvation is an important issue, obviously, and must never be deemphasized. But rebirth must be seen as a beginning, not an arrival. It provides access to the invisible world, the kingdom of God, of which we are to learn and experience and then share with others. Jesus Himself said it clearly before His ascension: "All authority has been given to Me in heaven and on earth. Go therefore and *make disciples* of all the nations, baptizing them in the name of the Father and the Son and the Holy Spirit, *teaching them to observe all that I commanded you*; and lo, I am with you always, even to the end of the age." [Matt. 28:18–20, New American Standard Bible]. The commission was to make followers and learners—converts—and to teach them the principles of the kingdom. Entry into the body of believers was not enough. They were to learn how to live in this world. . . . The invisible was to rule the visible. Christ has authority over both. (p. 51, emphasis in original)

62. Ibid., p. 82.

63. Ibid., p. 201.

64. Ibid., p. 82.

65. Ibid., p. 83.

66. Ibid.

67. James Poniewozik, "10 Questions for Sean Hannity," *Time,* November 11, 2002.

68. Quoted in Mark S. Zaid, "The New, Unabashed McCarthyism: A Review of *Treason: Liberal Treachery from the Cold War to the War on Terrorism* by Ann Coulter," originally published by Findlaw.com and reprinted with permission at Yurica Report, http://www.yuricareport.com/RevisitedBks/ZaidonCoulterTreason.htm.

69. Scalia, "God's Justice and Ours."

70. Ibid.

71. Ibid.

72. Williams, "Infallible Justice."

73. Scalia, "God's Justice and Ours."

74. Ibid.

75. Ibid.

76. Williams, "Infallible Justice."

77. TheocracyWatch.org, "The Rise of the Religious Right in the Republican Party," http://www.4religious-right.info/texas_gop.htm, provides the following excerpts from the platform of the Republican Party of Texas:

"The Republican Party of Texas reaffirms the United States of America is a Christian Nation. . . ."

1. GOVERNMENT:

"We reclaim freedom of religious expression in public on government property, and freedom from government interference. Support government display of Ten Commandments."

Dispel the "myth" of the separation of church and state.

A strong and vibrant private sector [should be] unencumbered by excessive government regulation.

Oppose Campaign Finance Reform.

Oppose any form of gun control.

Abolish:
- Bureau of Alcohol, Tobacco and Firearms;
- Position of Surgeon General;
- EPA;
- Department of Energy; Department of Housing and Urban Development;
- Department of Education; Department of Commerce and Labor; National Endowment for the Arts.

2. ECONOMY:

Abolish the dollar in favor of the gold standard.

Abolish the IRS.

Eliminate income tax, inheritance tax, gift tax, capital gains, corporate income tax, payroll tax and property tax.

Repeal minimum wage law.

". . . gradually phase out Social Security tax for a system of 'private pensions.'"

3. UNITED NATIONS:

". . . We immediately rescind our membership in, as well as all financial and military contributions to the United Nations."

We should ". . . evict the United Nations from the United States and eliminate any further participation."

4. FAMILY:

We believe that traditional marriage is a legal and moral commitment between a man and a woman.

We recognize that the family is the foundational unit of a healthy society and consists of those related by blood, marriage, or adoption.

The family is responsible for its own welfare, education, moral training, conduct, and property.

"The practice of sodomy tears at the heart of our society . . ."

"The party oppose[s] decriminalization of sodomy."

Oppose all forms of abortion—even in cases of rape or incest.

"We unequivocally oppose United States Senate ratification of the United Nations Convention on the Rights of the Child."

5. EDUCATION:

"We call for the abolition of the US Department of Education and the prohibition of the transfer of any of its functions to any other federal agency."

Support official prayer in public schools.

Oppose Early Childhood Development Programs.

"We support . . . a program based upon biblical principles. . . ."

Terminate bilingual education.

"Since Secular Humanism is recognized by the United States Supreme Court as a religion . . . Secular Humanism should be subjected to the same state and federal laws as any other recognized religions."

6. THE ENVIRONMENT:

Oppose the "myth" of global warming.

Reaffirm "the belief in the fundamental right of an individual to use property without governmental interference."

Oppose EPA management of Texas air quality.

7. THE MIDDLE EAST:

". . . Jerusalem is the capital of Israel . . ." therefore, the United States should move its embassy from Tel Aviv to Jerusalem.

To read the complete platform, go to Platform Committee, "2002 Texas State Republican Party Platform," http://www.texasgop.org/library/RPTPlatform2002.pdf.

78. Duncan, "Moses' Law for Modern Government."

79. North, "The Covenantal Wealth of Nations."

80. Katherine Yurica, "Rogue Republican Dons in Congress Tear Up the Constitution, Exclude Democrats, and Accept a New Title: 'The Godfathers,'" Yurica Report, December 29, 2003, http://www.yuricareport.com/Corruption/RogueRepublicanBillsUnconstitutional.htm.

81. North, "The Covenantal Wealth of Nations."

82. Ibid.

83. Ibid.

84. Ibid.

KATHERINE YURICA was educated at East Los Angeles College, USC, and the USC school of law. She worked as a consultant for Los Angeles County and as a news correspondent for *Christianity Today* and as a freelance investigative reporter. The author of three books, she is also the publisher of the *Yurica Report*.

Yurica recorded and transcribed 1,300 pages of Pat Robertson's television show, *The 700 Club*, covering several years in the mid-1980s. In 1987, she conducted a study in response to informal inquiries from the staff of the Subcommittee on Oversight of the House Ways and Means Committee of the US House of Representatives, which was investigating whether television and radio ministries were violating their tax-exempt status by conducting grassroots political appeals, endorsing candidates, and making political expenditures as defined under Section 527 of the IRS code. The Subcommittee on Oversight published Yurica's study of *Federal Tax Rules Applicable to Tax-Exempt Organizations Involving Television Ministries* on October 6, 1987, Serial 100-43 (published in 1988).

Part III
Global Humanism

14.

Global Humanism
Paradox and the
Concept of the Future

Harvey Sarles

*I assert that a key component of the Humanist project must
be the socio-political task of bringing into effect humanistic
changes in one's own society. When we put our priorities on
working towards greater political and economic democracy
at home (and we all have much further to go in this regard),
we contribute directly to the Humanist goal of giving our
fellow citizens greater power and control over their own
lives.*

—Don Page

Is this *the* moment in history when the ideas of humanism, based on an inclusive rationalism, might be introduced into the context of a global society? These ideas certainly seem to be universal in scope as they underlie the idea of human rights. And they are at least theoretically inclusive as applying to all people(s) in all places: a sense of individual rights and responsibilities; a global conversation concerning the ways in which we/they want to govern ourselves; a government representing all people in a singular republic, thus a global democracy.

This is a time when the world's greater and lesser political entities (countries, city-states) and traditions now meet in the large, but also in the small of interpersonal acts and interactions in many regions and most cities of the world.[1] Through developments in communication and transportation, we now form an increasingly cosmopolitan population, which

---

© Harvey B. Sarles, Professor of Cultural Studies and Comparative Literature, University of Minnesota.

meets frequently in actual interaction and in the global instantaneity of television and virtual reality.

This is also a time when the world's greatest gathering traditions and ideas are exchanging and changing. West meets East as South affects North. Western (Judeo-Christian-Islamic), Confucian, Buddhistic, Amerindian, and African concepts express themselves in politics, in medicine, in ecology, in economics, in intellectual exchanges and critiques that affect us in myriad and complex ways. Television, conversation, movies, journals, theater, talk; the cosmopolitan buzz grows more intense each day.

In some contexts, these ideas expand and enlarge all our thinking. In others, they seem to conflict and compete as each of the large traditions that have had the conceptual power to gather large numbers of persons wants to claim its own authority within the obviousness of its pronounced truths and histories.

It is in this setting, in this moment of great gathering and/or conceptual conflict or competition, that we address the possibility of global humanism. It is in this moment that there is competition for ideas, that there are also potential *openings* for the development of creative ideas. Can we develop a notion of global humanism that is inclusive more than competitive, that might grow beyond the particularities of various world traditions to become more truly global?

An initial difficulty is that humanism is at some variance with the range of world histories and traditions in which our ideas of universality may be seen as an imposition of Western and/or American ideas upon the rest of the world: an intellectual and political colonization more than concepts that might be more truly global and free of the traditions in which they originally gained meaning and power, a new form or cloak of power grab. Global humanism may well be associated early and directly with the prevailing world political economy and opposed (even adapted) within the various traditions . . . as they are—that is, the concepts of individual freedom and integrity that underlie humanism are derived particularly from Western history, irrespective of their potential global application.

Alternatively, we may be able to develop a global humanism that is not bound to the ideas of any tradition but cuts more to some core of human experience. Can we somehow relook at the human condition—outside any oppositional derivation of humanism—and attempt to see what gathers and creates meaning in the human condition?

If so, can we find gathering ideas that we can still see as a global humanism, rather than as some ideas wrenched from contexts of Enlightenment, universal rationality, and so on?[2] Can we, that is, circumnavigate cultural, political, and historical issues in order to explore and establish a global humanism? How can some—at least partially—very different traditions come together in some unity of humanism, with a sense of positive virtue more than hegemonic yearnings?

I suggest that each of the successful world traditions (cultures, civilizations) has similar or mutually understandable ways and ideas of considering the nature of the human. The openings for new ideas, therefore, reside somewhere in the loci of the definition of being human as they have been formulated in different contexts. I place these ideas within the pragmatism of James, Dewey, and G. H. Mead.

PREFACE

Humanism is a movement that has attempted to *return* to us humans the power and definition of our being: a return to or a reprieve from Western philosophical and religious texts and traditions, and from religious and political structures which those texts and their important interpreters support. It is a return from narrative or textual notions of our being to the human condition and human experience as we live it in the present age.[3]

Since the Enlightenment, humanism has focused on fairly specific human abilities, especially the ability of each of us to reason out the world and our being within it, and has concentrated on science and the scientific method to distill and clarify the ways in which we can obtain truth about the world and potentially about the human.[4] In addition, the notion of human reason based upon science has underwritten the authority to justify this approach to knowledge.

Humanism developed from a critique of the human condition, in a (Western) historical setting in which the definition of the world and our place within it had been dominated for many centuries by a deific conception of the world and of our being within it.[5] Humanism has opposed the idea that we and our place in the world were created by a transcendent being, a god, an agency outside of any particular experiencing, usually outside of time.[6]

In the more philosophical (less religious) renderings of the human condition, authority over our being was located in the great thinkers and texts of ancient times. Experiencing the present was to be understood within the contexts of what particular thinkers of other eras considered essential or central to the human condition. Generally, these textual traditions tended either to diminish the importance of human experience in the living or to locate the central issues and reasons for our being in times (and texts) long gone or places far away.

Humanism, in particular, developed from a direct engagement with the deific textual traditions that attempted to locate truth and being within the ancient textual ideas that the essence of being human is in having reason or in being capable of rationality. For humanism, the world, not ancient texts, was to be the locus of our understanding. Methods of science were to be the modes for obtaining knowledge and understanding of the world and of our place within it.

However, in replacing being within the world and, potentially, within human experience, humanism has developed less from some sense of its own integrity. Rather it grew to a large extent from an oppositional notion, opposing the idea of deity to control our lives, individually and collectively.[7] Within the Western, Judeo-Christian tradition the notion of opposition, of either/or, has seemed correct as humanism and theism appear to collide quite clearly and obviously.[8]

At this point in our thinking toward a global humanism, it seems important to critique whence our ideas have derived but particularly to begin to rethink the nature of the human. What needs to included in such a study, and how do we go about it?

Some questions to rethink our thinking:

- How do we think about a global humanism in the context of the world's traditions?
- Does humanism easily and directly expand, or does it have *different* resonances as it claims to have a place in the thinking of non-Westerners and to expand to include potentially all the people in the world?[9]
- Is humanism clearly *universal*, following some usually Western notions of human being and knowledge? Witness the current arguments with China and other countries over questions of human rights.[10]
- In attempting to expand an idea of humanism derived from Western ideations, is it reasonable or legitimate to expand humanism to the entire world?
- How can we go about seeking some core aspects of human nature that might resonate globally, yet still develop a recognizable humanism that expands the concepts of individual, rationality, and human understanding?

To wedge ideas into this *opening* moment, this essay will consider the world's traditions with some claim to look at them from continuing human experience rather than from or within the histories that are usually invoked to tell us how the world is and what the place of humans within it.

INTRODUCTION

The world is rapidly becoming smaller, people(s) and ideas interacting everyday in real and in computational time. There is an increasing sense that all is becoming one: a global society.[11] A process; an inevitability; a necessity?

What sort of world would we—or they—have? Can we form a singularity that is not dominated principally by political economy—transnational corporations—or by some religious and/or political totalitarian? Can we find and live in any harmony dominated, say, by a universal golden rule: a rational humanism supporting a participatory democracy, extended to the sense of the universality of objective knowledge? Or do we witness the rise of forms of cultural hegemony that are less inclusive and tolerant? Will an emerging global culture look like a democracy, a world in which each person has some say? A top-down despotic rule of control and power? Orwellian anarchies of misfitted ambitions; an aristocracy of . . . ?[12]

To the pessimist, it seems somehow inevitable that one or another tradition will attempt to take over, either on purpose or in the sense that one or another thought system will seem, say, *obvious* or *necessary*. Obvious because the thinking we are doing has so limited possibilities that kingship or aristocracy . . . vaguely, possibly, some sense of democracy . . . might emerge and hold, at least for a while. Necessary, because anarchy might spread amoebalike throughout the world over issues of water, pollution, or power, and we will have to forestall and placate the angers and frustrations that may engage us fairly full-time in interventions, close and far.

The alternative of the realpolitik of political economy[13] is that a small number of transnational corporations will take over in some still-being-determined limited set of cartels: look at your clothing labels. There are also pessimistic theories that the future will see an increasing number of anarchic, small wars similar to Somalia, particularly over water: gangs, tyrants, localisms, fundamentalisms. Or the world will break up or re-form into its ancient traditions, much as in Orwell's *1984*.[14]

For the more optimistic, the facts of our cosmopolitan global communication seem hopeful. A global melting pot has very real dimensions for many people. In the context of these global gatherings, can we begin to imagine and construct a globality, a sense of being and governing that would be more inclusive, a sense of some-think to which we could adhere, with which we could agree? What might that be like? How can we even go about thinking about a sense of globality that would include, that is, all human beings into some confederation of being, ideas, geography (property, ethnicity, history, language . . .)? A global humanism?

One senses the impetus and inertia of the will to power of each of these traditions that has been successful in gathering peoples to its ideations; that when this will to power meets the other similarly motivated and successful traditions, they will likely compete rather than join or complement. West and East, North and South, the very obviousness of opposition will drive each tradition into its history for roots and redefinitions of the world and the place of the human within it: Witness the current *returns* of American neoconservatives to Plato and the Great Books and of fundamentalists to the Bible, especially the Book of Revelation. Witness the various nativist and nationalist movements all across the world.

But there is also a vast and growing cosmopolitan awareness of the ideas and traditions of the world's constellations of being and meaning. We are, remarkably, able to communicate to a large extent with everyone and can at least find glimmerings of what is common to all humans. There is ample evidence of some commonalities of human nature: experience, abilities, practices, virtues. Human grounds for a global sociality are, that is, apparently available, irrespective of history and polity. The path: from commonality to communality.

Can we move global thinking? Better, can we move study and understanding in the direction of an inclusive humanism rather than yield the powers of definition to one or another tradition, to some (likely) corporate forms or religio-philosophical presumptions that will tend to favor some oligarchic or totalitarian grab for ultimate power: actual and/or definitional?

Are we humanists prepared to debate the notion that a universalizing humanism may itself be seen as the attempt of one tradition to captivate all others, lending its power willy-nilly to some larger forces of political economy or (an anti-)religio-philosophy?

This all on the table, I propose that global humanism ought to examine what it is within the human condition and in various traditions that gathers people(s) into communities of activity, polity, and understanding. How can we infer from our tendencies to join with others and to think in particular modalities, to outline a global architectonic?

GLOBAL COMMONALITIES

In this essay, I will explore two aspects of the world's traditions:

1. What are the conditions—attractions, promises, worldviews—that have attracted and held very large numbers within commonality and loyalty to different traditions and ideas of government/governance?
2. What are the primary architectonics of such traditions: the sine qua non, the obvious, perhaps the necessary ideas in whose terms different people(s) develop and live particular senses of their meaning, identity, and outlook or worldview?

I will attempt to step outside, as it were, of the *structural thinking* of the (historical) world's traditions and direct our attention to common aspects of human experience.[15] Rather than dealing with (apparent) differences between religions or philosophies, I will ask what it is in common experience that moves us toward notions of a gathering transcendence: a sense of identity with some concept beyond oneself and one's significant others. I am less concerned with particular facts of history than with the human dialogues in which we continue to emerge as thinking-acting persons. This approach will, I hope, become clear in its exposition.[16]

The principal conditions that have gathered people(s) in common in the largest and most successful populations have been, I will claim, *transcendent* or *utopic*. These traditions hold out the promise of meaning, the possibility that something good, better, wonderful will happen . . . if their followers cling to these traditional outlooks. Concepts of heaven, of nirvana are examples of utopic promises *beyond* life; while the Jews and Confucians seem to find and continually open (often transcendent) possibilities *within* life—by a covenant with their community for the Jews and a sense that the best is yet to be (*L'chaim!*), or by remaining *on the way*, in Confucian lines of thought and doing.

The conceptions of the human of any global society that might have continuity and the hegemony of any singularity of outlook and practice must proffer a worldview that includes a promise of utopic futurity to its practitioners-believers-followers,[17] else we will be continually in combat with anarchy and its attendant attempts at mind control.[18]

What are these commonalities, at various levels of universality? Are they principally, as in Western religio-philosophic history, those characteristics of human nature that particularly differentiate us from other species and are particularly *mental* within ideas of Platonic oppositions?[19] (Complicating this question, but necessary for our pursuit of global humanism, is the Western idea that there are ways of ascertaining some outside truth in consonance with a reality that includes the human condition.)

Indeed, I think this is the most usual line of inquiry about the human condition deriving from this outlook of the West and will resist it in this chapter: call it the search for human *universals* . . . based, ironically in this context, on Western ideas of the uniqueness of human nature: different from all other species on the basis of language and rationality. We Westerners have utilitized this (narrow) notion of the human to extend our ideas to the world in some melange of rectitude, necessity, and inevitability.[20] Each tradition takes its ideas, creates the straw persons of different modes of thinking, and either defends or replaces the Other with its own sense and defense of polity and human nature.[21]

Instead, I will attempt to show how human experience (as opposed to Platonic *essentialism*) is most widely conceived and understood as the ways in which different traditions deal with what I will call *life paradoxes*. Paradoxes are arenas of (usually) paired experience that have different faces or outcomes: life/death, male/female, sleep/wakefulness, one/many, change/permanence, form/content, and so on. They number, say, about two dozen.[22] They are found, I claim, in all human experience, in languages and cultures, and extend into the experiencing of our being.

Human experience with and within these paradoxical axes is common to all of us. It is the raw material, as it were, for our being; the relief against which religious and other narrative traditions have found their ground: much of what I am calling human architectonics. We actually gather our ideas of, or define, reality to some large extent within the context of (experiential) life paradoxes.[23]

This is to say that the quickest/most efficient/most revealing ways into the understanding of the different world traditions, in their present forms, at least, is through a probing of paradoxes. Which of these life paradoxes are most important in particular traditions? Which of them are backgrounded or not much recognized in any tradition?[24] My observation/ understanding is that the very idea of reality for different traditions settles upon the issue of which paradoxes are foregrounded in any system of thought/being.

The second principle in the grasping of different traditions is in their handling of the various paradoxes they have chosen to highlight or background: do they *resolve* these paradoxes or do they *complementarize* them (e.g., yin and yang)?

For example, Western thought has chosen wakefulness as the central definitional element of reality, whereas the Amerindian tradition seems to have carved out sleep and the dream state (a Western imposition?) as the life experience in which our spirit is free to wander from us (human) to our animal-companion-spirit (Nahual). Jews concentrate upon life and its celebration, but let death recede, whereas Christianity focuses upon death as the overarching truth of our being and reads into life the notion of it being chimerical and essentially a preparation for (life after) death. These are both example of traditions in which paradox is to be resolved as the principal(?) architectonic of the tradition.

In the Confucian tradition, now more than ever entering our thinking, paradox is more usually complementarized: yin/yang; study the *I Ching* to think about when is the moment for change, or not. Both are—the issue of our being is more in the living experience and its study: not whether change is, but whether just now, or not.

I opt for the recognition and study of paradox in our lives in developing the conceptual apparatus for a global humanism. Included in this thinking are an expansion of the (usual) ideas of nature that have framed our thinking until now, including a move toward a critical naturalism, rather than wandering upon the shaky grounds of cultural relativism that recent notions of multiculturalism have urged upon us versus a restricted notion of absolutism that Western thinking seems to have imposed upon our thinking.[25]

In addition, I urge that we develop and sustain the notion that meaning and futurity—the heart of any *useful* utopic outlook—lie within human experience. Here, I proffer the notion that the world is intrinsically secular-humanistic—but there are certain relationships and tasks that are *sacred within the secular*.[26]

Here I want to domesticate the term *sacred* to life experience rather than yielding to some notion that sacred represents some transcendence that is intrinsically outside of human experience. The term represents the Nietzschean notion that overcoming our experience is a continuous yearning of or directive for the human condition.

SOME BACKGROUND

Conceptually, the idea of any actual globality appears to be quite recent. Perhaps only since 1969, when the first astronauts stepped on the surface of the moon and looked back, have we been truly capable of containing the entire earth in our minds' eyes.

By now this concept seems to have become more realizable with the advent of CNN and ITN, the television news sense that events anywhere on earth are immediately available to our witnessing and human testimony. This is to say that the concept of globality is by now more or less firmly graspable in our collective human mentality.[27]

Much of this conceptual expansion has been due, in complex causal webs, to technological developments in transportation, communication, and information that have effectively shrunk the world. All the peoples on earth are effectively—often actually—right here and now in our towns and businesses and classrooms. Money flows each day in enormous amounts across all the boundaries formerly thought to enclose the ideas of nation-states, all now less well-bounded and permeable—ideas as well as the city-state.

The outlooks and practices of other global traditions interact with ours, framing and placing into some critical constructions the ideas from the Western tradition that had become obvious and commonplace . . . to us. We begin to hear insistent notions from Asia, whose populations far outnumber the West, but also from Africa and from indigenous America. There is occurring some mixing, blending, contrast, and competition of and for ideas and outlooks in the context of a global, cosmopolitan world.

On grounds of common humanity, but also within the contexts of ecology and the human problematics of teaching and curing, of meaning and identity, ideas from other traditions now enter our thinking continually, often subtly. Practice and thinking in medicine changes day by day: some epic battle depicted recently by Andrew Weil as the (ongoing) competition between Asklepios and Hygeia over the nature of *curing* sickness and *maintaining* health.[28] Over half the visits to curers these days are to practitioners of *alternative* medicine, it is being claimed widely: "alternative" presumably being somehow different from ideas and practices that have developed within Western-scientific medicine: *from* pathology versus *toward* wellness; curing versus/or teaching.

This is to say that it is timely to consider how ideas from the entire globe enter into one another—competing, complementing, altering, expanding, passing each other by: not only pathology versus wellness, but also in many of the other arenas in whose terms we gain meaning and worldviews.

Problems in pursuing this goal include the temptation of each way of thinking and of each worldview to impose its ideas on everyone else—if only from the presumption that its way is the right way or the only way to be, and to think about, being. Arguing within these traditions will immerse us forever in what appear to be details of history and habits of thought. Can we break through or bypass such details to see the human condition more, say, *directly*?[29]

LIFE PARADOXES

It is my observation/suggestion that the most direct or easiest way to begin to enter the variety of the world's traditions is to attempt to see past or through various practices and philosophical histories. Studying how different people(s) of the world deal with various life paradoxes seems to be the most direct way of doing this. My observation of paradox—which was awakened during a two-year stint of linguistic fieldwork among the Mayan Indians of Southern Mexico—began with the (dim, at first) understanding that the sleep/dream state of these people is not a commentary on their waking life, as it is for us.[30]

It has—for them—a full sense of being. Living in the same compound with several Mayan persons, I gradually realized that their dream life is very important to their experiencing of life. On gathering words for a dictionary, I found that the words for sensory experience had their grounding in a vocabulary which was—for them—located within sleeping states.

Thence began a stream of thinking about why Western thought has considered wakeful experience to be the reality, and dreams apocryphal or commentary. From this comparatist positioning,[31] I began to note that Western thought since Plato, at least, considered permanence more real than change; men more rational than women; the universal more actual than the individual object. Historically, there had been a large shift from the notions of change of Heraclitus to the enduring via Parmenides and Pythagoras. In the most current thinking, chaos theory and the notion of the vast change coming after the millennial moment of 2000, Heraclitus is regaining prominence.

Reading in other traditions—meeting thinkers of other philosophical outlooks—I began to realize that various thinkers come to their notions of reality from their parents and culture. And to a very large extent, presumptions of reality, of worldview, are merely presented to children as their ongoing actuality: The parental response to the inquisitive child's *why* is usually *because* (I say so). Slowly, again, I began to wonder and realize that one could make a first quick cut of understanding into other traditions, if one could but discern which of the life paradoxes was foregrounded within these traditions: life or death (death is the reality of Western thought/Christianity; life an illusion or preparation for a return of the soul to heaven), and so on.

After spending some time studying tai chi and reading Confucius, I began to wonder, as well, if the Confucians weren't taking some of these paradoxes and treating them in a *complementary* fashion—permanence and change, yin and yang—rather than finding some necessity to *resolve* them. It became clear, as well, in tai chi, that the possibilities of growth and improvement—knowledge of the forms, practice, and understanding of the martial arts—continues to grow indefinitely: the master/mistress of the form who reaches some venerable age is beyond vulnerable—glimpses of a transcendent notion, but within life.

Rethinking Amerindian notions, it appears that they—as we—tend to resolve various paradoxes but on different *sides* than we do, but they share with us the wish or need to resolve rather than to complementarize.

At any rate, within the context of thinking about global humanism, the study of paradox seems a most useful and potentially productive mode or site for us to cut through or to bypass the ideas of the traditions that will otherwise block us from moving toward ideas that might unite the world's peoples: We seem to see the world at the level of basic assumptions in terms that conflict or compete much as they might be complementary; or we Westerners see mysticism where others find direct meaning; or . . .

So I propose that in thinking about global humanism, it is worth our while to ponder, observe, read, study how other traditions and our own come to think about foundational issues in whose terms we cast the reality of the world and of the human condition. Here, the nature of life paradox would be a primary study in designing a global humanism that could grow to include all the people(s) of the world.[32] Else . . . else we will be caught at a level of thinking which will likely result in Orwell's standoff of three civilizations fuming at one another.

LOOKING OUT FOR THE FUTURE

The other contention I have concerning the commonalities of the world's traditions which have been successful in gathering large numbers of people over time, is that they somehow promise a good and hopeful future. In the West, we might refer to this as utopic or transcendent: a time when all will be good, and we will do well; a return to heaven for Christians, the idea for Jews that the best is yet to be; for Buddhists that nirvana is a great release from life conceived as a burden, for the Confucianists that if we remain on the Way, life will increasingly reward us.

There is, apparently, something in the human condition about futurity and its promises and possibilities, that *works* to gather people; to gather persons beyond the families and small, direct-experience communities into the imagined communities that have become the city-states' foundational thinking for our notions of the body politic.[33]

The ideas that have worked to gather peoples and their notions of self-definition, their sense of belonging to and covenant with particular others, their willingness to become subservient to institutions and ideations, have been notions that transcend individual lives. They are stories, offerings, ideas that some usually collective futurity promises, insures, and guarantees that life will be good, better, . . . wonderful. These are notions of the future that we would think of as utopias, loci of increasing wonder and power that often appeal to us as aspects of some transcendence: transliterated often as a time or aspect of being that has its own power—the deity; or in some sense of Emerson, Thoreau, or Nietzsche in which we overcome our earlier being each day.

Why/how utopic ideas *work* is another ground for our study toward a global humanism.[34] Probably some aspect of the urge toward a moving/growing future derives simply from our own (individual) development and growing up. We are urged to become adults in each community within various contexts of growth and towardness.

This urging, which each of us takes on within senses of conscience and responsibility, does not simply disappear upon reaching maturity. I take this to be a major psychological etching toward transcendence, making it at the least attractive to search for meaning within the larger sense of political community/tradition that have collected and held vast numbers of followers.[35]

Those transcendent or utopic notions of futurity most familiar to humanism offer a resolution within the paradox of life and death, on the side of death being the ultimate: the soul's return to heaven of Christianity and Islam, the deliverance of nirvana for the South Asians. The Jews and Confucians find their utopias within life: The best is yet to be, and on the Way to true knowledge, a promise is made that existence/experience holds out the promise of . . . improvement, a good life getting better.

The promise of humanism has itself been utopic. The notion of *progress* has been the principal utopic fuel driving the engine of modernism and the reasoned understanding of nature and human nature. And, it should be noted, an increasing loss of faith in the idea of progress is presently weakening the gathering force of humanism on its home ground—a loss requiring ongoing critique and study to rethink the grounds of humanism in all contexts, especially as we are experiencing an attempt to reground reason and authority within narrativity rather than nature in the name of postmodernism and fundamentalism.[36]

What I propose, therefore, is less any particular solutions that might establish and perpetuate a global humanism than modes of being, studying, and living with a major focus on our experiencing, rather than modes than have been chosen historically to bolster our human senses of knowing and control.

Some thinking about transcendent/utopic models toward forming, establishing and maintaining a global humanism:

The openings of this global moment include the idea that the various competing traditions are actively receding in their demands upon their people(s), tending to place many of the world's persons in a cosmopolitan setting and sensibility.[37] This is to say that establishing a global notion such as humanism has a fairer possibility of realization than in any other era so far. Something of global dimension *will happen* in the near future. It is timely to have this discussion at this moment in what is soon to be global history.

In a global future, one holds out the promise that the world/life will have the active possibility of moving beyond present experience. As children are promised the place and privileges of adulthood, the ideas of a hopeful futurity and the possibility of a meaningful life well lived need to be embodied in the ideas and practices of a global humanism: meaning in the present and well promised in the future; remaining in actual and realizable potential. Any attempt to present or create a utopic or transcendental idea of being outside human experience (deific, mystical . . .) leads us back to the histories and belief systems that will continue to divide us.

In order to avoid the likelihood that most attempts to deal with transcendence/utopia lead fairly directly back to themes and variations of the traditions that we hope to bypass, I propose that we consider and study the idea of human experience at some depth and with a breadth that attempts to be world-inclusive.[38] What do we mean by the concept of global virtues; how do we find the common spaces of the prevailing world traditions?

The study of experience—the notion of the human, caught so far in the paradox of being or doing—takes us fairly directly to the pragmatist tradition from C. S. Peirce and William James to John Dewey and G. H. Mead. Humanism rests in no small measure on the importance of the individual, and it will find itself in conflict with other traditions in which the idea of the individual is often submerged to history and tradition.

In the Enlightenment idea of the individual as particularly rational, using nature to define being and a method for knowing, the concept of the individual is usually taken as a given: a primary, a presupposition. This idea of individuality has been at war with most Marxist ideas, and will conflict with various of the world's traditions that consider the individual subservient to larger-gathering ideas. Sociality, in these modes of thinking, is either primary or a derived necessity in the vein of thought from Hobbes and/or Rousseau, projecting society as a necessary evil to control life's threatening vicissitudes: so-called *natural* law.[39]

Instead, recent scientific observations of the human condition—relating humans to our nearest related species—indicate that humans are, like all these other species, social as well: social by-our-nature. Sociality is not a human cultural invention; rather, it is our nature. We are not survivable except within the experience of human parenting. However, most of our ideas concerning the human condition are themselves derived from Western thinking about human uniqueness, not from the observational-experiential study of humans.[40]

G. H. Mead's writings offer us a direction of understanding this apparent paradox:[41] that the individual is indeed a strong aspect of our existence but that the individual is *emergent* from sociality. Our upbringing is not, then, merely toward becoming rational, but becoming rational is itself a statement about the ways in which different traditions regard the nature of human development toward becoming a *reasonable* adult.

Development includes a *reading-into* each child/person the character that one sees, as well as who we would have them become. That is, the individual is continually reincorporated into social being. Different societies (traditions) do this quite differently, but they all seem to act essentially within the nature of human experience that Mead outlined. Any move toward a global humanism has to move critically beyond the ways and beliefs of each tradition in order to see what is most generally and actually human;[42] not just the implications of different traditions' ideas of the human (derived especially from their favorite paradoxes and how the tradition has incorporated them into its philosophies).

Experience is not simply what one knows about the (external) world but *how* one is and knows: My most general critique of humanism-so-far is that we tend to remain stuck in our notions of knowing, within the Western dualistic opposition between a (hard) mechanical body and a (soft) mentalist idea of the stuff of consciousness and rationality.[43] It is particularly important and timely to study one's own (and others') *bodily knowing* in order to begin to broaden our ideas of knowing and meaning to encompass a more global understanding of human understanding: tai chi, yoga, but also Alexander technique as outlined by John Dewey . . . and more, lest we remain forever ensnared in (fairly parochial) arguments within a couple of favorite Western paradoxes: change and permanence, and the one and the many.[44]

The notions of utopia and transcendence are intimately coupled with questions of meaning and being, especially of becoming, hope, and futurity. Aspects of the realization of the openings of these times has the problematic side that the openings often occur because issues of meaning and futurity come into some crisis. While globality and cosmopolitanism are themselves hopeful for many persons, many others find these times undercutting to their ideas of meaning and futurity: for example, returns to nativism, fundamentalism, nationalism, historicism, and more promising themes and variations upon global anarchies rather than any inclusive globalism, or the emergence of some totalitarianism in the name of religion or political economy (or another form of *necessity*).

How/who might take some advantage of the openings that we may discern in this moment of a possible global humanism? We might begin by gathering those who have already begun to see the world as their locus of being and futurity: world federalists, human rights persons (Amnesty International), those who work and imagine the world is their place of operation—the International Monetary Fund and the World Bank, the United Nations, the world's religions, and so on. My concern is that most of the members of these organizations conceptualize the idea of globality already within prevailing ideas, seeking for power/control or to diffuse that which they see as damaging or otherwise worrisome. (It would certainly be interesting and educational for the Humanist Institute to call such a meeting. Count me in!)

Who will help create the idea of a global humanism? Where do we find the inspired and inspirers of the future, the hopeful, particularly those who have themselves survived life's vicissitudes and come to the table anew, almost every day? I propose that they include the thinkers and teachers (and mothers) and all those who take care, the ecologists and sustainers of the world and its bounties, in the attempt to create a world of vision beyond the usual and everyday of here and now, of only a few yesterdays, and a sense that tomorrow will take care of itself. We must create a sense of vision that will gather and sustain, else we will tend to furrow the world into narrow modes of opportunism where the worries of anarchism and small ambitions will cause attack and/or retreat on the smaller scales of nation and corporation and the views of the narrowers.

How can we do this? I, reacting to my cultural-critical observations and analyses, worry that any world vision we dream up will tend to be restricted by the sorts of boundaries we carry already in our thinking. Concerned as well that this moment in (Western, at least) history is a time of reaction to a vast surplus of world labor and the radically changing nature of work, we find ourselves in a moment when the future appears *unscripted*, especially to its young. That is, the very idea of futurity has become unclear and blurred. Thus, my election for the sorts of persons who would most help to develop a global vision are those whose work and thinking is already committed to *guaranteeing the future*: for example, teachers who include others in their thinking in the context of teaching as dialogue.[45]

(Master/great) teacher model: Some of the world's traditions focus a great deal of authority (and prestige) on their senior population, especially those who are seen to be teachers. In effect, these persons act to insure (ensure), to inspire, even to guarantee the idea of futurity. The Confucian model is, for example, to show that the tai chi master/mistress is capable of such great knowledge that he/she holds out a direction and promise of important abilities for younger persons. The Sufi master is sought out for those who wish to grow in the direction of whatever is thought to be wisdom. In some senses, these persons are *more* than others (authority, skill, knowledge, wisdom). In effect, teachers act as sacred persons within a secular (humanist) world: those who engage in dialogue, interaction— the sacred being those arenas/persons in dialogues in which the learners yield or surrender some of their power to their teacher or curer (or parent) temporarily, in order to grow more than they would . . . on their own.

We will have to debate how this idea of teacher might fit into any global humanism. It conflicts with the idea of the universal rational as it creates/admits that there are persons of privilege (with special responsibilities) in society: at least during certain periods of life experience—not too different from Plato's notion of the philosopher king, but with the proviso that the teacher's influence or power is limited and directed eventually toward subverting her or his being, enabling students to explore their own powers; accepting Freire's challenge and not oppressing the future because we act out of our own earlier pedagogical oppression.[46]

Might it (also) include the ecologists, those whose observations already cross the very idea of geographical boundedness, and . . . ?

QUESTIONS IN LIEU OF A CONCLUSION

Some continuing issues for discussion (soon):

- What is the positive in the transcendent? Progress, futurity/hope, wisdom (integrity, honesty . . .)?
- How do we *market* these ideas to the people(s) of the global society?
- Are they/we already in the mood to think globally, a new gathering idea for a next millennium?

Short of crises—anarchies over water, land, and religious or other disputes threatening all-out wars; takeovers of business as many in the South/third world seem to think is already the global situation—it is difficult to discern any great outcry for a world order that is any more clear and definite than the rough and ready situation that prevails at this moment.

It will be good to find some celebratory glue pots that will bind us all together in some sense that is positive and not merely defensively reactive. No doubt this takes leadership as well as ideas. Perhaps some global leadership will invent itself in this moment of openings, when some students begin to see themselves globally. I think I begin to see some already, developing the imagination, the richness of what might be, considering what is and what promises to be that they find odious and closing to a rare moment of vast, that is global, opportunity. Sustainability, ...

- How do we diffuse the histories and traditions which will find their turf shrinking, if this is to occur, this global humanism?
- What can draw people(s) beyond the personal testimony of those who would breathe life into futurity and globality: global teachers? Else we fall into histories and traditions, competitions based on pre-global visions, or global depictions of an always collapsing earth.
- How could a global humanism resist the temptation to react to any criticisms as forms of anarchy?
- If we have trouble (since Plato's *Laws*, at least) with the problems of virtues and vices of those who (would) have power, can we (as it

were) remold the human to be beyond the temptations which have corrupted us since?

- How can "love one another and live the Golden Rule" be translated into any ongoing actuality that might continue to engage its . . . citizens?
- Would a (hopefully small) crisis enable/pursuade us to see some more necessity in a global humanism: ecological, geological, political, economic, toxicological? What then?
- Can we evolve some new ways of thinking about stability, of meaning and purpose, so we can avoid the Scylla and Charybdis of Hesse's *The Glass Bead Game*[47] or the millennial-prophetic mystics whose idea of transcendence will overwhelm life itself either in mysticisms or in attempts to control all of being? That is, as we enlarge our thinking from city-state to global, how will we reenvision being and becoming? The temptation has often been to diminish human experience, and this may only hurry this process, perhaps especially for those who would substitute the robotic human E.T. for the one of flesh and blood who is only too liable to the vicissitudes of the climates of opinion.
- How/where do different traditions come together—one notion of openings?

NOTES

1. Do we even know how to think globally, or do we find our theories of society, behavior, and politics bound within various theories that presume a world composed of city-state entities: large, but always with the presumption of other similar city-states outside variously friendly, competitive, dangerous . . .? That is, there may be no real precedent idea for considering globality except as an extrapolation of how we (any tradition) thinks about its ordinary.

2. In *The Clash of Civilizations and the Remaking of World Order* (New York: Simon and Schuster, 1996), Samuel Huntington cautions us against the universalist ambitions of Western thought (hegemony?): "Western belief in the universality of Western culture suffers from three problems: it is false; it is immoral; and it is dangerous. . . . Spurred by modernization, global politics is being reconfigured along cultural lines. Peoples and countries with similar cultures are coming together . . . fault lines between civilizations are becoming the central lines of conflict in global politics." Quoted in William H. McNeill, "Decline of the West?" review of *The Clash of Civilizations and the Remaking of World Order* by Samuel Huntington, *New York Review of Books*, January 9, 1997, p. 18.

3. The notion of *return* implies one or both of the ideas that human experience has been depicted as and interpreted as in texts: (1) Historically, humans were more in tune with our experience until writing and textuality essentially froze the nature of our being; or (2) in our own experiencing, we tend to waver or to include our sensory-bodily-intellectual readings of the world and us within it, as well as seeing ourselves within literary/textual enscriptions of our being with which we either match actuality or interpret actuality within such representational terms. Humanism has as often used philosophical-conceptual renderings of the human condition to tell us *how* we are as to examine or appeal to our ongoing experience.

4. There are some current disagreements about the cleanness of truth obtained by scientific methods, especially as questions of the objectivity of the human observer elide into the politics of who gets to do science. My suggestion in this arena is that we need to do a lot of thinking/studying the human condition in order to more fully understand the nature of human nature, particularly as it reflects our notions of being in pursuit of science.

5. The nature of human nature and of the human condition is central, in my view, to this discussion. Who and how we are, in our individual and social contexts of being, is the locus of the question of human experience. How we think about our being, what issues seem central or peripheral or merely absent from discussion, frame the questions we ask about our being.

Western thought, for example, has set much of the definition of the human in the context of how we are unique and different (presumably) from other species, especially our thinking: thus, most of the philosophical discussion about humans devolves upon language and rationality, aspects of the humanly *unique* mind. How we are actually, in our more comprehensive experience, reveals that much is absent from the study of our being human and paves an easy road for us to extrapolate from narrow Western ideas of the human to the entire global population. See my *Language and Human Nature: Toward a Grammar of Interaction and Discourse* (Minneapolis: University of Minnesota Press, 1985) for a critique of this thinking.

6. The time paradox—change versus permanence—is perhaps the most central paradox with which I will be dealing in this chapter. It is worth raising our awareness of the paradoxical nature of many of the central issues of humanism as the chapter moves toward an incorporation—rather than a resolution—of various *life paradoxes.*

7. It continues to be a temptation, sometimes a necessity, to battle theism with seemingly endless attempts to refute the idea of a transcendent deity . . . as if it were possible to solve this issue once and for all. I take the position that human experience (within the larger contexts of life upon earth) is what there is and that we need to examine the human condition/human nature as cleanly as possible by observation and rethinking and begin to extricate ourselves from arguing against particular traditions of thought about humans (deific or not) in order to derive some essential humanism.

8. Universals and the claim that some ideas apply to everyone can be seen as the attempt to find what is in common to all humans, implying an ongoing study of human nature and of the human condition. Or—more likely as it derives from a Western opposition to deific thinking—it fits into a fairly specific mode and history of thinking about humans that has dominated thought about humans since Plato but particularly developing since the early Middle Ages. It has been based on a notion of human individualism as a given, on what has been considered or assumed to be uniquely human (different from all other species) and on various political and moral ideas that have blended Plato's and Aristotle's ideas of the human as intrinsically consisting of mind and of body, with most of our thinking about humans deriving from or existing within this oppositional thinking. Other traditions do not seem to think about the human within this form of (easy) oppositions, and their relations between, say, morality and politics seem quite different from the Western model. In this context, the idea of a global humanism could be seen as a Western attempt to universalize its thinking from a position of arrogance much as from reason and knowledge.

9. Humanism's claims to be rational and universal may have a more complex status once it moves from a Judeo-Christian context to other settings where the traditions of thought and history are different from the West, especially where humanism does not easily or directly *oppose* a theistic tradition.

10. The issues that have arisen in the context of human rights seem (to me, at least, having been trained within Boasian cultural anthropology) to be an aspect or derivation of humanism. Boas and his students, especially Margaret Mead and Ashley Montagu (who, with Pedro Comas, drafted the United Nations Human Rights Declaration), directly attempted to bring all humans into the human family. This had not been the case until well into the twentieth century. By the mid-1960s, the last of the aboriginal peoples of the world (the Australians) came to be thought of as essentially a single family with the fame of tennis player Evonne Goolagong. Since that time, battles over inclusivity have continued: In this country, civil rights battles continue concerning women, ethnic minorities, and various of the physically and intellectually handicapped—many of whom were considered *freaks* or beyond the pale of educability until quite recently. Boas's plan was to consider the three-part aspects of being human: physical (race), language, and culture. His work (and that of his students) has turned out to be quite inclusive, with continuing attacks from various quarters, especially within the context of deterministic biopsychology. The arguments against human rights—and, by extension, against global humanism, I think—are against any universality of human nature or thinking on the grounds of cultural perspectives or differences that are held to differ from tradition to tradition or from differing histories—one of the reasons why this chapter will attempt to probe the human condition to explore global humanism rather than trying to place humanism *against* various (cultural/philosophical) traditions.

11. This is not to deny that there are dominant groups everywhere (business, government, etc.) trying to control flow of information.

12. Many of the ecologically aware members of movements that support global sustainability worry less about cultural or conceptual ideas and more that global resources supporting our vast populations will soon come into crisis: water, climate, food. If they are approximately correct, questions of the politics of global humanism will take on some urgency in the near future. From personal discussions with Rod Sando, commissioner of the Minnesota Department of Natural Resources and a champion of global sustainability.

13. By the notion of realpolitik of political economy, I suggest that the global sense of political economy that now seems to rule our thinking seems—for the moment at least—to be at a similar level of the obvious as the ideas that our intellectual traditions grant to our thinking. If it seems compelling in this moment, other ideas could as easily have pervaded. It is in this rethinking of realpolitik that I seek other notions of what is human nature.

14. See Huntington, *The Clash of Civilizations and the Remaking of World Order*, reviewed in *New York Review of Books* by W. H. McNeill, January 9, 1997, pp.18–22 (note 2, above).

15. The temptations to take on various (often oppositional) ideas in order to justify and/or define humanism are great: the seemingly endless task of disputing the idea of deity, of fighting/arrogating the great prophets—Christ, Mohammed, Buddha, Confucius, et al.—or, in this tradition, of seeking guidance or certitude in the ancient philosophers over the meaning of our ongoing experience. In my view, a viable notion of humanism will (must?) be centered in the ongoing present.

16. I locate myself and this chapter in the context of pragmatics, especially of George Herbert Mead. Perhaps the major shift in thinking from the (rest of the) Western tradition, is in the conceptual apparatus of our individualism: Mead's idea is that we are (primarily) individuals but that this individuality is *emergent* from social interaction rather than primarily a given of our existence.

17. The idea of *progress* has been adapted within humanism as its transcendent offering. The current climate of cynicism/nihilism seems to undermine the idea of progress, undercutting rationality/science as the authoritative routes to truth and weakening the power of humanism to represent a sense of *the good life* and to gather great numbers of adherents.

18. The necessary literature here includes the utopic and dystopic narratives that have and continue to shape our time. I have been particularly influenced by the concerns of Orwell and the various shapings of mind control and of the antibureaucratic dialogues of Kierkegaard, Gogol, Kafka, Dostoevski, and Borges.

19. Leaving us frequently within either an often morbid history of bodily differences, which have been regularly cast within racial and slavery narrative structures, or a philosophical necessity to hierarchize the capabilities of various populations to think but also to rule or be ruled. This is currently playing out in some

(ancient) battle between a mechanical/material approach to our being of neuropsychology and a mentalist approach of critical theory. The truths of the human condition are often obscured on this battleground.

20. We can account for our rationality without invoking human uniqueness based on little actual knowledge of the abilities of other species. See my manuscript, "To Tell the Truth," submitted to the Humanist Institute in 1998.

21. An important conceptual history to restudy stems from Aristotle's *Politics*, in which he takes Plato's oppositional ideas of mind and body and places them in the context of polity, where it becomes inevitable that monarchy becomes the rule. Humans begin as anarchical creatures and become social, as Rousseau spins this tale. Instead, observation of other species strongly indicates that we are social by our nature, making individuality a necessary topic for observation and discussion: another reason why I claim we have to rethink our Western tradition lest global humanism become another form of philosophical imperialism.

22. The ontological status of life paradoxes I'll leave somewhat dubitable: whether statements about the world, the human experiencing the world, or . . .? What seems to be true is that all(?) humans *recognize* pretty much the same paradoxes within their life experience.

23. They also often form the bases for what we usually think of as logical categories from Aristotle (*Organum*) to the present. But they are foundational to the development of our individuality: see my *To Tell the Truth*. The paradoxes are located in the very learning of language and are thus universal to this process. See "Question-Response System," chapter 9 in my *Language and Human Nature*. An example of a logical category that is not a life paradox is the question of the one and the many, which is solved by every child before age two but remains problematic to logicians.

24. The idea that we can infer from our experience in the West to the remainder of the world through our own ideas of religious transcendence or of human universals derived from notions of human uniqueness due to mental-linguistic properties, seems anthromorphic and not very revealing of different traditions.

25. Harvey B. Sarles, "Cultural Relativism and Critical Naturalism," in *Cultural Relativism and Philosophy: North and Latin America*, ed. Marcelo Dascal (Leiden: E. J. Brill, 1991), pp. 195–214.

26. In contexts such as curing, teaching, parenting, friendship—in which one person regularly *yields* power to another at least temporarily, toward future growth, I see these relationships as sacred within the secular. As teacher, for example, I use the power given to me by students toward their growth and development, eventually subverting my power; similarly with curers.

27. We need to remind ourselves that most of our thinking habits—even about globality—developed during times that were not conceptually global. Rather, most of our thinking about sociality and politics was developed during periods of ideation when the city-state was presumed to be a natural, perhaps obvious, form of social arrangement. This thinking about who we are and where

we are included the idea that there were other similar loci outside of boundaries of our being somewhere, someone . . . a citizen/subject of . . . . The very idea of global thinking therefore resides in and is an extension of thinking about being within the idea of city-state. Blame it on, or locate it within, say, Machiavelli's *Discourses*. (Don't we need to read together?) Here much of our thinking is bound within ideas deriving from Aristotle's *Politics*, including Hobbes's analysis (*Leviathan*) and Rousseau's that society is somehow antihuman, antinatural (*The Social Contract*). Modern, observational ethology says this is ideology rather than the truth of our being.

28. Andrew Weil, *Spontaneous Healing* (New York: Ballantine, 1995).

29. I appreciate that what I am referring to as *details* of history are regarded as reality and actual history to most people. On the one hand, I apologize for my presumptuousness. On the other, I propose that a deeper comparative thinking about the human condition and human nature than has been the practice within any tradition up to now can enable us to see much more clearly what is in common to us all and how the different traditions have gained their footings.

30. I was gathering the dictionary not from concepts—which I could never have known from my background—but from the sounds/phonemes that I was attempting to systematize in schemata such as consonant-vowel-consonant and came upon a number of such sensory terms serendipitously.

31. My training as a comparative linguist is the undergirding for this position. I was trained to suspend my own languaging in order to enter into the cognitive abilities of speakers of other languages and understand the world of sound as they conceptualize it in their own languages. Then I would return to my English languaging and be able to see both their languaging and my own within a comparative framework. Similarly with a cognitive anthropology, toward a way of seeing my own ordinary—here, a probing of why Western thinking has taken reality to be the waking state—and the beginning for me of a long intellectual historical journey back to Heraclitus and forth to the present.

32. I think this is at its base a rational study of human nature and the human condition. It will reveal, for example, that our construction of the human individual as the base of being and of our institutions needs to include the fact that we are—by our nature—social beings. That is, we have to review our own philosophical and traditional presumptions in beginning to consider other traditions—else we will oppose, and conflict, and enter into a popularity contest rather than a reasoned discussion of the human condition. In following G. H. Mead in thinking that our individuality is emergent rather than a given, I can make a strong case that fundamental notions of reality are generated from a social grammar rather than our usual thinking that humans have a given matrix for language. See *Language and Human Nature*.

33. See Benedict Anderson, *Imagined Communities: Reflections on the Origin and Spread of Nationalism* (London: Verso, 1983).

34. See Harvey B. Sarles, "The Ideal" (Foundations Project, 1998 MS).

35. It is important for humanists to critically review the utopic sorts of stories that have informed our own tradition, cast usually within the progress of the human from (primitive) nature toward civilization. While these have usually paralleled the development from infant to adult, they have been derived particularly from the philosophical traditions of Plato and Aristotle as they have played out variously over the past two millennia plus. They are based to some (large) extent on a particular notion of human uniqueness, derived in turn from a largely misinformed idea of other species. In this context, we Western thinkers have often applied our thinking about globality and humanity to other traditions and have misunderstood and misestimated their ideas, within our terms: Notions of civilization, development, and so on, may derail our attempts to universalize global humanism as we tend to estimate others with respect to historically derived ideas of our own being—rather than, for example, looking at ourselves from the perspective of other species being as different from us as Plato and Aristotle claimed. That is, we need to rethink what we have meant by human nature in global and comparative contexts. For a critical and corrective view of the origins of human intelligence and an experiential explanation of our rational dispositions, see Peter J. Wilson's *The Domestication of the Human Species* (New Haven: Yale University Press, 1988). He claims that we became geometric thinkers as we became domesticated, living in permanent settlements where there were literal walls: We learned, for the first time, here and there, and became Euclidean in our lookings-out. In the contexts of globality, these ideas of being may well have altered.

36. See Jean-François Lyotard, *The Postmodern Condition: A Report on Knowledge*, trans. Geoff Bennington and Brian Massumi (Minneapolis: University of Minnesota Press, 1984). This can be appreciated in several contexts: internal weakenings and external attacks upon science from the humanities and from religious scientific creationism; a rise in cynicism and nihilism; a rising interest in the spiritual.

37. Remembering as well that many of the world's peoples find themselves increasingly resistant or marginalized in this globalizing moment.

38. My reading and study in various world traditions so far leads me to think that (most of) the traditions rely for their architectonics—their underlying ideas about the world—upon ideas of human experience and how to understand what and how they provide meaning to being. The attempt here: to enter meaning and experience at a level or place which, again, bypasses the traditions that have developed from various underlying notions of how we are and how we are to be. Hopefully this will develop into/devolve from ideas that are, say, more basic to the human condition because they derive from very general ideas and observations. I will claim, as well, that there exist elements of human experience that have not been much observed or granted their due importance in the construction of meaning and being: for example, the (central) importance of the (human) face in our knowing others and ourselves and the idea that individuality is emergent rather than given.

39. In the pursuit of global humanism, it will be necessary to critically review our own Western tradition, in order to see, for example, that this notion of *natural law* is itself derived especially from Hobbes's *Leviathan*. That is, we must study critically the history, sociology, and politics of ideas.

40. Harvey B. Sarles, *Ethology and the Philosophy of Language: Handbuch Sprachphilosophie*, ed. M. Dascal, D. Gerhardus, K. Lorenz, and G. Meggle (Berlin: De Gruyter, 1995), pp. 1700–1708.

41. An apparent paradox, because we have *not* so far considered that the individual is emergent from sociality, an idea that gathers power from the observation of related species, then the return to observing the human.

42. See Harvey B. Sarles, "Reality" (Foundations Project, 1998 MS).

43. *Hard* and *soft* are references to some of the binds humanism finds itself in: *hard* referring to a mechanical-material model of the bodily being that we are, and *soft* referring to ideas of rationality and human uniqueness. The rub is that both of these are crucial aspects of humanist thinking, usually invoked in noncompetitive contexts so we hardly notice the contradictions in our loyalties. Obviously we are (both) bodily and thoughtful and have hoist ourselves on the petard of our own traditional thinking.

44. John Dewey, "Three Prefaces to Books by Alexander," in *The Resurrection of the Body* by F. M. Alexander (New York: University Books, 1969), pp. 169–84.

45. Harvey B. Sarles, *Teaching as Dialogue: A Teacher's Study* (Latham, MD: University Press of America, 1993).

46. See Paulo Freire, *Pedagogy of the Oppressed*, trans. Myra Bergman Ramos, 30th anniversary ed. (New York: Continuum, 2000).

47. Hermann Hesse, *The Glass Bead Game (Magister Ludi)*, trans. Richard and Clara Winston (New York: Picador, 2002).

HARVEY SARLES has a PhD in anthropology from the University of Chicago. His theoretical work follows the pragmatist G. H. Mead, borrowing Mead's notion of the individual emerging from social interaction and placing it in the context of the body as well as language: gestures, experience, a grammar of question and response. Sarles, the author of *Nietzsche's Prophecy: The Crisis in Meaning*, considers this book as his central work as a cultural critic. Moving from a description of the crisis through questions about the nature of meaning, it attempts to describe the technology and intellectual-cultural questions of meaning and finally offers some directions out of current dilemmas toward the development of meaning within a hopeful futurity.

15.

Eliminating the Cult of Nationalism

Innaiah Narisetti

Nationalism is an infantile disease. It is the measles of mankind.

—Albert Einstein

NATIONALISM

Manabendra Nath Roy, the humanist revolutionary and philosopher, called nationalism an antiquated cult[1] (in 1938 on the eve of World War II). A person who is born by accident in a country is taught that his birthplace is pious and holy and that person must be prepared to sacrifice his or her life for the motherland. In the cult of nationalism, geography is given religious sanctity. "Right or wrong, my country first" becomes the slogan. When national hysteria is whipped up, only demagogues profit, and many will seek to justify their actions in the name of patriotism. Politicians and rulers use nationalism for perpetuating their own ends. People are fooled with all sorts of national slogans. No wonder, then, that Samuel Johnson cautioned that patriotism was the last refuge of a scoundrel!

Extreme nationalism as seen in Nazism in Germany and Fascism in Italy were the bloodiest (and most crudely capitalist) phases in Europe in recent history—they were also reactionary. While extreme nationalism led to fascism, the cult of Superman itself grew out of Fascist and Nazi philosophies. Earlier philosophers such as Schopenhauer provided the philosophy for the cult. There were literary people like Carlyle who justified the cult of hero and superman. Spiritualism added the necessary pep to the cult of the nation. Thus, the cultural groundwork was laid for the triumph of this authoritarian, collectivist, irrational ideologies. Fascism and Nazism swore by nationalism, sought the people's support, and exploited their weaknesses by pandering to their prejudices. In the case of Hitler, the National Socialists came to power through democratic means of voting, showing that an entire people can be manipulated into supporting a self-destructive ideological and cultural dictatorship.

Setting aside extreme forms of nationalism, I believe that even moderate nationalism is not compatible with internationalism. As long as nation-states continue, it will not be possible to create world government, an institution desired by many humanists. This is because nation-states defend and promote their own military interests by arming themselves and guard their own economic interests by imposing trade barriers. Often, their acts are against the interests of other nations and peoples, and at times against the interests of their own citizens. The international order is damaged by nations singularly pursuing their own interests, as we see all too often happening in the modern world. During wars, national frenzy is rampant everywhere. People die for the sake of their country. One's own country is placed above all else. Even children are dragged into war and abused by making them accept this ideal of sacrifice for the nation.

If the history of nations is traced, it is easy to understand that national boundaries often change and then the loyalties of the people must change, as well. After each war, national boundaries are redrawn, especially if the war involves territorial dispute. What happens to the previous piously held nation's geography?

The history of the former superpowers that divided the world is instructive to show that national boundaries are temporary and constantly evolving.

The Soviet Union, of course, no longer exists. After the Communists established their mighty government in Moscow in 1917, they redrew the map of many nations forcibly. Many neighboring nations were amalgamated into the Soviet Union under one red flag. Latvia, Lithuania, Estonia, Georgia, and Kazakhstan came into the Soviet fold. Again after glasnost and perestroika (under Gorbachev), the Communist world shrank, and nations redrew their boundaries.

The United States of America is also very different today from what existed when the Pilgrims entered America from Europe in the seventeenth century. The union began with thirteen states. Much later, the United States of America emerged with fifty states. It developed a national anthem, a national flag, and several slogans that are inscribed on coins and paper money. The United States put the nation above the individual and demanded the sacrifice of the sovereign individual at the altar of nationalism.

Yugoslavia has totally changed since the death of its Communist ruler, Marshal Tito. Serbia, Montenegro, and Croatia became separate nations. Also in Central Europe, Czechoslovakia was broken into the Czech Republic and Slovakia in 1993. Before these events, the great Berlin Wall crumbled, and the two Germanys reunited as soon as East Germany's Communist government collapsed. In Asia, the two Vietnams have become one country. Most national identities have been shaped by history and many kept in place by force. The reality is that everywhere, national boundaries are redrawn, and as anthems and maps change, so also do national virtues. The myth of eternal nations, is solely a creation of rulers.

There are 191 member nations in the United Nations. Each nation has its own flag, anthem, and geographical boundaries. Every nation claims greatness on many accounts, though many nations cooperate more internationally than they did before the advent of the international institutions.

RELIGION AND NATIONALISM

It is true that the sanctity given to a nation may play some role in consolidating some forces in society and even yield some benefits, as happened in the twentieth century when many nations rebelled against colonialism, imperialism, and foreign dominance and exploitation. However, soon after a people achieves political independence, nationalism develops into a myth and a cult.

A typical example would be India. Historical India is quite different from the present-day geographical and political entity. Conquest brought vast areas of land under the rule of emperors. Under colonial British rule, India changed its geographical boundaries radically after a period of consolidation. At the time of World War I there was no Pakistan, no Sri Lanka, no Myanmar: the whole land was India and all nationalists offered their loyalty to India. But by the time the British left India in 1947, those three nations had been carved out of India. Still later, Bangladesh emerged out of Pakistan. All these countries now have their own nationalist rhetoric, and citizens swear loyalty to the new political entities.

In India, as in Pakistan, nationalism uses religion as a tool and an instrument to consolidate its position. Humanists recognize that nationalism and religion have the same appeal. Both are based on collective identities and marginalize the individual. They treat the individual as of no consequence. They seek to mediate with a mythical entity on behalf of the people for a supposed better future for the people. While political parties are the instruments of nationalism, priests are the instruments of religion; and together they make a potent combination. As radical humanists often point out, the freedom and sovereignty of humans was robbed by religions in earlier days and political parties in modern days. Religions did it in the name of God. Political parties do it in the name of delegation of power. While religion theoretically can go beyond nationalism, in practice nationalism and religion are hand in glove, because religion adapts itself to suit national needs.

After independence, extreme Hindu nationalism in India—which had long existed—started gaining strength and took the name and shape of *Hindutva*. Because Pakistan was created on the basis of Islam, many Indian extremists would like to see India as a Hindu homeland. In their minds, Indian culture is equated with Hinduism. A leading ideologue and political leader from the extreme right calls for cultural nationalism, in which Christians and Muslims in India would be asked to adopt *Hindu* culture to prove their identity and national spirit. The advocates of *Hindutva* claim that they are democratic and that their ideas have popular support.

Many religions treat humans as sinners or as unworthy of any dignity other than that which is given them by a god. The morals, values, and principles of religions are oriented toward service of God. The intermediary institution of priesthood was created to negotiate, to interpret God's commands to humans. Most religions are stumbling blocks to implementing human rights, children's rights, human values, and morals. It is an uphill struggle to break the religious chains around humans and make them free. The minds of humans are polluted with religious superstitions, blind beliefs from childhood. Even scientists are sometimes unable to overcome the indoctrination of their childhood and are caught in these religious cobwebs. This is antithetical to the concept of modern society, but the intimate connection between religion and the identity of a nation makes reform very difficult.

Nationalism presents similar problems. A scourge of nation-states is the system of political parties. Political parties are created to capture power, claiming to represent the best interests of the people. They appeal in the name of the nation, attracting voters with manifestos and promises of a bright future. Elections are held periodically to get the consent of people and elect the representatives. In this process, the sovereignty of people is delegated to the representatives. Political parties vie with each other to lure the voters with all sorts of slogans. People cannot go and sit in parliaments or senates to monitor their day-to-day affairs. Hence, they prefer the representatives to act on their behalf. In this process, the elected representatives become powerful and, in due course, act as though they are the masters. Ultimately, a leader emerges as a very powerful charismatic person with enormous powers. That process leads to corruption. To remain in power and to win elections continuously, the persons in power compete in raising more attractive slogans and give false promises. Visions of great nations and great history are propagated.

Political parties enter into every walk of life. In due course, they also enter religion. Political parties forget the secular principles of separating religion from state. Religion, in turn, demands promises from political parties during elections. Thus, religion enters politics indirectly. Religion wants the political parties to respect beliefs, holy books, and superstitious commands. Most religions obstruct the laws of abortion and opposes birth control. Religion opposes euthanasia. Religion opposes teaching of evolution in schools. Religion demands prayers in primary schools. There is no end to religious demands from political parties. To get votes, the parties promise whatever the religion demands. Thus the collective notions and irrationality that power either a nation-state or a religion are detrimental to human freedom. These myths should end so that humanism can help create world citizens and a cosmopolitan atmosphere.

We have a long way to go, but that is a desirable and prosperous way, indeed.

NOTE

1. Manabendra Nath Roy, *Nationalism: An Antiquated Cult* ([Bombay]: Radical Democratic Party, [1942?]).

INNAIAH NARISETTI grew up in Patareddi, India. He received both an FA (father of arts) and BA at Andhra Christian College, Guntur, in 1958. During his college years, Narisetti actively participated in student movements, political movements, and literary movements. His PhD is in science, more specifically in the areas of determinism, space-time, second law of thermodynamics, modern biological progress, new quantum theory, and theory of relativity. He runs the Radical Humanist Association in India and has written for many magazines in India and the United States, including *Free Inquiry*.

16.

Political Humanism in Africa in the Twenty-first Century
A Nigerian Perspective

Leo Igwe

*We [must] work to humanize the earth through specific proj-
ects related to health, education and other vital issues, while
at the same time working to better ourselves through
increasing self-knowledge. Self-knowledge involves a conscious effort to understand and transform ourselves, towards
the goal of personal unity and self-liberation. This dual-
focus—changing society and changing ourselves—is the
most meaningful and revolutionary form of human activism.*

—Mission Statement of the Humanist Movement of Africa

Political humanism stands for the perception of government and deployment of state power that draws on humanist ethics and morality. The humanist ethical system maintains that human beings can be good without believing in God or relying on any superhuman power. It espouses the cultivation of what humanist philosopher Paul Kurtz calls "common moral decencies": personal integrity, truthfulness, benevolence, self-respect, and so on. Humanist morality is based on human needs and experience, informed by reason and science, and driven by compassion and empathy.

Humanists reject the supernatural (or mystical) view of reality, of social organization, and of ethics. Political humanism therefore provides an alternative to political religionism—political animism, political Judaism, political Christianity, political Islam, and other contraptions of faith or theology that seek to influence, control, or direct the affairs of the state. Humanist political philosophy defends the ideals of secularism and of separation of church (mosque, temple, shrine) and state.

In virtually all ages, the religious worldview has held sway in politics, government, and statecraft. Godmen, women, and the clergy—popes, prophets, bishops, priests, sheikhs, and gurus—have, through their political plots and intrigues, dictated and manipulated the instruments of government to suit the doctrines and dogmas of their faiths. Consequently, the perspectives of humanists—atheists and agnostics—have been shut out or completely ignored. Political views of humanists have been demonized. And humanist individuals are deemed unworthy of holding public posts and offices. Political humanism aims at counteracting this religionist conspiracy. It seeks to restore to political reckoning and respectability the views and out look of nonreligious people. To this end, political humanism articulates the views, interests, and positions of humanists and seeks to ensure that such perspectives influence the instruments of government and public policy.

AFRICA AND THE CHALLENGE OF POLITICAL HUMANISM

Discussing the place of humanism in African politics presents a difficult challenge because Africa does not have a distinct tradition of humanism—atheism, agnosticism, and religious skepticism. Instead, Africa has a long and deep tradition of religious piety, obscurantism, and mysticism (Africans are among the most religious people in the world). African thought and culture are permeated by antihumanistic tendencies—theism, supernaturalism, occultism, dogmatism, and superstition.

These forces govern all aspects of people's lives. They guide and inform the politics and governance. And there is one African country where this god-politics is fully at work with all its dilemmas, disruptions, and devastations. That country is Nigeria.

RELIGION AND POLITICS IN NIGERIA

Nigeria is Africa's most populous—and dare I say most religious—country. In Nigeria, belief in God is paramount. More than 90 percent of the citizens belong to one of at least three religions: Islam, Christianity, and traditional religion (animism). Northern Nigeria is dominated by Muslims, southern Nigeria by Christians, with a number of animists in the southwest and Middle Belt regions. As in other African countries, religion prevails in all aspects of the people's lives and heavily influences the management and deployment of state power and authority.

The dominant religions animism, Islam, and Christianity have been strong determinants of the people's political choices, power distribution, and social organization. And these we shall discuss as political animism, political Islam, and political Christianity.

Political Animism

Before the arrival of the alien religions—Islam and Christianity—most inhabitants of what is today known as Nigeria were animists. People worshiped assorted spirits and deities, including Amadioha, Ahiajoku. Sango, Ogun, and Ifa. Traditional religion was the basis of sociopolitical organization and administration of the different empires, kingdoms, and fiefdoms that existed in the region before Arab and Western colonialization.

Under political animism there is some distinction between the shrine and the state, between the powers of the priests and those of the kings and rulers. But in actual fact, the powers of the kings are subordinate to those of the priests, who are believed to be representatives and mouthpieces of the gods and clan spirits. The kings consult the gods through the priests to know their will concerning any matter that affects the society. No policy or decision is made unless it receives the blessings of the gods. Among the Yorubas, for example, it is traditionally the Ifa—not the people—who ultimately determines who becomes the Oba (the Yoruba name for King). All decisions of the people are subject to ratification by the gods. Politically, animism held sway in Nigerian communities till the invasion of Islamic religion.

Political Islam

Islam came to Nigeria around the eleventh century through Muslim traders and jihadists as part of the Arab colonialism of Africa. But the Islamic faith owes its currents political dominance in northern Nigeria to the 1804 jihad of Usman Danfodio (1754–1817). Danfodio was a member of a Muslim brotherhood called Quadiriyya. He studied under a famous teacher at Agades, where he got in touch with the imperialist trend then stirring throughout the Islamic world. Danfodio returned to Gobir, one of the Hausa states, where he launched a jihad against the Hausa kings, whom he accused of corruption, impiety, heresy, and adulteration of Islamic principles. His bloody revolution swept through the Hausa land

and beyond to Adamawa in the east and old Oyo in the west. Danfodio removed the Habe kings and appointed his Islamic followers as emirs (kings) of the conquered states and established his own political kingdom, the Sokoto caliphate, which administered on the basis of his "purist version of Islam" and sharia (Islamic law).

This Islamic political structure remained in place in spite of the colonization of northern Nigeria by the British in the late nineteenth century and its eventual amalgamation with southern Nigeria in 1914 because the British colonialists, in line with their policy of Indirect Rule, did not interfere with the Islamic political institutions. They administered northern Nigeria through such traditional rulers as emirs and alkalis.

The only aspect of the political system that the British tampered with was the Islamic law, which they made subservient to the British legal and justice system. They expunged aspects of the law that they considered repugnant to natural justice and humanity, and initiated a process of legal reform that culminated in the replacement of the sharia criminal code with the penal code—a modified version of the sharia law—in 1960.

The Quest for Sharia

Sharia is central to political Islam because it is the tool with which Islamic theocrats tyrannize over the lives of Muslims and non-Muslims. The abrogation of the sharia criminal code by the colonialists did not go down well with Islamists in Nigeria. Muslim activists describe it as an act of humiliation from a non-Islamic power. They regarded its substitute, the penal code, as a colonial imposition and a device to get rid of the Islamic law. And thus began the quest to restore and implement sharia law in Nigeria. The agitation for sharia was not pronounced during the first republic because Nigeria at that time practiced a regional system of government and northern Nigeria was under a pro-Islamic government of the Northern Peoples Congress (NPC), led by Alhaji Ahmadu Bello, a descendant of Usman Danfodio. But the event that actually marked the commencement of the sharia politics was the 1977–1978 Constituent Assembly, which was convened by Gen. Olusegun Obasanjo's military administration to debate on a draft constitution for the country as part of the program for a return to civil rule. But the delegates were divided over the adoption of sharia, and ultimately most of the Muslim delegates from northern Nigeria, led by Alhaji Shehu Shagari, staged a walkout to protest the rejection of the Islamic law.

It took the intervention of the then–head of state, General Obasanjo, to broker a compromise and resolve the stalemate. Sharia was eventually enshrined in the nation's constitution, but its application was restricted to Islamic personal matters. This constitutional provision for sharia still fell short of what the Islamists wanted—full sharia. The 1989 Constituent Assembly did not allow for debate on sharia because sharia was one of the issues classified by the Armed Forces Ruling Council as a "no-go area." But in 1999, the Islamic law took the political center stage again following the country's return to civilian rule.

Gov. Ahmed Sani of Zamfara unilaterally adopted sharia as state law and declared his state an Islamic state. During his election campaign, Governor Sani told the people of Zamfara that there was much suffering in the land because they had strayed from the path of sharia. He assured the poor, the sick, the jobless, the uneducated, that once elected into office he would implement sharia and their problems would be over. The adoption of sharia in Zamfara led to widespread agitation for the Islamic law in other northern states, but few other Muslim majority states adopted the law. Initial attempts to implement the law in Kaduna led to bloody riots and clashes between Christians and Muslims. In reaction, the Nigerian government ordered the "erring states" to return to status quo ante, but the directive was largely ignored. Instead, it led to more pro-sharia riots and demonstrations.

Amid the crisis and confusion, some Muslim politicians came together and formed the Supreme Council for Sharia (SCS), under the leadership of Ahmed Datti, a former presidential aspirant. The SCS was founded to promote the implementation of sharia nationwide. Today, sharia is fully operational in at least twelve states in northern Nigeria. A few other states have introduced varying degrees of Islamic theocracy at the local level, thanks to political pressure from the SCS.

Islamic Organizations

Politically, Islam owes its firm grip on the north not only to the jihad of Usman Danodio but also to the overt and covert plots, intrigues, and campaigns, sometimes violent, of a number of Islamic groups and organizations. They included Jama'atu Nasril Islam, Society for the Victory of Islam (JNI), Supreme Council for Islamic Affairs (SCIA), Muslim Students Society (MSS), Shiite Muslim Brotherhood, Izala, and Quadiriyya and Tijaniyya sects, among others. But politically, Islam faces a serious threat and challenge from the other alien religion . . . Christianity. The Christian faith has its stronghold in southern Nigeria.

Political Christianity

Christianity was introduced in Nigeria by missionaries from Europe in the late nineteenth century. The Christian religion owes its rapid spread and expansion to the aggressive evangelization strategies of the different missionary groups from Great Britain that invaded the country. One of the most powerful tools of Christian evangelization was the establishment of mission schools and colleges, which served as tools for the conversion of Nigerian "heathens."

More important, the mission schools served as breeding grounds for Christian-oriented politics and a Christian political elite that took over from the colonialists at independence. All Nigeria's foremost nationalists, including Herbert Macaulay, Nnamdi Azikiwe, Ahmadu Bello, Tafawa Balewa, Obafemi Awolowo, and Michael Enahoro, were products of Christian mission schools and colleges. So, by independence, Christianity had become a major force in Nigerian politics. For instance, during the first republic (1960–1966) the National Council of Nigerian Citizens, based in the south, could not take any action against Catholic authorities who were maltreating and discriminating against Protestants. The authorities turned a blind eye to the actions of Catholic nuns and nurses who deprived non-Catholic patients and expectant mothers of health-care services and subjected children of non-Catholics to forced baptism and conversion.

In the former western region, with an approximately equal number of Muslims and Christians, politics was Christian oriented. All members of the political elite were products of mission schools. And out of the regional party's inaugural and executive membership, only two were Muslims.

Much more than the regular level, Christian religious politics provided a counterweight to the political intrigues of Muslim Jihadists from the North. But Christian politics was never coordinated until the formation of the Christian Association of Nigeria (CAN) in 1976, which was formed to serve as the political voice of Christians—to articulate, present, and represent their views, interests, and positions. CAN therefore became for political Christianity what the SCIA, JNI, and SCS have been for political Islam.

The Secular Question

One issue has always pitched Christian politicians against their Muslim counterparts in Nigeria—whether Nigeria should be a secular state that is not biased for or against any religion or belief system. A secular government has no religious or ideological character. It is religiously neutral. Islamists in Nigeria argue that the nation is not a secular state. In fact, Muslim politicians and ideologues do not want to hear the words "secular" and "secularization." Islamic writer Ibrahim Sulaiman describes secularization as "a bastard of Christianity" and "a machinery to blackmail Muslims, impede the progress of Islam, and reduce it to an earthly concept." According to Alhaji Lateef Adegbite, the secretary general of the SCIA, secularism is antithetical to Islam. This view was echoed by Mohammad Embeay, who said that "to call Nigeria a secular state is to say at least not a correct [statement] if not a blatant lie, a great falsehood and a great disrespect to the Muslim community in Nigeria. For it is too obvious and unequivocal that Islam and secularism are two parallel lines that never and will never meet."[1]

But Christian politicians insist that Nigeria is a secular state and have used that argument to block the plots and schemes of Muslim politicians to make Nigeria an Islamic state. Nevertheless, Christian support for a secular Nigeria is not based on a genuine commitment to a Nigeria in which the political order steers clear of religious matters. States in the Christian-dominated south are hardly secular. And Christian groups have not opposed state sponsorship of Christian pilgrimages, purchase and distribution of Bibles, decoration of state capitols during Christian festivals, the recent handover of schools back to the missions, and other policies and programs that violate the principle of separation of church and state.

Christian support for a secular Nigeria is mainly for the following reasons: First, Christians in Nigeria do not have a centralized political structure or tradition such as the Muslim Sokoto Caliphate to fall back on. And second, due to the high population of Muslims—50 percent—Christians feel that they would be disadvantaged if Nigeria were run along religious lines.

Thus, in spite of Nigeria's claim to be a secular state, religion has continuously played a prominent role in its politics and government since independence. In the first republic, the governments of the eastern and western regions were pro-Christian, while that of the northern region was pro-Islam. The leader of the Northern Peoples Congress, Alhaji Ahmadu Bello, was a Jihadist, and, as the premier, he swore to continue the Islamic theocracy of Usman Danfodio. Bello's theocratic track record was so pronounced that after his death on January 15, 1966, the newspaper *Drum* (based in southern Nigeria) published a cartoon in which Bello was floating in limbo and confessing his sins of mixing politics and religion and playing the roles of a prophet and a Caesar. During the Nigerian civil war, the leader of the now-defunct Biafran Republic, Col. Odumegwu Ojukwu, used religion in his war propaganda to rally global support for the mostly Christian Biafrans, whom he said were being massacred by Islam-dominated Nigeria because of their faith. And in the early 1970s, the government of Gen. Yakubu Gowon, a Christian, took over schools from the Christian missions and other voluntary agencies in what was widely seen as a gesture of appreciation to the Islamic north for their support during the war. Still as part of its religious politics, Gowon's government secured for Nigeria an observer status at the Organization of the Islamic Conference (OIC)—an organization meant for Islamic countries—and created the Pilgrims Welfare Board to cater to the needs of Muslim pilgrims. In 1976, the army chief of staff under Obasanjo's military administration, Brig. Gen. Musa Yar'dua invited Christian religious leaders to a meeting at the Dodan Barracks—the seat of the military government—to seek their opinions on the National Pledge to be recited in the schools. The pledge, which was unanimously endorsed by Christian and Muslim religious leaders, ends with a prayer, "So help me God"—a line deliberately crafted to appeal to the sentiments of religionists.

During his time as president of Nigeria (1979–1983), Alhaji Shehu Shagari tried to establish an Islamic Affairs Board to regulate Islamic matters and a counterpart board for Christians, but the idea was opposed by Christians on the grounds of constitutional prohibition of governments meddling with religious matters. In 1986, President Ibrahim Babangida (1985–1993) attempted to make Nigeria a full member of the OIC, but the move was fiercely opposed by Christians. Strangely enough, Gen. Sanni Abacha (1993–1998) stirred the country away from the religious politics of his predecessors. His government clamped down on the Shiite Muslim brotherhood led by Ibrahim El-zak-zaky, which was campaigning for the institution of an Islamic state.

But the current civilian administration, elected in 1999, has further eroded the constitutional line separating religion and state. apart from the sharia being implemented in the north, President Obasanjo has created a largely Christian-oriented government at the center. Immediately after his inauguration, President Obasanjo built the Aso Rock Chapel in Abuja, which is being maintained with state money. The "born-again" president has gone to the extent of making Christian prayers and revivals part of state functions and activities.

In truth, Nigeria's secular project is in danger. Islamists are strongly opposed to it, while Christian support for it is dubious, hypocritical, and even mischievous. But secularism is one thing Nigeria needs in order to thrive and prosper because it offers a political framework for the peaceful and harmonious coexistence of individuals of all religions and beliefs. The time has therefore come for Nigerian humanists to rise up and defend, enlarge, and enhance their heritage.

HUMANISM AND POLITICS IN THE TWENTY-FIRST CENTURY

In the various manifestos, declarations, and affirmations, humanists have articulated far-reaching goals, visions, and aspirations. But what is now left for them is to apply these ideals to the needs and problems of their societies and, in so doing, change the world. To achieve this, humanists must be actively involved in politics. In the past, political apathy has done the humanist cause a great disservice. Humanists need to articulate policies that can enhance public good and development. This will entail building coalitions and proposing bills to safeguard and defend human rights, democracy, secularism, and open society. Humanist groups need to lobby their governments on such humanist issues as separation of religion and state, family planning, birth control, sex education, and civil liberties.

Religious fanatics often capitalize on socioeconomic difficulties to foist their political agenda on gullible masses. Humanists must also articulate programs that address the social and economic needs of the people. Such programs should include the alleviation of poverty, ignorance, diseases, and unemployment and the eradication of superstition, promotion of the scientific temper, technological intelligence, and productive use of energies that are most often dissipated in religious fanaticism and terrorism.

Particularly in Africa, humanists need to support the cause of secularization reformation. The African continent has not experienced the transformation Europe underwent during the renaissance. Africa entered independence with a lot of optimism and high expectations about its future, but these hopes have been dashed and squandered thanks to the parochial, ethnoreligious politics of its leaders.

Humanists therefore need to support groups and governments committed to African enlightenment and universal humanism. Humanist politics must also include campaigns against religionist governments such as the one in Khartoum, the Lord's Resistant Army in Uganda, the ethnic militia in the Great Lake Region, and Islamic militant groups in Algeria and Egypt.

In Nigeria, humanists must campaign against political Islam and sharia law. They should oppose, among other things, state sponsorship of pilgrimages, state funding of sharia courts and religious charities, and other government policies that undermine the separation of religion and state. Politically, humanists should work to build and realize a Nigeria and a world in which people of all racial and ethnic groups and all religious and nonreligious affiliations can live together freely, peacefully, and productively. To achieve such a vibrant political humanism requires an active humanist movement. Humanists need to strengthen organized humanism in their different countries, so that in Nigeria, for instance, the Nigerian Humanist Movement could do for political humanism what the SCIA, SCS, and JNI are doing for political Islam and the CAN for political Christianity.

Religion has caused—and is still causing—darkness, decay, and misery in Africa. Much more than slavery, racism, or colonialism, the religious faiths have been responsible for the underdevelopment of Africa and the black world. Africa is in dire need of a rational alternative to the corrupt and mistrusted political ideologies of religionists, a program that will facilitate the restoration of African humanity and human rights and bring about African emancipation, development, and progress. And this, I submit, will constitute the agenda of political humanism in Africa in the twenty-first century.

NOTE

1. Mohammad Embeay, quoted in the *Guardian* (Lagos), July 11, 2003.

LEO IGWE is executive secretary of the Nigerian Humanist Movement and director of the Center for Inquiry–Nigeria. He is a board member of the Atheist Alliance International and the International Humanist Ethical Union growth and development representative for sub-Saharan Africa. Igwe is the editor of the *Humanist Inquirer* and the author of several articles on African humanism, skepticism, and freethought.

17.

Democracy versus Secularism in the Muslim World

Taner Edis

I find it incomprehensible that we are still at that stage where they still believe in [creationism]. Materialism is so evident to me; how can they not believe it? It's beyond reason. It's such a violation of reason. In many parts of the Muslim world, that's what holds them back.

—Tariq Ali

T he Muslim world is in crisis, and we know the remedy. Or so many people seem to be saying these days.

Among Muslims themselves, What is to be done? is a perennial question. Around them they notice poverty, corruption, and humiliation in the face of Western military and commercial power. To solve these problems, some call for adopting Western ways in the most important practical aspects of life, reducing Islam to a personal belief—a mere cultural flavoring. Some dig in their heels, rejecting the modern world and claiming that a falling away from traditional Islam is the root of all Muslim misfortune. Most others, including those we humanists call "Islamic fundamentalists," try to find a way toward development without sacrificing their Muslim identity.

Westerners also seem to be full of advice for Muslims. After all, we usually notice Islam as a problem. Islam always seems to be associated with terrorism, political instability, dictatorial regimes, oppression of women, or immigrant communities with extreme ways of life. So conservatives recommend that Muslims adopt Western political and economic ways, especially freer markets. Some of our more extreme commentators think that conversion to Christianity would be the best solution to Muslim woes. Many leftward-inclined thinkers, in contrast, hold Western imperialism responsible for the crises that Muslims face. In their view, the first step to improving the lot of Muslims would be for Western powers to quit manipulating Muslim countries. Some leftists even admire Islamist rhetoric for its supposedly liberatory aspirations and its seeming aura of cultural authenticity.

Humanists, not being a particularly large or powerful group, can do little to shape debate over the crises of the Muslim world. However, this powerlessness does not stop us from being ambitious. After all, we think we have much to offer to humanity as a whole.

To begin with, political secularism seems a good prescription for Muslims.[1] Trying to run modern states while remaining shackled to medieval religious laws is a bad idea; theocracy is a dead end. Muslim countries, though they have had a later start than Western states, can surely come to acknowledge the virtue of allowing individual freedom in religious belief while preventing any one orthodoxy from prevailing in matters of government. Adopting secular government would be a giant step forward in improving human rights and the prospects for democracy in Muslim-majority countries. Even devoutly religious people can accept that genuine faith flourishes when individuals are free to choose, without having religion imposed on them by their government.

In fact, many humanists would like to see the Muslim world coming to embrace much of the European Enlightenment that we admire. Economic development, an expansion of individual liberties, democracy, an explosive growth in scientific knowledge and technological capabilities—these and a host of other benefits most Muslims themselves acknowledge as real achievements are what humanists identify as legacies of the Enlightenment. With the Enlightenment, we stopped priests from running the show and elevated the consent of citizens over the will of divinely appointed monarchs. Just as Christianity and Judaism were reformed and tamed in the industrialized West, we believe Islam can also be modernized. And, we may add, Islam is in desperate need of a reformation.[2] The cultural climate in Muslim lands must become more humanistic.

All this is well and good, and perhaps in some ideal world it would even be good advice. However, Muslims bring a different history and social context to their encounter with the modern world; the historical accidents that secularized Western politics need not be repeated for Muslims. Today, the reasons many Westerners find to be ambivalent about our Enlightenment legacy resonate even more strongly in Muslim lands. And though many Muslims also desire freedom of conscience and democracy, in the Muslim world such ideals more often conflict with secularism than support one another in the way we have become accustomed to in the West.

SECULARISM FROM ABOVE

Muslim-majority countries *are* in trouble. Most struggle with dire poverty; the exceptions are oil-rich states that are wealthy but make no creative contributions to human culture.[3] They are either undemocratic or have the formal apparatus of democracy with serious imperfections in practice. Corruption runs rampant. Whenever these countries come into competition with Western powers, the results are dismal.

Militarily, Muslim states are dependent, often negligible. In terms of scientific and technological productivity, tiny Israel is more significant than most Muslim nations. Many, even those sometimes considered relatively advanced like Turkey, are colonies in all but name.

This crisis, however, is not new. Ever since their first encounters with a newly industrialized West, Muslims have come out on the losing side. What is to be done? is a two-centuries-old question for Muslims.[4] And it has long been clear to many in the ruling elites that Muslim countries had to accept some degree of Westernization or risk enslavement if not annihilation. Having suffered lopsided defeats on the battlefield, military officers were typically at the forefront of reform. Starting from the mid-nineteenth century, they pushed their countries to adopt Western knowledge and institutions. They often faced significant opposition from traditional religious elites. The perception of the military and bureaucratic elites—probably an accurate one—was that without a concerted, state-organized effort to join the modern world, the crisis they were facing would become a much more complete disaster.

Part of the package of Westernization was secularizing government. Turkey, the remnant of the crumbled Ottoman Empire that had ruled over a good part of Muslim lands, took secularization to its farthest when the new Republic of Turkey took shape in the 1920s and 1930s. Rapid modernization required a true cultural revolution, breaking the power of the religious leaders who presided over a peasant society. Catching up to the twentieth century meant repressing traditional religion, concentrating power in a superficially Westernized bureaucratic elite, and even trying to impose a reformed sense of religion from above. Turkish Republicans declared that Islam from now on would be a purely personal affair between each individual and his or her God, with no influence on affairs of state or indeed any important worldly concern. They even attempted to make this reformed religion an instrument of cultural modernization, bringing Islam under the tight control of a national Directorate of Religious Affairs, suppressing most other expressions of Islam.

The elites of many other newly independent Muslim states emulated Turkey, which they admired for defeating the imperial powers. But not a few also resented Turkey for trying to shed its Muslim character and join the West, so the new Muslim states typically did not go as far as Turkey; they retained a diminished role for Islamic law and acknowledged a vaguely "Islamic" character for the state. Nevertheless, modern secular politics appeared to have the upper hand. Into the 1960s and beyond, efforts to overcome the crisis in Muslim lands took their ideological flavors from nationalism or even socialism; political Islam did not appear to be a significant force. Secularization seemed to be taking root in public life.

It did not work.[5] Secularization from above had some partial success: It occasionally produced some enduring modern institutions and sustained ruling elites eager to join the modern world. Upwardly mobile men put on suits and ties and women uncovered their hair. However, the secularized elites, who were rarely immune to corruption, ruled over a resentful population who had never relinquished their traditional religiosity.

Conservative Islam went underground; though its public expression was suppressed, it never became a modern individualist religion on the model of an eviscerated Protestantism. All this might not have mattered much if secular elites could have delivered on their promise that their form of modernization would overcome Muslim humiliation and bring prosperity and security. What modernizing Muslim countries such as Turkey ended up with instead was a prosperous elite who were estranged from the conservative religious culture of the bulk of the population.

RE-ISLAMIZATION FROM ABOVE

Devout Muslims naturally resisted the secularization imposed on them. Traditional peasant societies led by religious scholars, however, could not oppose the power of a modern state apparatus. Consequently, what developed out of the traditional, devout culture was not a reassertion of old-fashioned Islam but what became known as Muslim fundamentalism. Fundamentalists are creatures of today's world; from their new structures of religious authority to their urban constituencies, they are a distinctly modern way of opposing the Enlightenment ideals and political behavior humanists so often take for granted.[6]

Fundamentalism spawned political Islam. And in the 1970s and 1980s, political Islamists began to have serious dreams of attaining power. Many thought that since Westernization and secular government were imposed on an unwilling population from above, the way to right this state of affairs was to take control of the state. This notion of "Islamization from above" has deep roots in Muslim history; the orthodox Islamic political ideal demands a state ruled by Muslims who implement Islamic law and provide the conditions necessary to propagate Islam in a population that need not be majority Muslim. However, the practical impetus to the dream of seizing state power came with the Islamic Revolution in Iran. Though Iran is not a typical case and the circumstances enabling its revolution will not easily materialize elsewhere, many Islamists took heart that a revolutionary overthrow of their secular elites was possible.

Some advocates of Islamization from above worked through the military; in places like Pakistan, they even found partial success. Some took to terrorism and achieved nothing concrete even though government efforts to root them out usually took the form of massive repression and state terror, increasing the alienation felt by nonviolent conservative Muslims. Some Islamizers attempted to work through the political process, aiming to take over the state apparatus gradually. Their intellectuals denounced democracy as a Western abomination elevating the will of humans over the law of God, declaring that sovereignty ultimately belonged to God, not the people. This form of Islamist politics, however, was usually either defeated by entrenched secular elites or else reached a stalemate.

ISLAMISTS EMBRACE DEMOCRACY

Islamization from below worked much better. Islamic charity workers organizing social services for slum dwellers did not attract media attention as terrorist cells bent on overthrowing the government did, but they were much more successful. By the 1990s, the political landscape in most Muslim countries had taken on an overtly Islamic color because the everyday culture in these countries had become much more explicitly and *publicly* Islamic. The more ambitious Islamist political movements were blunted, absorbed into the system, or simply defeated by force. In Turkey, Islamist hopes for taking over the government and imposing Islam from above were repeatedly thwarted by a military that had held onto its secularist tradition. But other developments made it much more difficult for secular elites to impose their vision on the population at large.

One opportunity for re-Islamization of society came as an unintended consequence of economic globalization. In Turkey, as national-scale industries were gobbled up by multinationals and brands like Coca-Cola displaced what used to be indigenous consumer products, smaller, more regionally based economic enterprises found an opening. These local suppliers to the giants were not only regional but they were the instruments of upward mobility for a new elite that had much deeper roots in traditionally religious local cultures. Islamist politics united this new Islamic business class with the huge population of recent immigrants from rural areas into urban slums, papering over their conflicts of interest. Islamic political identities now had real muscle; they could not be as easily suppressed as before.

This muscle, however, did not prevent Islamist aspirations for taking over the state from failuring repeatedly. As a result, many Islamist movements around the world have begun to emphasize their popular support. Instead of propagating theologically purist fantasies of Islamic states, they play identity politics and present demands for democratic freedoms. Secular elites are not about to be swept away with a revolution. The distinctly Islamic form of economics that Islamist thinkers have long been fantasizing about will not work in the context of global capitalism, which in any case has presented opportunities for a conservative Islamic elite. So Islamists have begun to make peace with democracy and with global capitalism. Many have toned down their anti-Western rhetoric, becoming content to act as administrators of a neocolonial order as long as they can represent authentic-seeming local cultural identities.[7]

Today, the new generation of Islamic thinkers rarely denounce democracy as a Western hoax. Instead, they raise the banner of democratic freedoms against an oppressive secular state. They demand their right to live as Muslims without submerging their religious identity when they enter the public sphere. Living a genuinely Islamic life means submitting to Islamic law and forcing Muslim communities to live by secular, one-size-fits-all laws, interfering with their religious freedom. Furthermore, if a clear majority wants the laws they live under and their political life in general to express a shared moral culture, it is only the tyranny of a powerful elite that prevents them from attaining their goal. Indeed, secular elites have regularly had to resort to antidemocratic and even military means to prevent Islamic political demands from being realized. When Islamist activists complain of state-sponsored oppression, their complaint is not imaginary.

The new democratic Islamic rhetoric reflects not only the success of re-Islamization from below but also the failure of Islamist attempts to control the state. Politics in countries like Turkey are often a heavy-handed identity politics, with raging culture wars, in part because in today's global economy, Muslim-majority states without oil wealth have very little freedom to adopt policies that are not dictated by financial markets and the International Monetary Fund. Presenting different cultural options is about all that different political parties *can* do. But identity politics also exploits a difficulty inherent in the liberal democratic political philosophy that humanists take for granted. Since we set so much store in individual choice and the freedom to fashion one's own identity and live according to it, we tend to present the demands of communal ideologies as claims for individual freedom. Ensuring the secular nature of the state, however, is impossible without interfering with an individual's desire to live according to the comprehensive norms of a religious community.[8]

We tend to portray secularism as a position neutral between religions. It is not. Most religions are not individualistic, and they come with substantive political prescriptions for the faithful. Secularism in government is neutral only between religions that conceive of people as individual choice makers. Religions that forge strong communal identities operate at a disadvantage in a modern secular state; secularism does privilege the nonreligious—and the liberal Protestant and the New Ager—over conservative Catholics and orthodox Muslims.

Muslim countries confront this difficulty, but it is not entirely unknown to democratic Western countries. Consider the problems of allowing space for tight-knit communities, such as the Amish or orthodox Jews, in the United States. In a large country, small groups such as these can be handled as exceptions; larger groups can be assimilated into a wider culture with a healthy dose of multiculturalist rhetoric that papers over the fact that even though their religions look superficially different, everyone is expected to aspire to the same bland suburban consumerism. Nevertheless, multiculturalism and identity politics put a strain on liberal political systems and Enlightenment ideals even close to home. Europeans, in particular, have the very vexing problem of how to deal with large Muslim immigrant communities that demand the right to live according to their communal religious norms as a matter of individual liberty.[9]

Today's Islamist politics, then, incorporate a genuine democratic impulse; their demands for cultural space and community rights are fully part of their democratic thrust. Even here in the West, the cutting edge of democratic theorizing has acquired a postmodern color, recognizing that a notion of freedom that covertly assumes everyone must be a liberal individualist consumer is too narrow, that it can easily become oppressive when it ignores the communities and nonnegotiable, unchosen identities that people bring to politics.

Unfortunately, the Enlightenment ideals that humanists hold dear can best flower in a social environment not dominated by a small set of unchosen and usually religious identities. The Islamic vision of protecting communal freedoms from state interference has a way of leading not to a totalitarian theocracy but to localized rule by the clergy of religiously delineated communities.[10] In fact, Islamists often advocate just such an arrangement.

Western nation-states after the Enlightenment solved the problem of intercommunal conflict by separating government from religion, but Muslim multinational empires of the past found a very different means of preventing strife. The Muslim ideal has usually been a limited overall government concerned primarily with keeping the peace in a society where different communities live according to their own religious laws with minimal outside interference. While individuals live in a stifling environment dominated by their rabbis, mullahs, and priests, *community members* in such an arrangement are freer to live according to deeply felt religious identities than is the case under a liberal secular order.

WHAT ARE THE PROSPECTS FOR SECULARIZING ISLAM?

Muslim have problems, but recommending our typical humanist vision of democracy, human rights, and a secular state as an immediate solution to these problems is at the least naive. An Enlightenment political culture took root in Europe as a historical accident. A stalemate in religious conflicts led Westerners to remove government from the dominance of any

one theological point of view, and the humanist impulse of the Enlightenment generally went hand in hand with an increasing democratization of
political life. In Muslim history, secular government arrived as an imposition from above. It never grew popular roots. Where it survives, it is continually adulterated and kept in place by coercive means. As devout populations become better able to resist elite rule, as they are able to realize
their hopes for more democratic self-expression, we can expect governments in the Muslim world to become *less* secular. For example, in Turkey,
which has had the longest-running experience with the deepest form of
governmental secularism, democratization of politics has invariably meant
religious conservatives gaining in power. Turkish secularists, now long
accustomed to lacking popular support and being propped up by the military, wistfully speak of the "Anatolian Enlightenment" that flowered in the
1920s and 1930s. The Turkish experiment with the Enlightenment has
failed. The Turkish people, when given the opportunity, have indicated a
desire for a state that explicitly acknowledges and supports at least a moderately Islamic identity.

This is not to say that humanist thought can contribute nothing to the
Muslim world, or that there is no prospect for humanist developments
over a long enough term. However, any progress in this direction will not
come from above through the hand of elites, nor can it be imposed on
Western imperialist terms like those that the United States might attempt
in connection with its ill-conceived recolonization of Iraq. Whatever limited prospects exist for secularization and humanist ideals must be rooted
in the hopes that Muslims themselves harbor for a better future.

All is not bleak when we look in this direction. After all, though Muslims remain exceptionally devout by Western standards, religious skepticism is not completely unknown in the lands of Islam. And the desire to
keep spiritual beliefs at a remove from daily politics is even more common
despite the present dominance of the view that Islam is a comprehensive
way of life that does not separate the religious and the worldly.

One impetus toward secularism comes, curiously, from Iran.[11] That
country's experiment with clerical rule has been dismal; many Iranians
who grew up after the Islamic Revolution would like to move toward a less
explicitly religious form of government. This desire is particularly significant because Iranians have always been intellectual leaders in the world of
Islam.

Another source of humanism is indigenous religious heterodoxies in
Islam. For example, the Alevi sect in Turkey has always involved a kind of

religious humanism, very different in belief, attitude, and practice from orthodox Islam. Though commanding the allegiance of only about a quarter of the population, and certainly as supernaturalistic as any religion, Alevism at least means a ready-made constituency for secularism if only as a way of preventing orthodox Muslims from totally dominating public life.[12]

Islamist movements themselves can be secularizing forces in the long run because they are so much a product of modern life. While any Islamist success in its from-the-bottom democratic incarnation will mean more religion in public life, turning to identity politics also means that Islamists have to acknowledge the legitimacy of other communities, backing away from making claims to order social life for everyone. The critical question is whether Muslim cultures will change in the direction of more fragmented identities for individuals, so that religious or ethnic affiliation is not as determining as it still is. The pressures of modern economies and urban life make this a distinct possibility.

These are only examples that indicate opportunities for a humanistic approach to take hold in Islamic lands. There is nothing inevitable about this possibility, and today the best bet is that conservative religiosity will continue to dominate the scene for many generations. Nevertheless, Western humanists can do something to help with the crisis of Muslim countries. Restraining the imperial ambitions of our own political and religious conservatives would be a good start.

Perhaps more important, however, is our ability to uphold Enlightenment political and social ideals as something people from different cultural backgrounds might want to adopt. There is nothing more heartening to Muslim conservatives than signs that the Enlightenment is faltering in the West. The international bullying in which the United States is engaged certainly makes few friends among Muslims. Curiously, however, Islamists can also point to the public devoutness and bellicose fundamentalism that is so influential in the United States as a positive development—an illustration that secularism is failing even in the West, that worldly power and a rampant religiosity go together.

We cannot meaningfully intervene in the Muslim world; we can only present a good example. But first we must get out own house in order.

NOTES

1. See, for example, Roy Brown, "Opposing Political Islam," *Free Inquiry* 24, no. 1 (2003): 49.

2. This is not only a humanist wish; some liberal Western Muslims also call for reform. See, for example, Irshad Manji, *The Trouble with Islam: A Muslim's Call for Reform in Her Faith* (New York: St. Martin's Press, 2004).

3. See United Nations, *The Arab Human Development Report 2002: Creating Opportunities for Future Generations* (New York: United Nations Development Program, Regional Bureau for Arab States, 2002) and *The Arab Human Development Report 2003* (New York: United Nations Development Program, Regional Bureau for Arab States, 2003).

4. Bernard Lewis, *What Went Wrong? Western Impact and Middle Eastern Response* (New York: Oxford University Press, 2002).

5. See L. Carl Brown, *Religion and State: The Muslim Approach to Politics* (New York: Columbia University Press, 2000).

6. Gabriel A. Almond, R. Scott Appleby, and Emmanuel Sivan, *Strong Religion: The Rise of Fundamentalisms around the World* (Chicago: University of Chicago Press, 2003).

7. Ali Bayramoglu, *Türkiye'de Islami Hareket* [Turkey and the Islamic Movement]: *Sosyolojik Bir Bakis (1994–2000)* (Istanbul: Patika Yayincilik, 2001).

8. Liberal notions of democracy and secularism can clash, especially in a Muslim context. See Nuray Mert, *Islam ve Demokrasi* [Islam vs. Democracy]: *Bir Kurt Masali* (Istanbul: Iz Yayincilik, 1998).

9. At the time of this writing (January 2004), the head covering for female Muslims in educational settings is generating controversy in France and Germany, as well as in Turkey (where it is a continual flashpoint in the culture wars). The French are considering banning the display of such religious symbols in public schools either by students or teachers.

10. L. Carl Brown, *Religion and State: The Muslim Approach to Politics* (New York: Columbia University Press, 2000). It can be tempting to call traditional Islam "totalitarian" as Ibn Warraq has done in *Why I Am Not a Muslim* (Amherst, NY: Prometheus Books, 1995), chap. 6, but this view is not strictly correct.

11. See Abdolkarim Soroush, *Reason, Freedom, and Democracy in Islam* (New York: Oxford University Press, 2000).

12. There is even a leftist literature that describes Alevism as a kind of secular humanism; see, for example, R. Yürükoglu, *Okunacak En Büyük Kitap Insandir: Tarihte ve Günümüzde Alevilik* (Istanbul: Alev Yayinlari, 1990). Though exaggerated and historically incorrect, such writings at least indicate the presence of a humanist constituency.

Taner Edis was born in Istanbul to Turkish and American parents. After completing his undergraduate work at Bogaziçi University, he received his PhD from Johns Hopkins University in 1994 in theoretical and computational condensed matter physics. He has since written numerous articles, particularly on the topic of antievolutionary thought, appearing in the *Skeptical Inquirer, Reports of the National Center for Science Education,* and *Skeptic.* His critique of "Intelligent Design" in the March 2001 *Skeptical Inquirer* attracted national media attention, including notice in a front-page *New York Times* article of April 8, 2001.

Edis's book *The Ghost in the Universe: God in Light of Modern Science,* a defense of a naturalistic view of the world, was published by Prometheus Books and received the Morris D. Forkosch award for best humanist book of 2002.

18.

The Israeli-Palestinian Conflict
Can We Find a Humanist Solution?

Barry F. Seidman

There is a great deal of discouragement and lethargy in Palestine, and also elsewhere in the Arab world. So much has been written and proclaimed about the new era of peace, the benefits of peace, the economy of peace, etc., that with five years of non-peace, people are understandably disaffected, fed up with lies, fed up with Israeli arrogance, fed up, above all, with their own sense of powerlessness and failure.

–Edward Said, concerning the Oslo Accords

I should much rather see reasonable agreement with the Arabs on the basis of living together in peace than the creation of a Jewish State. Apart from practical considerations, my awareness of the essential nature of Judaism resists the idea of a Jewish State, with borders, an army, and a measure of temporal power, no matter how modest. I am afraid of the inner damage Judaism will sustain.

– Albert Einstein

Commonalities. This is what many humanists tend to search for in their fellow beings. Human traits that we share—from cooperation to competition to curiosity—we often argue, can be better evidence of our common humanity than our dissimilarities can. Although this notion is probably true, our awareness of it does not necessarily lead to establishing any sort of common ground. Indeed, what it can predict for us is quite the opposite. Too often for my tastes, people superficially admit similarities while remaining keenly focused on seemingly drastic differences. This tendency creates a mental block in the minds of people with opposing viewpoints to the similarity of their humanity. In essence, they cannot see the humans for the population.

One similarity that seems to exist among all humans is their tendency toward complex psychological behavior created by severe circumstances. One such behavior is the victim/oppressor cycle that so many members of our species get caught up in. When oppressed or abused *by* others, humans can often themselves become the abusers *of* others if the opportunity arises. We see this trait individually with victims of child abuse and culturally all around the globe. As a person born to parents who practiced Judaism, I have often wondered how one of the most repressed "peoples" in history could stomach treating others in the fashion of any one of their oppressors. From the Egyptians to the Romans to the Inquisitions in medieval Europe to the Nazi-caused Holocaust, I firmly believed as a youngster that no Jew would do—could do—what men like Ariel Sharon have done.

Can it be, I began to ask myself not so long ago, that the millennium-long persecution of the Jews had finally, ultimately created a people who have seen fit to turn the tables on their own neighbors? Like Japan outlawing the production of nuclear weapons after the vicious attacks on Hiroshima and Nagasaki almost sixty years ago, I would expect Jews to abhor and vehemently resist becoming oppressors of any other culture. But to my shock and dismay, many Jews support Israel's wars against the Palestinians while defending Israel's "right to exist" as if it were the Palestinians who invaded and occupied *their* lands.

There are many psychological and sociological studies on the victim/oppressor cycle, but the science involved lies outside the scope of this chapter, which investigates the roots of the Israeli-Palestinian conflict so as to both better understand how this conflict came to be and to determine in what ways a humanist viewpoint can—based on previous efforts—help end the conflict, as well as teach future societies how to avoid this kind of cycle of violence itself. I have found that many ways to rectify the situation are embedded in the history itself, buried in the formulation and application of the "problem." Our leaders, then, can either learn from the past or condemn their people to everlasting war and violence.

As for humanist solutions, humanism is a philosophy based on reason, evidence, and a one-world (planetary) cooperative politic; thus far, all other attempts have failed. Maybe it's now time to examine what humanists have to offer.

EARLY HISTORY

As I implied earlier, no humanist solution to conflict can be possible without understanding the history of conflict. What is the crux of this decades-long battle in the "Holy Lands"? Some humanists would point to religion as a main cause, and they would not be wrong to do so. As in Ireland, India, Pakistan, and many other epicenters of violence, people's beliefs in "sacred lands" and "holy texts" feed off of old fears and instincts, creating a fierce territorialism. The "Us versus Them" mindset is no more obvious than when "gods" are pitted against each other. In the case of Israel, the teaching of most Jews for centuries that Jews are "God's chosen people" has surely played a role in creating the arrogance of the current apartheid politics in that country.

Flipping the coin over, one must recognize that Muslim fundamentalism and the belief in an afterlife in which martyrs reign supreme is probably the main reason suicide terrorism flourishes as it does. That God cannot exist in the naturalist universe humanists live in is irrelevant because doctrines of faith naturally run counter to the real world. That every other religion has similarly self-congratulatory religious myths burdened with thousands of contradictions in logic and practice is also irrelevant because believers believe *in spite of the evidence and not because of it.* So a solution born from "accepting" atheism or agnostism, or even education in biblical criticism, will not help us to help those trapped within such beliefs. Instead, all we can do is to understand that both Jews and Muslims have a religious stake in Palestine/Israel—as do Christians, in fact—and that any solution that allows all three religions to peacefully coexist would be a good thing. In short, neither science nor atheism is the answer . . . not yet, at least. Humanism is more than either, and it must be based on the evidence. So, a brief history lesson, including an understanding of the Zionist mission, is in order.

Between 3000 and 1100 BCE, Canaan covered what is today Israel, the West Bank, Lebanon, Syria, and much of Jordan. Those who remained in Jerusalem after the Romans expelled the Jews (in the second century CE) were mostly farmers, either pagans or converts to Christianity and descendants of Arabs, Persians, Samaritans, Greeks, or old Canaanites tribes.[1] The kingdoms of David and Solomon, on which the Zionists base their territorial claims, lasted for less than eighty years. The Jewish kingdoms from David's conquest of Canaan in 1000 BCE through the destruction of Judah in 586 BCE lasted 414 years.[2]

Fast-forwarding, Palestine became an Arab and Islamic country at the end of the seventh century CE. In the early sixteenth century, Palestine became a province of the Ottoman Empire, but it remained both Arab and Islamic. Even by the 1880s, when the Jewish colonists first began immigrating to Palestine, the country was mostly Arab. In 1931, the Jewish population in Palestine was less than 175,000, while the Arab population was over 1 million.[3] By 1947, Jews owned about 6 percent of the land.[4]

What were the early reactions of the Palestinians to the new European Jewish (not ancient Hebrew) immigrants? What was the attitude of the settlers toward their hosts? First, we should know just who these settlers were. Zionism was originally a Christian ideology in England. According to Christian myth, come the end-times, the Jews will either have to convert to Christianity to be saved or die horribly. But the Jews must return to biblical lands for all this to happen. The Christian Zionists managed to convince then secular Jew Theodor Herzls of the benefits of a Jewish "homeland" and a movement was born.[5]

I wonder whether Herzls, was told about the religious intentions of the Christian Zionists, and if he was, whether he cared? Today, the Christian Right in America is still paying for Jews to move to Israel to fulfill their biblical destiny. Politically, this movement reveals itself via George W. Bush's policies toward Israel.

In a recent article by Rick Perlstein for the *Village Voice*, an e-mail message sent by Pentecostal minister Robert G. Upton concerning meetings between the Apostolic Congress and the Bush administration was leaked to the press. Upton's argument was that the United States must back a one-state plan in which Israel should do whatever it can to end the Palestinian cause. Perlstein writes, "Three weeks after the [e-mail message], President George W. Bush reversed long-standing US policy, endorsing Israeli sovereignty over parts of the West Bank in exchange for Israel's disengagement from the Gaza Strip."[6]

The Apostolic Congress dates back to 1981, when, according to its Web site, "Brother Stan Wachtstetter was able to open the door for Apostolic Christians into the White House."[7] Some Jews seem to be sympathetic to this virulent form of Christian Zionism; Ariel Sharon still works with the Apostolic Congress to build his fundamentalist, anti-Palestinian state. A Jewish group called Americans for a Safe Israel is another example of this unholy alliance. Its executive director, Helen Freedman, confirms the increasingly Christian cast of her coalition: "We have many good Jews, of course, but they're in the minority."[8]

According to Perlstein, Freedman "laughs off concerns that, for Christian Zionists, actual Jews living in Israel serve as mere props for their end-time scenario: 'We have a different conception of what [the end of the world] will be like. . . . Whoever is right will rejoice, and whoever was wrong will say, "Whoops!"'"[9]

The Palestinians had no problems with the Jewish settlers until they learned of their long-term plans for the neighborhood. There was Palestinian "anti-Semitism," but no people would be prejudice-free when their land is invaded by foreigners with the intention of setting up their own sovereign state. The expulsion of peasants from their lands and the Zionist refusal to employ Arabs worsened relations.

There was certainly no pretense about what the Zionists wanted. Zionist writer Ahad Ha'am says, "Serfs they [the Jews] were in the lands of the Diaspora, and suddenly they find themselves in freedom [in Palestine]; and this change has awakened in them an inclination to despotism. They treat Arabs with hostility and cruelty, deprive them of their rights, offend them without cause, and even boast of these deeds."[10] And in 1921, Dr. Eder—a member of the Zionist Commission—told the court of inquiry, "[T]here can be only one National Home in Palestine, and that a Jewish one, and no equality in the partnership between Jews and Arabs, but a Jewish preponderance as soon as the numbers of the race are sufficiently increased."[11]

The origins of the conflict—it seems to me—lie in a desperate movement by a people (the Jews) who suffered greatly in Russia, Europe, and other areas of the world—especially under Nazism when more than 6 million Jews were murdered—who turned to ancient mythology and, as their fellow Europeans had done in America, Africa, and India, decided on colonization. With that decision came the colonialists' mentality. Thus the Israeli-Palestinian conflict was born.

From those days on, several peace "solutions" were offered—often by outside forces—to try to fix the many problems that colonization often leads to. From 1948 to 1967 and from 1967 through today, events occurred that we must understand when considering our humanist solution.

1947–1967

In response to tremendous pressure in post–World War II America from Jewish lobbyists (and non-Jewish lobbyists for Jewish causes), President

Harry Truman decided that a partition plan was called for in Palestine. To the powers-that-were in 1947 America, Truman said, "I am sorry, gentlemen, but I have to answer to hundreds of thousands who are anxious for the success of Zionism. I do not have hundreds and thousands of Arabs among my constituents."[12] The Zionists accepted this response in public but had other goals in mind. In 1938, during earlier partition proposals, David Ben-Gurion of the Zionist movement stated, "When we become a strong power after the establishment of the state, we will abolish partition and spread throughout all of Palestine."[13]

The Arab rejection of any partition was born of the fear that though the Jews were to own only 10 percent of the land, they would become the ruling power. By denying the Palestine Arabs, who formed two-thirds of the population of the country, the right to decide for themselves, the US-led United Nations violated its own charter upholding the right of all people to self-determination. The inevitable result was war.

Who struck first? The Mufti leader in Palestine by the name of Haj Amin al-Husseini called Palestinians to war against partition, but very few Palestinians responded. Arab armies did cross the border in 1948, after Israel declared its independence, but this declaration came three and a half months before the date specified in the partition resolution.

The United States had proposed a three-month truce on the condition that Israel postpone its declaration of independence. The Arab states accepted the truce but Israel rejected it, in part because it had worked out a secret deal with King Abdullah of Jordan. In this deal, Abdullah's Arab Legion would invade the Palestinian territory assigned to the Palestinian state but would not attack the Jews.[14] During the battle, most of the major Zionist military attacks on Palestinians occurred in the territory given to them.

In 1948, Israel declared its statehood. About seven hundred thousand Palestinians fled or were expelled. The Israeli government claimed that Palestinians chose to leave Palestine voluntarily, instructed to do so via radio broadcasts from Arab leaders so they could clear a path for their army. But the British and US governments monitored all radio broadcasts from the area and found no evidence of any such orders.[15]

In December 1948, the UN General Assembly passed Resolution 194, which declared that "refugees wishing to return to their homes and live in peace with their neighbors should be permitted to do so" and that "compensation should be paid for the property of those choosing not to return." Although this resolution has been overwhelmingly adopted year after year, Israel has not responded. Indeed, Israel has chosen to ignore all UN resolutions relating to reparations. From 1955 to 2002, the UN passed seventy-four resolutions aimed at making Israel respect international law and bringing justice to the Palestinian people. Israel has ignored every one of them.

Of course, UN resolutions mean nothing if they cannot be enforced, and enforcement requires the cooperation of the UN Security Council members, including the United States. And though the United States, the chief supporter of Israel, enforced every one of the UN resolutions against Iraq—even going so far as to make it impossible for Iraq to comply with the resolutions, then using force to punish them—the United States, according to the US State Department, vetoed more than twenty-five resolutions concerning Israel from 1982 to 1992 alone.[16]

In June 1967, Israel launched a war seizing all of Palestine (the West Bank, including East Jerusalem, from Jordan and the Gaza Strip from Egypt), along with the Sinai Peninsula (from Egypt) and the Golan Heights (from Syria). Many Palestinians, some living in cities, towns, and villages and some in refugee camps, came under Israeli control. Israel justified the war as self-defense, which was reasonable since Egypt and Jordan were threatening to attack Israel. However, this does not correlate with what Israel did to the Palestinians. As Middle East scholar Stephen Shalom wrote, "A people do not lose their right to self-determination because the government of a neighboring state goes to war."[17]

After the war, Israel confiscated more than 52 percent of the land in the West Bank and 30 percent of the Gaza Strip. Between 1967 and 1982, Israel demolished more than one thousand Palestinian homes on the West Bank, and more than three hundred thousand Palestinians were detained illegally.[18] Psychologist Samir Quota reports that, as of 1996, "90 percent of children two years old or more have experienced—some many, many times—the [Israeli] army breaking into the home, beating relatives, destroying things. Many were beaten themselves, had bones broken, were shot, tear gassed, or had these things happen to siblings and neighbors. . . ."[19]

SOLUTION ONE? THE OSLO ACCORDS

The Palestine Liberation Organization (PLO) was formed in 1964, and in 1969 Yasser Arafat became its leader. The PLO had many factions, each with different tactics (including hijackings) and different politics. At this time, the PLO took the position that Israel had no right to exist and that only Palestinians were entitled to national rights in Palestine.

This position was the mirror image of the official Israeli view of the Palestinians—both the right-wing Likud party and the Labor party argued that the PLO should not be recognized under any circumstances, even if it renounced terrorism and recognized Israel, and that a Palestinian state in any part of the occupied territories was unacceptable.

In 1993, forty-five years after Israel became a state, the first plan to bring peace to the region was introduced. The Oslo Accords consisted of "Letters of Mutual Recognition" and a Declaration of Principles. As part of this plan, Arafat agreed to recognize Israel's right to exist, accepted various UN resolutions, and renounced terrorism and armed struggle. Israeli prime minister Yitzhak Rabin agreed to recognize the PLO as the representative of the Palestinian people and to negotiate with them. Israel did not agree on the right to a Palestinian state, however. The Declaration of Principles was signed on the White House lawn on September 13, 1993.

September 1995 brought Oslo II. This new agreement divided the occupied territories (not in including East Jerusalem) into three zones, Areas A, B, and C. In area A, the Palestinean Authority (PA) was given civil and security control but not sovereignty; in area B, the PA would have civil control and the Israelis security control; and area C (which included the settlements, connecting roads, and most of the valuable land and water resources of the West Bank) was under full Israeli control. The Gaza Strip, with a population of over a million Palestinians, was the home of sixty-five hundred Israeli settlers, who occupied 20 percent of area C. Palestinians thus had very limited autonomy and no sovereignty in the Gaza Strip. The PA now had to control quite poor and understandably angry Palestinians.

In 1995, a right-wing Israeli assassinated Rabin, and Shimon Peres succeeded him as prime minister. Peres had little regard for Oslo, wanting any future Palestinian state to be located only in Gaza. Then, in 1996, Likud's Benjamin Netanyahu, who was openly opposed to the Oslo accords, was elected prime minister. Netanyahu ignored the already agreed-upon Israeli troop withdrawals from occupied territory, continued building settlements, stepped up the policy of sealing off the Palestinian enclaves, and refused to begin the final talks required by Oslo.

Ultimately, through all these changes, the number of Israeli settlers (beginning in 1993) in the West Bank and Gaza grew from 110,000 to 195,000 and in annexed East Jerusalem during the same period, the Jewish population rose from 22,000 to 170,000.[20] Thirty new settlements were

established, and more than eighteen thousand new housing units for settlers were constructed.[21] From 1994 to 2000, Israeli authorities confiscated
thirty-five thousand acres of Arab land for roads and settlements.[22] Oslo II
was a failure.

SOLUTION TWO? CAMP DAVID, 2000

In March 2002 the *Washington Post* claimed that the US-led Camp David
meetings in July 2000 saw Israel for the first time offer "extraordinary con-
cessions" to the Palestinians.[23] Other US papers printed editorials claiming
that Arafat's "recalcitrance"—his supposed arrogant walking away from
Israeli peace proposals without even making a counteroffer—doomed the
Palestinians to continued victimhood.

The Camp David plan called for Israel to withdraw completely from
the Gaza Strip, but allowed it to annex strategically important and highly
valuable sections of the West Bank (retaining "security control" over other
parts), thus making it impossible for Palestinians to travel or trade freely
within their own state without permission from the Israeli government.
Israel also demanded that Arafat sign an "end-of-conflict" agreement
stating that the decades-old war between Israel and the Palestinians was
over. Arafat's notoriety for being a poor diplomat aside, the substance of
this lopsided plan resulted in the Camp David meeting ending with failure
on July 25, 2000.

Former president Jimmy Carter said of Camp David, "It is unlikely that
real progress can be made . . . as long as Israel insists on its settlement
policy, illegal under international laws." Israeli peace activist Uri Avnery
explains, "In this fight, we are Goliath and they are David. In the eyes of
the world [outside the United States], the Palestinians are fighting a war of
liberation against a foreign occupation. We are in their territory, not they
in ours. We are the occupiers, they are the victims. This is an objective situation, and no minister of propaganda . . . can change that."[24]

On September 28, 2000, Sharon, as a member of Parliament, accompanied by a thousand-strong security force, dared to visit to the site of the
Al Aqsa mosque in Jerusalem. The Israeli-provoked second Intifada began
on September 29, 2000, after Israeli troops opened fire on Palestinian rock
throwers at the mosque, killing four and wounding more than two hundred. According to Amnesty International, by March 2002, more than one
thousand Palestinians had been killed, "including more than 200 chil-

dren, unlawfully, by shelling and bombing residential areas, random or targeted shooting . . . by extrajudicial executions, and during demonstrations."[25]

Ariel Sharon was the commander of an Israeli force that massacred more than seventy civilians in the Jordanian village of Qibya in 1953. He was defense minister in 1982 when Israel invaded Lebanon, causing the deaths of almost twenty thousand civilians. In September 1982, Lebanese forces "switched sides" and allied themselves with Israel to murder hundreds of Palestinian noncombatants in the Sabra and Shitila refugee camps, a crime for which an Israeli commission found Sharon to bear indirect responsibility. On February 6, 2001, in a special election, Sharon was elected Israel's prime minister.

UNDERSTANDING FUNDAMENTALISM

Before bringing us up to date with George W. Bush's "Road Map to Peace," it may be prudent to talk a bit about religious fundamentalism. Not Islamic fundamentalism—for unlike Osama bin Laden, the Palestinians are not Islamic terrorists. Instead, it may be interesting to look briefly at Jewish fundamentalism. Since September 11, the American media have bombarded readers and viewers with memes about the evils of Islamic fundamentalism and the terrorism that these supposedly backward Muslims inflict on innocent people everywhere. Again, there *are* elements in the Islamic world (e.g., bin Laden) that advocate for the killing of noncombatant infidels (non-Muslims) in the name of Allah. There are also those who have legitimate political grievances with the West who use religion to "motivate" terrorists to sacrifice themselves for "the cause." Some of the Palestinian suicide bombers may fall into this category. As an atheist and secular humanist who has studied the effects of religion on society from the Crusades and the Inquisitions to 9/11, I have no lingering doubts of the destructive power of religious fundamentalism. This is why I want to address for a moment a religion not often associated with fundamentalism—Judaism.

The fundamentalist wing of the Jewish religion is very influential in Israel. Indeed, it is the ideological basis of the settler movement in the West Bank and Gaza. According to the late Israel Shahak and Norton Mezvinsky, the Talmud states that two contrasting kinds of "souls" exist in the world: Jewish and non-Jewish.[26] The difference between a "Jewish soul" and that of a non-Jew is similar to the difference between a human "soul" and that of a cow. Following this tradition, the code of Maimonides and the Halacha state that a Jew who kills a non-Jew is exempt from human punishment and has not violated Jewish religious law.[27] This deep-seated notion has led to tremendous human rights abuses and cannot be ignored as part of why Israel does what it does in Palestine. As I have often explained to religious friends and family members baffled by my atheism, irrational beliefs often lead to irrational actions.[28] (For more on this, read Shahak and Mezvinsky's book, *Jewish Fundamentalism in Israel.*)

SOLUTION THREE? THE ROAD MAP TO PEACE

The "road map" is not a treaty. Its sponsors describe it as a "performance-based and goal-driven" plan. It requires action by the Palestinian Authority and government of Israel on a wide range of security-related, humanitarian, and policy matters.

If George W. Bush's "Road Map to Peace" were a humanist response to the conflict, it would first have to convince nervous, misinformed Americans that Israel would not be destroyed in the advent of a Palestinian state. It must expose the religious fundamentalist mindset not only of Islam, but also among Jews in Israel. Years of pro-Israel, anti-Arab, anti-Muslim propaganda and slanted media coverage in the United States have led many people in the United States, particularly American Jews, to think that if Israel acts in accord with international law, it will eventually disappear into a river of anti-Semitism. For many Jews, the very real, unforgettable horrors of the Holocaust still prey on their minds, so much so that it is hard to see that the victims of yesterday may have become the oppressors of today, and that fundamentalism cuts both ways.

It is said that conquerors like to justify their conquests by claiming a threat to security. The United States made such a claim to justify attacking Iraq in 2003 *even though no threat existed from Saddam Hussein*. Israel used this same excuse to avoid returning the Sinai to Egypt or pulling out of Lebanon. But Israel *did* work with Egypt and *did* leave Lebanon eventually, and its security was enhanced rather than harmed as a result.

Indeed, those who are worried about Israel should remember that Israel is the region's only nuclear power. In fact, it is the strongest military power in the entire Middle East by far. Surely Israel does not need to occupy the neighboring territory of militarily primitive people (Palestinians) to achieve security. Indeed, pulling out of the occupied territories would probably be a better guarantee of peace and security for the Israeli people. Nor is allowing people who have been expelled from their homes the right to return such a wild idea. Both Palestinian officials and the Arab League have often said that the right of return should be implemented in a way that would not create a demographic problem for Israel.

It could be argued, too, that an officially Jewish state is antidemocratic—a theocracy based on ancient myths and prejudices. Indeed, Shalom wonders, "Why should a Jew born in Brooklyn have a right to 'return' to Israel while a Palestinian born in Haifa does not?"[29]

It is true that Hamas (which was originally supported by Israel because its leaders were opposed to the PLO) and a few other, smaller Palestinian groups object not only to the occupation but also to the very existence of Israel, but that position is a minority view among Palestinians. As Shalom points out, "If there were a truly independent Palestinian state, one can assume that Hamas would find far fewer volunteers for its suicide squads."[30] The ability to implement peace seems to be in the hands of the occupiers.

International "donors," "quartet members," and neighboring states also have obligations—to fund Palestinian reforms, to provide international political support, and to end any public or private financing of armed Palestinian groups. However, no bans on the financing of the Israeli war machine are mentioned.

Human Rights Watch, a human rights advocacy group, is concerned that the road map, like with all past proposals, may ignore basic human rights. Phase I of the road map states that Israel will take no action that might undermine the trust of the Palestinians, including deportations, attacks on civilians, confiscation and/or demolition of Palestinian homes and property, or destruction of Palestinian institutions and infrastructure. HRW argues that

> the language of (Phase I) misstates the gravity of the offences it describes. All of these actions, they say, violate international humanitarian law: some are even war crimes. HRW points out that their inclusion in the roadmap text is a necessary (and overdue) step towards promoting IHL [International Humanitarian Law] standards, and that "they cannot be negotiated away or made contingent on steps taken by another party.[31]

These concerns are only a few of the many that HRW has with the road map. As it happens, the road map may be permanently stalled as of this writing, not due to a failure of its application but due to Israel's vengeful attacks on Palestinian civilians every time Hamas commits another crime. What Israel seems never to learn is that Hamas will not go away *until* peace is agreed upon by both sides. Again—mutual peaceful, cooperative coexistence will soon negate the need, or tolerance by the Palestinians, for Hamas and other violent groups.

The Israelis must end their vicious Old Testament "eye-for-an-eye" policies (often disguised as security tactics) if they want to achieve peace at all. Is this a hard pill for Israel to swallow . . . to turn the other cheek when Hamas continues to try to end the peace movement? No. It is what an occupying nation *must* do if it wants to end the cycle of violence. Israel has brought terror upon itself by the very nature of its existence and actions. It is time to right the wrongs it has done and takes the first real steps toward peace.

Toward this peace, HRW offers several suggestions for Israel, the United States, and the Palestinians to consider. These suggestions include the need to

1. Clarify immediately and publicly that obligations under international human rights and humanitarian law are not subject to negotiation or reciprocal action by the other party. . . .
2. Require that all parties investigate and bring to justice those who have committed war crimes or other breaches of IHL. Where necessary, this should include
   a. Provision of necessary technical and financial assistance;
   b. Ongoing monitoring of the caseloads, timelines, and outcomes of investigations of the Judge Advocate-General's Office of the Israel Defense Forces and the Department of Investigation of Police Misconduct of the Ministry of Justice.[32]

As of this writing, (June 2004), one major obstacle in the road map may be the building of Israel's own version of the Berlin Wall. In an effort to calm its citizens—a false calm though it may be—Israel is building what it calls a "separation fence" between itself and the Palestinians. Professor Yigal Bronner at Tel-Aviv University writes:

> The wall that is under construction will lead to the annexation by Israel of a considerable percent[age] of the West Bank. On the western, Israeli, side of the fence hundreds of thousands of Palestinians will remain. On the eastern, Palestinian, side, there will be thousands of Jewish settlers. [Sharon's] idea is not of one fence but rather of, at least, two sets of walls. While one of them, the one on the west side, will steal as many kilome-

ters as possible of Palestinian land alongside the Green Line, the other—on the eastern side—will annex the remoter settlements, like Ariel and Kiryat Arbah. Between these two walls there will be various types of obstacles, fences and trenches. This set up will irreversibly turn the West Bank's centers of population into isolated human cages. What this amounts to is not a state but a smattering of ghettos.

The walls that Sharon is building now are intended to render Israel's hold over the land it captured in 1967 irreversible. They are the last nail in the coffin of the two-states solution.[33]

So is this the end of the peace movement? Maybe, maybe not. A new plan was signed in Geneva on December 1, 2003, by leading Israeli and Palestinian political figures. Former president Jimmy Carter, who was present at the ceremony, said "It's unlikely we shall ever see a more promising foundation for peace."[34] The fifty-page document, which addresses the rights and concerns of both the Israelis and the Palestinians, has been endorsed by British prime minister Tony Blair, Egyptian president Hosni Mubarak, former Soviet leader Mikhail Gorbachev, Russian foreign minister Igor Ivanov, longtime German foreign minister Hans-Dientrich Genscher, former South African president F. W. DeKlerk, and UN secretary general Kofi Annan.

The agreement calls for Israel to withdraw from the Gaza Strip and West Bank. Jerusalem would become the cocapital of Israel and Palestine, with Israel controlling the important Jewish holy sites and Palestine controlling the major Muslim and Christian holy sites. The international community would aid Palestine in disarming and disbanding all of the private militias and terrorist groups.

The two exceptions to a full Israeli withdrawal from these areas include the Latrun area in the West Bank and a section around East Jerusalem where a large number of Jewish-only settlements have been built. As Stephen Zunes points out, these exceptions represent a major concession on the part of the Palestinians because these settlements are in direct violation of the Fourth Geneva Convention, as well as UN Security Council resolutions 446, 452, 465, and 471.[35] The most important concession from the Palestinians will be the waiving of the right of refugees and their descendants to return to what is now Israel proper.[36]

Yet the United States does not seem ready to let this proposal work. US State Department spokesman Richard Boucher dismissed the peace plan as "a private effort."[37] The Bush administration's position is that the "real" peace talks will have to be US-led, and such talks would not even begin until there was a cessation of Palestinian violence. Nothing was said, as usual, of Israeli violence. Even the Israeli lead negotiator admitted, "The Geneva Initiative will not be accepted by Washington."[38]

HUMANISM, ANYONE?

This essay began with my suggestion that there may be a humanist solution (or solutions) to this conflict. Some possible solutions have indeed been explored. The place to start for Israel, and for Jews all over the world, must be to acknowledge that there never was a "divine right" given to those who practice the Jewish faith to be in that part of the world or to force on that part of the world a Jewish theocracy. Zionism—in practice—is clearly not about saving the Jewish people from extinction after the Holocaust and finding a safe haven for Jews to live but about the domination of a mythical "Promised Land."

Look at this closely. The Zionists came from European and Russian heritages, far removed from those peoples who lived thousands of years ago in what is now Israel. The misguided notion that Jews are a "race" or that Judaism is in one's genes, like skin or eye color, has led many to believe that anyone born to a person who practiced Judaism is "naturally" a Jew. The idea that his or her "soul" belongs in Israel is even more absurd. Judaism, like Christianity, is a philosophy, a mind-set (dogmatic as it may be), and nothing more or less. The kind of misunderstanding of science and humanity that we are witness to is truly appalling in this time and age—over a hundred years post Darwin.

Similarly, the Muslim fundamentalism of Hamas, as backward as any religious fundamentalism anywhere, needs to be understood as a Frankenstein's monster of Israel's own making (as Saddam Hussein and bin Laden are America's monsters) and not as representative of the majority of Palestinians. Hamas leaders need to be dealt with as Osama bin Laden ought to be, as criminals and not as representatives of an entire people—a notion some Israeli leaders still cling to in justifying the murder of innocent people in the name of security.

A "real" road map to peace must acknowledge this distinction, as well as the real causes of the 1947 and 1967 wars. Its formulators must understand why Oslo and Camp David were too lopsided to work. A real road map to peace must also comply with international law and human rights (as put forth by HRW). It must focus not only on the horrors of suicide bombings but also on the damage of Palestinian society via Israeli colonialism that led to the mess in the first place. The damage must then be assessed and reversed. Where there is no healing, no understanding, no chance for reconciliation . . . there is no chance for peace.

A TRULY BRIGHT IDEA

An experimental commission called the Truth and Reconciliation Commission of South Africa (TRC) was set up in Africa in 1996. The TRC's method is to bring together all the players involved in those many years of apartheid in South Africa for full disclosure. Once the oppressors admit their deeds in honest and open discussion—once there is genuine regret and a willingness to work toward a better future—then both sides work with the commission and other organizations (including, in this case, the American Association for the Advancement of Science's Science and Human Rights Program) to heal the nation. Thus far it seems to be working. A humanistic response to that decades-long conflict has proven helpful.

Why can't such a reconciliation be considered for Israel and the Palestinian people? Here, even more than in Africa, *both sides* have committed over a thousand atrocities as the result of one group's desire to create a theocratic homeland. What if Israel came forward in the sprit of the TRC and finally admitted all it has done to the Palestinians that led not only to the suicide bombings and other acts of terrorism but also to wars involving other Arab nations, Europe, and the United States. Perhaps it is time for the United States to support such a commission and see to it that both Jews and Palestinians work on reconciliation and healing.

Indeed, as with the Geneva talks in 2003, the United States may be the key, after all. After much of the goodwill toward America was squandered away by George W. Bush and his cowboy imperialist policies post-9/11, he can help to reverse his tragic leadership by making a real effort to work for peace in Israel, the occupied territories, and the entire Middle East. The United States must work—within international law, and with the United Nations and the rest of the world—to rebuild Afghanistan and Iraq, to rebuild Palestine, to persuade Israel to retreat to the 1967 borders. Peace might just break out if Israel uses its resources to help the United States in this endeavor while engaging with the Palestinians in dialogue that can help the two peoples learn to live together.

Peace . . . really? Yes, really. Rectifying the extremely poor situation the Palestinians have been put into can eliminate in short order the popular support for extremist groups like Hamas. But to do so requires a reformation in Israel. Men like Sharon need to be removed from office—as they got in only by creating the situations that led to the fear that in turn supports their hard-line policies. The United States must encourage Israel to move more to the Left or, once and for all, eliminate the funding of Israel and quit blocking the UN sanctions against it. The United States must lead by example.

Section VI of *Humanist Manifesto 2000* states:

> The overriding need of the world community today is to develop a new planetary humanism—one that seeks to preserve human rights and enhance human freedom and dignity, but also emphasizes our commitment to humanity as a whole. The underlying ethical principle of planetary humanism is the need to respect the dignity and worth of all persons in the world community.[39]

It is time we put our money where our manifestos are because a humanist solution to this conflict is the only one that can succeed.

NOTES

1. Joseph Albright and Marcia Kunstel, *Their Promised Land: Arab versus Jew in History's Cauldron* (New York: Crown, 1991), quoted in Jews for Justice in the Middle East, *The Origin of the Palestine-Israel Conflict*, 3d ed. (Berkeley: Author, 2000), http://www.cactus48.com/truth.html.

2. Ilene Beatty, "Early History of the Region," *Arab and Jew in the Land of Canaan* (Chicago: Regnery, 1957), quoted in Jews for Justice in the Middle East, *The Origin of the Palestine-Israel Conflict*.

3. Edward W. Said, *The Question of Palestine* (New York: Vintage, 1992), quoted in Jews for Justice, *The Origin of the Palestine-Israel Conflict*.

4. Ibid.

5. Theodor Herzls, born in 1860, was a journalist and playwright in Paris for a Viennese newspaper. He founded organized Jewish Zionism in 1897.

6. Rick Perlstein, "The Jesus Landing Pad," *Village Voice*, May 18, 2004, http://www.villagevoice.com/issues/0420/perlstein.php. Policy switch benefits Israel because the Christian fundamentalists favor the elimination of all things Palestinian, which is consistent with Sharon's own position.

7. "About Us," Apostolic Congress, 2004, http://www.apostoliccongress.com/about.html.

8. Helen Freedman, quoted in Perlstein, "The Jesus Landing Pad."

9. Ibid.

10. Ahad Ha'am, quoted in Sami Hadawi, *Bitter Harvest: A Modern History*, 4th rev. and updated ed. (New York: Olive Branch Press, 1991).

11. David Eder, quoted in Hadawi, *Bitter Harvest*.

12. Harry S. Truman, quoted in Roselle Teikener, Samir Abed-Rabbo, and Norton Mezvinsky, eds., *Anti-Zionism: Analytical Reflections* (Brattleboro, VT: Amana Books, 1989).

13. David Ben-Gurion, quoted in Noam Chomsky, *The Fateful Triangle: The United States, Israel, and the Palestinians*, updated ed. (Cambridge: South End Press, 1999).

14. Jews for Justice in the Middle East, "Statehood and Expulsion: 1948," *The Origin of the Palestine-Israel Conflict*, http://www.cactus48.com/statehood.html.

15. Erskine Childers, paraphrased from Hadawi, *Bitter Harvest*.

16. US State Department, www.state.gov/p/na/oi/israel.

17. Stephen R. Shalom, "Background to the Israel-Palestine Crisis," *Z Magazine*, May 2002, http://www.zmag.org/shalom-meqa.htm.

18. Zachary Lockman and Joel Beinin, eds., *Intifada: The Palestinian Uprising against Israeli Occupation* (Boston: South End Press, 1989).

19. Samir Quota, quoted in *Journal of Palestine Studies* (Summer 1996): 84, cited in "The Tragedy of Palestine," Islamic Circle of North America, http://www.icna.org/tragedy_of_palestine.htm.

20. Edward Said, "Palestinians under Siege," in *The New Intifada: Resisting Israel's Apartheid*, ed. Roane Carey (New York: Verso, 2001).

21. Sara Roy, "Decline and Disfigurement: The Palestinian Economy after Oslo," in Carey, *The New Intifada*.

22. Ibid.

23. Editorial, *Washington Post*, March 13, 2002.

24. Uri Avnery, "12 Conventional Lies about the Palestine-Israeli Conflict," Talking Points, Palestine Media Watch, http://www.pmwatch.org/pmw/talking points/.

25. Amnesty International, 58th UN Commission on Human Rights (2002), Background Briefing, IOR 41/004/2002, March 11, 2002, quoted in Shalom, "Background to the Israel-Palestine Crisis."

26. Israel Shahak and Norton Mezvinsky, *Jewish Fundamentalism in Israel*, 2d ed. (London: Pluto Press, 2004).

27. The works of Moses Maimonides (Mishneh Torah) is a major code that covers all of Jewish law. It is a part of the *Halachah*, which means "Jewish Religious Law." For more, see Jews for Justice in the Middle East, "Jewish Fundamentalism in Israel," *The Origin of the Palestine-Israel Conflict*, http://www.wrmea.com/ Jews_for_Justice/fundamentalism.html.

28. For an updated idea of what it's like to be a Palestinian in Israel, see Naama

Yashuvi, "2003: The State of Human Rights in Israel," Electronic Intifada, February 10, 2004, http://electronicintifada.net/v2/article2423.shtml.

29. Shalom, "Background to the Israel-Palestine Crisis."

30. Ibid.

31. Human Rights Watch, "The 'Roadmap': Repeating Oslo's Human Rights Mistakes," Human Rights News, 2003, http://www.hrw.org/backgrounder/mena/israelpa050603.htm.

32. Ibid.

33. Yigal Bronner, "A Fence of Deception: The Truth about the Wall," Counterpunch.org, September 23, 2003, http://www.ccmep.org/2003_articles/Palestine/092303_a_fence_of_deception.htm.

34. Jimmy Carter, quoted at a press conference near the UN before the Geneva Initiative, in December 2003.

35. Stephen Zunes, "Israelis and Palestinians Attempt to Jumpstart the Peace Process despite Washington's Support for Sharon," FPIF Commentary, December 3, 2003, http://www.fpif.org/commentary/2003/0312genevapeace_body.html.

36. Ibid.

37. Ibid.

38. Ibid.

39. *Humanist Manifesto 2000*, page 23 in this volume.

RECOMMENDED READING

Ackerman, Seth. "The Myth of the Generous Offer: Distorting the Camp David Negotiations." *Extra!* July/August 2002. http://www.fair.org/extra/0207/generous.html.

Bronner, Yigal. "A Fence of Deception: The Truth about the Wall." Counterpunch.org. September 23, 2003. http://www.ccmep.org/2003_articles/Palestine/092303_a_fence_of_deception.htm.

Jews for Justice in the Middle East. *The Origin of the Palestine-Israel Conflict.* http://www.wrmea.com/jews_for_justice.

Perlstein, Rick. "The Jesus Landing Pad." *Village Voice.* May 18, 2004. http://www.villagevoice.com/issues/0420/perlstein.php.

United Nations. "A Performance-Based Roadmap to a Permanent Two-State Solution to the Israeli-Palestinian Conflict." UN NewsCentre. http://www.un.org/media/main/roadmap122002.html.

United Nations High Commissioner for Human Rights. "Grave and Massive Violations of the Human Rights of the Palestinian People by Israel." Resolution S-5/1 of the fifth special session of the Commission on Human Rights. October 19, 2000. http://www.unhchr.ch/Huridocda/Huridoca.nsf/(Symbol)/E.CN.4.RES.S-5.1.En?Opendocument.

Yashuvi, Naama. "2003: The State of Human Rights in Israel." Electronic Intifada. February 10, 2004. http://electronicintifada.net/v2/article2423.shtml.

BARRY F. SEIDMAN is the New Jersey Coordinator for the Center for Inquiry–Metro NY. He received his MA in science journalism from New York University in 1998 and has written for *Biotechnology Today*, Oncology.com, *Free Inquiry*, *The Skeptic UK*, and *Skeptical Inquirer*. He has also published a chapter in an anthology titled *Opposing Viewpoints: Death and Dying*. Seidman is the producer of *Equal Time for Freethought*, a live radio program on WBAI-NY covering the scientific, philosophical, and humanistic aspects of the freethought world.

19.

Worldly Humanism versus the Empire Builders

Edward Said

The problem of promoting a humanist agenda today is that we live in deeply antihumanist times. In the eyes of many, the "arrogance" of humanism is responsible for most of the ills of the world, from third-world poverty to environmental depredation. And where once antihumanism was the province of reactionaries, today it is at the heart of supposedly "progressive" movements—antiracism, anticapitalism, environmentalism.

—Kenan Malik

Nine years ago I wrote an afterword for *Orientalism* which, in trying to clarify what I believed I had and had not said, stressed not only the many discussions that had opened up since my book appeared in 1978, but the ways in which a work about representations of "the Orient" lent itself to increasing misinterpretation. That I find myself feeling more ironic than irritated about that very same thing today is a sign of how much my age has crept up on me. The recent deaths of my two main intellectual, political, and personal mentors, Eqbal Ahmad and Ibrahim Abu-Lughod, has brought sadness and loss, as well as resignation and a certain stubborn will to go on.

In my memoir *Out of Place* (1999) I described the strange and contradictory worlds in which I grew up, providing for myself and my readers a detailed account of the settings that I think formed me in Palestine, Egypt, and Lebanon. But that was a very personal account that stopped short of

© 2003 by Edward Said, reprinted with the permission of the Wylie Agency, Inc.

all the years of my own political engagement that started after the 1967 Arab-Israeli war.

Orientalism is very much a book tied to the tumultuous dynamics of contemporary history. Its first page opens with a 1975 description of the Lebanese civil war that ended in 1990, but the violence and the ugly shedding of human blood continues up to this minute. We have had the failure of the Oslo peace process, the outbreak of the second intifada, and the awful suffering of the Palestinians on the reinvaded West Bank and Gaza. The suicide-bombing phenomenon has appeared with all its hideous damage, none more lurid and apocalyptic, of course, than the events of September 11, 2001, and their aftermath in the wars against Afghanistan and Iraq.

As I write these lines, the illegal imperial occupation of Iraq by Britain and the United States proceeds. Its aftermath is truly awful to contemplate. This is all part of what is supposed to be a clash of civilizations— unending, implacable, irremediable. Nevertheless, I think not.

I wish I could say that general understanding of the Middle East, the Arabs, and Islam in the United States has improved somewhat, but alas, it really hasn't. For all kinds of reasons, the situation in Europe seems to be considerably better. In the United States, the hardening of attitudes, the tightening of the grip of demeaning generalization and triumphalist cliché, the dominance of crude power allied with simplistic contempt for dissenters and "Others" has found a fitting correlative in the looting and destruction of Iraq's libraries and museums. What our leaders and their intellectual lackeys seem incapable of understanding is that history cannot be swept clean like a blackboard, clean so that "we" might inscribe our own future there and impose our own forms of life for these lesser people to follow.

It is quite common to hear high officials in Washington and elsewhere speak of changing the map of the Middle East, as if ancient societies and myriad peoples can be shaken up like so many peanuts in a jar. But this has often happened with the "Orient," that semimythical construct which since Napoleon's invasion of Egypt in the late eighteenth century has been made and remade countless times. In the process, the uncountable sediments of history, which include innumerable histories and a dizzying variety of peoples, languages, experiences, and cultures—all these are swept aside or ignored, relegated to the sand heap along with the treasures ground into meaningless fragments that were taken out of Baghdad.

My argument is that history is made by men and women, just as it can also be unmade and rewritten, so that "our" East, "our" Orient, becomes "ours" to possess and direct. And I have a very high regard for the powers and gifts of the peoples of that region to struggle on for their vision of what they are and want to be.

There's been so massive and calculatedly aggressive an attack on the contemporary societies of the Arab and Muslim for their backwardness, lack of democracy, and abrogation of women's rights that we simply forget that such notions as modernity, enlightenment, and democracy are by no means simple and agreed-upon concepts that one either does or does not find like Easter eggs in the living room. The breathtaking insouciance of jejune publicists who speak in the name of foreign policy and who have no knowledge at all of the language real people actually speak has fabricated an arid landscape ready for American power to construct there an ersatz model of free market "democracy." You don't need Arabic or Persian or even French to pontificate about how the democracy domino effect is just what the Arab world needs.

But there is a difference between knowledge of other peoples and other times that is the result of understanding, compassion, careful study and analysis for their own sakes, and, on the other hand, knowledge that is part of an overall campaign of self-affirmation. There is, after all, a profound difference between the will to understand for purposes of coexistence and enlargement of horizons and the will to dominate for the purposes of control. It is surely one of the intellectual catastrophes of history that an imperialist war confected by a small group of unelected US officials was waged against a devastated third world dictatorship on thoroughly ideological grounds having to do with world dominance, security control, and scarce resources but disguised for its true intent, hastened, and reasoned for by Orientalists who betrayed their calling as scholars.

The major influences on George W. Bush's Pentagon and National Security Council were men such as Bernard Lewis and Fouad Ajami, experts on the Arab and Islamic world who helped the American hawks to think about such preposterous phenomena as the Arab mind and a centuries-old Islamic decline that only American power could reverse. Today bookstores in the United States are filled with shabby screeds bearing screaming headlines about Islam and terror, Islam exposed, the Arab threat and the Muslim menace, all of them written by political polemicists pretending to knowledge imparted to them and others by experts who have supposedly penetrated to the heart of these strange Oriental peoples.

Accompanying such warmongering expertise have been CNN and

FOX, plus myriad evangelical and right-wing radio hosts, innumerable tabloids, and even middle-brow journals, all of them recycling the same unverifiable fictions and vast generalizations so as to stir up "America" against the foreign devil.

Without a well-organized sense that these people over there were not like "us" and didn't appreciate "our" values—the very core of traditional Orientalist dogma—there would have been no war. So from the very same directorate of paid professional scholars enlisted by the Dutch conquerors of Malaysia and Indonesia, the British armies of India, Mesopotamia, Egypt, and West Africa; the French armies of Indochina and North Africa, came the American advisers to the Pentagon and the White House, using the same clichés, the same demeaning stereotypes, the same justifications for power and violence (after all, runs the chorus, power is the only language they understand) in this case as in the earlier ones.

These people have now been joined in Iraq by a whole army of private contractors and eager entrepreneurs to whom shall be confided everything from the writing of textbooks and the constitution to the refashioning of Iraqi political life and its oil industry.

Every single empire in its official discourse has said that it is not like all the others, that its circumstances are special, that it has a mission to enlighten, civilize, bring order and democracy, and that it uses force only as a last resort. And, sadder still, there always is a chorus of willing intellectuals to say calming words about benign or altruistic empires.

Twenty-five years after my book's publication, *Orientalism* once again raises the question of whether modern imperialism ever ended, or whether it has continued in the Orient since Napoleon's entry into Egypt two centuries ago. Arabs and Muslims have been told that victimology and dwelling on the depredations of empire is only a way of evading responsibility in the present. You have failed, you have gone wrong, says the modern Orientalist. This, of course, is also V. S. Naipaul's contribution to literature, that the victims of empire wail on while their country goes to the dogs.

But what a shallow calculation of the imperial intrusion that is, how little it wishes to face the long succession of years through which empire continues to work its way in the lives, say, of Palestinians or Congolese or Algerians or Iraqis. Think of the line that starts with Napoleon, continues with the rise of Oriental studies and the takeover of North Africa, and goes on in similar undertakings in Vietnam, in Egypt, in Palestine, and, during the entire twentieth century, in the struggle over oil and strategic control in the Gulf, in Iraq, Syria, Palestine, and Afghanistan. Then think of the rise of anticolonial nationalism, through the short period of liberal independence, the era of military coups, of insurgency, civil war, religious fanaticism, irrational struggle, and uncompromising brutality against the latest bunch of "natives." Each of these phases and eras produces its own distorted knowledge of the Other, each its own reductive images, its own disputatious polemics.

My idea in *Orientalism* is to use humanistic critique to open up the fields of struggle, to introduce a longer sequence of thought and analysis to replace the short bursts of polemical, thought-stopping fury that so imprison us. I have called what I try to do "humanism," a word I continue to use stubbornly despite the scornful dismissal of the term by sophisticated postmodern critics.

By humanism I mean first of all attempting to dissolve Blake's mind-forg'd manacles so as to be able to use one's mind historically and rationally for the purposes of reflective understanding. Moreover, humanism is sustained by a sense of community with other interpreters and other societies and periods: Strictly speaking, therefore, there is no such thing as an isolated humanist.

This it is to say that every domain is linked to every other one, and that nothing that goes on in our world has ever been isolated and pure of any outside influence. We need to speak about issues of injustice and suffering within a context that is amply situated in history, culture, and socioeconomic reality. Our role is to widen the field of discussion. I have spent a great deal of my life during the past thirty-five years advocating the rights of the Palestinian people to national self-determination, but I have always tried to do that with full attention paid to the reality of the Jewish people and what they suffered by way of persecution and genocide.

The paramount thing is that the struggle for equality in Palestine and Israel should be directed toward a humane goal, that is, coexistence, and not further suppression and denial. Not accidentally, I indicate that Orientalism and modern anti-Semitism have common roots. Therefore it would seem to be a vital necessity for independent intellectuals always to provide alternative models to the simplifying and confining ones based on mutual hostility that have prevailed in the Middle East and elsewhere for so long.

As a humanist whose field is literature, I am old enough to have been trained forty years ago in the field of comparative literature, whose leading ideas go back to Germany in the late eighteenth and early nineteenth centuries. Before that I must mention the supremely creative contribution of

Giambattista Vico, the Neopolitan philosopher and philologist whose ideas anticipate those of German thinkers such as Herder and Wolf, later to be followed by Goethe, Humboldt, Dilthey, Nietzsche, Gadamer, and finally the great twentieth-century Romance philologists Erich Auerbach, Leo Spitzer, and Ernst Robert Curtius.

To young people of the current generation, the very idea of philology suggests something impossibly antiquarian and musty, but philology in fact is the most basic and creative of the interpretive arts. It is exemplified for me most admirably in Goethe's interest in Islam generally, and Hafiz in particular, a consuming passion which led to the composition of the "West-Östlicher Diwan," and it inflected Goethe's later ideas about *Weltliteratur*, the study of all the literatures of the world as a symphonic whole that could be apprehended theoretically as having preserved the individuality of each work without losing sight of the whole.

There is a considerable irony to the realization, then, that as today's globalized world draws together in some of the ways I have been talking about here, we may be approaching the kind of standardization and homogeneity that Goethe's ideas were specifically formulated to prevent. In an essay he published in 1951 entitled "Philologie der Weltliteratur," Erich Auerbach made exactly that point at the outset of the postwar period that was also the beginning of the cold war. His great book *Mimesis*, published in Berne in 1946 but written while Auerbach was a wartime exile teaching Romance languages in Istanbul, was meant to be a testament to the diversity and concreteness of the reality represented in Western literature from Homer to Virginia Woolf; but reading the 1951 essay, one senses that for Auerbach the great book he wrote was an elegy for a period when people could interpret texts philologically, concretely, sensitively, and intuitively, using erudition and an excellent command of several languages to support the kind of understanding that Goethe advocated for his understanding of Islamic literature.

Positive knowledge of languages and history was necessary, but it was never enough, any more than the mechanical gathering of facts would constitute an adequate method for grasping what an author like Dante, for example, was all about. The main requirement for the kind of philological understanding Auerbach and his predecessors were talking about and tried to practice was one that sympathetically and subjectively entered into the life of a written text as seen from the perspective of its time and its author (*einfühlung*). Rather than alienation and hostility to another time and a different culture, philology as applied to *Weltliteratur* involved a profound humanistic spirit deployed with generosity and, if I may use the word, hospitality. Thus the interpreter's mind actively makes a place in it for a foreign Other. And this creative making of a place for works that are otherwise alien and distant is the most important facet of the interpreter's mission.

All this was obviously undermined and destroyed in Germany by National Socialism. After the war, Auerbach notes mournfully, the standardization of ideas, and greater and greater specialization of knowledge gradually narrowed the opportunities for the kind of investigative and everlastingly inquiring kind of philological work that he had represented, and, alas, it's an even more depressing fact that since Auerbach's death in 1957, both the idea and practice of humanistic research have shrunk in scope as well as in centrality. Instead of reading in the real sense of the word, our students today are often distracted by the fragmented knowledge available on the Internet and in the mass media. Worse yet, education is threatened by nationalist and religious orthodoxies often disseminated by the mass media as they focus ahistorically and sensationally on the distant electronic wars that give viewers the sense of surgical precision but in fact obscure the terrible suffering and destruction produced by modern warfare. In the demonization of an unknown enemy for whom the label "terrorist" serves the general purpose of keeping people stirred up and angry, media images command too much attention and can be exploited at times of crisis and insecurity of the kind that the post-9/11 period has produced.

Speaking both as an American and as an Arab, I must ask my reader not to underestimate the kind of simplified view of the world that a relative handful of Pentagon civilian elites have formulated for US policy in the entire Arab and Islamic worlds, a view in which terror, preemptive war, and unilateral regime change—backed up by the most bloated military budget in history—are the main ideas debated endlessly and impoverishingly by a media that assigns itself the role of producing so-called experts who validate the government's general line. Reflection, debate, rational argument, moral principle based on a secular notion that human beings must create their own history have been replaced by abstract ideas that celebrate American or Western exceptionalism, denigrate the relevance of context, and regard other cultures with contempt.

Perhaps you will say that I am making too many abrupt transitions between humanistic interpretation on the one hand and foreign policy on the other, and that a modern technological society that along with unprecedented power possesses the Internet and F-16 fighter jets must in the end be commanded by formidable technical-policy experts like Donald Rumsfeld and Richard Perle. But what has really been lost is a sense of the density and interdependence of human life, which can neither be reduced to a formula nor brushed aside as irrelevant.

That is one side of the global debate. In the Arab and Muslim countries, the situation is scarcely better. As Roula Khalaf has argued, the region has slipped into an easy anti-Americanism that shows little understanding of what the United States is really like as a society. Because the governments are relatively powerless to affect US policy toward them, they turn their energies to repressing and keeping down their own populations, which results in resentment, anger, and helpless imprecations that do nothing to open up societies where secular ideas about human history and development have been overtaken by failure and frustration, as well as by an Islamism built out of rote learning and the obliteration of what are perceived to be other, competitive forms of secular knowledge. The gradual disappearance of the extraordinary tradition of Islamic *jihad* or personal interpretation has been one of the major cultural disasters of our time, with the result that critical thinking and individual wrestling with the problems of the modern world have all but disappeared.

This is not to say that the cultural world has simply regressed on one side to a belligerent neo-Orientalism and on the other to blanket rejectionism. The 2002 United Nations World Summit in Johannesburg, for all its limitations, did in fact reveal a vast area of common global concern that suggests the welcome emergence of a new collective constituency that gives the often-facile notion of "one world" a new urgency. In all this, however, we must admit that no one can possibly know the extraordinarily complex unity of our globalized world despite the reality that the world does have a real interdependence of parts that leaves no genuine opportunity for isolation.

The terrible conflicts that herd people under falsely unifying rubrics like "America," "The West," or "Islam" and invent collective identities for large numbers of individuals who are actually quite diverse cannot remain as potent as they are and must be opposed. We still have at our disposal the rational interpretive skills that are the legacy of humanistic education, not as a sentimental piety enjoining us to return to traditional values or the classics but as the active practice of worldly, secular, rational discourse. The secular world is the world of history as made by human beings. Critical thought does not submit to commands to join in the ranks marching against one or another approved enemy.

Rather than the manufactured clash of civilizations, we need to con-centrate on the slow working together of cultures that overlap, borrow from each other, and live together in far more interesting ways than any abridged or inauthentic mode of understanding can allow. But for that kind of wider perception we need time and patient and skeptical inquiry, supported by faith in communities of interpretation that are difficult to sustain in a world demanding instant action and reaction.

Humanism is centered upon the agency of human individuality and subjective intuition rather than on received ideas and approved authority. Texts have to be read as texts that were produced and live on in the histor-ical realm in all sorts of what I have called worldly ways. But this by no means excludes power, since on the contrary I have tried to show the insin-uations, the imbrications of power into even the most recondite of studies.

Last and most important, humanism is the only and, I would go so far as saying, the final resistance we have against the inhuman practices and injustices that disfigure human history. We are today abetted by the enor-mously encouraging democratic field of cyberspace, open to all users in ways undreamed of by earlier generations either of tyrants or of ortho-doxies. The worldwide protests before the war began in Iraq would not have been possible were it not for the existence of alternative communities all across the world, informed by alternative information, and keenly aware of the environmental, human rights, and libertarian impulses that bind us together in this tiny planet.

EDWARD SAID was born in 1935 in Jerusalem, Palestine. In the 1947 parti-tion of Palestine, he and his family became refugees and moved to Cairo, where they lived with relatives. As a young man, he attended the Juilliard School of Music and became quite skilled at playing the piano. He gradu-ated from Princeton University, where he received his master's degree and then attended Harvard University, where he received his PhD. His disser-tation was on Joseph Conrad. He took a position as a professor of compar-ative literature at Columbia University where he became the holder of an endowed chair in English and comparative literature. He was also a former president of the USA Modern Language Association; a prolific author of books and articles, both scholarly and popular; a frequent lecturer and commentator on radio and television, and a sometime diplomatic inter-mediary and congressional witness.

A one-time member of the Palestine National Council, Said resigned in 1991 in protest against the Oslo agreements, which he thought distorted the real path to peace. On July 17, 2002, Said cofounded the Palestinian National Initiative, or Mubadara, a recently established democratic opposition movement in the realm of Palestinian domestic politics, along with Dr. Mustafa Barghouthi, Dr. Haidar Abdel-Shafi, and Ibrahim Dakak. Among Said's many books are *The Question of Palestine*, *Orientalism*, *Blaming Victims*, and *Reflections on Exile*. Edward Said died from leukemia in 2003.

Part IV
Revisioning Humanism

20.

No More Walls
Humanism's Role in Building Lasting Coalitions

Madelyn Hoffman

A human being is part of the whole called by us universe, a part limited in time and space. We experience ourselves, our thoughts and feelings as something separate from the rest. A kind of optical delusion of consciousness. This delusion is a kind of prison for us, restricting us to our personal desires and to affection for a few persons nearest to us. Our task must be to free ourselves from the prison by widening our circle of compassion to embrace all living creatures and the whole of nature in its beauty. . . . We shall require a substantially new manner of thinking if mankind if to survive.

—Albert Einstein

FINDING OUR COMMON HUMANITY

Long lost sisters: It was October 1999. I was about to fulfill a lifelong dream and travel to Ukraine as part of a delegation of grassroots environmental activist women from America. We were heading to Kiev to meet grassroots environmental activist women from Ukraine, Belarus, and Moldova. I had dreamed of this moment many times over the course of my life because all four of my grandparents were born in that part of the world, which at times was part of the Soviet Union and at other times part of Poland.

I was born in November 1956, at the height of the cold war. While I was able to meet three of my grandparents and others who had immigrated to the United States from the former Soviet Union, I knew very little about life there. However, I did know (at least I heard it repeatedly from my own government) that we couldn't trust the Russians, that they hated what America stood for, and that if we didn't stand prepared to fight anywhere in the world against the Russian aggressor, we would certainly lose our freedoms sometime in the near future.

In elementary school, I participated in drills that we were told would protect us in the event of nuclear war. It wasn't until much later that I realized that these drills would do no such thing. However, in third grade we sat dutifully in the hallway with our hands over our heads, hoping that we would be saved in the event a nuclear bomb was dropped on us. Later, I realized that rather than cover my head with my hands to keep an atomic bomb from incinerating me, I would do much better by trying to get both the US government and the Soviet government to reduce and ultimately eliminate their nuclear arsenals.

I learned about the dangers of nuclear weapons. I learned that many Russians were as frightened as I was of being annihilated by an exploding atomic bomb. And I learned that my government was using my fear of people I didn't really know to provide the rationale for continued development of nuclear weapons and for interventions in parts of the world I didn't know much about. Ultimately, they were succeeding in building a huge wall between my past and me. This wall wasn't physical and thus couldn't be dismantled piece by piece. I longed to visit the Soviet Union and see firsthand where my ancestry came from.

After the Berlin Wall fell, my dream had a chance to become a reality. Finally, at forty-three, I was ready to make my first flight to Ukraine.

*   *   *

I've taken you through all of this because it's important to understand what was in my heart and mind when I stepped off the plane in Ukraine. It is important to understand the role that government can play in keeping people separated from one another and dehumanizing those we are never allowed to understand because we rarely see them portrayed as human. It is important to understand this because what was happening to us in America was simultaneously happening to our counterparts in the former Soviet Union, as if the citizens from either country were some kind of demon.

*   *   *

Ukraine: After a day or two of getting acclimated to our new surroundings, the delegation of six American women stood face to face with about two dozen women from Ukraine, Belarus, and Moldova. More than the language barrier standing between us, there was the barrier of misinformation and mistrust created by our respective governments. Fortunately, interpreters were standing by, waiting for us to approach one another. Getting right down to business, one woman from Belarus began by asking me what I thought of the US bombing of Kosovo.

Gulp! I took a deep breath, and told her I was opposed to it. There *had* to be a better way. I told her about my friend from Serbia who shared with me what it is like every night for her family to worry about bombs dropping in the street.

Pause. The interpreter translated my words.

Then, suddenly, the tension in the air dissipated. The Belarussian woman relaxed, smiled broadly, and gave me a big hug as the walls between us tumbled down. Instead of continuing to believe that all Americans were in favor of the bombing, she now realized that some indeed were not. In that moment, we found, lost in years of propaganda, our common humanity. We reached out past years of misrepresentations and lies and found in each other new friends.

My two-week trip included many similar moments. I found myself crying in both deep sadness and overwhelming joy. I began to realize that so much time had been wasted because of fear and unfounded hatred. I realized how many people were harboring animosity toward other people without having the first idea why. And, finally, I was shown most vividly how, if we are given an opportunity to discover others for ourselves, we can easily and without much commotion discover the humanity in each of us.

Virtually every experience I had in Ukraine allowed me to treasure the heritage I had been denied for so long. That realization still holds great significance for me because it is evidence that humanism must inform our politics and because it shows that humanists must do whatever we can to break down the walls that keep us all separated from one another. Planetary humanism cannot take hold if the human species is not united.

*   *   *

In this essay, I will illustrate why it is that I believe a humanist must be politically progressive. I will focus primarily on two issues that mean a great deal to me, the environment and peace. Not only do I have strong commitments in these two areas, but also I have put these commitments into action and have organized around both—as the director of the Grass Roots Environmental Organization from 1983 until 1998 and as the director of New Jersey Peace Action since August 2000. It is my hope that the combination of intellectual analysis and discussion of organized political action and activism will persuade the reader that humanism and progressive politics are a potent and essential combination.

While I will focus only on these two issues, this kind of analysis could easily be extended to many other areas of current interest, such as globalization, economic and social justice, education, criminal justice, poverty, and hunger. But since I have only taught about such things and have not organized political action around these issues, I leave it up to the reader to see how the principles of humanism enumerated in the areas of environment, peace, and justice can be applied to these other extremely important issues.

WHAT IS HUMANISM?

According to the Canadian Humanist Association, humanism is a nontheistic, nonreligious ethical philosophy based on the principle that human beings are responsible for giving meaning and purpose to their own lives. The humanist ethic aims at the full development of *every* human being to his or her fullest potential. In order for that fullest potential to be reached, it is my belief that other principles must also apply.

1. We must understand that no human being is superior to another human being.
2. While many factors cause us to take certain actions, ultimately we must take responsibility for our actions and be held accountable for the consequences.
3. One human being or group of human beings cannot develop to his/her/their full potential by taking an action that prevents another human being or group of human beings from developing to his/her/their fullest potential.
4. Full development as a human being does not imply unlimited

freedom to act in any way we choose. We must understand that we are all citizens of the world and thus are interconnected.

5. We understand that human beings are not superior to the environment but a part of it—thereby affected by everything we do *to* it.

6. We must understand that what happens to one species on this planet also happens to us. The biodiversity on earth is maintained through a delicate balance and thus must be treated with extreme care.

7. We must understand that we don't actually own *anything* but we must care for everything.

HUMANISM AND ISSUES OF WAR AND PEACE

There is no realm in which these principles can be seen more clearly than in the way in which nations attempt to resolve international conflict. As was evident during the cold war, and now again during the so-called war on terror, it is all too easy for a country to promote its own sense of superiority to the detriment of others. It is all too easy to invoke the need for "patriotism" in order to blind people to the damage being done domestically and abroad in their name.

A short quotation from Martin Luther King Jr. about US involvement in Vietnam embodies many of these principles:

> Somehow this madness must cease. We must stop now. I speak as a . . . brother to the suffering poor of Vietnam. I speak for those whose land is being laid waste, whose homes are being destroyed, whose culture is being subverted. I speak for the poor in America who are paying the double price of smashed hopes at home and death and corruption in Vietnam. *I speak as a citizen of the world, for the world as it stands aghast at the path we have taken. I speak as an American to the leaders of my own nation.* The great initiative in this war is ours. The initiative to stop it must be ours. (Emphasis mine)[1]

Some people may argue that the United States didn't start the "war on terror." However, others suggest that George W. Bush's statement that "you're either with us or you're with the terrorists," just an hour after the first tower had been hit, shifted the focus immediately away from self-examination and reflection to a mentality that put American interests and American lives above all others. Only one member of the Senate or House of Representatives, Rep. Barbara Lee of California, had the courage to speak out on the danger of allowing the executive branch virtual carte blanche to determine when and how to respond to the events of September 11, 2001.

Because of this acquiescence, very little time was taken to debate whether a full-scale military operation in Afghanistan was the best option. Worse, the decision to invade Iraq was made quickly, under enormous political pressure and without much debate. Thus, a discussion of the real consequences of both actions on the countries involved *and* the rest of the world never occurred.

Robert Jensen, associate professor of journalism at the University of Texas at Austin, clearly delineates the dangers of placing one's country and its needs above the needs of all other countries:

> If in the end we are just Americans, if we cannot move beyond patriotism, then we cannot claim to be internationalists. And, if we are not truly internationalist in our outlook—all the way to the bone—then I do not think we truly call ourselves people committed to peace and justice. . . .
>
> If freedom and democracy are not unique to us, then they are simply human ideals, endorsed to varying degrees in different places and realized to different degrees by different people acting in different places. If that's true, then they are not distinctly American ideals. They were not invented here, and we do not have a monopoly on them. So, if one is trying to express a commitment to those ideals, why do it in the limiting fashion of talking of patriotism? . . .
>
> This is both a struggle to save ourselves and a struggle to save the lives of vulnerable people around the world. We must say goodbye to patriotism because the kind of America the peace-and-justice movement wants to build cannot be built on, or through, the patriotism of Americans.
>
> We must say goodbye to patriotism because the world cannot survive indefinitely the patriotism of Americans.[2]

One important aspect of Jensen's thinking is that no one country has a monopoly on the values many of us hold dear, such as real freedom and true democracy. In fact, there are people all over the world who work for freedom and democracy every day. Instead of rallying behind a flag and a country—any country—whose motives are suspect, it makes sense to find those people, whoever they are and wherever they live, and build alliances with them in our desire to build a better world.

Hiding behind hastily adopted and blind patriotism, it is all too easy for a country to live according to the "ethic" of might makes right. In addition to the poor logic, acting according to that maxim leads to the *breakdown* of whatever sense of community exists. Having the military power to defeat any identified enemy, real or imagined, does not give to a country an inherent right to impose its values or interests on the weaker nation. Just as the US Constitution was designed to protect the minority from the tyranny of the majority, so is international law designed to protect the smaller, less-developed nations from the actions of larger, more aggressive ones, looking to expand their influence and economic power.

Booker Prize–winning author Arundhati Roy points out the dangerous absurdity of thinking in terms of retaliation and vengeance and demonstrates the impossibility of achieving *justice* in this manner. In very powerful language, filled with poetry and irony, Roy also shows the arrogance and inhumanity behind the assumption that lives of those in *your country* are worth more than lives of those in *another's country:*

> In 1996, Madeleine Albright, then the US Secretary of State, was asked on national television what she felt about the fact that 500,000 Iraqi children had died as a result of US (U.N.) economic sanctions. She replied that it was "a very hard choice," but that all things considered, "we think the price is worth it." . . .
>
> So here we have it. The equivocating distinction between civilisation and savagery, between the "massacre of innocent people" or, if you like, "a clash of civilisations" and "collateral damage." The sophistry and fastidious algebra of infinite justice. How many dead Iraqis will it take to make the world a better place? How many dead Afghans for every dead American? How many dead women and children for every dead man? How many dead Mojahedin for each dead investment banker? As we watch mesmerised, Operation Enduring Freedom unfolds on TV monitors across the world. A coalition of the world's superpowers is closing in on Afghanistan, one of the poorest, most ravaged, war-torn countries in the world, whose ruling Taliban government is sheltering Osama bin Laden.[3]

What gives Madeleine Albright, or any other American for that matter, the right to proclaim that the loss of five hundred thousand children's lives is a price worth paying, no matter how honorable the cause?[4] (And, in the case of Iraq, there are many questions about how honorable the cause.) Surely, it is not sufficient to answer that Albright has the right to say that because she is American and America has the ability to defeat the Iraq mil-

---

itarily or that, honorable cause or not, no country or group of countries like the United Nations can or will stop America. If the roles were reversed and an Iraqi said the same thing about the loss of Kuwaiti or Israeli lives, there would be no end to the outrage from this country. If one country's anger is legitimate in the face of such tragedy, then another country's anger in the face of similar tragedy is also legitimate, whether the country has been ravaged by twelve years of sanctions or twenty years of war.

It is all too easy for a country to get locked into its particular worldview and to attemp to sell others on the notion that is the best and its worldview superior to that of anyone else. One of the most frightening moments I have experienced since the tragic events of September 11, 2001, came in a moment when it seemed that morality and ethics had been turned completely on their heads.

It was January 2002. I was addressing a chapter of the Mensa Society, made up of people with high intelligence quotients. It was one of the first times I had spoken in public about the events of 9/11 and this nation's reactions to it. Like almost every thinking person, I was still trying to make sense both out of what happened to us *and* what we were doing to others in response.

I spoke of the tragic loss of nearly three thousand people on American soil as a result of the planes flying into the World Trade Center, the Pentagon, and a field in Pennsylvania. I called the actions a terrible crime against humanity. It was imperative that *those responsible be brought to justice* through what even Secretary of Defense Donald Rumsfeld admits is the most effective means, international cooperation, international intelligence, and international police work. "The military isn't organized to do manhunts," he was quoted as saying.[5]

Then I echoed something that members of an organization called September 11th Families for Peaceful Tomorrows said to approximately thirty peace activists at a vigil held on a cold autumn night in November 2001 in the parking lot of a New Jersey mosque. David Portorti, whose older brother was killed in the attack on the World Trade Center, spoke of the day he told his mother the terrible news of her son's death. According to David, his mother doubled over in pain, as if she had been kicked in the stomach, and cried. When she finished crying, she sat up and said, "I don't want any other mother anywhere else in the world to feel the pain I feel today." Although nearly crippled by grief, this mother thought of others in her situation around the world and, in her own way, implored her government not to respond by war and the loss of additional innocent civilian lives. Predictably, the words and beliefs of this organization of families of those killed in the attacks of September 11 get very little coverage in the mainstream media. Yet, in a very real sense, who else had as much authority to speak about how to respond than those who lost loved ones in the attacks?

This philosophy was underlying my presentation to the Mensa Society that January day. I was concerned that the full-scale military action against Afghanistan had resulted in the loss of many innocent lives, without necessarily stopping violent attacks against the United States.

I was appalled to learn that, when asked the number of civilian casualties, Rumsfeld stated emphatically, "We're not counting civilian casualties. Neither are the Afghans. We don't know how many civilians have died."[6] The moral high ground is lost instantly by the dismissive nature of that comment, particularly when the military claims to be taking every precaution to minimize civilian casualties. We can do better than that, I reflected.

When I had finished, one woman approached me. She asked me if I knew how many civilians had died in Afghanistan. I said that I didn't know the exact number, but that Professor Marc Herold from the University of New Hampshire had culled through many newspaper articles in the region and had been able to corroborate enough stories to estimate that between three thousand and four thousand civilians had died.

This woman looked me squarely in the eyes. I saw her eyes widen. I was prepared to hear her express surprise and say something like, "I never imagined there would be so many!" Instead, she said, "Good! Kill them. Kill them all!" I mentioned that many of the dead were children. She continued, "Good! By the time they are five, they already hate us."

Some of the people standing around us nodded their approval of her statement. At that precise moment I asked myself a very disturbing question. How had it happened that a perspective based on limiting civilian casualties and going straight to the heart of the problem carried less moral weight than a statement advocating the deaths of many, if not all, of a population not well known to us? This question has been haunting me ever since.

It soon became apparent that in the face of overwhelming grief and anger at what happened to *us*, some folks—even those most gifted—lost their sense of humanity. I am reminded of lyrics from a Bob Dylan song, "With God on Our Side."[7] I'd heard it many times before September 11, 2001, but after the war against Afghanistan, born-again George W. Bush's self-appointed mission to rid the world of "evildoers," and Rumsfeld's comments, Dylan's words held even more meaning. While his lyrics refer to World War I, Dylan's song could easily apply to the war in Afghanistan (and months later, the invasion of Iraq).

Just what are we fighting for? There are elements of a "holy war" in the US response to 9/11. Could that be why we are not counting civilian casualties? Could it be that we don't want to know? How can this be justified when we're still mourning almost three thousand casualties of our own? More than two years after 9/11, Osama bin Laden still runs free. Our political leadership acts as if the attacks give us not only the moral right but also the absolute right to claim resources that we proclaim we need as our own. Henry Kissinger once stated, "Oil is too important a commodity to leave in the hands of the Arabs."[8]

If we look at the overall distribution of the world's resources, we uncover some disturbing facts. The United States, and countries with our level of affluence, account for just 20 percent of the world's population. However, we control 80 percent of the world's resources, leaving the other 80 percent of people to share the other 20 percent of resources or to become dependent on the overdeveloped world. Many of the resources controlled by the first world resulted from various forms of colonization of second- and third-world countries. If we are ever to stop the cycle of violence, it is imperative that we address these gross inequities between rich and poor nations. Otherwise, we're sure to see an increasing number of battles over resources.

Indeed, we act as if we are perplexed at how *our* oil got under *their* sands. The arrogance that convinces one nation of its presumed superiority is the same arrogance that convinces one race of its presumed superiority to another. That arrogance translates into repression of many types, bolstered by and transforming into racism.

Which brings us to the "war against Iraq." Many people believe it began on March 20, 2003. However, what amounted to an illegal invasion of Iraq was just the final stage in a twelve-year siege against that country, which began right after the end of the Persian Gulf War of 1991.

There *is* hope for humanism and a humanist ethic to emerge from this unnecessary invasion, despite what ultimately happened. On Saturday, February 15, 2003, perhaps 30 million people gathered in many cities around the world to protest what was still just a proposed unprovoked invasion of the sovereign country of Iraq. Millions of people in Great Britain, Spain, and Italy took to the streets to protest the unjustified, illegal, and immoral planned action of the Bush administration and Tony Blair's government.

In another instance of ethics being turned upside down, the Bush administration praised the prime ministers of all three countries for having the "courage of their convictions" and being capable of standing up to public sentiment. It would have been more appropriate for those millions of people speaking out to be praised for practicing their democratic rights.

As a matter of fact, the *New York Times* did just that. On February 16, an article in the *Times* stated, "There are now two superpowers in the world. The first is the United States. The second is that of global public opinion [public opinion against the war]."[9]

The worldviews of these two existing "superpowers" clash in many ways. The Bush administration used the events of September 11, 2001, to trumpet the greater value of American lives and thus, the intensity and importance of America's grief. The Bush administration used the events of September 11, 2001, to proclaim the superiority of the American military and to flex its muscles militarily whenever it feels justified in doing so. The Bush administration has used the events of September 11, 2001, to proclaim the United States and its allies as "civilized" nations and anyone refusing to go along as part of the "uncivilized" world. The Bush administration also used the events of September 11, 2001, to justify steady erosion of civil rights and civil liberties, as expression of dissent and concern can now be defined as a threat to national security. In other words, the events of September 11, 2001, have provided the Bush administration with the perfect platform to promote their agenda of superiority and domination such that they will be given permission to gain greater control of some of the world's most precious resources. In the Middle East, the two resources of most concern are oil and water.

The counterweight to that attitude is the millions of people around the world who gathered in opposition to the invasion and remain in opposition to such action. While they would not all consider themselves humanists, it is easy to spot many elements of humanism in their position. And, while the Bush administration can throw on a humanist cloak when it suits them by talking about the so-called liberation of the Iraqi people, the clear and consistent humanist message comes from those who opposed the invasion.

Why is that? Those opposed to the invasion of Iraq reject the philosophy that the "ends justify the means." If we strip away the nationalities of all involved and describe the invasion of Iraq in nonnationalistic terms, many people would agree that the invasion was unethical, immoral, and illegal. It violated international law, justification for it was based on lies, and the stated reason for invasion was far from the real purpose behind it. As historian and novelist Tariq Ali writes, "In the clash between a religious fundamentalism—itself the product of modernity—and *an imperial fundamentalism determined to 'discipline the world,'* it is necessary to oppose both . . ." (emphasis mine).[10]

The recent capture of Saddam Hussein must be looked at through the same humanist filter. While most opponents of the invasion of Iraq did not consider Saddam Hussein the world's most benevolent dictator, those same opponents understood the danger behind allowing one militarily powerful country to determine when and how and under what conditions certain leaders may maintain their leadership position in the world.

For a good twenty years, Saddam Hussein was "America's dictator." When he no longer served America's interests, he was dispensable, regardless of what international laws had to be violated and how many lives had to be sacrificed.

Imagine the following scenario. People in countries targeted by the United States as members of the "axis of evil" turn America's words right back at us. The United States, they say, has more weapons of mass destruction than many countries combined. The United States is threatening to use those weapons should it decide that it is at risk of attack some time in the indeterminate future. We must take its threats seriously, they reason, because that particular nation is also the only nation ever to have used nuclear weapons, resulting in approximately two hundred thousand people dying instantly and countless others dying the long, slow death of radiation poisoning. Its president defies international law and is slowly denying his citizens many of their constitutionally guaranteed civil rights and civil liberties. For the overall security and prosperity of the world, they conclude, a regime change is required.

If the actions of the United States against Iraq are justified, the only thing stopping these countries from acting on the same reasoning is their lack of military power and economic strength. It is dangerous to make decisions in this manner. Just because we live in a country that can back up its rhetoric with military might does not mean that we are acting in the best interests of the international community. In fact, it is quite the contrary.

The capture of Saddam Hussein took place as the result of an illegal, immoral, and unjustified invasion. His capture must be looked upon in that light and not used to obscure and erase the memory of how it happened. In addition, the humiliating images of Hussein at the mercy of his

American captors and projected on television screens throughout the world reinforce the paternalistic American attitude expressed by Kissinger, that oil is too important to be left in the hands of the Arab world, and that the United States has a right to claim Iraq and Iraq's oil as its own.

When one nation puts itself above all others, it encourages other nations to do the same. In this ever-shrinking world, more accessible to everyone through electronic communications, nations need to act with even more consideration of the consequences of their actions. That which leads a person to sacrifice his or her life will not be stopped through more violence and a show of military prowess. Valuing one set of lives more highly than another set of lives and acting as if one's country has a monopoly on all that is "good" creates a problem for the rest of the world.

Is the world safer post-9/11? Many Americans state that they feel safer today than they did on September 11, 2001, because no further acts of terror have taken place on American soil. There is a terrible irony in this proclamation of victory. There have been almost daily attacks on Americans on Iraqi soil and frequent attacks on Americans in Afghanistan. India and Pakistan came to the verge of nuclear war about a year after September 11, 2001. There have been two recent attempts on the life of Pervez Musharraf, prime minister of Pakistan.

While the Israelis and Palestinians have been fighting over land, resources, and social justice since 1948, there appears to be a quantitative and qualitative shift in the violence since 9/11. The Israelis justify their actions by referring to America's "war on terror." They appear more emboldened in their words and actions as they draw parallels between their war and our war. The level of violence between the Israelis and the Palestinians has escalated since September 11, 2001, with no end in sight.

Longstanding and simmering tensions between India and Pakistan nearly came to a head a year after 9/11, raising new fears that their feud over Kashmir would result in a nuclear war. Tension between North Korea and South Korea has increased as well. And the list goes on. When the world's only superpower opts for a military response to international conflict and uses military force as the language of diplomacy, the whole world is encouraged to join in.

In view of the world situation, the fact that some Americans feel safer because no further acts of terror have taken place on American soil seems hollow and shortsighted. Nearly every day, Americans are being attacked and killed in Iraq. Many countries throughout the world that once sympathized with the United States after 9/11 are now frightened and critical of the United States for our actions in Iraq and our increasingly one-sided support for Israel in the Israeli-Palestinian conflict. There are attacks on our civil rights and civil liberties here at home, in the form of many provisions of the USA PATRIOT Act. Although it is tempting to feel complacent because one's own country hasn't been attacked a second time on its soil, it is also dangerous to ignore the increasing levels of violence worldwide. Instead, it makes better sense to understand how all these actions and situations are interconnected and to concentrate on finding ways to reduce violence and tension worldwide, not only on American soil.

HUMANISM AND UNIVERSAL PRINCIPLES: CHANGING THE PARADIGM

Much of the division and destruction accomplished through war and violence derives from the ability of some to convince others that there is an inherent difference between people of different cultures, religions, or countries. History is replete with instances of government's ability to "divide and conquer," to utilize the fears, jealousies, or insecurities of one group against another. As long as groups are fighting one another, those in power can maintain their power.

If we listen to those who would divide us artificially, through narrow and rigid doctrines, dogma, religious rhetoric, or stereotypes, we will never overcome the cycle of violence with something more constructive and affirming. If we let our own beliefs blind us to the humanity of others who do not share our beliefs, we allow those who would exploit our minor differences to continue to do so.

What we need instead is an awareness of the ways in which all humans are the same. We can start with the notion that all human beings are complex physically, psychologically, emotionally, and intellectually. Regardless of the specific characteristics unique to each individual, all human beings need certain material goods in order to survive. Satisfaction of material needs, together with access to certain intellectual, mental, and emotional stimulation allows humans to develop to their fullest potential. Recognizing and honoring similarities among human beings instead of concentrating on and highlighting the differences among people will give humanity an opportunity to devise a series of policies that encourage human development instead of policies that stunt that growth. In contrast, encouragement of greed instead of simple fulfillment of one's needs will, in the words of J. R. Seydel, "prevent a person or a group of persons from recognizing and enjoying their own wealth, and their greedy posture will cause them to resort to dishonesty, lying, cheating and stealing."[11]

So many of the measures used to determine the "success" of a society are tied to materials production and materials consumption. One's economic standard of living is measured, instead of the quality of one's life. If, instead, the human development index and other human development indicators (devised by the United Nations Development Program and first implemented in 1975) were used to determine the worthiness of a certain set of economic and social policies, we could be living in quite a different world.

The human development index and accompanying indicators measure the level of education attained by each person within the society being studied. They measure the amount of power held by women in the society relative to that held by men. They measure the society's ability to protect and preserve the environment and manage its resources.

It is possible through a democratic, decentralized commitment to raising the level of education for all, regardless of income level, to achieve high levels of education for all without spending millions of dollars.[12] It is possible to grant equal rights to men and women without a strong manufacturing sector or a steady consumer price index. The ability to protect the environment and preserve its resources is independent of the country's gross domestic product. Rather, these laudable goals can be achieved when they are established as a priority, regardless of a nation's per capita income.[13]

If we understand what one human being needs to function, then we can understand how to provide for that human being and for others. Policies can encourage and develop healthy relationships between and among humans within nations and between and among nations, instead of exploiting their differences. Policies can encourage cooperation instead of competition, mutual respect instead of misconceptions. In the process, both a unity of purpose and a unity of mind can be achieved.

Rabbi Arthur Waskow, director of the Shalom Center, said it most eloquently on September 12, 2001. I did not see this statement until about a week later. For the first time since September 11, I read a most human appraisal of what had happened on that day and how the world should respond. For the first time since the tragedies, I was able to cry.

> For much of our lives we try to achieve peace and safety by building with steel and concrete and toughness. *Pyramids, air raid shelters, Pentagons, World Trade Centers. Hardening what might be targets and, like Pharaoh, hardening our hearts against what is foreign to us.*

But the sukkah[14] comes to remind us: We are in truth all vulnerable. If "a hard rain gonna fall," it will fall on all of us.

Americans have felt invulnerable. *The oceans, our wealth, our military power have made up what seemed an invulnerable shield.* We may have begun feeling uncomfortable in the nuclear age, but no harm came to us. Yet yesterday the ancient truth came home: We all live in a sukkah.

Not only the targets of attack but also the instruments of attack were among our proudest possessions: the sleek transcontinental airliners. They availed us nothing. Worse than nothing.

Even the greatest oceans do not shield us; even the mightiest buildings do not shield us; even the wealthiest balance sheets and the most powerful weapons do not shield us.

There are only wispy walls and leaky roofs between us. We are, in fact, one interwoven web of life. I MUST love my neighbor as I do myself, because my neighbor and myself are interwoven. If I hate my neighbor, the hatred will recoil upon me.

What is the lesson, when we learn that we—all of us—live in a sukkah? How do we make such a vulnerable house into a place of shalom, of peace and security and harmony and wholeness?

The lesson is that only a world where we all recognize our vulnerability can become a world where all communities feel responsible to all other communities. And only such a world can prevent such acts of rage and murder. (Italics mine)[15]

If we do not act as Rabbi Weskow advises, societies will find it necessary to construct a wall to protect themselves from others. The wall and the electronic fence being constructed by Israelis to keep themselves separate from Palestinians and to "address matters of national security"[16] is one such example. Construction of this proposed four-hundred-kilometer wall appears to be an easy way out. It appeals to those who have lost patience with negotiations and seems to eliminate the need to truly understand one's adversary.

Many Israelis and Americans hold one prejudice that is helping to construct the wall—the belief is that it is impossible to negotiate with the Palestinians because "they don't value life the way we do." This conclusion is derived from viewing "suicide bombers" at work. At the same time, the Israelis and Americans ignore those elements of their own behavior that devalue human life, like failure to count or acknowledge civilians killed by US or Israeli military action, or refusal by the United States to participate in the International Criminal Court, or the rare and gentle rebuke by the United States of Israeli conduct in the occupied territories of the West Bank and Gaza. And, more important, the superpower and its ally ignore the ongoing injustices that have left the Palestinian people bereft of their culture, denied them their history and made economic survival virtually impossible. While suicide bombing and its consequences are deplorable, it is not enough to simply condemn and then increase the violence without addressing the root causes of the actions. Nor does it move matters forward to demonize an entire people and subject them to collective punishment and hatred. A lesson can be learned from South Africa's Truth and Reconciliation Commission—based on understanding the truth about what happened under apartheid and finding ways of reconciliation, not an endless cycle of retribution and revenge.

Certainly the Palestinians value life as much as anyone else does. A Palestinian mother informed of the death of a son or daughter will cry uncontrollably, and just as the mother of an American soldier killed in Iraq will find a way to honor that death, so will the mother of a Palestinian killed in a suicide bombing. Without that justification, the tragic death of a son or daughter will become completely meaningless. No parent can live with that.

Construction of a wall between two peoples in conflict with one another does nothing to resolve the injustices that cause that conflict. Building the wall will not end the violence, nor will it build understanding between those peoples in conflict. The wall will create a false sense of security for the Israelis. It will be a poor substitute for understanding the basic human needs driving the conflict, thus preventing identification of a real solution to the problem.

Ultimately, it is the discovery of our common humanity and the basic human needs that are being left unsatisfied by our respective governments that will enable people to stop being territorial and instead to advocate for solutions that transcend national boundaries. This process rehumanizes our adversary. At the same time, in discovering compassion and empathy, we rehumanize ourselves.

HUMANISM AND THE ENVIRONMENT

Changing our view of our relationship to other human beings is the first step toward achieving genuine peace and security throughout the world. Of course, this view of other human beings also helps in establishing healthy economic relationships, dealing with poverty and world hunger, and developing a more human-based system of criminal justice.

However, there is one more step humanity must take in order to pre-serve and protect the environment around them—the world. Environ-mental scientists call it "changing the paradigm" and describe it this way: The old paradigm establishes human beings as separate from and masters of their environment. The old paradigm is built on the premise that of all living creatures, humans are the only ones that can think about themselves and that are aware of how the rest of the creatures function and operate.

While this premise may be true, having that awareness and conscious-ness gives humans a special responsibility as well. It allows humans to understand that all elements of the ecosystem function together, that if one part of the ecosystem is sick, all other parts are affected. If the global temperature is rising, weather patterns all over the world are affected. If species of animals are becoming extinct through human activities or if rainforests are being chopped down at alarming rates, everything else on the planet is affected.

Once humans have accepted the ethic that no one human being is superior to another, it is a small but very important step to accept the prin-ciple that no human being is superior to any other living organism and that all living organisms exist in an intricate series of interconnected rela-tionships. This understanding becomes a new paradigm, one that replaces the notion that everything on the planet is here to assist humans with one that requires human beings to think about their connection and relation-ship to everything on the planet, from animals to plants to insects to woodlands, rainforests, and oceans.

Shortly after the events of September 11, 2001, the US Senate and US House of Representatives had a chance to take an action that would, over time, significantly reduce our need for oil, either foreign or domestic. The legislature was considering a bill to establish a minimum fuel-efficiency rate of thirty-five miles per gallon for all new vehicles. In an action that made no sense environmentally, yet total sense economically, the Senate rejected this bill, offering the rationale that "they did not want to interfere with the soccer mom's freedom of choice."[17]

I wish someone would explain to me how requiring the automobile manufacturers to build more fuel-efficient vehicles interferes with "freedom of choice." The technology is currently available to build many types of vehicles capable of achieving such fuel efficiency, including sport utility vehicles. And, for those vehicles for which it is not available, it would seem a worthy endeavor to conduct research with the goal of finding that technology. Given the current state of the world and the dangers involved in trying to obtain more oil to satisfy the US appetite, all possible resources should be poured into finding ways to reduce our dependence on oil, not only through increased fuel efficiency but also through nonoil-based alternatives.

The legislature's unwillingness to mandate higher fuel-efficiency standards is immediately beneficial only to the oil and automotive industries. It presupposes that this government will be able to obtain the necessary oil to fuel both industries whenever and wherever it pleases. The inner logic behind this action (and others like it) can only lead to ultimate environmental and economic disaster.

Many actions could be taken today to stave off environmental disaster in the future. And, for those who do not believe the warnings, these actions still make sense if we allow the new humanist paradigm to inform our decisions. And for those who do not yet accept the humanist paradigm, common sense would result in taking precautionary measures.

Being embroiled in a "war without end" and a war that, according to Vice President Dick Cheney, will probably "not end in our lifetimes" and the Bush administration's current philosophies do not permit us to adopt this new paradigm.[18] We have replaced the cold war with this so-called war on terror. Developing policies while preparing for and waging war may have an untold impact on the environment. As Albert Einstein once said, "You cannot simultaneously prevent and prepare for war." He was referring to the political momentum that is built up during preparations for war. That political momentum is incompatible with the momentum or will needed to live at peace. However, his words could also be applied to the environmental impacts of war.

Preparation for modern warfare has meant, at least until 9/11, building bigger and more powerful weapons. Since 1945, it has also meant building nuclear weapons, as many countries scrambled to keep up with the United States and the former Soviet Union. Fear of being left out and thus vulnerable to the most deadly weapon currently known sparked a nuclear arms race in many parts of the world.

The development and construction of nuclear weapons brings with it potential and often actual damage to the environment through research at nuclear weapons laboratories and, in the case of the new nuclear weapons sought by the Bush administration, a resumption of nuclear testing. Yet, the current administration is lobbying hard for the funds to develop and test more deadly nuclear weapons, inappropriately called "mini-nukes." Cluster bombs and daisy cutters, though conventional weapons, devastate both the people near them and the environment surrounding their point of impact.

War also means waste. Who can forget scenes of oil fields burning in Iraq during the Persian Gulf War of 1991? Not only are precious resources destroyed in war but also the destruction of those resources often adds to the environmental dangers faced by the world's inhabitants.

Research is uncovering serious environmental and health consequences related to the use of depleted uranium as a coating for missiles. Physician, humanist, antinuclear campaigner, and Nobel Peace Prize nominee Helen Caldicott writes about the use of depleted uranium during the Persian Gulf War of 1991:

> In 1991, during Operation Desert Storm, American tanks fired 14,000 depleted uranium anti-tank shells.... The air force tank-killer planes fired approximately 940,000 30-mm depleted uranium rounds in combat, totaling 564,000 pounds of depleted uranium that either hit their targets or were scattered over the desert floor.... At the end of the operation, between 300 and 800 tons of uranium 238 with a half-life of 4.5 billion years lay across the battlefield of Iraq, Kuwait and Saudi Arabia, never to be retrieved, in spent rounds, in solid and powdered form, in various states of decay and dispersal.[19]

The Campaign Against Depleted Uranium further explains:

> Depleted uranium was first used on a large scale in military combat during the 1991 Gulf War, and has since been used in Bosnia in 1995, and again in the Balkans war of 1999.[20]

> A sub-commission of the United Nations Commission on Human Rights appointed a "rapporteur" to investigate the use of depleted uranium weapons among other types of weapons, after passing a resolution which categorised depleted uranium weapons alongside such as nuclear, chemical and biological weapons, napalm, and cluster bombs as a "weapon of indiscriminate effect."[21]

According to Caldicott, having an indiscriminate effect means they fail the following tests:

1. The temporal test: their effects continue after the war ends;
2. The environmental test: they pollute food, water and soil;

3. The humaneness test: they have effects beyond those necessary to achieve military objectives;
4. The geographical test: the particles can potentially travel to non-combatant countries.[22]

The United States and other countries known to be using depleted uranium in their arsenals—the United Kingdom, France, Russia, Greece, Turkey, Israel, Saudi Arabia, Bahrain, Egypt, Kuwait, Pakistan, Thailand, Iraq, and Taiwan—utilize this waste product of the nuclear industry, a form of "enriched uranium," by producing so-called depleted uranium weapons. Enriched uranium is uranium in which the proportion of U-235 (to U-238) has been increased above the natural 0.7%.[23] While many scientists, lobbyists, and politicians worldwide call for a moratorium on the use of depleted uranium until the environmental and health effects can be determined, no action has been taken to prevent the use of missiles coated with depleted uranium.

Veterans of the Vietnam War had to deal with the potential health effects of being exposed to Agent Orange, a defoliant used to strip trees of their foliage so that Americans could see their "enemy" better. Veterans of the Persian Gulf War, the war in Bosnia and Kosovo, and the conflict in Iraq in 2003 are already dealing with the potential health effects of exposure to depleted uranium.[24]

These concerns compound the tragic legacy of war. Not only do we mourn the human casualties caused by the fighting itself but also there may be countless casualties, both human and environmental, caused by the materials used in war. Yet, when a declaration of war is contemplated, the environmental consequences are rarely factored into the equation. These consequences are faced on the battlefield. They are also faced wherever the materials are produced. Those working to manufacture Agent Orange for use in the Vietnam War or those involved with handling depleted uranium and producing depleted-uranium-coated missles are also potentially at risk. Also at risk are those who live near to the facilities producing the weapons and herbicides. Currently, there is a bill in Congress, HR 1483 (the Depleted Uranium Munitions Study Act), sponsored by Rep. Jim McDermott (D-WA), which calls for study and resolution of medical and environmental consequences of exposure to depleted uranium, potentially addressing some of these concerns.

The message is clear. Unless we adopt a humanist ethic in resolving conflicts around the world, we stand to fuel the cycle of violence. An intensified cycle of violence means destruction of much that we value, not the least of which is our basic humanity: our ability to show compassion, to understand the truth, and to work for justice.

And while some leaders may use the language of humanism to justify their actions, it is imperative that we look past those words to uncover our leaders' true motivation. Unless we do that, we may find ourselves living in a world beyond recognition, where the only ethic at work is might makes right or the end justifies the means.

As residents of one of the countries in a position to make decisions that affect the rest of the world, it is tempting to bask in the glory of being on the "winning side." However, for the sake of all humanity and the good of the planet, we must guard against that mentality. In fact, our position of power demands that we exercise even greater responsibility in determining our actions around the world. Echoing Einstein, we require a substantially new way of thinking if we are to survive. That way is humanism.

$$*\quad*\quad*$$

Standing Tall?

How do you
Stand tall
Without falling?

How do you
Stand tall
Without making others
Feel small?

Can you raise
The good
Without standing above?

Can you appreciate
The best
Inside
Without boasting
Or being
Too loud?

Inside . . . . Outside
The Twin Towers
Stood tall. . . .

Taller than
Any other
Edifice
Of metal
And glass
On the face
Of the earth
They pierced
The sky.

For some,
Symbols
Of everything
Terribly right.
For others,
Symbols
Of everything
Terribly wrong.

Targets
Struck
Fallen
Collapsing
Beneath their weight
Supports
Melting
In intense
Heat.

To stand tall
With dignity
To stand tall
With humility
To stand tall
Without

Looking down.
Does anyone know
How it can be done?
Will we ever learn?

Smoke rising
From the rubble
What's happening
In the rubble?
I hope
Something changes.

Slowly,
So very slowly,
The spirit
Inside
Is sitting up

The spirit
Outside
Is beginning
To take notice

Bubbling up
Clearing away
Emerging. . . .

A quiet courage
An unspoken confidence
A feeling of peace
A feeling of place

One still
Bound
To the ground
But one
That soon
May run
Truly free.[25]

NOTES

1. Martin Luther King Jr., *The Trumpet of Conscience* (New York: Harper and Row, 1968). Quote accessed on http://www.mccsc.edu/~bhsntech/backup/quotes.html.

2. Robert Jensen, "Saying Goodbye to Patriotism," *Counterpunch,* November 12, 2001, http://www.counterpunch.org/jensen12.html.

3. Arundhati Roy, "The Algebra of Infinite Justice," *Guardian* (UK), September 29, 2001, http://www.guardian.co.uk/saturday_review/story/0,3605,559756,00.html.

4. Madeleine Albright, quoted on *Sixty Minutes,* May 12, 1996.

5. Donald Rumsfeld, originally quoted in the *Newark (NJ) Star Ledger,* February 2002, and repeated in Ann Scott Tyson, "Does bin Laden Matter Anymore?" *Christian Science Monitor,* March 1, 2002, http://www.csmonitor.com/2002/0301/p01s02-usmi.html.

6. Rumsfeld, quoted in Ian Traynor, "Afghans Still Dying as Airstrikes Go On. But No One Is Counting," *Guardian* (UK), February 12, 2002.

7. Bob Dylan, "With God on Our Side," lyrics at http://www.bobdylan.com/songs/withgod.html.

8. Henry Kissinger, quoted in Hans von Sponek and Denis Halliday, "The Hostage Nation," *Guardian* (UK), November 29, 2001.

9. Patrick E. Tyler, "A New Power in the Streets," *New York Times,* February 16, 2003, front page.

10. Tariq Ali, *The Clash of Fundamentalisms: Crusades, Jihads, and Modernity* (London: Verso, 2002), acknowledgments.

11. J. R. Seydel, "Universal Cosmic Law: The Seven Principles," 1996, http://www.pymander.com/AETHEREAL/PRINC~1.htm. The Seven Universal Principles are Mentalism, Correspondence, Vibration, Polarity, Rhythm (the cycles), Cause and Effect, and Gender.

12. "The People's Campaign" and "Overview of the People's Campaign," in T. M. Thomas Isaac and Richard W. Franke, *Local Democracy and Development: The Kerala People's Campaign for Decentralized Planning* (Lanham, MD: Rowman & Littlefield, 2002), pp. 5–8.

13. Ibid.

14. The sukkah is a hut, constructed during the Jewish holiday of Sukkhot, which lasts just one week. Even though the sukkah is used within a religious context, it can be instructive to a secularist as well.

15. Arthur Waskow, "The Sukkah and the World Trade Center," Shalom Center, http://www.shalomctr.org/index.cfm/action/read/section/HOLI/article/peace42.html.

16. James Rodgers, "Israeli Security Fence Casts Shadow," BBC News World Edition, July 29, 2003, http://news.bbc.co.uk/2/hi/middle_east/3106583.stm.

17. "Shame on the Senate, Killing CAFE Standards," TomPaine.com, http://www.tompaine.com/feature.cfm/ID/5258.

18. Dick Cheney, quoted in Frida Berrigan, "Halliburton's Axis of Influence," In

These Times, March 28, 2003, http://www.inthesetimes.com/comments.php?id=138-010C. Quote is from October 2001.

19. Helen Caldicott, *The New Nuclear Danger: George W. Bush's Military-Industrial Complex* (New York: New Press, 2002), pp. 151–52.

20. Also in Iraq in 2003.

21. "Introduction," Communities against Depleted Uranium, http://www.cadu.org.uk/intro.htm

22. Caldicott, *The New Nuclear Danger*, p. 157.

23. Information and Issue Briefs: Glossary, World Nuclear Association, http://www.world-nuclear.org/info/inf51.htm.

24. Introduction, Campaign Against Depleted Uranium, http://www.cadu.org.uk/intro.htm; Caldicott, *The New Nuclear Danger*, pp. 158–61.

25. Poem © Madelyn Hoffman.

MADELYN HOFFMAN has been the executive director of New Jersey Peace Action since August 2000. Before holding this position, she was the director of the Grass Roots Environmental Organization of New Jersey for fifteen years. She worked with over two hundred citizens' groups from every part of New Jersey around issues of toxic chemical pollution affecting their communities. Before holding that position, Hoffman was a community organizer for the Ironbound Community Corporation in Newark, working with senior citizens living in public housing projects and with residents concerned about toxic chemical pollution in the neighborhood. Hoffman is also an adjunct professor of ethics, public speaking, and American national government. She was Ralph Nader's vice presidential running mate for New Jersey in 1996, and the New Jersey Green Party candidate for governor in 1997.

21.

Facing Facts

Policy Implications of the Humanist Commitment to Science

Thomas Clark

> *Science is the foundational structure of humanism, and consequently the growth of humanism is dependent upon the growth of public recognition, understanding and acceptance of scientific knowledge.*
>
> —Florien J. Wineriter

THE SCIENTIFIC BASIS OF NATURALISM

Humanism, at least of the secular, naturalistic variety, is predicated on the idea that reliable knowledge of the world is best attained via science—the empirical, experimental, and intersubjective investigation of phenomena. Allegiance to science is an expression of the basic human need to predict and control circumstances to bring about outcomes we desire. Responsiveness to the way the world is, as opposed to the way we might want it to be, is a cognitive trait that obviously serves complex organisms such as ourselves well in the quest for survival. Science is the culturally evolved refinement of such responsiveness, and it has turned native human curiosity into a powerful tool of prediction and control while giving us a coherent, unified picture of the world.

The ultimate constituents of the universe, according to science, are those microlevel phenomena described by physical theory, and the rest of what exists is, in one way or another, composed of these constituents. The scientific mode of knowing thus leads to an overarching ontological naturalism, in that whatever science incorporates into its explanations is likewise incorporated into a single, natural world, not divided into two distinct realms, the natural and the supernatural. The latter division is the hallmark of nonempirical, nonexperimental epistemologies, those driven by a commitment to revealed knowledge, authoritative texts, personal revelation, and traditional worldviews that often ascribe supernatural status to gods, spirits, souls, and other nonphysical entities.

Because of their commitment to science as an epistemology, secular humanists tend toward a nondualist, naturalist conception of ourselves as embedded in nature. There is nothing that fundamentally sets us apart, or above, the natural world. We are fully physical, caused creatures, even in our highest capacities, and the various characteristics of persons, whether idiosyncratic or universal, are entirely a function of the environmental and genetic situation in which they develop.

But at the start of the twenty-first century such a view is held by a small minority, at least in the United States. Human nature, it seems, prevents the optimally rational allegiance to science that secular humanists hold as the ideal epistemic commitment. The overriding desire for survival implanted in us by evolution generates the opposite, antiscientific tendency: the wishful thinking that denies the empirical evidence that we are simply material creatures doomed to die and disappear. Hence the widespread, often religiously expressed supposition that the causal physical story told by science can't be the whole story; there's something within us that transcends nature and survives death, namely the supernatural soul.

This soul, this mental essence or nonphysical agent, escapes being fully included in the natural order. But not only does it survive death, it has contra-causal free will (what philosophers sometimes call libertarian free will), the capacity to cause without itself being fully the causal product of surrounding and prior conditions. Like God, it is causally *privileged* over the rest of nature. I will call this commitment to the soul and contra-causal free will the dualist stance, since it supposes that we are of fundamentally two natures, the natural and the supernatural.

NATURALISM, ATTITUDES, AND SOCIAL POLICY

Because they imply radically different things about ourselves as agents, these two fundamentally different worldviews, the nondual, naturalist stance and the dualist, supernaturalist stance, help drive deeply divergent attitudes and social policies. The naturalist stance, based in science, acknowledges that human beings and their successes and failures are completely a function of prior and surrounding conditions, both genetic and environmental. Human behavior is the result of complex interactions between an individual's biology and his or her upbringing, education, peer group, community, and other factors, many of which are potentially affected by social policy. In seeking to explain and ameliorate substandard social conditions and criminal behavior and to create a more flourishing society, those inclined toward a naturalist view of human nature will be led to consider, in the light of scientific findings, all the factors that influence individual growth and community health.

Likewise, when evaluating the impact of policies on persons, societies, and the planet, secular humanists will seek out the best available empirical evidence that bears on a policy's effects. Moreover, their acute and steadfast appreciation of causality leads, or should lead, to a compassionate understanding of those who, by virtue of their genetic and environmental circumstances, end up on the bottom rungs of the economic ladder or who exhibit dysfunctional or antisocial behavior. After all, there but for the luck of the environmental and genetic draw go you or I, experiencing the same deprivation and dysfunction. By virtue of this causality-based empathy and compassion, the naturalist stance *motivates* humanists toward progressive social policies that work to maximize opportunity for the disadvantaged while simultaneously showing the effective *means* of personal and social change based in a scientific understanding of human behavior.

The dualist stance, in contrast, leads in much the opposite direction, both in terms of the perceived effectiveness of policy interventions and the motivation to implement them. Dualists suppose that there is something—the freely willing, supernatural soul—that acts independently of heredity, environment, and any and all policy initiatives. True, as partially material creatures we are to some extent influenced by those factors cited by naturalists but as partially *supernatural* creatures we can transcend any and all influences in making choices in life, should we choose to exercise our capacity for free choice.

Despite the impact of various influences upon us, we essentially create ourselves and our character by virtue of having contra-causal free will. What we do, and the sorts of people we become, is therefore essentially and finally up to us. So however much society invests in creating conditions under which people might become productive, flourishing individuals, the soul has the final, determining say on behavior. If such is the case, then social policies that seek to ameliorate conditions that give rise to crime and economic inequality can have only limited effects, in which case why invest much time and energy on such policies? Because individuals, not social conditions, are the ultimate determining factor behind success in life, then it really isn't within our capacity to help much, and so it's really not that much our concern or responsibility. Belief in free will, therefore, lets us off the hook with respect to others' welfare.

Not only can the dualist view undercut the perceived efficacy of social policies, and thus our motivation to pursue them, it suggests that the less fortunate simply deserve their lot in life. As freely willing agents, we alone merit ultimate credit and blame for success or failure in becoming morally upright, productive, gainfully employed citizens. Those who are poor are ultimately at fault for not having competed successfully in the marketplace of education, jobs, and careers, and those that end up in the criminal justice system are likewise the ultimate, buck-stopping source of their offenses and so deeply deserve punishment. The homeless, Ronald Reagan famously said, simply choose to be homeless, and addicts, because they simply refuse to stop using drugs and alcohol, deserve to die of needle-borne diseases, overdoses, or liver failure. Those who succeed in life, on the other hand, are fully deserving of whatever rewards they can lay their hands on, including, for instance, the hugely inflated salaries of corporate CEOs and university presidents, and the vast unearned income from stock trade windfalls. The differential outcomes following from failure and success are just deserts for the differential exercise of free will, not disparities stemming from social conditions that should be remedied via social policy.

CRIMINAL JUSTICE

Some of the starkest differences in policy objectives driven by the naturalist and dualist conceptions of human nature are found in the arena of criminal justice. The last quarter of the twentieth century in the United States saw an increasing emphasis on nonrehabilitative punishment as the preferred "get tough" response to crime. The American criminal justice system underwent a retrenchment in training programs and substance abuse treatment for offenders, reductions in inmate amenities, and sometimes even the denial of basic privileges such as exercise, books, and television. There was a corresponding increase in punitive control, such as maximum security units, solitary confinement, and physical restraints. Criminal sanctions on juveniles became more severe, even as juvenile crime declined, and many states passed "three-strikes" laws, some of which permit sentences of up to life for simple theft. High rates of mental illness and addiction in prison suggest that mental and behavioral disorders figure prominently in the cause of crime, but these remain notoriously unaddressed by the criminal justice system.

Underlying such policies are more or less unquestioned retributive attitudes supporting harsh sanctions, attitudes stemming from a dualist conception of the criminal, who freely chose to become an offender. If criminals, not the conditions that produced them, are seen as the ultimate source of their criminality, then they are deemed deserving of punishment on grounds that they could have overcome their environmental and biological circumstances but simply and willfully refused to do so. This sense of strong ultimate desert is used to justify both capital punishment and incarceration far more punitive than necessary for rehabilitation or deterrence. Such punishment simply models and perpetuates violent, retaliatory behavior, leaving in its wake vast and unnecessary suffering.

To the extent that criminality and harmful deviance are understood to arise from individuals' undetermined, freely willed choices, their actual biological, social, and economic causes will necessarily go unexplored and unaddressed. The myth of contra-causal free will essentially releases us from the obligation to thoroughly investigate and remedy the origins of maladaptive and antisocial behavior, which lie in mental illness, poverty, child abuse, lack of education and economic opportunity. Free will is the bottom-line excuse and justification for harsh and ineffective criminal justice policies that guarantee continuing high levels of dysfunction and alienation and that perpetuate the cycle of crime and punitive response.

The scientific view that people don't create themselves but instead are fully included in the causal matrix of environmental and biological conditions can help to defuse retributive blaming focused on the person alone. As the metaphysical assumption of free will is questioned and replaced with a naturalist understanding of how offenders are shaped by their genetic and environmental circumstances, retributive attitudes should soften, which in turn will help reduce the demand for capital punishment and punitive prison conditions. Simultaneously, more attention will be paid to the factors that generate criminality. Under pressure from naturalism, the aims of criminal justice will shift from the retributive imposition of just deserts to policies that support the prevention of crime and recidivism, rehabilitation of offenders, and victim restoration and reconciliation. These policies will do far more to increase public safety than the punitive orientation of our current criminal justice system. Such reforms have long been contemplated, of course, and some are underway, but the secular humanist commitment to the science of human nature adds a powerful rationale for their adoption.

As of this writing (June 2004), there is evidence that under severe budgetary constraints brought about by the recession of 2001, some states are reconsidering "tough on crime" criminal justice policies. It turns out that long prison sentences for nonviolent offenses, such as drug possession, are simply too expensive to justify their punitive objectives, even for those who favor punishment over treatment or training. The financial incentive to be "smart on crime," therefore, is shifting attention away from the merely retributive aims of criminal justice to the practical, pragmatic aim of keeping the peace cheaply.

It turns out that *less*-punitive criminal justice policies, involving alternatives to incarceration for nonviolent offenders and rehabilitation for those who must be incarcerated, may well be more economical and more effective. It is to be hoped that the budgetary inducement to rethink retributive justice will carry over into an increased appreciation of how more humane criminal justice polices—those that emphasize prevention, rehabilitation, and community restoration—are indeed smarter, more efficient policies. A naturalistic understanding of ourselves will help accelerate this process.

SOCIAL INEQUALITY

During the 1980s and 1990s, voter support of get-tough criminal justice coincided with declining enthusiasm for public programs designed to address unequal opportunities in access to housing, education, job training, child care, and other necessities strongly associated with economic success in life. The 1960s vision of a "Great Society" in which government would play a central role in equalizing opportunity was, by the end of the century, largely usurped by a narrower, private-sector philosophy in which individuals sink or swim in competitive market economies without much government assistance. Efforts to better the lot of those born into disadvantaged circumstances are now more likely to be dismissed as paternalistic infringements on a person's right (and obligation) to be a self-sufficient self-starter than praised as altruistic attempts to level the playing field.

Helping to motivate this retrenchment is the widespread assumption of libertarian, contra-causal freedom, the Western radical individualism that supposes that persons are at bottom self-made. This assumption works to justify and excuse the increasing differences in material well-being and social advantages that have followed the dismantling of the Great Society. On this dualist understanding of ourselves, those that fail economically fail partially because of a willful refusal to apply themselves or follow the rules. Since it was their *choice* not to get ahead, they deserve their impoverishment. Likewise, those that succeed deserve their riches, however excessive or disproportionate, since they made themselves who they are. The huge and growing inequalities between rich and poor, driven by conservative policies such as tax cuts for the wealthy, welfare reform, and disinvestments in public infrastructure and education, are tolerated partially because many people believe that they reflect differences in metaphysical merit derived from the differential exercise of free will. Inequality, at bottom, is simply the reflection of what people deserve.

To the extent that economic and social inequalities are believed to result from human choices unaffected by surrounding conditions (the definition of libertarian freedom), such inequality will be perceived as the natural outcome of self-originated individual differences, not as anything that could or should be remedied by social policy. Progressive social interventions, therefore, will be thought capable only of operating around the margins of what is essentially up to human free will. The free will assumption, therefore, disempowers and defeats interventions to reduce inequality *in advance* by implying that they cannot be effective or that they somehow infringe on our right to ultimate self-determination. (Of course if we really had contra-causal free will, our self-determination couldn't be infringed upon.) In contradicting the myth of radical individualism, inclusive naturalism shows that a person's economic and social success is entirely a function of family status at birth, innate talents, access to education and other social resources, and numerous other environmental and biological factors, not free will. As John Rawls put it in *A Theory of Justice*:

> It seems to be one of the fixed points of our considered judgments that no one deserves his place in the distribution of native endowments, any more than one deserves one's initial starting place in society. The assertion that a man deserves the superior character that enables him to make the effort to cultivate his abilities is equally problematic; for his character depends in large part upon fortunate family and social circumstances for which he can claim no credit. The notion of desert seems not to apply to these cases.[1]

If we take science as our guide to truth, successful individuals can no longer claim that their riches are deserved in the deep, metaphysical sense of having created themselves and their success ex nihilo. There are no literally self-made men or women. Nor can those who end up on the bottom be blamed for their failure on the grounds they could have chosen otherwise, given the circumstances that obtained. Social and economic inequality will be understood as the luck of the draw, a matter of environmental and biological conditions, not a matter of self-created will and hence not a reflection of metaphysical merit.

Accepting a naturalist view of ourselves will therefore weaken justifications for inequality based on the notions of deserved success and deserved failure. Those of us living comfortable lives will see that, but for circumstances, we, not they, would have been denied such comforts, and this insight will increase our empathy for the less fortunate. It will undercut support for social policies that have generated huge discrepancies in wealth and opportunity, while increasing support for interventions that improve both opportunities and outcomes for the disadvantaged. Although incentives must still exist to encourage hard work, initiative, and risk taking, they need not, and should not, result in a grossly skewed distribution of resources. Inclusive naturalism will shift the justification for having a reasonable standard of living from what's *deserved* to what's *needed* to live a fulfilled, satisfying life. It will also challenge the implicit assumption that nearly unlimited riches in the hands of a few is an acceptable outcome of a just economic system.[2]

There are many other arenas in which naturalism suggests progressive policy reform, including our approaches to such behavioral issues as mental health, addiction, obesity, and learning disabilities. Whenever the individual's free will is assumed to play a role in causing behavior, as it often is in these domains, the secular humanist response should be to challenge that assumption, and initiate a scientific investigation into the actual causes. Such inquiry will serve to reduce the stigma surrounding the behavior in question since it will no longer be considered to originate from the individual alone. This view helps to supply the empathetic motivational *basis* for pursuing nonpunitive, rehabilitative interventions. And by illuminating the causal story of how interventions actually work (or don't work, as is too often the case), naturalism will make them more *effective*. An increase in the awareness and acceptance of an inclusive, thoroughgoing naturalism, therefore, should result in the adoption of progressive social policies and humane behavioral interventions that work better than those premised on the existence of free will.

THE PROSPECTS FOR NATURALISM

If naturalism is both true and effective as a basis for enlightened social action, the question arises of how secular humanists can promote naturalism within a culture that seems increasingly inimical to science and critical thinking. The challenge to free will, like earlier secular humanist challenges to God, the supernatural, and the paranormal, will not receive a warm welcome given the widespread assumption that contra-causal freedom is the basis for all we hold dear. In fact, the scientific threat to our cherished causal exceptionalism is already beginning to spark anxiety in some quarters. Dr. Frederick K. Goodwin, organizer of a 1998 conference titled *Neuroscience and the Human Spirit*, put it this way in his opening remarks:

> Do . . . scientific advances challenge the first principles that the majority of our citizens believe provide the very foundation upon which our civilization rests—free will and the capacity to make moral choices? . . . Does this growing understanding of genetic and environmental influences on human behavior leave any room for free will? . . . How can the ever-mounting discoveries of biological, genetic, and environmental factors shaping human behavior be integrated into our culture without contributing to further erosion of individual responsibility? . . . To the extent that our choices are not truly free, it would seem that we have less moral responsibility for them.[3]

Some philosophers, notably philosopher Saul Smilansky, claim that although inclusive naturalism is true, it is dangerous and counterproductive to make it widely known. He recommends that the truth about free will be kept an academic secret, so that what he considers to be the *fictional* but nevertheless irreplaceable basis for morality and values remains intact.[4] Daniel Dennett, also warns about the "environmental impact" of spiking the myth of libertarian freedom. Demoralization might ensue, he worries, if people mistakenly conclude that they've lost something essential when they cease to believe that they're causally privileged.[5]

Such concerns suggest what must be done to make the naturalist view of ourselves palatable: Secular humanists must defuse the common "determinist anxieties," as they might be called, that arise when we discover that we are entirely natural creatures. Just as they strive to show that we can be good without God, they must also show that we can be moral, effective, and fully individual agents without belief in free will. In addition, they must also demonstrate—as I have attempted to do in discussing criminal justice and social inequality—the positive motivational and practical benefits of taking a consistently scientific, causal view of ourselves. Allaying anxieties and showing the positive consequences of naturalism will help to generate acceptance of a worldview that, although empirically well founded, now has barely a foothold in a public consciousness dominated by the myths of free will and radical individualism.

Although the topic is beyond the scope of this chapter, anxieties about determinism having to do with responsibility, morality, individuality, personal efficacy, and rationality (to name some of the fears most frequently encountered) can be successfully addressed. To do so requires showing how, in each case, the assumption of a freely willing agent is unnecessary for a self-image that supports robust and socially adequate conceptions of moral agency, cognition, action, and personhood. As Dennett has put it, nothing *valuable* gets lost in this revised picture of ourselves—everything we need is afforded under naturalism, and the myth of contra-causal freedom ultimately does far more harm than good.[6]

Facing the naturalistic facts about ourselves, including the sometimes emotionally fraught denial of free will, involves a firm commitment to science as one's epistemology. Secular humanists, nearly universally, find this commitment to be second nature, but many will find it sorely tested as they confront the initially discomfiting realization that we are not exceptions to causality. Nevertheless, as the beneficial personal and social implications of a fully consistent naturalism sink in, accepting this truth about ourselves will become easier. Secular humanists will be in the vanguard (as they always have been) in this next revolution in our understanding of our place in the universe. Their humane motives, reinforced by the empathy generated by taking the fully causal view, will ensure that the immense power of causal understanding will be used wisely as we seek to create a more flourishing, sustainable world.

For the majority not committed to science as the route to truth, naturalism stands as a clear threat to some dearly cherished notions of human nature and the proper social order. Their response to the view proposed here is likely to be increasingly heated denials that science does or should have the final say about who we are, and a more fervid embrace of dualistic faiths that proclaim human causal exceptionalism. The ideologically driven rejection of naturalism in the face of our increasing scientific understanding of ourselves may well emerge as the defining schism of the culture wars.

In facing such opposition, secular humanists must apply the same causal thinking that informs their approach to all other phenomena. Understanding the various factors that contribute to supernatural thinking, including needs for emotional security, lack of education, and growing up within religious traditions, will help humanists to avoid the counterproductive demonization of their opponents. Supernaturalists, like naturalists, are fully caused to believe and act as they do, and do not willfully choose to remain unenlightened. An intelligent, empathetic appreciation of the causal story behind supernaturalism itself will allow secular humanists to be more skillful and more humanistic in their quest to make known the virtues—and truth—of naturalism.

NOTES

1. John Rawls, *A Theory of Justice* (Oxford: Clarendon, 1971), p. 104.
2. Indeed, the marginal utility (the immediate added subjective value) of an increase in resources, for example, a $10,000 tax credit or government grant, is far greater for those who have little than for those who have much, so an objective increase in the net quality of life across economic strata is achieved via redistributive policies.
3. "Does Neuroscience Threaten Freedom and Dignity? Analysis and Comment on a 1998 Conference Hosted by the Ethics and Public Policy Center, Naturalism.Org, http://www.naturalism.org/neurosci.htm.
4. Saul Smilansky, *Free Will and Illusion* (Oxford: Clarendon Press, 2000), pp. 225–33.
5. Daniel C. Dennett, *Freedom Evolves* (New York: Viking, 2003).
6. Daniel C. Dennett, *Elbow Room: The Varieties of Free Will Worth Wanting* (Cambridge, MA: MIT Press, 1984), pp. 4–6. Readers are referred to some recent literature on coming to terms with determinism and naturalism, including such works as Dennett's *Freedom Evolves*, Owen Flanagan's *The Problem of the Soul*, Steven Pinker's *The Blank Slate*, my articles on naturalism for the *Humanist* and *Free Inquiry*, and other publications available at www.naturalism.org.

THOMAS CLARK is director of the Center for Naturalism and can be reached at his Web site, www.naturalism.org. Before this endeavor, Clark was a research associate at Health and Addictions Research, Inc. in Boston, a nonprofit firm that conducts research and evaluation in the addictions, behavioral health, and criminal justice. Among many other projects, HARI has conducted prevalence surveys of adolescent substance use in Massachusetts and participated in the National Institute on Drug Abuse's Community Epidemiology Work Group (CEWG) on illicit drugs in the United States. Through his involvement in both these groups, Clark learned about addiction, patterns of substance use, and drug policy. He began to approach these issues from a naturalistic stance, one that questions absolutist pronouncements about the evils of altered consciousness while still taking very seriously the health consequences of drug use, especially for developing adolescents.

22.

Making the Humanist Commitment a Viable Political Instrument

Agwonorobo Eruvbetine

Mere propaganda for an alternative society is not enough. The complexities of the current situation demand that the Left practice what it preaches. . . . [I]t must try to mount a logic of humanism and solidarity in the territories and spaces which it holds.

—Marta Harnecker

INTRODUCTION

The task of making the humanist commitment a viable political instrument is a daunting one indeed, especially if the envisaged leap into the political arena is to be propelled by corporate bodies like the humanist movement or its cognates. Not only are humanist organizations oriented toward the avoidance of partisan politics, they espouse ideals that are essentially theoretical constructs. The notional ideals are, of necessity, sketched in broad strokes, providing an ingenious way of glossing over dissension-triggering details and purveying a semblance of ideological unity. Moreover, humanist statements avoid situations in which direct engagements with issues are called for. This strategy steers humanists clear of the inevitable, context-specific problems in the practical application of theories to real social circumstances. The strong belief in an open-ended approach to issues, central to humanism, seems incapable of producing political leadership. Since unresolved controversies permeate most humanist groups, it is quite natural to keep the group intact by boldly articulating ideas that are as general as possible.

While the application of broad strokes to the generation, expression, and projection of a single, broad-spectrum opinion on behalf of all humanists can weather potential waves of emotional and intellectual battles and maintain a reasonable following, it hardly suffices to sustain the complex process of gearing human groupings for active participation in politics. For any humanist political rallying call to succeed, it must rise above ambiguity-laden declarations of values. Existing proclamations of cherished core principles come across to a discerning audience as hollow and lacking in specifics. Subtle codes, which build imprecision into well-crafted ideals, serve as safety valves against such eruptions as may compromise the integrity of touted humanist ideological standpoints. And yet, these same safety valves conceal undercurrents of turbulence.

These hidden sources of instability explain why whenever humanists, under the aegis of an organized entity, endeavor to present to the world an *agreed-upon position* on a particular subject, a cacophonous heteroglossia of opposing voices come to the fore. These voices of conceptual and motivational diversities often render impotent the seemingly common humanist view on whatever issue is on the political front burner. The true test, then, is that of harmonizing the viewpoints to build a meaningful base for a practical and worthwhile political venture.

THE PRIVATE/PUBLIC DIVIDE

The present state of affairs in which the humanist ideologue is plagued by an endless *signifying play* introduced into it by generalities can at best guarantee only a surface sturdiness of any machinery put together for a political mission. This situation will continue to subsist as long as the perceived import of quite a good number of humanist pronouncements remains sufficiently hazy, accommodating as many interpretations as suit wide-ranging sensibilities. This lack of a *holding center* is responsible for widening the gap between private and public standards—a widening of gap that poses a dilemma for all who seek to convert humanist creeds into viable tools for human development. For instance, the strident extolling of personal freedoms creates an atmosphere in which personal freedoms invariably hold sway over public ones, generating tensions that have far-reaching implications for democratic processes. Such an atmosphere either relegates the culture of *majority rule* to the background or constantly pitches the individual against the society. The logical fallout of this rather inadvertent humanist endorsement of an uncompromising individualism, buoyed by *unbridled* personal freedom, is the fostering of a discontinuity between private and public ideologies and moralities. Since this discontinuity is habitually compounded by a clash of interests, it follows that the humanist ethos, more often than not, comes across as being fundamentally more suited to private than to public life. Yet politics remains a public affair.

The real issue, then, is that of the tension between the private and public domains of existence. Since humanists usually let the individual assume the commanding role, it is not surprising that personal perspectives dictate articulated political values and create a milieu in which humanists work at cross-purposes that are devoid of true moral significance. Explosive encounters (mainly debates but possibly actions) result from this situation. Debates and actions sometimes degenerate into appalling exhibitions of deep-seated intolerance that run counter to the humanistic tenet of the warm accommodation of contrary views. This trend often leads to inaction.

Properly used, the humanist accommodation of plural views can be regarded as an operational principle that should facilitate activities in the public sphere. This principle can, however, be misused in the sense that plural views may be given equal weighting and made to pull in different directions, signaling the existence of irreconcilable outlooks. The acceptance of pluralism becomes an acceptance of the overriding of the public by the personal domain. These diametrically opposed stances tend toward an anarchic multiplicity that ingeniously consigns the community culture to the backwoods as individualism reigns unchallenged, fueling the divisive tendencies that have scuttled and are still likely to scuttle humanist involvement in politics.

The private/public divide is at the root of intended differentiations that are reflected in the naming of humanist associations. For example, *secular, atheistic, agnostic,* and *religious* humanists are so designated, it is said, to set the groups apart on the basis of highly treasured differences in perspective. On the surface, these nomenclatures and what they represent seem to provide the basis not only for intergroup delineation but also for intragroup solidarity. At a deeper level, however, the individual groups lack ideological unity, especially on the issue of religion. This lack of coherence is partly traceable to the fact that religion is a highly personal matter, governed by faith and belief that hardly yield to meaningful debates and logical resolutions.

Hence only diehard fanatics are imbued with the kind of unusual steadfastness that can act in pretended ignorance of the difficulties attendant on making religion a political panacea. Is it any surprise that this scenario makes most religious attempts to engage public issues problematic?

RELIGIOUS DISCOURSES

Religious discourses among humanists and the controversies they generate may well provide the best means for seeking a point of convergence of ideas because they usually focus on the public application of religion. This is so because in overt personal performances, many a nonreligious humanist is impatient with all those who would discern any form of supernatural influence in human affairs. And yet in covert personal encounters, humanists are not shielded from the occasional admission of the reified nature of human idealisms. Perhaps freeing human beings from the unwritten code of the public dramatization of personal freedoms may initiate the stepping out from individualist cocoons that is necessary for straddling the private/public divide. It would then open up the possibility of applying the principle of openness to different views. This spirit of cooperation, when exercised in the examination of religion and its input into public life, would foreground the fact that virtually all religions, in their genuine manifestations, are guided by the quintessential humanist ethos. This approach to religion paves the way for humanists to retain their individuality and still participate in public life—a necessary prelude to political relevance.

Bridging the private/public gap in this manner demonstrates that contesting and affirming the reality of otherworldliness (and its input into human affairs) are not as mutually exclusive as they sound. Points of contact definitely exist in religious and nonreligious positions—contact points that can enable coherent political action. The shared beliefs about what humane individuals and societies should be provide the basis for a politically viable culture that would thrive if the supernatural were always regarded as having great affinity with the ideal *possibilities* projected by humanists. When this attitude is made to prevail, the notion of otherworldliness can then be interpreted in a manner that serves the political needs of believers and nonbelievers alike.

The supernatural or ideal is then conceived of as a literal reality for the religionist and as a symbolic reality for the nonreligionist. Such an interlacing of secular and religious idealisms informs the civilized practice, in democratic institutions, of encouraging the coexistence of all faiths. The belief underlying this practice is that all true faiths are committed to uplifting the human psyche through material and nonmaterial means, for the attainability of the good life. The uplift of humanity makes a belief or nonbelief in the *divine* inconsequential to the ideology of secular state-hood and political governance. This is the kind of approach to issues that humanists should model their political ambitions on.

POLITICS

Politics is essentially a public and not necessarily private or personal affair. At its best, it entails the effective management of civic life, the forte of which is the fashioning and operating of institutions conducive to the synchronization of individual and social interests. Politics strives to create room for the myriad competing, and sometimes colliding, needs, and beliefs and thrusts of persons and communities within the framework of social control systems that facilitate meaningful coexistence. It seeks to evolve and put in place structures of power relations that are created out of mutual trust. To ensure the smooth operation of these structures, politics provides and positions policies and laws that, through covert and overt combinations of moral suasion and state power or force, channel the potential (and sometimes actual) destabilizing forces into constructive factors of personal and social endeavor.

Since the main task of politics is that of harmonizing individual and social freedoms by smoothing out the ragged edges that too often involve the inadvertent pitching of private against public interests, it follows that realistic politics thrives on making decisions on definite political issues, mapping out feasible courses of action, and enabling their implementation in tangible fashions. In real politics, specific methods are put in place for managing dissensions and inching discussions, debates, and negotiations toward a kind of closure, which, while it serves as the basis of action, does not disrespect or absolutely silence contrary positions. This is so because political closures are arrived at, despite disagreements, through either consensus, compromise, or majority opinion.

Any foray of humanists into real politics must embrace the democratic processes for arriving at a closure on hotly debated issues. These procedures facilitate political decision making in ways that must, of necessity, reconstruct the humanist belief in *diversity of opinion, including differences among its members* into a vehicle capable of presenting a unifying vision that can galvanize action. All opinions are entertained in discussions motivated by the need to arrive at a conclusion in favor of one opinion or a conflation of numerous opinions as a means of moving toward an acceptable focus for all discussants. Such a consensus should always be the ultimate goal of any political debate embarked on to determine a particular policy or course of action within a specific time frame. Conflicting views are useful for processing ideas and converting them into definite principles for administering polities. Indecision and its corollaries of inaction and instability are political time bombs that are assembled, planted, and detonated when debates become ends in themselves.

LEADERSHIP

Since politics is a public affair, public spirit is required of political leadership that is sustained by consultation and devotion to the common agenda. The democratic procedure appears to be the best mode of power management that thrives on keeping leaders in check and preventing them from making their private agenda that of the public. By guaranteeing the involvement of all stakeholders in government activities, the electoral procedure keeps the leader in check through constant monitoring and close communal scrutiny of policies and projects.

Given the public role of political leaderships, it is imperative that good leaders should align their individualism with the public culture toward handling social matters. Manifestations of extreme individuality detract from good leadership. Even when a personal vision springs from supposedly noble ideas, it is still absolutely necessary that the vision be put to test by subjecting it to the democratic process. If the leader, through the consultative course of action, is unable to convince the citizenry of the nobility of a particular mission, he or she is obligated to defer to the view of the majority (or to a majority of the people's true representatives). The humanist proclivity toward respecting the individual dream may not be sufficient to challenge the reasonableness of making the leader defer to what the electorate approves of. Examples of individuals who have changed the course of history for the better notwithstanding, the truth remains that unilateral actions have done more harm than good to the world.

Absolute individualism has great potential for creating a self-centered leadership pattern capable of foisting dictatorship on large and small groups of people. This is tantamount to appropriating the public domain for private use through clever manipulations of the system. The unleashing of personal whims on the social sphere by self-willed leaders entails seizing the public institutions and reconfiguring them to uphold personal dreams. This approach to politics—a negative manifestation of the predominance of individualism—invariably proves to be a disastrous way of bridging the public/private gap. History abounds with examples of individuals who projected their pet visions into the public domain and held large populations hostage. For example, Hitler was so convinced of his personal superiority and that of the Germans that he projected it into a public credo that plunged the world into a nightmare. The single-minded manner in which Hitler pursued his dream through the ruthlessness of the force available to the state had disastrous effects on all its victims.

There is always danger in an individual being able to subvert viable political machines and use them to enforce his or her convictions. Whether the beliefs are good or bad is of little importance. To be in a position to impose one's will on citizens abrogates the rule of law and negates the principle of collective responsibility. Self-centered leadership is ruinous to society. In most cases, this aberration results both from placing too high a premium on the individual and from the egoistic individual's inability to engage the public domain in the true spirit of cooperation. Since dictatorship is the logical outcome of the bloated presence of the individual in the public sphere, it is the duty of humanists to address this issue in the bid to be part of partisan politics.

SKEPTICISM

Individualism is also made to occupy center stage in the greatly prized principle of skepticism. Skepticism has a high potential for confusion, which is usually actualized whenever personal flirtations with free expression of misgivings metamorphose into fervently held beliefs that assume the status of endemic superstitions. These kinds of belief, enveloped in the aura of mysterious certainty, pitch many a humanist against entrenched truths and practices. Ordinarily, there is nothing untoward about expressing doubts or misgivings. Applied responsibly, skepticism provides the basis for a comprehensive examination of issues that fosters ideological dynamism in the political sphere. If skepticism questions the veracity of certain ideas and brings the structures that support them into the limelight for closer scrutiny, then it is of immense usefulness in politics. But if skepticism holds most of the ideas that lend meaning to people's lives up to ridicule or seeks to dismantle structures that have long provided many people with a sense of stability without providing compelling alternatives, then its role in politics is suspect.

Quite often individuals derive great fulfillment from being skeptical about operational political modes. But this vigorous interrogation of the status quo must serve a purpose. There must be methods for fashioning skepticism and its attendant defense of alternative viewpoints into props that can support enhanced operational realities. This approach to debate guarantees that possibilities arising from specific political projects are comprehensively examined before a particular option is endorsed. At any point in the envisaged humanist forage into politics, this approach to issues should guide deliberations. This strategy somewhat provides a means of harnessing the multiple and sometimes contradictory signals beamed out in the *Humanist Manifestos* into constructive and practical governance enterprises.

HUMANIST OPTIMISM

The humanist creed in the twenty-first century is a complex reiteration of Enlightenment optimism that emphazises the positive prospects of human beings and how they contribute to the actualization of potentials for progress, that is, the personal and social ascent toward humane existence. History and technological advances have hardly corroborated this optimism. Human beings seem to have failed woefully in managing the past in a manner that makes for progress toward truly civilized individuals and societies. Technical advancements have complicated the equation further by their potential, if misused, to destroy the world. Since politicians play a major role in powering human and material development, the lack of real advancement toward the envisaged ideal statehood serves as a grave indictment. Even now, there are no known ways to bring about a systematic evolution that corroborates this humanist optimism. Rather, what stares us all in the face are clear and abundant memorials of mankind's failure to deliver on promises of security and development, as well as personal and social well-being.

If the optimism about the fate of the human species is to be demonstrated in concrete terms, then some extraordinary actions need to be taken to motivate individuals and groups to make this optimism materialize. As long as a coherent political posture remains problematic, it is impossible to determine whether a humanist instrument in governance is sufficient to produce the radical outlook and political action that will make the desired difference. Even with the passage of time—this being the twenty-first century—the administration of human affairs remains as difficult as when social life commenced. As the course of human history reveals, the myriad problems associated with human existence have defied lasting solutions. A humanist political equation, even if it is attainable, may not fare better than all previous and present approaches to political business. Yet the humanist optimism persists.

INSTITUTIONALIZATION

Politics entails the establishment of institutions charged with specific responsibilities for generating and implementing policies and projects. Each institution is founded upon clearly defined principles and operational modes. The key issue is that institutions require a very high degree of conformity from those who are part of or benefit from them. If humanists are to ensure that these institutions work for the generality of the populace, they must rise above their nonconformist posturing. They must seek ways and means of educating themselves on how to overcome self-centeredness and become part of a team. Cultivating the team spirit will ensure that, within political and other associated establishments, public concerns are paramount.

Many structures for managing power in the public sphere already exist and some of them have set patterns of operation. Humanists need to understand these structures intimately in order to realign them in the task of governance. If some existing institutions need to be dismantled, the dismantling must result from a thorough knowledge of the workings of the system and a better system to replace the old one must be available. Moreover, those involved in the dismantling process must be cognizant of the traumas that accompany drastic changes and make provisions for handling the situation in a humanely competent manner.

TENTATIVE STEPS

Perhaps the best way to approach the issue of humanists becoming politicians and humanist groups committing themselves to partisan politics is to take tentative steps in the management of social organizations that directly affect the lives of the general population. Awkward as it may sound, humanist organizations have no institutions that engage the society directly. There are no known schools, colleges, hospitals, industries, or even rituals that bear the authentic organizational stamp of humanism. These institutions touch people's lives in multiple ways. They meet day-to-day needs, inculcate values, provide cultural signatures, offer hope, inform aspirations, and generally define the basis for meaningful human existence. Humanists have neither founded such institutions nor certified existing ones as meeting their standards of excellence as enshrined in the *Humanist Manifestos*.

With little or no tangible experience in the founding, running and/or supporting of these developmental agencies, it is unlikely that humanists would succeed in managing partisan power configurations. The first step toward becoming a force to be reckoned with in civic life is that of building and running such essential public institutions. This step would serve as a useful prelude to an active participation in real politics. Being proprietors and executors of human development projects would be a direct means of meeting societal needs and training personnel for governance. Aspiring politicians in the humanist fold need to experience the realities of managing human beings within a public system. Their success or failure in such endeavors would predict the likelihood of success or failure in the larger polity.

By being involved in the business of these human development agencies, humanists would learn to rise above egoistic and autonomous concepts of selfhood and its implied privacy. They may then be in a position to embrace notions of the individual as a social construct. This viewpoint is desirable because an individual, even in his or her most intimate personal experiences, behaves in ways that reflect h is or her culture. For this reason, the public realm is a most potent power in creating human consciousness and behavior. Humanists must establish and run civic institutions, such as schools and colleges, that facilitate the building of personalities in order to gain real insight into the working of political organizations. These institutions will provide political microforums for humanists.

Real politics is the macroforum for putting together the individual consciousness. The recognition of this fact would make humanists lean toward accepting the socially constructed nature of individuals and eschewing theories of personality that tend to alienate the individual from society. This outlook would power their active participation in the construction of personalities suited to civic life as well as creating civic environments suited to individuals.

CONCLUSION

Issues related to the beliefs of humanists have been briefly explored in this chapter to reveal how they can hamper or facilitate a humanist incursion into real politics. The conclusion reached after weighing the possibilities for success or failure in making these ideas blueprints for politics is that humanist ideas need to be focused on specifics, individualism must engage the social sphere, privacy must synchronize with company, skepticism must strive to overcome its proclivity toward anarchy, active political adventure should be preceded by involvement in human development plans, diverse perspectives must not be ends in themselves, debates should serve as catalysts in the determination of viable options, binary positions need to be reconciled, and decisions made must be respected by all stakeholders to ensure success in the formulation of workable political systems

And yet the nagging questions remain. Is it possible to streamline the various ideas that make up the humanist commitment in ways that reorganize, animate, and concretize them into bases for the establishment of humanist political parties with clearly defined visions? Can well-articulated political programs spring from the manifestos? Is it possible that these programs will elicit from a majority of adherents the support, enthusiasm, and near single-minded commitment necessary to political success? Will such a commitment guarantee the capability to manage power proactively within the matrix of democratic institutions? In what ways will a humanist venture into politics benefit of humanity? This essay, and the book it is part of, is an attempt to answer some of the questions. The rest is up to you.

AGWONOROBO ERUVBETINE was born in 1946 in Uduere, Nigeria. He had his university education at both the University of Lagos (BA and MA) and the University of Alberta, Canada, from which he obtained his PhD in English.

A university teacher since 1972, he progressed through the ranks to become a professor of English at the University of Lagos in 1991. His research interests over the years have been in the areas of the theory of literature, the Romantics, and the Moderns—areas of interest in which he has many publications. In the past few years, however, his interest has revolved around the input or role of humanism and humanistic management in the generaration of viable options for the solution of human problems and the enrichment of life. This new interest has produced a book of collected essays edited by him titled *The Humanistic Management of Pluralism: A Formula for Development in Nigeria.*

23.

Interest-Group Politics and Humanism

Tim Gordinier

Interest groups are the instruments through which American pluralism is expressed.

—James Madison

INTRODUCTION

I was watching a well-known politician being interviewed on television the other day when the interlocutor's questioning abruptly shifted to matters of faith and religion. Without hesitation, the politician, whom I suspected of having little or no religious belief, recited what appeared to be a carefully prepared statement professing his reverence for God and the efficacy of prayer.

I had just witnessed another instance of self-inoculation: the obligation of all serious politicians to let current and potential supporters know that religion is essential or central to their lives, even if it isn't. As a humanist and political scientist, I don't feel shocked, betrayed or even angered when I witness this all-too-common charade. Perhaps I'm a little saddened that nonreligious politicians still have to resort to deception in order to attain higher office, but like most humanists, I understand that this is the realpolitik of the moment. So be it. If we have to continue to deny ourselves in order to get this nation to move forward, then that is a small price to pay.

Or am I being too defeatist? It's not as if this nation has not made progress when it comes to the politics of inclusion. If the candidate I had seen on TV had been black, female, or of some nonmainstream religious affiliation—or even gay—there would still have been a fair chance that prejudice would not have stood in the way of his getting elected—even if he had the ability to hide his affiliation but chose not to do so. But to run for office and admit that he is nonreligious? He might as well not have bothered in the first place.

True, the nonreligious are not totally marginalized. After all, we can still seek a political career if we pretend to be devout, though we often, like other minorities, have to vote for surrogates, not for one of our own. There also have been no real *legal* efforts, at least recently, to deny us the franchise, or to prevent atheists from coming out of the closet to make a (futile) attempt to seek office. The nonreligious can even vote as a bloc, though most studies show that they don't, even though such a bloc would be quite large and formidable—by last count 9 to 20 percent of the population depending on what poll you read and how nonreligion is defined. This failure of nonbelievers to join ranks is, in itself, not surprising. Not all atheists are humanists, after all. And some who identify themselves as humanists often are libertarians, or even objectivists, who don't support a "progressive" political agenda.

The whole episode got me thinking about the freethought movement and its potential to win the hearts and minds of the American people. Why is it that the nonreligious have not made any serious inroads politically in this nation as compared with other Western democracies, most of which long ago accepted nonbelief as just another viewpoint and a secularist language as the norm by which political commerce is transacted? Is there something in the very fiber of America that makes this a deeply religious nation where atheists are regarded like moral lepers, even among people who otherwise might be regarded as tolerant and open-minded? Why was it that even progressive-minded politicians felt that they needed to race to the steps of Capitol to recite the Pledge of Allegiance after the *Newdow* decision?[1] If this action is an accurate portrayal of their beliefs, where does that leave the humanist community as far as participating in democracy and doing so in a visible, viable manner is concerned?

A DIFFERENT FOCUS

Perhaps we need to shift at least some of our focus from electoral politics to interest-group politics. Although I tell freshman students in my Political

Science 101 course that interest-group politics is the kind that takes place between elections, that definition is not totally accurate. Interest-group politics does not stop on a dime when voters begin to consider how to cast their ballots. Rather, it occurs in addition to voting, when organized groups attempt to influence policy by gaining discreet access to elected officials.

Is it democratic? In some ways it is not. Often the groups pressuring politicians represent only a small segment of the population and wield influence far beyond their numbers. Often this kind of politics leaves out the average citizen because the issues are too complex, requiring specialized lobbyists who comprehend legislative legalese and consequently can finesse our democratic institutions to their clients' benefit. Often there is no spokesperson for a particular point of view or life-stance, especially for those groups that are most in need of having their cause championed.

The potential for any group to get a hearing in a representative's office is supposed to be a given, and that does seem to have a democratic flavor to it. We all can visualize a kind of Norman Rockwell picture of a citizen meeting with her local congressperson, posing for a photo, smiles all around. But such encounters may be no more than simple courtesy to give constituents a fair hearing, not a definite sign of "pressure" politics. After all, most politicians probably forget your name two seconds after they shake your hand. This kind of participation signifies little more than getting something off your chest, which, though valuable as a cathartic, really does not do much to advance your cause. Interest-group politics, if it is truly going to live up to its name, involves educating and pressuring politicians to adopt or change their position on some issue.

Even if, theoretically speaking, politicians took all their visitors seriously and all groups had access to elected representatives, the playing field would not necessarily be level. In other words, not all groups are viewed as equal by the powers that be. However, under the pluralistic model used by political scientists, most pressure groups are considered to be roughly equal. What one group lacks in money another might make up for in numbers, or passion, or expertise. Still, the pluralistic model is often derided as being an idealization or even an outright myth. We all know that banks and big corporations, or the AARP, have more clout than the lobbies for the homeless, PETA, or graduate assistants. All groups are not created equal after all.

But inequality is beside the point. The real question should be: Is interest-group politics a game that humanists should be playing? And if so, are we up to it? And how should we go about it?

The answer to the first question, in my opinion, is a definite yes. The answers to the second and third questions are a little more complicated and call for some serious reflection.

HUMANISM'S IMAGE

One of the first questions we might ask about a particular interest group is whether any impediments hinder or prevent it from engaging in this type of political activity. For most of us in the humanist movement, the answer seems as obvious as it is distressing. We seem to have been hobbled right out of the starting gate because of the religious fervor of this nation, which appears to have become more tolerant of non-Protestants over time—even to the point of grudgingly accepting Islam—yet also seems to have placed a limit on that tolerance so that it does not extend to the nonreligious. But this outlook is by no means the entire picture. I would say that we have a number of related but distinct problems besides the way others perceive us. The most important of these is a self-image problem.

Humanists are often viewed within their own community, and not altogether unfairly, as humorless, ivory-tower eggheads afraid to get their hands dirty by involving themselves in the messy business of politics. We're supposed to be straight-talking rationalists, after all, and politicking usually involves strategic manipulation of mass opinion and less-than-straightforward machinations of the political system. On the one hand, we seem unsuited to this activity because it involves behaving in ways that go against the very principles we supposedly stand for—it's almost as if genetics had predisposed humanists to being alienated by the whole prospect of engaging in interest-group politics.

On the other hand, we can alloy our rationalism with a little pragmatism, and ask why we should unilaterally disarm and put ourselves at a disadvantage to other groups, especially right-wing religious groups, that have done such a good job of mobilizing their own troops. And it might do something to our dour, staid image if we started getting involved and schmoozing it up a little with elected officials instead of engaging in a constant, self-defeating introspection that leads to paralysis by analysis and bouts of hand-wringing.

But is the above depiction accurate? In fact, couldn't it be argued that it is close to a caricature because humanists are a varied lot and contain within their ranks many who are not afraid to roll up their sleeves and play the game? Isn't this fact evident everywhere we look?

But how do we go about playing the game if we're considered so far outside the political mainstream that even progressive groups are cautious about being associated with us? Again, remember how fast congresspersons from both parties—liberals and conservatives alike—ran to recite the Pledge of Allegiance after the Ninth Circuit Court decision. In other words, we have to contend with that other image problem—the image of the movement from the outside looking in, in addition to our own sense of group insecurity and rigidity. If that is a more serious problem, what concrete steps must we take to become more like other interest groups, so that politicians and others don't ignore us even if they would prefer to?

The answer is not unfathomable, nor does the remedy require a prodigious effort on our part to *begin* to change things. In fact there are time-honored tricks of the trade that other groups have plied to increase their influence on the American electorate.

CONCRETE STEPS

A good place to start is to simply pay our dues like every other group and help out our natural allies with their agendas. Doing so does not require compromising our principles. We are naturally linked to progressive organizations that fight against discrimination based on race, gender, sexual orientation, and so forth, because we, the humanist community, regard such forms of prejudice as driven by irrational religious dogma. We need to start coalition building and do more lobbying. But how do we get these people to value our world stance, if they are not already humanists? How do we get them to see the rights and interests of the nonreligious as being intimately connected to their own destinies?

In interest-group politics, the difference between protest groups and a mass movement is that the former appeals primarily to oppressed groups and to very few others. In contrast, a successful mass movement occurs when a group can also appeal to those outside the group—who will remain outside that group—for support.

The civil rights movement in the sixties was more or less successful because it not only galvanized African Americans into action but it was supported by progressive whites through the appeal to some shared or "universal" value such as equality or fair play. Note that whites had to remain whites. Straights who support gay rights will not become gay to support the movement. Atheists, too, should not expect to win over people by making them atheists, though we do have a sizable group of freethinkers or "Brights" (a new term some use instead of "atheist") who are not "joiners" and who could possibly be a great resource if they could somehow be tapped.

But my main point is that proselytizing new members to the humanist movement is not only unnecessary, it may even be counterproductive. In fact, we should be ready to make common cause with virtually any group, on whatever issue and even send out the message that we will gladly work with religious organizations that preach tolerance, compassion, charity, and other humanistic values; that, at worst, our disagreement with these organizations is a friendly one, no more serious than that between a Jewish and a Christian neighbor who debate theology as a pleasant, over-the-fence pastime.

Unsuccessful protest movements such as children's rights advocates or People for the Ethical Treatment of Animals (PETA) have not been able to make the case for shared values in the way that the civil rights movement did. At least not yet. Most Americans realize that making "discriminatory" laws to protect youth is far different from making laws that classify people on the basis of race, class, or sex. That's why a person has to be a certain age to drink or to drive a car. In many cases a child cannot, by definition, give informed consent to engage in an activity such as sex with an adult. As far as animal rights are concerned, people who don't hunt, trap, or fish will usually tolerate those activities if they are practiced in a humane way. That acceptance may change with time, or it's possible that groups fighting to change those attitudes and behaviors may never appeal to a larger audience.

Which boat is the freethought movement in? Can humanism appeal to those outside its group to become a successful mass movement?

We have a history in this country of simultaneously supporting religious freedom and religious "privatization." Freedom *from* religion seems like a cause that even a religious person might support if the message was couched in a way that made it seem less threatening. It seems likely that we can make a pretty good case that separation of church and state is to everyone's benefit and an accepted long-term value of most educated Americans, just as black civil rights leaders such as Martin Luther King Jr. could appeal to legal equality and equal opportunity to reach white America.

And more important, even if some people don't like us, we need to at least earn their grudging respect. Reciprocity usually works in the American system of logrolling and compromise because of its practical implications if not because it nurtures empathy over time. Others will come around on our behalf because eventually they will owe us their support—not just other interest groups but elected officials as well, who self-interestedly begin to view us as a political wellspring to be tapped.

Machiavelli once asked whether it was better to be loved or feared. While both were advantageous, he said, it was ultimately better to be feared. That observation is not far from the truth as far as humanists are concerned, though I would prefer to use the term "respected" in place of "feared." However, we have the almost contradictory objective of reaching out to the masses to show that we don't bite, that we are in fact, just like other Americans in most ways that are relevant, such as living our lives in an ethical manner.

Let's get back to our image problem—partly of our own making, partly of others' making—and realize this: that just like racism and sexism, prejudice against the nonreligious will never be eradicated completely in some circles. Deep-seated prejudice will continue to fester. Atheists are not trustworthy. Atheists are immoral. Atheists will engage in any behavior because they are not restrained by the carrot and stick of an afterlife judgment. We may have to live with these attitudes even as gays may have to live with the fact that among some groups they will only, at best, be legally tolerated.

We may never receive the same kind of respect that abortion rights advocates get from moderate Republicans or that the Dalai Lama gets from the religious mainstream. Atheists, like convicted criminals, are forever in the position of having to explain that they have rights, even though they aren't guilty of some crime. This lack of respect is partly due to the negative definition of atheism, but only partly.

To overcome this widespread prejudice, we may have to rely on being more feared than loved. But how do we do that without alienating allies? As I said earlier, winning allies among progressive groups is not impossible. We share similar objections to irrational and invidious forms of discrimination. We know that humanists can join in coalitions with other progressive groups. But is the reverse true? Will the mainstream come some day to view us as being part of itself?

We need to let politicians—even those who don't like us—know that we have clout. We need to self-identify and be identified by others as a constituency, like the Gray Panthers or the gay rights movement, whose participants vote often and have long memories. That does not mean we can't belong to other constituencies; it just means politicians have to take note that, like gays, blacks, women, retired people, and people with disabilities, we are a serious contender for bloc voting. We also need to let them know that we have economic power and that we are politically active. A good lobbyist brings along constituents on her trips to the legislature whenever she can. She lets the elected officials know that many voters in the legislator's district belong to that pesky group and that they do more than just vote. Local humanist organizations certainly can be tapped for this purpose when we begin to engage in interest-group politics.

Finally, we need to work hard and be patient—and not expect overnight success from such endeavors. Many of the most prominent lobbying groups have been at it for years and are only now beginning to see their labors bear some fruit. It takes time and effort to build a track record that allows a group to network with other progressive-minded groups. It also takes time to gain a critical mass of experience, to make solid allies, and to learn valuable lessons about what works and what doesn't work in the political arena. Time will tell whether we are successful in this endeavor, but one thing is certain: If we don't play the game of interest-group politics, we will continue to remain on the periphery, with ourselves as much to blame for our marginalized circumstances as the deep-seated prejudice that put us there in the first place.

NOTE

1. *Newsday v. United States*, 292 F.3rd 597 (9th Cir. Cal. 2002).

TIM GORDINIER is the director of public policy and education at the Institute for Humanist Studies. Gordinier is primarily responsible for spearheading the institute's legislative agenda. In particular, Gordinier focuses his efforts on the New York State Legislature, lobbying legislative officials on such matters as separation of church and state and other humanist-related issues. He collaborates in the formation of coalitions with other organizations in the Capital District area to promote progressive causes. Finally, he works with other institute staff to advance the institute's Continuum of Humanist Education (COHE) program.

Gordinier received his doctorate in political science from the University at Albany in May 2000, focusing on constitutional law and specifically on the religion clauses of the First Amendment. His dissertation tackled the controversial question of how far the First Amendment protects religious groups.

In 2003, Gordinier was named to the board of directors of the New York American Civil Liberties Union (ACLU).

24.

Revisioning Humanism

Building Foundations for Peace and Human Rights

Riane Eisler

We must, each one of us, pledge ourselves to action in helping to move humankind towards a way of living where the humanistic family ethic overlays the nationalistic, linguistic, religious, and ethnic differences that separate us. We work toward the time when the world will be at peace and human energy will be focused on the needs and well-being of all members of a single family, a time when we will enjoy and celebrate our unique differences while exalting the importance of our human similarities, a time when we will acknowledge the basic human needs that unite us including our mutual concerns for the futures of our children, our grandchildren and our great-grandchildren who constitute the future.

—Gerald A. Larue

Humanism is founded on the belief that we can live together in more peaceful, mutually respectful, humane ways. Today, many people, including some humanists, feel hopeless about achieving this goal. They point to all the insensitivity and cruelty around us, the political regressions to strongman rule, the worldwide escalation of violence. They note that, despite international treaties and United Nations declarations on respect for human rights, brutal human rights violations continue unabated. They lament that, despite countless international peace conferences and treaties, and despite the millions of people in the antiwar movement, warfare and terrorism are still daily facts of life. They worry that in our time of nuclear and biological weapons and ever more efficient conquest of nature, we may be heading toward mass extinction.

We certainly have ample grounds for concern, but the situation isn't hopeless. The problem isn't that humanism has failed. It's that the movement to a more humane society is incomplete. There are lessons to be learned from science and history. If we take a systemic, long-range view, we can reformulate the humanist agenda to lay the missing foundations for a more peaceful and equitable future.

REASSESSING HUMAN NATURE

Much of what we've been taught says violence, selfishness, and oppression are just human nature. The message is that nothing much can be done about them. Traditional religious stories tell us that we're flawed by original sin or by bad karma we carry from earlier lives. More recent secular stories—even stories accepted by some people who consider themselves humanists—have the same general import. War, we're told, is a millennia-old evolutionary adaptation; men are innately violent because of testosterone; the overriding human motivation is selfishness. Whether we know it or not, we're run by selfish genes.

However, whether we're violent or not isn't a matter of ancient genetic imperatives. Certainly we have the genetic capacity for violent behavior. But in the course of evolution we also acquired the genetic capacity for nonviolent, caring, empathic, and loving behavior. Nor does testosterone cause violence. Indeed, studies show that sometimes low levels of testosterone lead to irritability and aggressive feelings. A study at the National Institute for Mental Health conducted by Elizabeth Susman and colleagues, for example, found that aggression in boys was associated with *lower*, rather than higher, testosterone levels.[1]

Even when people carry genes that predispose them to violent, antisocial behavior, these genes alone don't explain these behaviors. A low-activity version of a gene called monoamine oxidase A, or MAOA, has been implicated in a higher propensity for violence. But a study of men with this gene variant found that this gene alone does not predict who will become violent. Only those men who were mistreated as children—which the researchers defined as having been rejected by their mothers, physically or sexually abused, or subjected to frequent changes in their primary caregivers—were more likely to engage in antisocial behavior, including violent crime, as adults.[2]

Recent research in neuroscience verifies that what matters is the interaction between genes and experience.[3] And this is particularly true of what we experience in our early years. A pioneer in the study of the neurochemistry of abused children, Dr. Bruce Perry, found that children who are abused or who grow up in violent environments are predisposed to become abusers because their brain neurochemistry tends to become programmed for fight-or-flight at the slightest provocation.[4]

This doesn't mean that all children who are abused or witness violence replicate these behaviors; on the contrary, some grow up to be adults who not only eschew violence but empathically work against violence. However, psychological research shows that many people who are violent were themselves victims of violence. And historical and sociological research shows that whether habits of violence are developed, institutionalized, and even idealized is largely a cultural matter.

Throughout history and across cultures, the most violently despotic and warlike cultures have been those in which violence, or the threat of violence, is used to maintain domination of parent over child and man over woman. We see this connection in the European Middle Ages, in Hitler's Germany, and in some so-called religious fundamentalist cultures today. It is a disturbingly familiar pattern, and if we don't learn from history, we're doomed to repeat it.

Yet while there is much talk about economic and social factors behind warfare and terrorism, the link between *intimate violence*—in home and school—and *international violence*—in terrorism and war—is still largely ignored. Unless we address this underlying issue, talk of a more peaceful and humane world will be just that—*talk*. To build cultures of peace and respect for human rights, this matter of the *foundations* we lay down in intimate relations must be vigorously addressed.

TRADITIONS OF DOMINATION AND VIOLENCE

Human society is based, first and foremost, on relationships between the female and male halves of humanity and on their relations with their sons and daughters. Our first lessons about human relations are learned not in the public but in the private or intimate sphere. As children, in our families and in other intimate relationships, we learn either respect for human rights or the acceptance of abuse and violence. While some people transcend teachings of violence and injustice, many carry these teachings into other relations and accept violence and injustice as "just the way things are."

The fact that intimate violence and domination provide a basic model for using force to impose one's will on others is recognized by those who seek to push us back. For example, the "culture wars" launched in the United States by the heads of the right-wing fundamentalist movement center on strengthening a male-headed family in which women must render unpaid services (with no independent access to income) and children of both sexes learn that orders from above have to be strictly obeyed on pain of severe punishment.

Viewed from the dynamic perspective of the cultural transformation theory I introduced in *The Chalice and The Blade* and other works,[5] this reinforcement of traditions of domination in gender and parent-child relations by those who consider rigid rankings of domination divinely ordained makes sense. It is a reaction to the growing challenge to traditions of force-backed domination in the so-called private sphere of our foundational, day-to-day interpersonal relations.

It is not coincidental that the 9/11 terrorists came from cultures in which women and children are literally terrorized into submission. Nor is it coincidental that the Taliban in many ways resemble the way society behaved in the European Middle Ages—a time when witch burnings, public drawing and quarterings, despotic kings, brutal violence against children, and male violence against women were considered moral and normal.

Throughout history, regimes noted for their repressiveness and official violence have made the return of women to their "traditional" (a code word for subservient) place in a male-headed family a priority. Even in democracies such as the United States, those who believe in the international violence of "holy wars" against "Godless enemies" oppose equal rights for women. In fact, the so-called Religious Right first became a major force in US policies in the 1970s when they organized to defeat the proposed Equal Rights Amendment to the US Constitution—a history lesson we should take note of. This regressive political bloc has pushed the United States back over the last thirty years to a degree that today threatens our basic liberties—not only reproductive freedom but even freedom of assembly, religion, and speech.

But while these threatening new developments are vociferously denounced by the humanist community, we give far less importance to the fact that a key objective of the Religious Right is returning women and children to a "traditional" family in which the father's word is law. And this objective isn't a secret. It's well known, for example, that the Religious Right tried to gut the Violence Against Women Act and even supported a

"Family Protection" Act that would have cut funding for battered women's shelters—protecting a family structure in which male "heads of household" can legitimately exercise violent and despotic control.

It's high time that traditions of domination and violence against women and children that undermine all efforts to build a truly humane world are strongly condemned worldwide—not only for the sake of those directly affected but because the connections between intimate and international violence today threaten us all. Humanists can—and must—lead the way in forcefully exposing these traditions for what they are: brutal practices to exert control through the infliction or fear of pain.

HUMAN POSSIBILITIES

Our world stands at a crossroads. On one side is the well-trodden path of violence and domination—of man over woman, parent over child, race over race, nation over nation, and human being over nature. This is the road leading to a world of totalitarian controls and ecological or nuclear disaster. On the other side lies a very different path: the road to a world in which our basic civil, political, and economic rights—including protection from domination and violence and, just as important, protection of our natural environment from man's fabled conquest of nature—will at long last be respected. This road can take us to a new era when partnership and peace, rather than domination and violence, are the norm.

I use the terms *domination* and *partnership* in a specific way. They describe two contrasting configurations or models of social organization that make it possible to see patterns not visible using conventional categories such as capitalism versus communism, religious versus secular, Right versus Left, East versus West, or North versus South.[6] These cultural categories describe whole social systems, including *both* the public sphere of politics and economics and the private sphere of family and other intimate relations.

In the domination model, the primary organizational principle is ranking, with rigid *hierarchies of domination* backed up by fear of pain. Human differences—beginning with the differences between male and female—are automatically equated with inferiority or superiority, with those deemed superior (such as men) dominating and those deemed inferior (such as women) being dominated. Power is equated with control, with power over others, and the "superior" capacity to inflict pain. In this model, human rights are, by definition, severely limited, as the whole system is ultimately held together by fear and force.

In the partnership model, the primary organizational principle is linking, with *hierarchies of actualization* in which power is designed to empower rather than disempower. Difference, again beginning with the difference between women and men, is not automatically equated with inferiority or superiority. Boys and girls aren't taught to divide humanity into in-groups and out-groups; both halves of humanity are equally valued and "softer," more stereotypically "feminine" values such as caring, non-violence, and empathy are valued in both men and women and can in fact (not just in rhetoric) be given social and economic precedence. While there is some violence, it does not have to be institutionalized or idealized to maintain rigid rankings of domination—whether of men over women, race over race, or nation over nation. In short, human rights are protected in both the so-called private and the public spheres.

Models are abstractions, and no society is just a partnership or domi-nator culture. But the degree to which a society orients to either end of the partnership-domination continuum profoundly affects all areas of our lives.

Contrary to what we have been taught, evidence from archaeology and myth indicates that for thousands of years in our prehistory many societies oriented primarily to the partnership rather than dominator model. In other words, strongman rule, whether in the family or the state, has not always been the human norm.[7]

There are also contemporary cross-cultural data on societies that orient more to the partnership model, cultures where there is a high degree of respect for human rights, nonviolence, gender equity, and policies that support more stereotypically feminine traits and activities in both women and men.[8] For example, in the Nordic nations there is a strong men's movement to disentangle "masculinity" from domination and violence, as well as laws prohibiting any violence against children in families. Not coincidentally, these nations also pioneered the first peace studies programs as well as fiscal policies that invest heavily in universal health care, child care, elder care, and other caregiving activities that in the domination model are considered "soft" or feminine and hence given low fiscal priority.

A detailed discussion of these models is beyond the scope of this chapter. The main point I want to bring out here is that if we look at the modern human rights and peace movements as key elements in the struggle to free ourselves from a domination model, we can see that the first phase of this movement challenged what we might term the top of the dominator pyramid: domination—and with it, institutionalized violence—in the public or political sphere.

And we can also see that the next essential step is the challenge to the base upon which that pyramid rests and continues to rebuild itself: domination and institutionalized violence in the private sphere of family relations, and even more specifically, in the day-to-day relations between women and men and parents and children.

THE INVISIBLE PANDEMIC OF VIOLENCE

It should be enough to say that intimate violence must stop because of the horrible damage it causes to the millions of children and women directly affected. But it has not been enough. Nor has it been enough to point to the massive economic and social costs of this violence, to the billions of lost lives and billions of dollars wasted because of this violence.

There are even people who still refuse to acknowledge the existence of intimate violence—even though it has been extensively documented. Here are just a few examples:

- According to the WHO (World Health Organization), each year 40 million children under the age of fifteen are victims of family abuse or neglect serious enough to require medical attention.[9]
- National studies from eleven nations show that 5 to 48 percent of women report having been abused by an intimate partner at some point in their lives. Localized studies in Africa, Latin America, and Asia report higher rates of physical violence—up to 58 percent of women.[10]
- According to the US Department of Justice, between 1995 and 1996, more than 670,000 US women were the victim of rape, attempted rape, or sexual assault.[11]
- Intimate violence is the single largest cause of injury to women in the United States.[12]
- In the United States, four million women a year are physically abused in intimate relationships.[13]
- From 40 to 60 percent of known sexual assaults are committed against girls fifteen and younger, regardless of region or culture.[14]

Another form of family violence, selective female infanticide and medical neglect, is also common in many world regions. In India's Punjab state, girls aged two to four die at nearly twice the rate of boys, and according to statistics released in 1995 (the year of the Fourth United Nations Conference on Women), deaths per year per thousand in Bangladesh were 15.7 for girls ages one to four versus 14.2 for boys. In Pakistan, the ratio was 9.6 for girls versus 8.6 for boys. In Guatemala, it was 11.3 for girls versus 10.6 for boys. In Egypt, it was 6.6 versus 5.6. And even in Singapore, which at that time had a strong economy, the ratio was 0.5 for girls versus 0.4 for boys.[15]

A huge number of female children are enslaved (often offered for sale by members of their own families) in the global sex industry, for example, in Thailand, India, and the former Soviet Union. The United Nations estimates that 2 million girls between the ages of five and eleven are introduced into the commercial sex market each year.[16] It is estimated that forty-five thousand to fifty thousand women and children are trafficked annually to the United States.[17] An estimated 100 to 132 million girls and women have been subjected to female genital mutilation (FGM) worldwide. Each year, an estimated two million more girls will undergo some form of female genital mutilation. In Egypt, 97 percent of women had undergone FGM according to a national study carried out by Demographic and Health Surveys in 1995.[18]

Lori Heise reported in 1992 that one in three women worldwide had experienced violence from a spouse or partner. Forty-two percent of women in Kenya admitted that their husbands regularly beat them. In Papua, New Guinea, 67 percent of rural women and 56 percent of urban women had been abused by partners.[19] A study from Lima, Peru, showed that one out of every three women in the city's emergency rooms was a victim of domestic violence.[20] According to estimates by then–US surgeon general C. Everett Koop in 1989, 3 to 4 million women are battered in the United States each year. In Bangladesh, husbands' murders of their wives account for half of all homicides. In Bombay, India, one out of every five deaths among women ages fifteen to forty-four resulted from "accidental burns"—that is, the infamous "bride-burnings" or "dowry deaths" that only recently attracted international media attention.[21] In short, violence against women and children is the most pervasive violation of human rights in the world today. But so ingrained is the idea that these are "just" women's issues and children's issues, that ending this pandemic of violence is even now a secondary issue for most national and international leaders.[22]

THE PROBLEM OF TRADITION

It's not easy for us to come to terms with the reality—and implications—of domination and violence in intimate relations. It's an emotionally charged subject. Besides, we have all—humanists included—to varying degrees been socialized to accept them, or, at best, to relegate them to the secondary status of "women's issues" and "children's issues."

But precisely for this reason, they must be addressed. The most important—and dangerous—matters are those that are not generally talked about. For most of recorded history, parental violence against children and men's violence against their wives was condoned. Those who had the power to prevent and/or punish this violence through religion, law, or custom openly or tacitly approved it. Even today, some religious teachers still insist that punitive violence by parents against children and men against women is divinely ordained. And, whether we are secular or religious, we all unconsciously carry these traditions.

It's hard to challenge traditions, even when they are inhumane. Doing so is often unpopular and can sometimes be dangerous, since domination and violence in intimate and intergroup relations are encoded in some religious and ethnic traditions. But if we don't address these cornerstones of violence and abuse, we will not have the foundations for a more equitable, peaceful, and sustainable future. The reason is that families in which men are ranked over women and children painfully learn that questioning orders from above is dangerous to their physical and emotional welfare, even survival, are central to authoritarian, warlike cultures and subcultures.

Beliefs about the legitimacy of men dominating women and of parents hitting children are central to the perpetuation of domination systems across the board. They maintain not only a dominator family structure but the larger social structure and the prevailing system of authoritarian values and beliefs. At the same time, the family is not only influenced by but also in turn influences the larger social structure and culture of which it is a part. What we see is a *transactive process* between families and cultures.[23]

We see this transactive process historically and cross-culturally.[24] In the violent and authoritarian Roman Empire, the male head of household had life-and-death powers, not only over his slaves but also over the women and children in his household. Similarly, under English Common Law, which was developed during a time when monarchs maintained their rule through fear and force, even extreme parental violence against children was lawful and husbands were legally permitted to beat their wives if they disobeyed them.

The connection between rigid male domination in the family and despotism in the state also helps explain customs such as the "honor killings" of girls and women by members of their own families and the stoning of women for alleged sexual offenses found in cultures and subcultures in which terrorism against defenseless civilians is seen as legitimate and honorable. Through the rule of terror in the family, both women and men learn to accept rule by terror as "normal," whether in their own societies or against other tribes or nations.

Fortunately not all people raised in violent households become violent and brutal. But studies such as the classic *The Authoritarian Personality*[25] document how individuals who participate in and/or acquiesce to authoritarianism, violence, and scapegoating in the state tend to be individuals from families in which authoritarianism, violence, and scapegoating were also the norm. In other words, such studies verify what common sense would tell us: that the link between cruelty and violence in the private sphere of the family and the public sphere of the state is all too real.

As psychotherapist Alice Miller has pointed out, if we examine the childhoods of brutal despots such as Adolf Hitler, we see yet another link between the institutionalization of domination based on cruelty and terror in child rearing and the institutionalization of domination backed by cruelty and terror in the state. The biographies of such demagogic archcriminals reveal that their cruelty and violence, particularly their violent persecution of "inferior" or "dangerous" people—be they Jews in Germany, blacks in the American South, or members of different religious sects or ethnic groups in other world regions—is in large part rooted in the violence and cruelty they experienced as children.

Intimate violence and abuse has long-term effects on the brain. Neuroscience shows that the stress of childhood abuse often affects the very structure of the brain. As Robert Post, chief of the US National Institute of Mental Health's Department of Biological Psychiatry, writes, the impact of stress occurs on the cellular level; it cranks up levels of gene-regulating transcription factors in ways that reconstruct the brain, with long-lasting consequences for neural function and behavior. As neuroscientist Debra Niehoff writes, "More constructive coping responses are lost, and the brain fixates on an increasingly smaller portfolio of counterproductive reactions. With fewer and fewer alternatives, violence, depression, and fear stop being options and become a way of life."[26]

THE MOVEMENT TOWARD PARTNERSHIP:
A CALL TO ACTION

From the very beginning, the reexamination—and rejection—of cultural and/or religious traditions have fueled the modern movement for human rights and democracy. The whole basis of humanism is the rejection of autocratic cultural traditions backed up by fear and force. The autocratic rule of kings was once justified, and staunchly defended, by religious authorities, who claimed that kings and other "noblemen" have a divinely ordained right to rule. It was also defended by secular philosophers such as Edmund Burke—who argued that the doctrine of "the rights of man would lead to the utter subversion, not only of all government, in all modes, but all stable securities to rational freedom, and all the rules and principles of morality itself."[27] This kind of rhetoric is all too familiar, as it is still used in our time to oppose "women's rights" and "children's rights" by some religious authorities and secular writers who claim that women's and children's rights are subversive of the moral order, a threat to family and social stability, and a violation of tradition.

Of course, every institutionalized behavior, including cannibalism and slavery, is a cultural tradition. Surely no one today would dare to justify cannibalism or slavery (which were once also traditional practices in some cultures) on cultural or traditional grounds.

That the subject of intimate violence is receiving more attention today reflects major changes in cultural values and beliefs as well as in the structure of social institutions, from the family and education to politics and economics. These changes toward more democratic values and institutions are part of the shift from a dominator to a partnership model of social organization as the ideal norm.[28]

But until now, the impetus for attention to violence against women has primarily come from organized action by women, particularly during the United Nations Decade for Women (1975–1985) and through subsequent national and international meetings, such as the 1993 UN World Conference on Human Rights in Vienna, which led to the 1994 UN Declaration on the Elimination of Violence against women, and the 1995 UN Conference of Women in Beijing. Similarly, children's rights activists have been the prime movers in bringing violence against children into national and international meetings and into the United Nations, as in the Convention on the Rights of the Child and UN documents, such as *We the Children: Meeting the Promises of the World Summit for Children 2001*.[29]

By contrast, those working to maintain and reinstate traditions of domination and violence in families have the support of many major national and international political and religious organizations. For them, maintaining and reinstating a strict father in control of families is a top political, cultural, and financial priority.

It's high time that progressives also make these "women's and children's issues" top policy priorities. If we continue to let the powerful, punitive father, rather than the nurturing parent, be the ideal norm, we cannot effectively counter the cultural drift back to powerful leaders who likewise rely on fear and violence to impose control. Nor can we realistically expect policies, such as universal health care, child care, and help for the poor, that reflect the ideal of a nurturing and caring parent rather than a punitive father.

This is one of the lessons from the last decades of the twentieth century—decades marked by massive regression to the domination model as so-called fundamentalists have invested enormous money and energy in returning us to the fundamentals of domination systems: strongman rule in the family, and with this, in the state and the world.

We urgently need an integrated progressive political agenda. With the specter of biological or nuclear terrorism and warfare hanging over us, many humanists have spoken out against traditions of international violence. It is time we join to raise our voices against the intimate violence that sparks, fuels, and refuels international violence.

We need a clear, long-term, integrated partnership political agenda. Those pushing us back already have an integrated agenda. They have invested billions on reframing the political conversation on their terms and with their terms. *Family values* masks an agenda to reimpose a traditional dominator family. They use the terms *freedom*, *free markets*, and *free enterprise* to mask an agenda that would give those on top freedom to control and exploit others. As linguist George Lakoff points out, we have to reframe the political conversation. This, too, is a central theme of my book *The Power of Partnership*, in which I propose alternative terms, such as *valuing families* and *fair markets* to this end.

Domination and violence in intimate relations and in international relations are as tightly bound together as the fingers of a clenched fist. We must revision the humanist agenda to no longer split off the rights of the majority—women and children—from the "important" issues. Only if we vigorously oppose intimate violence, abuse, and domination will we have the foundations for a better world. Humanists must to take a leadership role in laying these solid foundations for a more equitable and peaceful future.

NOTES

1. E. J. Susman et al., "Hormones, Emotional Dispositions, and Aggressive Attributes in Young Adolescents," *Child Development* 58 (1987): 1114-34.

2. Avshalom Caspi et al., "Role of Genotype in Maltreated Children," *Science* 297 (August 2, 2002): 851-54.

3. Riane Eisler and David Levine, "Nurture, Nature, and Caring: We Are Not Prisoners of Our Genes," *Brain and Mind* 3 (2002): 9-52.

4. Bruce Perry, "Childhood Trauma," *Infant Mental Health Journal* 16, no. 4 (1995): 271-91.

5. See, for example, Riane Eisler, *The Chalice and The Blade: Our History, Our Future* (New York: Harper and Row, 1987); Pat Barrentine, ed., *When the Canary Stops Singing: Women's Perspectives on Transforming Business*, 1st ed. (San Francisco: Berrett-Koehler, 1993); *Sacred Pleasure: Sex, Myth, and the Politics of the Body* (San Francisco: HarperSan Francisco, 1995); and "Human Rights and Violence: Integrating the Private and Public Spheres," in J. Turpin and L. R. Kurtz, eds., *The Web of Violence: From Interpersonal to Global* (Urbana: University of Illinois Press, 1997).

6. Eisler, *The Chalice and the Blade*; *Sacred Pleasure*; *Tomorrow's Children: A Blueprint for Partnership Education in the 21st Century* (Boulder, CO: Westview Press, 2000); and *The Power of Partnership: Seven Relationships That Will Change Your Life* (Novato, CA: New World Library, 2002).

7. See, for example, Eisler, *The Chalice and the Blade* and *Sacred Pleasure*; James Mellaart, *Çatal Hüyük: A Neolithic Town in Anatolia* (London: Thames and Hudson, 1967); Marija Alseikaite Gimbutas, *The Goddesses and Gods of Old Europe, 6500-3500 BC: Myths and Cult Images*, new and updated ed. (Berkeley and Los Angeles: University of California, 1982).

8. See, for example, *Sanday* 2002; and Eisler, *The Power of Partnership*.

9. United Nations, *We the Children: Meeting the Promises of the World Summit for Children 2001* (UNICEF/Kofi Annan), p. 73.

10. United Nations, *The World's Women, 2000: Trends and Statistics* (UN Stats Division), p. 153.

11. US Bureau of Justice Statistics, *National Crime Victimization Survey* (1997).

12. US Senate Committee on the Judiciary, *Violent Crimes against Women* (1993).

13. Commonwealth Fund, *First Comprehensive National Health Survey of American Women* (1993).

14. United Nations, *The World's Women, 1995: Trends and Statistics*, p. 158.

15. United Nations, *1995 Human Development Report* (UN Stats Division).

16. *State of the World Population, 1997*.

17. United Nations, *The World's Women, 2000*, p. 158.

18. Ibid., pp. 159-60.

19. Lori Heise, *Violence against Women: The Hidden Health Burden* (Washington, DC: World Bank, 1994).

20. C. Everett Koop, *The Surgeon General's Letter on Child Sexual Abuse* (Rockville, MD: US Dept of Health and Human Services, Public Health Service, Health Resources and Services Administration, Bureau of Maternal and Child Health and Resources Development, Office of maternal and Child Health, 1989).

21. Heise, *Violence against Women.*

22. See Eisler, *The Chalice and The Blade,* and Eisler, David Loye, and Kari Norgaard, *Women, Men, and the Global Quality of Life* (Pacific Grove, CA: Center for Partnership Studies, 1995).

23. See Eisler, *Sacred Pleasure;* "Human Rights and Violence"; and *The Power of Partnership.*

24. See Eisler, *The Chalice and the Blade; Sacred Pleasure; Tomorrow's Children;* and *The Power of Partnership.*

25. T. W. Adorno et al., *The Authoritarian Personality* (New York: Norton, 1982).

26. Debra Niehoff, *The Biology of Violence: How Understanding the Brain, Behavior, and Environment Can Break the Vicious Circle of Agression* (New York: Free Press, 1999), p. 187.

27. Edmund Burke, *Reflections on the Revolution in France* (1789; repr., New Haven, CT: Yale University Press, 2003).

28. See Eisler, *The Chalice and the Blade; Sacred Pleasure;* "Human Rights and Violence"; and Eisler, Loye, and Norgaard.

29. United Nations, *We the Children.*

RIANE EISLER is best known for her best-seller *The Chalice and The Blade*, which has been translated into twenty languages including Chinese, Spanish, Russian, and Japanese. She is internationally recognized for her groundbreaking research and her activism for human rights, peace, and equity. Her book *Tomorrow's Children*, which applies her research to education, was recently translated into Urdu for use in Pakistan. Her most recent book is the award-winning *The Power of Partnership*, a guidebook for individual and social transformation that applies her research to personal and political action.

A constitutional law expert and attorney in family law practice prior to her many years as a cultural historian and evolutionary systems scientist, Eisler has taught at the University of California and Immaculate Heart College in Los Angeles. She is a founding member of the General Evolution Research Group, a fellow of the World Academy of Art and Science and the World Business Academy, and the recipient of many honors, including the Humanist Pioneer Award, www.partnershipway.org.

25.

Reinventing Humanism

A Need for New Ideas

Arnell Dowret

> *"Poor human nature, what horrible crimes have been committed in thy name! Every fool, from king to policeman, from the flatheaded parson to the visionless dabbler in science, presumes to speak authoritatively of human nature. The greater the mental charlatan, the more definite his insistence on the wickedness and weaknesses of human nature."*
>
> —Emma Goldman

THE NEED FOR NEW IDEAS

In its major manifestos, humanism of the twentieth century makes a strong commitment "to promote social well-being," to "establish the conditions of a satisfactory life for all," to foster creativity and help to establish "a free and universal society in which people voluntarily and intelligently cooperate for the common good," "to elicit the possibilities of life," it calls for equal rights for both women and men to "fulfill their unique careers and potentialities," and to "humanize . . . conditions of work, education, . . . and play." It states that "[a]ll persons should have a voice in developing the values and goals that determine their lives." It takes extremely progressive positions on global economy: "[E]xtreme disproportions in wealth, income, and economic growth should be reduced on a worldwide basis." It declares its support for "a minimum guaranteed annual income," and a "transnational federal government."[1]

Humanism also asserts that the most effective approach to achieving such goals is through reason and scientific naturalism. There are many mainstream humanists, however, whose beliefs about the nature of humankind and understandings of human behavior are so traditional and uninformed by modern social science that they are hardly distinguishable from ideas that are based on faith. For this reason, humanism, thus far, has failed to promote a comprehensive philosophy and related set of practices that could actually help humankind progress toward the laudable goals that humanists endorse.

Even secular humanism, which ostensibly represents the strongest commitment to scientific naturalism and reason, fails to dispense with ancient and mystical beliefs in a human's ability to act independently of causes. Secular humanists are every bit as likely to pronounce the existence of free will as any priest or rabbi. The same is true regarding our failure to move beyond the effects of using antiquated terms to discuss human behavior. Rather than adapting language that describes human behavior based on its constructive or damaging impact, secular humanism continues to classify behaviors in primitive and simplistic terms, such as right and wrong, or good and evil. Although voluminous data exist that demystify and explain the causes of human behavior, most secular humanists instead continue to characterize human behavior using obfuscating language that is more consistent with a worldview based on a belief in the supernatural rather than one built upon science and reason.

Rather than discuss the developmental factors that are recognized as being highly accurate predictors of human behavior, secular humanists also promote archaic concepts of virtue, giving rise to sanctimonious speeches and essays extolling the importance of striving for excellence or the desirability of courage which, but for the absence of references to a supreme deity, are hardly distinguishable from speeches and essays made by any devout member of the clergy. Carrying on in the ancient tradition of their faith-based counterparts, secular humanists feel compelled to pronounce their "condemnation" of socially damaging behaviors. In fact, most secular humanists seem to simply accept the popularly held Judeo-Christian belief that while some people have "merit," others simply lack it, and that those meritorious people who "choose" to contribute to society deserve special rewards for their efforts.

With regard to our children, many secular humanists, like their religious counterparts, accept without question that in order to treat each other with caring and compassion, children must receive moral instruction, completely overlooking the fact that caring and compassion are the natural products of self-esteem, which develops as a result of a loving and supportive environment. Additionally, a majority of humanists do not seem to recognize that children are naturally curious learners and that the system of education which they are forced to endure is based on assumptions that are fundamentally nonhumanistic and factually erroneous, such as the idea that, unless forced to learn, children would spend their time unproductively, or that more testing facilitates a better education.

Our continuing acceptance of ideas that are anachronistic cannot lead to the creation of the society to which humanists aspire. To bring about the vast array of social changes that humanism claims to support, we must adopt a radically new set of ideas about the human experience, ideas that are consistent with modern social scientific research. Fortunately, a wide range of dramatically new and radical ideas and approaches to understanding humankind, and to realizing even the loftiest of humanistic goals, do exist.

While not specifically identified as part of traditional, or secular, humanism, many unprecedented social and political liberation causes have recently arisen, including movements that champion realizing human potential;[2] naturalism;[3] democratic education;[4] guaranteed minimum income; nonhierarchical institutions and social relationships;[5] prison reform and abolition of capital punishment; gender liberation and equality;[6] open source/free information, such as sharing freely "intellectual property";[7] slavery reparations;[8] and democratic transhumanism, the movement that regards human technological progress as a natural and integral extension of human evolution.[9] There are also many others. Progressive movements like these embody ideas and approaches that could move our humanist agenda forward by providing a progressive and dynamic new way of understanding our human experience, one that present-day humanism does not offer.

THE NEED FOR A HUMANISTIC CONSENSUS

Perhaps most essential to making humanism effective in bringing about a more humanistic society is the ability to articulate a common vision about basic human nature and the ways that humans behave. It is erroneous to assume that all who declare themselves to be "humanists" actually share a common understanding about the nature of humankind. In fact, many humanists assume that the essential drives of human beings are antisocial.

While it may seem ironic that those who call themselves "humanist" can harbor misanthropic views, misanthropic thinking is so fundamental to our mainstream culture, it is not difficult to understand why.

That human nature is inherently flawed or sinful, greedy, selfish, corrupt, duplicitous, and lazy is a primary idea both in Judeo-Christian philosophy and its secular counterpart, cynicism. Through the misanthropic lens, humans are seen as naturally possessing no desire to act in socially beneficial ways. This view assumes that only when great external pressure (such as the threat of eternal damnation or long prison sentences), is applied can the greedy, corrupt, selfish individual be kept from inflicting damage on others. Popular misanthropy regards the considerable economic pressure under which most people function as the most effective way to assure that people actually get up off their lazy butts and earn a living.

When someone behaves in a manner that is considered to be socially beneficial, the faith-based misanthrope attributes it to the person choosing to be influenced by a "higher power," the secular misanthrope to the person choosing to express natural greediness. In this way misanthropy ultimately justifies the violence of crushing poverty in the presence of excessive wealth by offering the rationalization that some people deserve great affluence as a reward for sublimating or repressing their base human instincts into making a valuable contribution to society.

Religions teach that this sad state of affairs is the way things have always been and always will be; humans are doomed to suffer forever unless they repent and overcome their base desires. This is seen as unlikely to occur until a supreme deity sets things right, subsequent to an apocalyptic annihilation of our evil human world. Cynics, despite viewing themselves as no longer under the influence of ignorant religious thinking, share a surprisingly similar view of humanity as being fundamentally greedy, selfish, ruthlessly corrupt, and irreparably hurling itself toward its own apocalypse-like self-destruction. The irrationality of misanthropy transcends one's stance on issues of faith. When it comes to the question of human nature and the ultimate fate of humanity, it's nearly impossible to distinguish between the views of a hardcore cynic and those of a faithful Christian.

Misanthropy justifies attitudes that are judgmental and self-righteous, promoting the idealization of the ruggedly independent individualist and giving rise to bizarre concepts of fairness embodied in such phrases such as "may the best man win," and "winner take all." Misanthropy is the predominant guiding philosophy of our culture, and it is instilled through a wide variety of religious and secular institutions. Misanthropic attitudes provide the central rationalizations for our class-stratified, intensely capitalistic culture. The impact of a misanthropic view of humankind on one's ideas about issues such as war, economics, and politics cannot be overstated. Misanthropy is the single greatest obstacle to the advancement of humanism and humankind.

To hold a misanthropic view of humankind is also to actively advance a deadly self-fulfilling prophecy. Both an overview of human history and considerable modern clinical research indicate the immense power of self-fulfilling prophecy. Our beliefs about our identity and our future significantly influence who we are and what our future will be. Through our continued misanthropic thinking, we guarantee that our antisocial culture will persist, advancing the cause of our own self-destruction.

Who will stand up for humankind against the unrelenting misanthropic onslaught? One would hope the answer can be "the humanists." Yet, if we are to be effective at persuading others to rethink their misanthropic assumptions, we first must challenge the misanthropic attitudes among ourselves.

NO ANIMAL ANALOGUE

For millennia humans have looked to the animal world to gain a better understanding of ourselves, yet it hardly seems that doing so has resulted in any consensus. Whether arguing that humans are inherently brutal and selfish, or that humans are inherently gentle and loving, those who have looked to other species to find justification for their viewpoint always seem to have found the evidence they sought, yet attempts to gain a greater understanding of our human experience by observing other species may be of little value.

Human evolution has resulted in humans possessing a combination of characteristics not present in any other creature. Certainly, many behaviors observable in animals can be considered to be analogous to those found in humans, yet, because of significant differences with regard to the complexity and/or intensity of those behaviors, and because there is no other single species in which a combination of all important human behaviors can be observed, there are many valid reasons to question the value of ideas we have about humans that are based on our observations of other species.

Further diminishing the significance of animal models are aspects of human experience that seem to have essentially no analogue throughout the rest of nature. One such manifestation relates to the question of being unguarded and vulnerable versus being well-defended. Unlike any other animal, a human individual possessing a greater than average amount, or intensity of, intellectual and/or emotional openness and sensitivity may find that those qualities greatly enhance his or her functioning and/or happiness; or may result in the complete opposite. To a large degree, this is determined by the individual's social environment.

Tough and aggressive behaviors may cause someone to be regarded as the hero of a group that has been stranded in the woods and is surrounded by wild animals. Those very same characteristics expressed in social circles of intelligent, urbane artists may actually be an impediment to gaining acceptance. Among humans, the degree to which it is advantageous to possess certain characteristics will depend on the degree to which an individual has access to the requirements for civilized living, such as adequate resources, safety, artistic expression, and individual fulfillment.

To be capable of realizing his or her full potential, a human being needs a great deal more than the satisfaction of basic survival needs and assurance that they will continue to be met. Humans also need appropriate intellectual stimulation and emotional nurturing to achieve the full range of functioning of which they are capable. To complicate matters, when we are provided with healthy nurturing, our general sensitivity to our world increases, as does our potential to experience pain. When, however, an individual receives sufficient high-quality nurturing, he or she will not only be highly sensitive but also (usually) resilient and strong.

Individuals who have had some important needs met, yet others not, can be of great value to the species, yet can be personally miserable. This phenomenon is also unique to humankind. In no other species that we know of could an individual live an entire life so replete with intellectual, emotional, and/or physical suffering that he or she might ultimately commit suicide, yet the same qualities that produced such anguish may have also enabled that person to make a significant contribution to the entire human species in the arts or science or some other area of human endeavor.

For all of these reasons, as well as those yet to be discussed, there are no animal models that mirror our comprehensive human experience. This observation is central to the understanding of the human experience expressed in this chapter. Accordingly, in addition to examining the human experience in a rational manner, uncolored by beliefs that are religious, supernatural, or cynical. This essay will avoid making assumptions about humanity based on the behaviors of nonhuman species, and instead restrict its focus to human behavior and history.

WHAT IS HUMAN NATURE?

When we inquire as to the basic nature of any given species, what we are really asking? We know that it is the nature of any species to behave in the manner that will most efficiently and effectively satisfy its needs. For any species to evolve successfully, a vast majority of its healthy adult members must possess the necessary physical and mental attributes required to accomplish this. Hence, when discussing any species' basic nature, we are actually referring to the basic characteristics that are essential to accomplishing the satisfaction of that species' needs, these would be the characteristics that we would expect to find in healthy adult members of that species.

On the most basic level, human beings have the same needs, or drives, as most other animals: the need to survive, the need to procreate, and the need for social contact. Additionally, however, humans have needs that appear to be unique. Our strong need for challenging intellectual stimulation drives us as it does no other creature; from our most distant origins, humans have exercised constant effort to satisfy their boundless curiosity. Our most unparalled and extraordinary need is expressed via the manner in which we pursue satisfying all of our human needs: organizing ourselves and manipulating our environment on an increasingly grand scale with ever-increasing intensity and efficiency.

Our attempts to satisfy our uniquely human needs result in humans behaving in ways that bear little resemblance to the behavior of any other creature. Since our earliest development, humankind has given rise to projects that transcend the life of any one human as all aspects of human endeavor are ongoing and transgenerational. Although our methods of pursuing these enterprises, and our objectives themselves, have been subject to perpetual revision, redefinition, and improvement, our ultimate goal remains undefined and open ended, with no imaginable point of achievement that could be regarded as ultimate and final; for no other existing creature is this true.

Satisfying the basic needs that we share with the rest of the animal world—the need to survive, the need to produce progeny, and the need to have social contact—would not require humans to possess attributes that are different from any other animal. To satisfy his or her uniquely human drives, however, a healthy and mature human must be constructive, creative, prolific, inclined toward cooperative behaviors, and sensitive to the other beings and the world around them. To satisfy their bursting curiosity, humans must also be naturally inclined toward rational thinking and developing effective methods of gathering reliable information.

While such characteristics are absolutely necessary to satisfy our uniquely human needs, what could possibly explain there being so few humans, if any, who actually fit the aforementioned description of a healthy human? Additionally, why have such socially destabilizing and destructive characteristics as greed, selfishness, irrationality, and the desire to dominate others been so chronic among humans in our past and in our world today?

OBSTACLES TO REALIZING HUMAN POTENTIAL

Humans possess the most sophisticated intellect of any animal we know. Our advanced intellect is the source of our unique human agenda; without it we would most likely care no more about activities such as computer science or space exploration than any other animal. Unfortunately, this same advanced intellect makes it possible for us to behave in egregiously antisocial and destructive ways that have no equivalent among other animals.

One feature of our advanced intellect is that we do not necessarily need to behave in response to conditions at any given moment; instead, our actions can be informed by abstract ideas that have little or nothing to do with immediate conditions around us. Simply because there is no nearby fire in need of extinguishing and no deadly disease threatening to spread rapidly, humans do not decide that there is no need to retain an ever-ready firefighting force, or to abandon disease prevention and control measures. Humans can engage in complex, resource-intensive efforts, over protracted periods, based simply on an idea that is not focused on conditions in the present moment.

Our ability to act in response to an idea, or to a projection of a possible future, not only facilitates innumerable survival-enhancing behaviors but also makes possible the satisfaction of a variety of human needs. Sadly, however, being able to ignore or dismiss what is actually happening "in the moment" also makes it possible for one human to subject another to sustained levels of agony and torment unparalleled throughout the rest of nature. Just as we can ignore our present sense of comfort and safety and preemptively act as if we were in danger, we can also ignore the cries of a suffering captive and focus instead on ideas that explain why this individual's suffering does not matter or is "deserved" because "he suffers for the glory of a god," or "for the greater good of humanity," or some other rationalization.

Over the millennia, successful application of our abstract thinking in areas of technological development slowly resulted in humans' moving away from lives in which almost all efforts expended were those essential for survival to lives in which ideas would play an increasingly important role. Human minds are easily possessed by ideas; whenever we are freed from focusing purely on surviving, our minds naturally gravitate to ideas. For this reason we are continually improving the quality of our lives and forever redefining our understandings of ourselves and everything around us.

This preoccupation with ideas, however, has put humans at the tremendous disadvantage of being vulnerable to hurtful and damaging ideas. Some of the most destructive behaviors of humans result from our uncritical acceptance of erroneous ideas and/or false information, such as the belief that it is wise to physically discipline children, or the belief in the inherent superiority of certain people and the inferiority of others, or that some deity has appointed one group to dominate another. Such false and destructive ideas tend to be perpetuated and to resist challenge, particularly when those in positions of power regard such ideas as advantageous to their ruling-class agenda.

Humans can think about the past and the future in a manner which no other animal can. Our advanced intellect enables us to analyze past successes and disappointments and learn how to ensure continued success or facilitate a more desired result in the future. While the constructive application of such abilities has enabled humankind to enjoy increasingly longer, healthier, and happier lives, the application of such abilities has also resulted in immeasurable damage not only to humankind but also to the world around us.

As in the animal world, resources for early humans were scarce and deprivation was common. An individual human or group of humans with superior physical and/or mental abilities would easily gain dominance over less able individuals or groups. Those in positions of dominance established institutions to ensure their continued preferential status and that such status would be conferred upon their descendants.

One of the results of humankind's ability to apply abstract thinking to the institutionalization of power is that many who wield power and enjoy preferential access to resources often lack the superior physical or mental characteristics requisite for those who dominate among animals.

While power held by the few may once have had a practical genesis, our monarchies, oligarchies, and other institutions of class stratification have ultimately empowered untold numbers of incompetent and, at times, savagely damaging individuals resulting in great social havoc and incalculable human suffering.

Additionally our inclination to do everything on an ever-increasingly grand scale has made our destructive behaviors terrible beyond all comparison. Clearly, our ability to think abstractly and take action based on such thinking has been a double-edged sword for humankind, resulting in both its greatest achievements and its cruelest depravities.

HUMANS ARE FRAGILE

The double-edged sword that our advanced intellect represents should not lead us conclude that human nature is neutral. Humans cannot be just as inclined to be destructive as constructive; given our unique human agenda, that would not make sense. What is clear is that our human minds are profoundly sensitive. The amount of nurturing and enlightened support needed to realize a human's socially constructive potential is more intense and complex than for any other being. The factors that can cause an individual not to reach his or her human potential are voluminous.

This situation is somewhat visible in modern society, where after more than a twenty-year childhood, many humans enter the adult world still essentially unprepared for what will be required of them. Furthermore, given the rapidity with which our modern society is hurtling into its future, many people have come to accept that our children and their children will at best glean only minimal benefits from the wisdom of their elders. While this phenomenon might seem to be purely modern, in actuality, our entire human journey has been embarked on under just such circumstances.

A JOURNEY WITHOUT PRECEDENT

Unlike all other species, which either inherit the instincts or receive the parental guidance that makes their goals and methods of accomplishing them clear, the ultimate goals of humanity are essentially undefined. Each human embarks on a journey that is unprecedented in its potential impact. As previously stated, the goals of the human endeavor are as infinite and open ended as the ever more complex means through which humans attempt to realize them. For this reason, humans became the only creature unable to inherit, from instinct or parental training, a complete set of comprehensive instructions specifying what they must do and the best method of doing it. Humans would be disconnected from the previously unbroken chain of information that provided those who preceded us with everything required to satisfy their needs.

One could compare humankind to children growing up without the benefit of effective parental guidance. In this respect all humans are, to some degree, functional orphans. In addition, humankind has emerged in desperation, ever conscious of being subject to sometimes critical limitations of resources.

What types of behavior should we expect from orphaned children, possessing perceptive and sensitive minds, growing up without effective direction, and terrified of the continual threat of harsh deprivation? As we view the nascent human experience in this context, our history, with its millennia of brutality and obsessive struggles for ultimate power, should not surprise us. Far more surprising is the considerable progress that humankind has made in relatively little time. To bring the nascency of the human journey into perspective, consider that on a scale on which the earth's actual age of 4.5 billion years is represented by only forty-five years, the entire existence of *Homo sapiens* would be represented by only four hours, and the industrial revolution would have begun just one minute ago. The progress that humans have achieved in satisfying our needs and in grappling with the complexities of the human condition in so short a time is truly awesome.

OUR AMAZING JOURNEY

Emerging from a faith-based and superstitious culture, reason-based thinking and human ingenuity have resulted in modern science. Today the application of science has enabled masses of people to experience the benefits of surplus resources, lower infant mortality, extended life expectancies, better health, increased leisure time, more nutritious and varied diets, access to a wide range of intellectual pursuit, and comforts and luxuries previously unimagined. Unfortunately, such progress has not been experienced in those parts of the world where the ruling classes believe that their power is best assured by keeping people harnessed to the yoke of faith-based thinking. Where humans have been encouraged to think rationally and to question and investigate their environment, however, the accomplishments and sensitivities of which we have shown ourselves capable portend extremely well for the future of humankind.

In places where technological progress has made it possible for the average person's daily life to advance from merely seeking to survive to actually living for fulfillment, an ever-increasing desire to diminish social inequities for all those who continue to struggle has commensurately emerged. Never before has the plight of the marginalized concerned so many mainstream individuals who have no direct interest in the situation. Never before have so many governments emerged that, at least in theory, agree to be held accountable to the will of the majority.

Additionally, even where humans continue to suffer the consequences of nonreason-based cultures, it is only a question of time before a rational progressive culture will prevail. The ubiquity of modern technology and the access to information it provides will ultimately transform every culture on our planet.

The trajectory of human progress is undeniable, and humanity is on an exponential upswing. Yet our culture remains steeped in misanthropy. Christians and cynics alike declare that humankind is doomed to abject obliteration. Many people who hold this view have children and/or grandchildren, and many have worked all of their lives building great projects, yet they seem to accept that it's perfectly rational for us all to believe that the world will destroy itself and there's not a thing we can do to stop it. Those who dare to suggest that humankind can achieve peace and happiness are ridiculed and dismissed, characterized as naive optimists with impractical "pie in the sky" ideas, as if to imply that sitting back in stoic resignation, accepting that our world is on the brink of irreversible cataclysm is somehow practical.

Contrary to such misanthropic worldviews, humankind is quickly closing in on ways of interacting with our environment that will make it possible to meet every humans' basic physical needs, such as the development of nanotech replication—construction at a molecular level—that will allow us to convert matter into whatever is needed. We are about to leave the history of human want and suffering behind us. To take full advantage of humankind's having attained the capacity to provide the basic conditions needed for the global realization of human potential and to ensure that our unprecedented power is fully directed to the satisfaction of human needs and not misapplied, humanism must become manifest and widespread. However, there are many obstacles to humanism's becoming a "popular" movement. For humanism to succeed it must change, it must rethink several of its most common assumptions.

SELECTIVELY NATURALISTIC

Present-day humanism has a difficult case to make in presenting itself as a rational alternative to religion because its own presumptions are rooted in religious thinking. It offers essentially traditional perspectives, minus a god and an afterlife. To become a truly naturalistic alternative, humanism must become internally consistent. It must drop its unscientific ideas about what drives human behavior. It must cease to promote ideas that fail to recognize the significance of human potential. Humanists must replace nebulous ideas about human nature with thinking that is naturalistic and prohuman. Secular humanism must recognize that when humans are the beneficiaries of an environment that meets their physical, cognitive, and emotional needs, their chances for realizing their full potential are greatest. This is not a belief faith, nor does it selectively disregard significant evidence to the contrary.

Decades of research in areas of scientific study as diverse as criminology, sociology, anthropology, and early childhood development have resulted in the compilation of voluminous data that confirm what should be obvious; the likelihood of realizing their full potential is reduced in direct proportion to the degree that people's physical, cognitive, and emotional needs are neglected. Humanists must recognize that, rather than being inherently greedy and indolent, people are potent, productive, and motivated to cooperate and contribute to the best of their abilities when properly supported.

An overwhelming misanthropic majority believe that, should the average person be given a stipend large enough to pay his or her bills with no expectations or requirements, that person would respond by sitting home and watching television all day or perpetually engage in some other self-indulgent activity. A secular humanist should be able to reason that such a view is erroneous. People who possess even a modicum of self-esteem simply could not be unproductive for any protracted length of time. Most people would find a way to contribute even if someone was actively trying to prevent them from doing so, if for no other reason than to preserve their own sanity. Humanists should reject the idea that people would not provide the contributions their society required without the specter of devastating financial hardship or the lure of exorbitant rewards. In an economy based on outdated principles, the perception of one person's merit and another's lack of merit could never justify suffering and deprivation in a world of staggering wealth.

Accepting Universal Causation

Humanists must also recognize the reality of universal causation—that human behavior, like everything else in our universe, is caused. We must separate ourselves from the common supernaturalistic assumption of humans being "causally privileged" to act in a manner that is contrary to causes: "contra-causal free will." The impact of acknowledging that human behavior is caused and not the result of some nebulous, unexplainable, magical free will would be tremendous, first and foremost because doing so would allow humanism to actually represent itself as offering a consistently naturalistic worldview rather than the selectively naturalistic view it presently supports.

Accepting the reality of universal causation humanism would also provide a truly reason-based rationale for a truly progressive and humane agenda for issues ranging from how to prosecute criminals to how to distribute resources. To better see how an entirely new and humane yet fully effective way to respond to social problems is possible, let's examine what might happen if we apply the understanding that even those who act in damaging ways do not do so out of a willful desire to be evil.

The response to individuals who, after a fair investigation with built-in civil protections, have been determined to have "caused" social or individual damage should be "damage control" or "harm reduction" designed to prevent any further destruction or hurt. Such social intervention could involve providing the treatment and support to enable the person to grow beyond the need to act in damaging ways and might result in that person's becoming empowered to eventually become productive.

Those who are believed to continue to pose a threat would have to be separated from mainstream society and have their freedoms limited, but even in these cases, society's response need not be violent and retributive. Once the types of functioning an individual cannot handle have been determined, focus should be concentrated on establishing those areas of functioning in which the individual has talent or potential, and in which the individual would not constitute a danger. While a causal understanding of behavior does not require vindictive reprisals, it does not in any way compromise the protection of society from abuse. It would set a highly humane standard for public policy and the role model effect that all public policy ultimately provides. Humanists could make it known that recognizing the decisive role that determinants play in the way we behave actually produces a much higher level of social accountability than we have in our present society.

Whether we acknowledge it or not, our social institutions set a tone and standard for behavior that is felt throughout our entire culture. The social role model which our current public policies provide is officially sanctioned violence and cruelty. Legitimized violence ranges from the devastating weapons we create to the barbaric way we treat wildlife, such as hunting it for sport, to the brutal manner in which we frequently neglect, deprive, or abuse the most defenseless members of our society—including the very elderly, the very young, and those suffering with mental illness or developmental or physical disabilities, and children—to our insistence on inflicting emotionally abusive, and frequently physically abusive, long-term punishments as retribution for committing crimes.

Almost 54 percent of US federal prisoners enduring appalling and inhumane punishments in our criminal justice system do so as a result of having committed crimes that stem from the problem of addiction to drugs that our society has arbitrarily made illegal.[10] Publicly sanctioned violence administered with righteous indignation also includes the anachronistic idea that because one person has murdered another it's perfectly reasonable for the state in turn to murder that person. Accepting the full implications of determinism would provide humanists with a scientific basis to argue for the immediate abandonment of all such primitive and rapacious public practices.

Real Empowerment

Understanding the role that determinism plays in our lives would also provide a nonsupernatural motivation to achieve greater personal empowerment. Once we accept that our behavior is the result of determinants, we become increasingly able to view ourselves objectively without the damaging effects of judging and hating ourselves. As soon as we reject the myth that whatever difficulties we have result from our own decision to bring such situations on ourselves, we can form a new and more realistic self-image.

People who have struggled with challenge after challenge might, for the first time, become able to appreciate the amazing strength and determination that they have repeatedly demonstrated but never acknowledged. When people realize that they are not to blame for who they are, the perpetual cycle of dysfunctional behavior contributing to feelings of inferiority and those feelings in turn contributing to evermore dysfunctional behaviors is broken.

Understanding the ultimate role that determinants play in our lives does not result in complacency or the abandonment of effort. Unlike faith-based ideas about human behavior, facilitating increased self-awareness and self-esteem actually makes significant personal growth and achievement a realistic possibility.

Challenging belief in free will, the most pernicious of all faith-based beliefs, is an essential part of what humanism must do if it is to become a consistent naturalistic worldview.

the Damage of Moral Judgments

After decades of observing and analyzing the way humans behave, social scientists have accumulated a great deal of data indicating that viewing behavior as good or evil or right and wrong is primitive, inaccurate, and ultimately unproductive. Additionally, an ability to commit an act that is "right" or "wrong" assumes freedom of choice, which is completely inconsistent with the reality of universal causation. It is perfectly reasonable to examine human behaviors in terms of their having greater or lesser potential to meet human needs. This type of analysis, however, is very different from, and should not be confused with, moral judgment.

Damaging or constructive behaviors are not the result of choosing to be good or bad but are the result of an individual's emotional health and sense of self-esteem. Such self-esteem develops after a person has received the meeting of his basic needs, and love. Labeling behaviors as right or wrong, like all shame- or fear-based motivators, is a hopelessly ineffective approach to achieving a cooperative and caring society. Such labeling not only fails to recognize the decisive role a person's self-esteem plays in his or her behavior; the judgmental labeling of behavior is actually quite adversative to the development of such self-esteem.

We can teach a child that it is wrong to kill a bird and therefore it should not be done, and if you do it you have done a bad thing. If the child is emotionally disposed to kill the bird and does so despite having learned that it is wrong, you now have two problems. The degree of aggressive feelings necessary for a child to kill an innocent animal in itself indicates a problem that needs to be addressed. In addition, thanks to labeling such behavior as "bad," a child who has committed such an act is quite likely to consider him or herself to be a "bad" person, reasoning "who else but a bad person would do bad things?"

This perception, which is very common among people who have acted in a way that violates what they have been taught to regard as the standards of "good" behavior, invariably results in lowering what is most likely an already inadequate level of self-esteem in the person committing the act in question. Labeling a person's behavior as "bad" can contribute to a negative self-image that often predisposes the person to continue to act as a "bad" person, frequently resulting in behaviors that become ever increasingly egregious.

This dynamic is abundantly evident among many families that are poor, and where the child's basic self-esteem needs are very poorly supported, if at all. In such homes, there is seldom a shortage of excessive moralizing by parents or grandparents, including regular exposure to Bible teaching and strict rules of conduct in the school. Yet despite the barrage of moral instruction, antisocial and damaging behaviors are much more likely to be committed by the product of such environments than by those who have had the benefit of an environment in which the child's development of high self-esteem was considered a priority.

Interconnection and the Extended Self

Understanding why we can expect people to act in caring and responsible ways, we can then see how moral instruction relates to appreciating a significant component of our human potential.

The ability to realize our human potential includes becoming aware that our sense of being separate from others, and from the world around us, is essentially superficial. Recognizing the interconnectedness between ourselves and the world around us greatly facilitates our ability to satisfy the drives that constitute our unique human agenda: to satisfy our endless curiosity, and to accomplish everything on an ever increasingly grander scale. A sense of interconnection enables an individual to relate to a wide range of experiences with a sense of awareness and urgency that is otherwise not possible. Those who are aware of their interconnection are more likely to stumble upon universally significant insights that may become manifest as invention, art, thought, or action and may represent an important contribution to the advancement of humankind.

Acknowledgement of one's interconnection also destroys the illusion that there can be any deep personal satisfaction when suffering surrounds us. In a humanistic context, ethical behaviors are promoted by encouraging the emotional growth and awareness of an individual to a point where he or she can recognize that in diminishing another we diminish ourselves. In a new and vital humanism, recognizing our inclination to feel such interconnection or an extended sense of self is the naturalistic alternative to religious ethics. Those who become aware of their interconnectedness realize that personal aggrandizement by ignoring the plight of others does not put them ahead, it is a zero-sum game. In fact, whenever one person diminishes another for personal gain, it is always a zero-sum game. The elevation one person might achieve is offset by the sense of loss they experience as he or she perceives a connection to the diminished party. Even when the person who gains does not personally perceive the offset caused by the loss of the diminished party, there is still no gain.

In order to be impervious to those diminished around them, a person must live with a sensitivity threshold that is significantly reduced from what it would naturally be in a healthy human. Whether the result of harsh developmental experiences or other causes, living with reduced sensitivity is costly. Occasionally, we may encounter a sensitive person bemoaning the difficulties that their sensitivities seem to cause in his or her own life. Yet while greater sensitivity might occasionally bring pain and discomfort, it also facilitates a fuller experience of being alive. This is why, despite such complaints, no healthy, intelligent person would voluntarily reduce his or her perceptive and/or cognitive abilities.

Those whose life circumstances have resulted in their not knowing such sensitivities have, in fact, already been reduced in their human potential; they were not allowed to develop an important way of experiencing the world that surrounds them, one that is highly valued by all who possess it.

Consider that for some people, the sight of a trapped suffering animal is a heart-wrenching experience, yet others do not share this empathetic reaction and many feel fine about setting the traps and killing or capturing a free animal. Yet the people who are likely to feel intensely saddened when they see an animal in distress are also far more likely than others to take delight in witnessing a wild bird taking off into flight or to feel great exhilaration when observing (from a safe vantage point) a mother bear nurturing her cub in a natural environment.

In the trapper and the hunter, the sensitivities that might engender such feelings must be sacrificed in order to allow the individual to function. In order to hurt others without feeling reduced, one must have lost or stifled the awareness of the vital connection between oneself and the world, that very same connection that can make life truly joyful. A humanistic ethic can be developed only by nurturing our natural inclination to see ourselves in the world around us; becoming evermore aware of our extended selves.

LIMITS TO THE EXTENDED SELF

It should be understood that having an extended sense of self does not mean that you confuse yourself for another person; the boundaries of our individual personalities do not become confused. Relating to the world around us with an extended sense of self is, however, not unlike the way that one might regard one of his fingers.

We seek to protect our fingers always. Even if we had nerve damage that prevented us from feeling sensation in them, were we to notice that one of our fingers were infected or at risk of injury we would act immediately to protect it. A person would resign himself to allowing one of his fingers to be harmed in only the most severe of circumstances, where protecting his finger could result in even more serious damage, or death: for example, if one had no other way to stop an infection from spreading throughout one's entire body; or if one's finger was caught in some machinery that threatened to seize even more of one's body. Only under such a desperate and brutal circumstance could an otherwise healthy individual be forced into accepting dismemberment. Such behavior can be seen in animals that, after being caught in the infamously cruel metal foot trap, eventually gnaw off their own foot in order to save themselves from starvation.

Our fingers, even our limbs, are not the seat of our consciousness, and, in that respect, they are merely appendages; they are not who we are, in the most essential, and indispensable sense; while people survive without legs, no one can survive without her head. Yet, although we survive the loss of a limb, our commitment to protect our fingers and limbs is, just short of avoiding death, inviolable.

To a person who feels a strong sense of interconnection to those around her, her relationship to others is equally inviolable. In contrast to the "every man for himself" message our rugged individualistic culture sends, the feeling of the extended self urges us to protect what we perceive to be the world around us as we would our own fingers.

Relating to the world with such a level of propriety would be over-ridden only in the most critical of situations: for example, in so devastating a drought that sharing one's water would result in watching one's own child dehydrate to death. While we might want to act in a loving and gen-erous way right down to our last sip of water, our most primary obligation is to protect the biological apparatus which contain us: our genes, and/or our genetic legacy, our progeny. This is a universal imperative which, when sufficiently threatened, will most likely override all else.

Sometimes, while trying to prove the inherent selfishness or corrup-tion of humankind, a person of misanthropic orientation will point to such a scenario, in which all of the necessary elements of civility are evis-cerated, and a human may be reduced to behaviors which are brutal and desperate, as if the way that people might act in such a situation substan-tiates the misanthropic point of view.

Dismissing the ways that humans behave when they are supported by the civilized environment that they are driven to create, the misanthrope is inclined to think that the desperate ways in which one may be driven to act in such devolved circumstances reveals the "ultimate truth" about human nature. Often, in such discussion, you'll hear the misanthrope say, "When you get down to it . . . ," which will be invariably followed by some declaration of humankind's innately flawed and antisocial nature. Such a misanthropic argument, relying on a debased situation that is artificial, extreme, and representative of precisely what all human effort is funda-mentally aimed at avoiding, exposes its invalidity.

Interconnection Every day, Everywhere

Fortunately, we who enjoy lives in which our basic needs are assured can experience an extended sense of self. In fact, the frequency of everyday random acts of kindness as reported on Web sites such as "Random Acts of Kindness" or "Pay It Forward" and the tremendous number of unpaid volunteers in a culture that mythologizes rivalry and self-sufficiency completely belies the falsehood of misanthropy.

Every day at any given moment, thousands of people are scrambling to help pick up the groceries that drop out of a stranger's bag, or staying with a victim of a crime or a sudden illness, or holding the door for the next person, or helping another person lift a heavy load, or leaving a fair tip in a restaurant they don't expect to revisit, or stopping to assist a stranded fellow motorist on a cold and rainy night. Even though our culture conditions us from a very early age to regard each other as adversaries and competitors in school, in sports, in dressing, and in dating, people in our culture continually demonstrate a strong inclination toward cooperative, sensitive, caring, and generous actions.

The variety and frequency of social and cooperative behaviors challenges the misanthropic assertion that we are a culture of whining victims, driven by a sense of entitlement. It is, of course, true that many people in our culture believe that they are being treated unfairly, and that the considerable inequity of our antisocial system fosters a great deal of resentment. The feeling of being taken advantage of is a normal state of affairs, and while this outlook may perhaps be indicative of emotional problems for some, given our society's class antagonism and the cruel economic setbacks in recent decades to many in the middle class and those who were already poor; widespread feelings of resentment are not unfounded. Add to these circumstances the extreme rise in the fortunes of those who were already on the top of the economic ladder, resulting in an unprecedented divide between rich and poor, it is not hard to see why many people who are disadvantaged and perceive what is happening are filled with anger and indignation.

Yet should the playing field appear to be more level, even disadvantaged people are inclined to act in supportive and giving ways. Frequently people who seem to have the least to part with will give with a degree of generosity that is proportionately far beyond the largesse of those who are far more affluent.

The prevalence of socially constructive and responsible behaviors within a culture that is so blatantly misanthropic, brutal, ruggedly individualistic, and self-righteous beckons us to consider how much greater the average person's sense of interconnection to others could be in a culture that actually supported such a perspective. Who will fight for such a world?

Humanists can, and, if we are to stand up for the things to which we've committed ourselves in writing, we must.

PROVIDING BETTER ANSWERS

Because it is based on assumptions that are faith-based, an erroneous misanthropic thinking results in mistaken analyses and useless solutions. If humanism adopts the ideas discussed in this chapter, it will be able to offer analyses of social problems that provide fresh insights, as well as solutions that are effective. An example of such problems and solutions relates to what is happening in our public schools.

It is well known that our nation's public schools are in crisis. They do not capture our children's imagination, nor do they nurture curiosity. They do not put children in touch with the wonder of being human, and they do nothing to promote our children's sense of interconnectedness to their world and to each other. While parents know that the schools are failing, the majority of them have no idea why. Rather than pointing the way to the democratic education movement, with its presumptions that children are naturally curious and natural learners, humanists remain silent. The only voice being heard is that of the religious fundamentalists, who want to force religion down our children's throats and use taxpayers' money to do it.

Instead of leading the progressive charge, humanists and freethinkers have spent recent years immersed in ferocious battles to keep religion out of our schools. When an incident such as the Columbine High School shooting brings home the degree to which our schools are failing, the religious fundamentalists have not hesitated to opportunistically use such a tragedy to further their own faith-based agenda. Hence, the revitalized call for school prayer; for the Ten Commandments to be posted in the halls, for "God bless America" signs to be displayed, and for keeping "under God" in the often-mandatory recitation of the Pledge of Allegiance.

To make matters even worse, some fundamentalists, such as David Nobel and Tim Lahaye, have declared that the public schools' adoption of a secular humanist agenda is responsible for promoting low morality and a cavalier disregard for social values. When we respond to such charges, secular humanists must make clear that if our schools were truly based on secular and humanistic principles, they would be incorporating a multitude of modern, effective techniques for strengthening self-awareness and sensitivity to others; they would relate the true wonder of our nascent human experience and convey the brilliance and magnificence that distinguishes the human enterprise. Most important, if our public schools were truly based on secular and humanistic principles, they would regard promoting the dignity and self-esteem of all students as their top priority. Making these points clear would be a more effective way to address the problems that concern parents, but because humanists do not aggressively advocate the progressive path, the religious fundamentalists are allowed to frame the discussion in a manner that results in humanism being attacked.

GETTING OFF THE DEFENSIVE

We must take the Christian Right head-on by identifying what needs to change in our society and show how those changes must be secular and humanistic if they are to work. With the charismatic passion of the late Carl Sagan, we must show how science is as inherently democratic and progressive as supernaturalism is elitist and reactionary. We must address such pressing social issues before tragedy strikes again and provides the fundamentalists with further opportunities to spew their reactionary venom. We must clearly identify the antihuman attitudes that influence the most damaging policies in our nation, not only with regard to public education but also with regard to such issues as illegal drugs, the belief in the long-term effectiveness of military solutions; and our self-serving meritocracy that forces the violence of poverty on all who are not deemed "worthy."

BUILDING A LIVING MOVEMENT

Perhaps most important, we must ask ourselves the question, "Do we really want to be a popular movement?" We cannot assume that the answer to this question is yes. Do the senior Caucasian male academics who gather for polite intellectual debates and conferences really want a dynamic widespread "people's movement humanism" filled with raucous teenagers and people who gesticulate and speak in your face? Are humanists willing to deal with the intensely tragic and utterly wacky circumstances that poor and marginalized people might sometimes bring to the mix? Can humanism tolerate getting messy, with babies crying and school-age children wreaking havoc?

As any one who has been to several meetings in the humanist community can see, at least here in America, it's difficult to imagine that most of the current participants in humanism would be able to appreciate such dynamics. Despite lots of saber rattling regarding huge expansion campaigns, by and large, the majority of those who frequent humanist events already appear to have the type of community they want.

The problem, of course, is that as long as humanism remains a practice characterized by its staid, cautious, bland, intellectual, and academically oriented approach, as long as its desire to wear the suit of respectability causes it to reject new and revolutionary thinking, humanism will remain impotent. Unless we can speak to the needs of families, unless we can see the age of the average participant at humanist meetings dip at least below fifty, unless we can win the hearts and minds of the masses, we can forget about the promises of humanism. Humanists also need to recognize that the cutting-edge work of building a better tomorrow is happening; it's just not people who identify themselves as humanists who are making it happen.

If humanism wants to be part of making that better tomorrow, it must apply the recommendations made in this chapter for philosophical consistency and then discover how its revitalized commitment to naturalism and a progressive worldview relate to those important progressive causes actively working for positive change right now. These movements include support for a universal guaranteed minimum income; democratic education; peer-to-peer/open source/free information; the end of capital punishment; progressive prison reform; community-based homecare for seniors and persons with physical and/or mental disabilities; global pacifism; single-payer universal health care; gender liberation; gay rights; slavery reparations; and democratic transhumanism. Ideally, a new and reinvigorated humanism will be able to provide such widely disparate causes with an underlying naturalistic philosophy that unites them all and supports their collective synergy.

In addition to changing its philosophy so that it is fully naturalistic and prohuman, and in addition to aligning itself with movements already fighting for a humanistic agenda, humanism must develop practices that speak to average people and offer them a vital alternative to traditional faith-based approaches. Each dollar, each hour, we invest in developing a comprehensive alternative to faith-based approaches is infinitely more valuable than equal amounts of time and money directed to knocking down established approaches that we know are flawed.

Our understanding of the inherent limitations of faith-based systems should enable us to develop an indisputably more fulfilling, more effective, and more compelling alternative—a comprehensive approach to meeting human needs, fully based in reason, as wide in its scope as the breadth of science. Such an approach should evoke a profound sense of interconnection and stirring emotional highs, which a scientific worldview can facilitate. We must inspire our freethinking and humanist communities by providing a less cerebral and more visceral connection to the wide range of comprehensive experiences that our reason-based orientation can support and inspire; humanism should offer meetings that are experimental and fun, providing an approach living one's life as a secular journey of discovery.

This approach, combined with the aforementioned recommendations, will breathe new life into our humanist cause and enable humanism to become the path that leads us into a future far more amazing than we could ever imagine.

NOTES

1. "A Humanist Manifesto," in Oliver L. Reiser, *Humanism and New World Ideals* (Yellow Springs, OH: Antioch Press, 1933); *Humanist Manifesto II* (Amherst, NY: Prometheus Books, 1973).

2. Human Potential: An empathetic approach to addressing the obstacles to living a life that is satisfying, and socially productive, by facilitating the fullest realization of each individual's abilities and talents possible and by promoting a heightened sense of interconnection between individuals and the people and the world around them.

3. Naturalism: The movement that challenges the commonly held supernatural belief that human behavior is not subject to and can function completely independent of the universal laws of cause and effect. See http://naturalism.org.

4. Democratic Education/Nonmanipulative Child Rearing: The movements that hold that the rights of children deserve no less protection than the protection we convey upon adults. These movements respect children and trust that their natural curiosity makes them their own best educators; they regard the role of teacher and school as providing only guidance and facilitation to a child's self-directed learning process. See A. S. Neill, *Summerhill* (Harmondsworth, England: Penguin, 1968).

5. Nonhierarchical Institutions and Social Relationships: The movement

that challenges the need for hierarchal relationships and asserts that the maintenance of such relationships interferes with a human being's natural propensity toward cooperation and that hierarchy is antithetical to achieving the full contribution of which each individual is capable.

6. Gender Liberation and Equality: Movements that do not support the expansion of male dominance and male cultural hegemony as the single cultural ideal to which both men and women must aspire. A true movement involving gender equality and liberation would hold in high regard those types of work and various roles which have traditionally been assumed by females as being just as important as the traditional roles and culture of males.

7. Open Source/Free Information/Peer to Peer: A movement in which people driven by nothing more than the desire to contribute to the betterment of all, freely share their intellectual property. It keeps alive some of the original vision of the way the Internet was to be a synergistic collective and open global project.

8. Slavery Reparations: The movement that seeks to readdress the significant but unappreciated and uncompensated contributions of those African Americans and Native Americans whose descendants remain primarily disenfranchised.

9. Democratic Transhumanism: Due to the imminent synergy of cutting-edge technologies such as genetics, artificial intelligence, nanotechnology, and cryogenics, humankind stands at the threshold of a dramatic transformation with the potential to eliminate deprivation and drudgery and facilitate an unprecedented universal standard of living which will offer a satisfying and empowered life to all.

10. Bureau of Justice statistics for the year 2001.

ARNELL DOWRET is a writer, radio host, and activist in the humanist community. Dowret cohosts WBAI's weekly radio program for humanism and scientific naturalism—"Equal Time for Freethought." He has been involved in human potential group work since 1972, developing "Secular Connections," an alternative experimental workshop originally offered by Center for Inquiry–Metro NY. Dowret's work has been featured in presentations to various schools and community groups in the Metropolitan New York area, including New York University, Columbia University, Princeton University, Rutgers University Newark, The Ethical Culture Society of Queens, The Secular Humanist of New York, The Humanist Society of Metropolitan New York, The New Jersey Humanist Network, and Long Island Secular Humanists. Dowret has been a contributor to *Free Inquiry*, and more of his writing can be found at www.secularconnections.org.

Suggested Reading

Allen, Norm, Jr., ed. *The Black Humanist Experience.* Amherst, NY: Prometheus Books, 2002.

Alley, Robert S., ed. *James Madison on Religious Liberty.* Amherst, NY: Prometheus Books, 1985.

Altemeyer, Bob, and Bruce Hunsberger. *Amazing Conversions: Why Some Turn to Faith and Others Abandon Religion.* Amherst, NY: Prometheus Books, 1997.

Aristotle. *The Politics.* Translated by Ernest Barker. Revised edition. New York: Oxford University Press, 1998.

Atran, Scott. *In Gods We Trust: The Evolutionary Landscape of Religion.* London: Oxford University Press, 2002

Barad, Judith, and Ed Robertson. *The Ethics of "Star Trek."* New York: Harper-Collins, 2001.

Barker, Dan. *Losing Faith in Faith.* Madison, WI: Freedom from Religion Foundation, 1992.

Barker, Ernest. *Social Contract: Essays by Locke, Hume, and Rousseau.* London: Oxford University Press, 1947.

Barrett, Michèle, and Duncan Barrett. *"Star Trek": The Human Frontier.* New York: Routledge, 2000.

Britt, Laurence. *June, 2004: A Political Novel.* Sarasota, FL: Book World Press, 1998.

Chomsky, Noam. *Fateful Triangle: The United States, Israel, and the Palestinians.* Cambridge, MA: South End Press, 1999.

———. *Hegemony or Survival: America's Quest for Global Dominance (The American Empire Project).* New York: Metropolitan Books, 2003.

———. *Media Control: The Spectacular Achievements of Propaganda.* New York: Seven Stories Press, 2002.

———. *Middle East Illusions: Including Peace in the Middle East? Reflections on Justice and Nationhood.* Lanham, MD: Rowman and Littlefield, 2003.

Chorney, Harold, and Phillip Hansen. *Toward a Humanist Political Economy.* Montreal: Black Rose Books, 1996.

Clark, Wesley K. *Winning Modern Wars: Iraq, Terrorism, and the American Empire.* New York: PublicAffairs, 2003.

Cole, David. *Enemy Aliens: Double Standards and Constitutional Freedoms in the War on Terrorism.* New York: New Press, 2002.

Coon, Carl. *Culture Wars and the Global Village: A Diplomat's Perspective.* Amherst, NY: Prometheus Books, 2002.

Cousins, Norman, ed. *In God We Trust: The Religious Beliefs and Ideas of the American Founding Fathers.* New York: Harper, 1958.

Dahl, Robert A. *How Democratic Is the American Constitution?* 2d ed. New Haven, CT: Yale University Press, 2003.

Dennett, Daniel C. *Freedom Evolves.* New York: Viking, 2003.

Detmer, David. *Challenging Postmodernism: Philosophy and the Politics of Truth.* Amherst, NY: Humanity Books, 2003.

Domke, David. *God Willing? Political Fundamentalism in the White House, the 'War on Terror' and the Echoing Press.* London: Pluto Press, 2004.

Drury, Shadia B. *Terror and Civilization: Christianity, Politics, and the Western Psyche.* New York: Palgrave Macmillan, 2004.

Einstein, Albert. *Einstein on Humanism.* Reprint. New York: Kensington, 1993.

Eisler, Riane. *The Chalice and The Blade: Our History, Our Future.* Cambridge, MA: Harper and Row, 1987.

———. "Cultural Transformation Theory: A New Paradigm for History." In *Macrohistory and Macrohistorians*, edited by Johan Galtung and Sohail Inayatullah. Westport, CT: Praeger Publishers, 1997.

———. *The Power of Partnership: Seven Relationships That Will Change Your Life.* Novato, CA: New World Library, 2002.

———. *Sacred Pleasure: Sex, Myth, and the Politics of the Body.* San Francisco: HarperSanFrancisco, 1995.

———. *Tomorrow's Children: A Blueprint for Partnership Education in the 21st Century.* Boulder, CO: Westview Press, 2000.

Eisler, Riane, David Loye, and Kari Norgaard. *Women, Men, and the Global Quality of Life.* Pacific Grove, CA: Center for Partnership Studies, 1995.

Fern, Yvonne. *Gene Roddenberry: The Last Conversation.* Berkeley and Los Angeles: University of California Press, 1994.

Francis, Diana. *Rethinking War and Peace.* London: Pluto Press, 2004.

Flanagan, Owen. *The Problem of the Soul: Two Visions of Mind and How to Reconcile Them.* New York: Basic Books, 2002.

Gaylor, Annie Laurie. *Women without Superstition: "No Gods—No Masters": The Collected Writings of Women Freethinkers of the Nineteenth and Twentieth Centuries.* Madison, WI: Freedom from Religion Foundation, 1997.

Grayling, A. C. *Meditations for the Humanist: Ethics for a Secular Age.* New York: Oxford University Press, 2002.

Holyoake, George Jacob, *The Origin and Nature of Secularism*, London: Watts, 1896.

Honderich, Ted. *How Free Are You? The Determinism Problem*. 2d ed. Oxford: Oxford University Press, 2002.

Hume, David. *A Treatise of Human Nature*. 1739–40. Reprint, New York: Clarendon, 1978.

Hutton, Will. *A Declaration of Interdependence: Why America Should Join the World*. New York: W. W. Norton, 2003.

Jefferson, Thomas. *Democracy*. Selected and arranged by Saul K. Padover. 1939. Reprint, New York: Mentor, 1958.

Johnson, Chalmers. *Blowback: The Costs and Consequences of American Empire*. New York: Metropolitan Books, 2000.

Johnston, Michael. "The Search for Definitions: The Vitality of Politics and the Issue of Corruption." *International Social Science Journal* 149 (1996): 321–35.

Jost, John T., et al. "Political Conservatism as Motivated Social Cognition." *Psychological Bulletin* 129 (2003): 339–75. http://psychoanalystsopposewar.org/resources_files/ConsevatismAsMotivatedSocialCognition.pdf.

Kaplan, R. D. *Warrior Politics: Why Leadership Demands a Pagan Ethos*. New York: Random House, 2002.

Kellner, Douglas. *From 9/11 to Terror War: Dangers of the Bush Legacy*. Lanham, MD: Rowman and Littlefield, 2003.

———. *Grand Theft 2000: Media Spectacle and a Stolen Election*. Lanham, MD: Rowman and Littlefield, 2001.

Kramnick, Isaac, and R. Laurence Moore. *The Godless Constitution: The Case against Religious Correctness*. New York: Norton, 1996.

Kurtz, Paul. *Eupraxophy: Living without Religion*. Amherst, NY: Prometheus Books, 1989.

———. *Humanist Manifesto 2000: A Call for New Planetary Humanism*. Amherst, NY: Prometheus Books, 2000.

Lamont, Corliss. *The Philosophy of Humanism*. 8th ed. Amherst, NY: Humanist Press, 1997.

Locke, John. *Two Treatises of Government: In the former, the false principles and foundation of Sir Robert Filmer, and his followers, are detected and overthrown. The latter is an essay concerning the true original, extent, and end of civil-government*. London: A. and J. Churchill, 1698.

———. *Two Treatises of Government and a Letter Concerning Toleration*. Edited by Ian Shapiro. New Haven: Yale University Press, 2003.

Macdonell, Diane. *Theories of Discourse*. Oxford: Basil Blackwell, 1986.

Mahajan, Rahul. *The New Crusade: America's War on Terrorism*. New York: Monthly Review Press, 2002.

Mellaart, James. *Çatal Hüyük: A Neolithic Town in America*. New York: McGraw-Hill, 1967.

Miller, Robert T., and Ronald B. Flowers. *Toward Benevolent Neutrality: Church, State, and the Supreme Court*. 5th ed. Waco, TX: Markham Press Fund of Baylor University Press, 1996.

Moore, R Laurence, *Selling God: American Religion in the Marketplace of Culture*. New York: Oxford University Press, 1994.

Niehoff, Debra. *The Biology of Violence: How Understanding the Brain, Behavior, and Environment Can Break the Vicious Circle of Aggression*. New York: Free Press, 1999.

Orwell, George. *1984*. 1949. Reprint, New York: Harcourt, 2000.

Parenti, Michael. *Superpatriotism*. San Francisco: City Lights Books, 2004.

Pereboom, Derk. *Living without Free Will*. Cambridge, England: Cambridge University Press, 2001.

Pigliucci, M. *Tales of the Rational: Skeptical Essays about Nature and Science*. Atlanta: Freethought Press, 2000.

Pinker, Stephen. *The Blank Slate: The Modern Denial of Human Nature*. New York: Viking, 2002.

Plato. *The Republic*. Translated by A. D. Lindsay. New York: E. P. Dutton, 1957.

Prestowitz, Clyde. *Rogue Nation: American Unilateralism and the Failure of Good Intentions*. New York: Basic Books, 2003.

Richards, Janet Radcliffe. *Human Nature after Darwin: A Philosophical Introduction*. London: Routledge, 2001.

Russell, Bertrand. *The Autobiography of Bertrand Russell*. London: Routledge, 1992.

Said, Edward W. *Humanism and Democratic Criticism*. New York: Columbia University Press, 2004.

———. *The Question of Palestine*. New York: Vintage, 1992.

Schick, Theodore, Jr., and Lewis Vaughan. *How to Think about Weird Things: Critical Thinking for a New Age*. Boston: McGraw-Hill Higher Education, 2002.

Shahak, Israel, and Norton Mezvinsky. *Jewish Fundamentalism in Israel*. 2d ed. Pluto Middle Eastern Studies. London: Pluto Press, 2004.

Singer, Peter. *A Darwinian Left: Politics, Evolution, and Cooperation*. New Haven, CT: Yale University Press, 2000.

———. *The President of Good and Evil: The Ethics of George W. Bush*. New York: Dutton, 2004.

Smith, George H. *Atheism, Ayn Rand, and Other Heresies*. Amherst, NY: Prometheus Books, 1991.

Taylor, Richard. *Virtue Ethics: An Introduction*. Amherst, NY: Prometheus Books, 2002.

Vidal, Gore. *Dreaming War: Blood for Oil and the Cheney-Bush Junta*. New York: Thunder's Mouth Press/Nation Books, 2003.

———. *Perpetual War for Perpetual Peace: How We Got to Be So Hated*. New York: Thunder's Mouth Press/Nation Books, 2002.

Waller, Bruce. *The Natural Selection of Autonomy*. Albany: State University of New York Press, 1998.

Wegner, Daniel. *The Illusion of Conscious Will*. Cambridge, MA: MIT Press, 2002.

Zunes, Stephen. *Tinderbox: U.S. Foreign Policy and the Roots of Terrorism*. London: Zed Books, 2002.